Humanism in Islam

Marcel A. Boisard

Humanism in Islam

American Trust Publications

First published in French under the name
L'Humanisme de L'Islam
by Albin Michel, 1979

This English translation is published by
The American Trust Publications
10900 W. Washington Street
Indianapolis, Indiana 46231

Library of Congress Cataloguing in Publication Data
87-070337
ISBN 0-89259-035-1
Printed in the United States of America

Publisher's Note

This is the English version of *L'Humanisme de l'Islam* prepared by the translators and editors of the American Trust Publications. The original French edition was published by Albin Michel in 1961 from Paris.

The American Trust Publications secured the rights of translation and publishing in March 1981. After six years of ups and downs, we are finally in a position to present it to the English-speaking readers. We hope that Dr. Marcel A. Boisard's work will be appreciated for its perceptive scholarship and his sincere desire to create a better world by increasing understanding between the Islamic aspirations of the Muslim people and the West.

INTRODUCTION TO THE
ENGLISH EDITION

The Meaning of Humanism

To strive for enjoyment and to flee from pain – with this lapidary sentence, two great materialistic thinkers, Epicurus in antiquity and Holbach in modern times, defined the basic principles of life, not only of human life but also that of animals. Materialism always stresses what is common to animals and humans, while religion stresses what makes them different. The meaning of some cults and religious prohibitions is only to underline these differences.

In its effort to emphasize the animal nature of human beings, materialism sometimes shows more than a common concern for truth.[1]

Darwin did not make man an animal, but he made him aware of his animal origin. Out of this "awareness," the others continued to draw the "appropriate conclusions," both moral and political: a human society is a flock in civilized form, and civilization is the human awakening which goes accompanied with the rejection of prohibitions, power over nature, living with the senses instead of the spirit, and so forth.

By establishing the unity (or continuation) between animal and man, evolution abolished the difference between nature and culture. Starting from a quite different point, religion reestablished this difference. Therefore, from the act of creation, man – and all culture with him – inexorably has opposed the whole development of human history. The divergence between culture and civilization began here. While Camus indicated that "man is an animal which refuses to be so,"[2] whitehead saw in this negation the essence of the religious attitude, this "great rejection."[3] Religion seems to say: look what the animals do, and do the opposite; they devour you should fast; they mate you should abstain; they live in flocks you should try to live alone; they strive for enjoyment and flee from pain you should expose yourself to difficulties. In a

---

[1]A good example of this is the stubborn insistence that sexual relations were completely free during a great part of prehistory. Every woman belonged to every man and every man to every woman. Engels openly admitted that there is no direct proof that it was really so, but still he continued to insist upon it in his *The Origin of the Family, Private Property, and the State*. Serbocroatian trans. (Zagreb: Naprijed, 1945), p. 28. Not scientific truth but ideological decision is the dscisive factor.

[2]Camus, *L'Homme révolté*.

[3]Alfred Whitehead, *Science and the Modern World* (New York: Mcmillan, 1926).

word, they live with their bodies, but you should live with your spirit.

Rejection of this zoological position, this "negative desire" which cannot be explained by Darwinian and rational theories, is the crucial fact of human life on this planet. This fact may be the human damnation or privilege, but it is the only specific quality which makes one a human being. There exists in reality both a complete parallelism and an absolute incongruity between man and animal. We find conformity in the biological, constitutional, that is the mechanical aspect, but on the other hand, there is actually no parrallel since an animal is innocent, sinless, and morally neutral like a thing. Man is never so and from the moment "animal became humanized," from the dramatic "prologue in heaven," or from the famous "fall to earth," man cannot choose to be an innocent animal. Man was set free without the option to return, and so every Freudian solution is excluded. From that moment on, he could no longer be an animal or a man; he could only be man or non-man.

If man was simply the most perfect animal, his life would be simple and without mysteries. Still, since he is not so because he is "a worm of the earth and a child of heaven" and because he was created, he is a disharmonious being, and "Euclid's harmony" is not possible. Not only our fundamental truth but also our sins and vices are based on the fact of the creation.

There we find our human dignity, moral striving, and tragedies as well as our dilemmas, dissatisfaction, damnation, cruelty, and malice.[4] An animal knows none of them and in this lies the meaning of this epoch-making moment.

The question of creation is really the question of human freedom. If one accepts that man has no freedom, that all his actions are predetermined – either by what is inside or what is outside of him – one may consider that God is not necessary for an explanation and understanding of the world. However, if one gives man freedom, if one considers him responsible, one recognizes the existence of God, tacitly or openly. Only God was able to create a free creature, and freedom could only arise by the act of creation.[5] Freedom is not the result or product of evolution. Freedom and product are disparate ideas. God does not produce or construct. He creates. We used to say the same for artists, for the artist who constructs does not create a personality but rather a poster of man. A personality cannot be constructed. I

---

[4]Compare the Qur'ān, ash-Shams: 7-8.

[5]Compare Karl Jaspers: "When a man really is conscious of his freedom, he at the same time becomes convinced of the existence of God. Freedom and God are inseparable," and further: "If the consciousness of freedom contains the consciousness of God, then there exists a connection between the denial of freedom and the denial of God." Karl Jaspers: *Introduction to Philosophy*, Serbocroatian translation. (Beograd: Prosveta, 1967), p. 158.

do not know what a portrait could mean without God. Maybe during this century, after a million years of continued civilization, man will succeed in constructing an imitation of himself, a kind of robot or monster, something very similar to its constructor. This human-looking monster may look very much like a man, but one thing is certain: it will not have freedom, it will be able to do only what it has been programmed to do. In this lies the greatness of Allāh's creation which cannot be repeated or compared with anything that has happened before or after in the cosmos. In one eon of eternity, a free being started to exist. Without a divine touch, the result of evolution would not have been man, but rather a more developed animal, a super-animal, a creature with a human body and intelligence but without a heart and personality. Its intelligence without moral scruples might even be more efficient but, at the same time, more cruel. Some people imagine this type of creature as coming from a far planet in the universe; others see it as a product of our civilization on some high level of development. There is such a creature in Goethe's *Faust*, but it is a quasi-man – a homunculus. It should be noted that there is no analogy between this cruelly indifferent creature, homunculus, and the worst criminal. Man can choose to go against the moral laws, but he cannot, as a monster, stay out of the moral sphere, beyond good and evil. He cannot "switch off" himself.

Practical moral experience shows that man has greater inclination to sin than to do good. His ability to fall deep into sin seems to be greater than to soar up into the heights of virtue.[6] Negative personalities always seem truer than positive ones, and the poet who describes negative characters has an advantage over the one who describes heroes.[7]

Anyhow, men are always good or bad but never innocent, and this could be the ultimate meaning of the biblical story about the fall, the original sin. From the moment of the expulsion from paradise, Adam (man) could not rid himself of his freedom, nor escape from the drama, to be as innocent as an

---

[6]Yusuf: 53.

[7]It is interesting to note the polemic that took place in China in 1974 about a Chinese novel from the fifteenth century, *The Water Boundary*, better known in the West in Pearl Buck's English translation *All Men are Brothers*. The novel, one of the best in Chinese classical literature, describes the revolt of the peasants against the imperial administration during the twelfth century. Because of its message that all men are brothers, the novel was cited as "a negative instructive example" of an "unclass approach" because "all men are not brothers," as stated during this polemic in 1974.

In Hungary, the Ministry of Education ordered the classification of all children according to the class they belonged to six categories "a" to "f." The reaction of the public, although very careful, showed that this classification was looked upon as a discriminatory measure. New forms or reasons for making differences among people are, no doubt, connected with official atheistic philosophy.

animal or an angel. He has to choose, to use his freedom, to be good or evil; in one word, to be man. This ability to choose, regardless of result, is the highest form of existence possible in the universe.

Man has a soul, but psychology is not the science about it. There cannot exist a science about the soul. Psychology deals with some forms of apparent inner life. This is why it is possible to talk about psychophysiology, psychometry, psycho-hygiene, and the physics of the psyche. The possibility of quantitative psychology confirms the thesis of the outer, mechanical, and quantitative, that is, the soulless nature of thought and feeling. Animal and human psychology may complement each other, for psychology has nothing to do with the soul, only with the psychological manifestations. John Watson wrote: "Human psychology, as understood by behaviorism, must be built upon the example of the objective and experimental psychology of animals, borrowing from its way of examining, its methods, and its aim. As such, there do not exist two types of psychology (human and animal), separated from each other by an iron curtain, not knowing each other; having basically different objects, methods, and aims, but only one psychology which takes its place among the natural sciences."[8] This quotation needs no comment. If we use Islamic terms, we may say that psychology is the science of the *nafs* and not of the *ruh*, that is, a science on the biological and not on the personal level. There are three circles (the mechanical, the biological, and the personal), which correspond to the three degrees of reality (matter, life, and personality). This way of thinking leads to the application of the scientific method, which always implies an absolute causality, and this by itself means the negation of freedom which is tthe essence of the soul. Our attempt to "study" the soul in psychology brings us necessarily to the negation of the "subject of this study." There is no way out of this bewitched circle.

The equality and brotherhood of people are possible only if man is created by God. The equality of men is a spiritual and not a natural, physical, or intellectual fact. It exists as a moral quality of man, as the human dignity, or as the equal value of the human personality. On the contrary, as physical, thinking, and social beings; as members of groups, classes, political groupings, and nations, people are always very unequal. If man's spiritual value is not recognized – this fact of religious character – the only real base of human equality is lost. Equality, then, becomes a mere phrase without a base and content and, as such, it will soon retreat, faced with the evident facts of human inequality, or with the natural human desire to rule and to obey and thus to be unequal. As soon as the religious approach is removed, the empty room is filled by different forms of inequality – racial, national, social,

---

[8] Watson, p. 158.

or political.

Man's dignity could not be discovered by biology, psychology, or by any other science. Man's dignity is a spiritual question. After "objective observations," it is easier for science to confirm the inequality of man, and so, "scientific racism" is quite possible and even logical.[9]

The ethics of Socrates, Pythagoras, and Seneca were not inferior to the ethics of the three revealed religions (Judaism, Christianity, and Islam) even though there remains one clear distinction: only the ethics of the revealed religions postulated clearly and without ambiguity the equality of all men as God's creatures. Even Plato accepted it as necessary that men were unequal. On the contrary, the cornerstone of the revealed religions is the common origin, and therefore the absolute equality, of all men. This idea has had a fundamental impact on all later spiritual, ethical, and social development of mankind. Moreover, the history of ethics seems to prove the connection between the idea of the equality of men and the idea of immortality – a topic which has not yet been studied enough. Religious and moral systems which do not recognize or, have a confused idea about immortality do not recognize this equality either. If there is no God, men are obviously and hopelessly unequal.

Nietzsche claimed that religions were invented by the weak to delude the strong. Marx maintained the opposite. If we accept that religions were imagined, Nietzsche's interpretation seems more convincing because only on religion could the weak base their demand for equality. Science and everything else except religion have confirmed their inequality.

Why are there so many handicapped people around the mosques, churches, and temples which we enter? Only the houses of God have opened their doors to the ones who have nothing to show and to prove, who are "poor in health and wealth," who are shut out from all the feasts of this world where one is asked for name, family, talents, and knowledge. The sick and the uneducated remain in front of the factory door, while the healthy and educated enter. But in the house of God, a poor and blind man can stand by the side of a king or a noble and he may even be better than they are.[10] The most important cultural and human meaning of the temples lies in this recurring proof of equality.

The utmost meaning of art is to discover the human quality in men who have been degraded by life and to find human greatness in the small, forgotten people – in a word, to reveal the human soul of the same value in

---

[9]Evolutionism can neither be reconciled with the idea of equality nor with the concept of natural human rights. The "égalité" of the French revolution is also religious in its origin.

[10]"Abasa: 1-9.

every human being. The lower the social status of a man, the more striking is the discovery of his dignity. French literature equally featured this in such personages as Quasimodo, Fantine, and Jean Valjean. In this lies the true value of classical Russian literature.[11]

Humanism is not charity, forgiveness, and tolerance, although that is the necessary result of it. Humanism is primarily the affirmation of man and his freedom, namely, that is, of his value as a man.

Everything that debases man's personality, that brings him down to a thing, is inhuman. For instance, it is human to state that man is reponsible for his deeds and to punish him. It is not human to ask him to regret, to change his mind, to "improve," and to be pardoned. It is more human to prosecute a man for his beliefs than to force him to renounce them, giving him the well-known chance called "taking into consideration his sincere attitude." So, there are punishments which are human, and pardonings which are most inhuman. The inquisitors claimed that they burned the body to save the soul. Modern inquisitors do the opposite: they "burn" the soul as the compensation for the body.

To reduce a man to the function of a producer and a consumer, even if every man is given his place in production and consumption, does not signal humanism but dehumanization.

To drill people to produce "correct" and disciplined citizens is likewise inhuman.

Education, too, can be inhuman: if it is one-sided, directed and indoctrinated; if it does not teach one to think independently, if it only gives ready-made answers; if it prepares people only for different functions instead of broadening their horizons and thereby their freedom.

Every manipulation of people, even if it is done in their own interest, is inhuman. To think for them and to free them from their responsibilities and obligations is also inhuman. Our quality of man obliges us. When God gave man the ability to choose and threatened him with severe punishments, He confirmed in the highest way the value of man as a man.[12] We have to follow

---

[11]In the essay "The Russians Point of View," Virginia Woolf describes this lively quality of classical Russian prose: "The soul is the leading character in Russian artistic prose. Delicate and subtle with Chekhov, deeper and greater with Dostoevski, inclined to violent and furious convulsion but always dominating ... Dostoevski's novels sow gales, whirlwinds of sand, gushes of water bubbling and gurgling, absorbing us. They consist of soul only." See Virginia Woolf, *The Common Reader* (New York: Harcourt, Brace & Co., 1925).
[12]"Verily, We have created man into toil and struggle .. Have we not made for him a pair of eyes? And a tongue and a pair of lips? And shown him the two highways. But he has made

the example set by God: let us leave man to struggle for himself, instead of doing it for him.

Without religion and the concept of man's ever-striving spirit, as stated in the "prologue in heaven," there is no authentic belief of man as the highest value. Without it, there is no belief that man as man is at all possible and that he really exists. Atheistic humanism is a contradiction, because "if there is no God, then there is no man either."[13] Also if there is no man, humanism is a phrase without essence. The one who does not acknowledge the creation of man does not understand the real meaning of humanism. Since he has lost his basic standard, he will always reduce humanism to the production of goods and their distribution "according to need." To make sure that all people are fed is of course a matter of great concern, but knowing affluent societies of today, we cannot be sure that in this way we would get a better and more humane world. It would be even less humane if the ideas of some people about general leveling, uniformity, and depersonification were put into practice. In such a world described by Aldous Huxley in *Brave New World*, there would be no social problems, and evenness, uniformity, and stability would reign everywhere. Nonetheless, all of us consciously or instinctively reject this vision as an example of general dehumanization.

"Man is a product of his environment" – this basic postulate of materialism served as the starting point of all subsequent inhuman theories in law and sociology, and of the practice of manipulating human beings, which in our time reached monstrous proportions during the time of Nazism and Stalinism. All other similar seductive theories of society's priority over individuals, of man's obligation to serve society, and so forth, belong here as well. Man must not serve anybody; he must not be a means. Everything must serve man, and man must serve God only. This is the ultimate meaning of humanism.*

'Alija 'Ali Izetbegovic

---

no haste on the path that is steep. And what will explain to you the path that is steep? It is freeing the bondman; or the giving of food in a day of privation to the orphan with claims of relationship. Or to the indigent down in the dust. Then will he be of those who believe and enjoin patience, constancy and self-restraint, and enjoin deeds of kindness and compassion" al-Balad: 8-17.

[13]Nikolai Berdyaev, *The Beginning and the End*, trans. R.M. French (New York: Harper, 1957).
(*) This piece has been taken from 'Alija 'Ali Izetbegovic's *Islam Between East and West* (Indianapolis: American Trust Publications, 1984).

*To my parents and
my wife Claude*

Contents

Chapter 5
THE UNIVERSE AND THE WORLDS

Chapter 6
THE REALITY OF ISLAM

EPILOGUE

Chapter 1

PERSPECTIVE

Law, along with mathematics, is
one of the surest means of making
us lose sight of the facts.

Charles de Guardia

The Universal Nature of the International System

It is clear that the organization of international relations is at present in a period of profound change which could lead to perceptible modifications within the structure of the established system. This transitional phase is in itself not unique, for there are numerous examples of such periods in world history. It is true that, as the development of civilization gradually takes its course, new problems arise to which solutions constantly have to be found. Rules and norms are supposed to be prescribed in accordance with the evolution of society; yet, the necessity of adaptation in our day and age seems even more urgent and more obvious than ever before.

This phenomenon has arisen for several reasons. On the one hand, the Second World War essentially shattered the entire structure of the law of nations, and its reconstruction has always been precarious since its foundations were not relaid with sufficient solidarity. Moreover, if the inspiration – often born in the very disasters which have befallen Western civilization – claims to be of a higher nature, the structure is nevertheless largely composed of shreds and decaying fossils salvaged from the monument which crumbled during the years 1939-1945. On the other hand, the process of decolonization, followed by an ever-growing realization by the newly formed states of the role they could possibly play on an international scale, exerted great pressure on the entire system of international relations. This issue is likely to continue to develop, feeding on itself, since it constantly exposes the fact that the basic premises of international law were postulated at a time when the European community believed that it alone was representative of the entire world. Still, it just so happens that certain expressions are the product of Judeo-Christian civilization and that particular attitudes which still prevail in our times are the response to problems which, historically speaking, faced the Western world alone. Over the last two decades new states have followed suit, although each individually wished to assert its own independence, all the time remaining in the cultural grip of the West. These non-European communities, united by similar economic problems – if not by a common ideology – are gradually becoming aware of the influence which they have been called upon to exert. They are therefore demanding that their own deeper aspirations be taken into consideration within the structural order governing international relations.

The issue at hand proves to be a most complex and major problem. It is not really certain that the effort to dewesternize – to decolonize, in actual

[3]

fact – the existing world structure, even if only in its outer form, would necessarily lead to the establishment of universal values or rules. When new moral demands are made, the "status quo" is upset, and this situation could ultimately bring about the disintegration or the rejection by certain states of the international community's organization. This international community would simply be considered as another "holy alliance" of powers ruling the world. This extreme situation is a threat to the existence of international solidarity, whose collapse could hardly be imagined at the present time. The acute nature of the problem thus becomes apparent, and cooperation between states becomes a necessity. However, this cooperation could not truly come into effect unless the present organization were to more readily accept new influences. Recent experience has brought into focus not only the difficulties of the undertaking, but also the reticence, and in reality the inability, on the part of the older nations to understand certain expressions of the aspiration toward justice or to even imagine accepting moral values which appear foreign to them.

If the present study has any aim whatever, it is primarily that of serving the West. Could this be called presumptuous? It is true that an unconscious feeling of fear and contempt can be detected in the attitude of Europe toward the "Third World." On the one hand, one finds a condescension stemming from an ineradicable ethnocentrism and nourished by memories of the past, or by "objective" considerations concerning the economic development of societies and also, perhaps, by an underlying racism. On the other hand, there is a fear, deepened by the misunderstood claims made by a certain demographic power belonging to that section of the world's population which possesses immense economic resources and, in particular, sources of raw materials and energy. This combination of two generally indivisible feelings, although vague in the individual European consciousness, is reflected in political authorities. Public reactions often lack courage and lucidity, a phenomenon typical of a civilization on the defensive. Culturally holding on to the past, satisfied with its present material achievements, and fortified by its position of military power, the West will in all likelihood have great difficulty in coming up with the intellectual honesty or sufficient realism to truly understand the great ideological enthusiasm, bubbling with old or new and often contradictory ideas, which is the motivating force of one part of humanity. This movement, which still has a relatively unassertive character in international relations, could quite easily represent a tidal wave which bears with it the threat of destroying and entirely carrying off the whole existing establishment.

Academic publications also bear the imprint of this same European ethnocentricity, and it would appear that those responsible for the education of future generations are not conscious of the fact that Western civilization on the whole is no longer accepted by the outside world. Modern writers who appeal to international law to open itself to new influences are few and far between.[1] In this day and age, it is still unquestionably maintained that "it is essentially due to Christian influence that warring peoples are obliged to respect certain judicial laws at a time of hostilities."[2] The origins of the rights of man are still traced back to Western civilization, the claim being made that "the English Magna Carta in the thirteenth century, then, toward the end of the eighteenth century, the Constitution of the United States and the Declaration of Citizen Rights in France, were the first systematic statements" of this law.[3] By failing to recognize set attitudes and laws in cultures other than those belonging to the Greek-Judeo-Christian tradition, a number of authors rather too hastily concluded that respect for the human creature was a product of Western thought.[4] The question, however, seems to have been badly posed. If history does, in fact, seem to ascertain that the first manifestations of the rights of man or certain obligations aiming at "humanizing" war appeared in Europe on the basis of "natural law" or of philosophical principles, then it is precisely because public conscience revolted against unacceptable conditions which still existed on that continent at that time: the absolutism and arbitrariness of the monarchy, bloody barbarism during wars between European countries, and the frightful massacre of nations in the newly discovered Americas. It is true that, in the name of Christianity, the "founders of the law of nations" attempted to impose certain rules toward the end of the Middle Ages. An identical motivation was evoked later again toward the end of the nineteenth century.[5] Juridical promotion and codification of norms inspired by the highest human values were, on the surface, the achievement of Europe, the imperial power ruling the world at the time, but a power

---

[1]The most outstanding exceptions are: Quincy Wright, "The Strengthening of International Law," *Recueil des cours de l'Académie de Droit international* vol. 3 (Leiden: Sijthoff, 1960), pp. 1-295. After this: Wright, "Strengthening," and, above all, Wilfred C. Jenks, *The Common Law of Mankind* vol. 26 (London: Stevens, 1958), 456 pages. After this: Jenks, *The Common Law.*
[2]Philippe Breton, *Le droit de la guèrre* (Paris: Armand Colin, 1970), p. 16.
[3]Henri Coursier, *Etude sur la formation du droit humanitaire* (Geneva: C.I.C.R, 1952), p. 99.
[4]Albert Verdot, *Naissance et signification de la Déclaration universelle des Droits de l'Homme* (Louvain: Nauwelaerts, n.d.), 356 pages. After this: Verdot, *Naissance.* This author, nevertheless, points out on page 10, "before expressing myself on this subject," it is necessary "to wait for the conclusions of more exhaustive research."
[5]Refer to Henry Dunant, *Un souvenir de Solférino,* according to *l'Avenir sanglant,* vol. 22 (Lausanne: Age d'Homme, 1969), particularly "Un christianisme blasphématoire," pp. 159 f. After this: Dunant, *Solférino.* Roger Boppe, *L'Homme et la Guerre.* Le docteur Louis Appia et les débuts de la Croix-Rouge (Geneva: Muhlethaler, 1959), p. 97 f. See also Herbert Maza, *Neuf meneurs internationaux*: de l'initiative individuelle dans l'institution des organisations internationales pendant le XIX et le XX siecle (Paris: Sirey, 1965), above all the second part, pp. 33-124.

which nonetheless had the sad privilege of being the amphitheater of most of the wars. Concrete facts such as these made it necessary to remind these "civilized nations" of certain principles since they, more than any other people, had violated the rules which they themselves had previously recognized and proclaimed to be true.[6]

Those authors who do not attribute the system of international moral attitudes to Christianity refer back to antiquity. Referring in particular to ancient Greece, they then jump right into "modern times" without any transition since they take it for granted that the so-called darkness of the Middle Ages had cast its shadow over the entire world.[7] Yet others subscribe to the widely accepted generalization that Hellenism and Judaism were the mainsprings of Western civilization.[8] Now, it is not a question of contesting the influences of Greek philosophy or of Judaism (or of Christianity, for that matter).[9] However, historical objectivity – or to be frank – plain justice, forces us to remind ourselves that the civilization which took charge of the Mediterranean culture for the seven centuries of the Middle Ages was that of Islam.[10]

This fact is accepted by most modern writers. Nevertheless, in most general works dealing with the development of the law of nations and of international morality, the contribution of the Muslim world is rarely mentioned. Yet, was it not this very world which collected, translated and commentated upon the writings of antiquity, leaving on them the imprint of its own genius before passing them on to the Western world of Christianity? Were Averroes (ibn-Rushd) and Avicenna (ibn-Sina'), along with other Muslim philosophers, not

[6]"Réaffirmation et développement des droits et coutumes applicables dans les conflits armés," Report presented to the 21st International Conference of the Red Cross, Istanbul, September 1969, (mimeographed), p. 50. After this: *Réaffirmation.*
[7]A simple consultation of the table of contents of works dealing with the elaboration of international law is illustrative. See, among others and for example, Jean Graven, *Le difficile progrès du règne de la justice et de la paix internationale par le droit*: des origines à la Société des Nations, ed. René Cassin, vol. 2: Amicorum Disciplinorumque liber (Paris: Pedone, 1970). After this: Graven, *de difficile progrès.* Charles Ruyssen, *Les sources doctrinales de l'internationalisme* 3 vols. (Paris: P.U.F., 1954, 1958, 1961). Also, Robert Redslob, *Traité de droit des gens.* L'évolution historique. Les institutions positives. Les idées de justice. Le droit nouveau (Paris: Sirey, 1950), particularly chapters 1 and 2. After this: Redslob, *Traité.*
[8]Julius Stone, *Human Law and Human Justice* (Sydney: Maitland, 1965), pp. 9, 21-22. After this: Stone, *Human Law.* See also Alfred N. Whitehead, *Adventures of Ideas* (New York: Free Press, 1967), pp. 11 f.
[9] We state immediately that we accept Islam as a divine revelation "sui generi," without considering the possible influences that Judaism or Christianity might have had upon it. See Hanna Zakarias, *Voici le vrai Mohammed et le faux Coran* (Paris: Nouvelles éditions latines, 1960), which is the most violent attack directed against the prophetic mission of Muhammad, whose role would have been to report the teaching which the Rabbi of Makkah lavished upon him.
[10]Jean Wolf, "L'héritage d'une civilisation qui domina l'univers," *Le Monde* 8/9 (June 1969).

the masters of thought for many generations in Europe? Was it not under the cultural influence of Islam that Hebraic philosophy was delivered from the burden of the Talmudic doctrine which had for so long weighed it down? Maimonides, the Jewish philosopher of the twelfth century whose influence greatly determined the direction taken by the Judaic and Western consciousness in general, lived in the land ruled by the Muslims. The enumeration of these various determining factors defines one of the main arguments of the present study: namely, the claim that the Islamic civilization most definitely made an important contribution to that system which ensures respect for human rights and which governs relations between peoples. Though this contribution may not truly have been wilfully ignored by Western writers, it remains the domain of specialists, never reaching the general public. The reasons for this neglect – or more exactly for this tacit denigration – are not entirely clear. Could it be that the ancient Greek complex with regard to the Orient lives on,[11] or that Christianity refuses to admit the validity of a monotheism which came after it, or is it that the European law of nations may at the outset have been established partially to unite the European peoples against Islam? The latter seems the most likely answer to us.[12]

This study is presented in a historical perspective, in the broad sense of the word. This approach seems justifiable on several accounts since it is history itself which in effect supplies the material necessary for the understanding and analysis of the law of nations. History places the concrete facts and the palpable manifestations of political or philosophical thought within the established normative structure. In all likelihood, jurists in general have committed a grave error of method by simply subjecting the law of nations to traditional techniques of juridical analysis and exegesis without refreshing their doctrine by a deeper knowledge of the phenomenon of international social relations.[13] International law, history, and political science are inextricably linked to one another. A more universal orientation in international morality should be implemented by systematic experimental research of social phenomena rather than by strict, cold, syllogistic reasoning, or by means of "rational intuition," the latter sometimes slipping into pure abstraction. The historian should therefore know the foundations of a civilization based upon religious belief, a civilization whose stamp is borne by the evolution of mankind and which is still in this day and age the source of the moral standards

---

[11]Amir M. Badi, *Les Grecs et les barbares* – L'autre face de l'histoire (Lausanne: Payot, 1963).

[12]"The Muslims are the natural enemies of the Christian community. They must, therefore, be fought, driven out, just as a civilized society fights and punishes the wrongdoers." Pierre Dubois, attorney of the king and author of a project of Christian federation at the beginning of the fourteenth century. Refer to Graven, *le difficile progrès*, p. 26.

[13]Pierre Vellas, *Droit international public* – Institutions internationales, 2nd edition (Paris: Librairie générale de droit et de jurisprudence, 1970), p. 36. After this: Vellas, *Droit*.

and main policies for millions of individuals. It is necessary to analyze the essential ideas of this civilization as well as their ultimate development, to elucidate in which terms this faith with its claim to universality has defined the place of the individual in society, and how it conceives the organization of relationships between peoples.

The international judicial doctrine is the outcome of a vast history of events as well as of constant and progressive philosophical research aiming at more justice and humanity, even if there has truly been a measure of philosophical regression or stagnation. From one culture to another, the elaboration of laws, whether written or unwritten, has followed two different courses, namely: either by coming into being autonomously and spontaneously, or by virtue of the unconscious reciprocal penetration and mutual exchange of ideas. Since international morality is primarily a human phenomenon, the various peoples of the world decreed laws which were similar, if not identical to each other, as the expression of basic values, without there having to be any actual reciprocal communication. Despite greatly diverging beliefs concerning man's ends, as expressed by various philosophical systems, religions, and ideologies, there is a common nucleus in what could appear to be the mind's perennial quest for a universal humanism. On the other hand, reciprocal interaction between institutions, their acceptance and assimilation by differing judicial systems, has been more frequent than is generally believed.[14] It would therefore be absurd to present Islam as being simply antagonistic to other contemporary doctrines and judicial structures.

For historically objective reasons, an international morality claiming universal import was formulated in Europe, a morality whose outward expression is probably peculiar and applicable only to Europe. Consequently, the judicial systems which grew from this morality are perhaps quite restrictive. If morality were to constitute the nucleus of the international system, the positive law of nations would seem to be its outer walls which were progressively built by those norms governing relations between the European states of the sixteenth century. The need to universalize the system has already been denounced. As far as Islam is concerned, a few writers have already shown the possible similarities or differences between Islam and the other major present-day ideologies.[15] Some of them have even claimed an understanding of how the Islamic system could be adapted to the problems of the modern world,[16]

---

[14]Georges Del Vecchio, *Philosophie du Droit*, translated from the Italian by J. Alexis D'Aynac (Paris: Dalloz, 1953), p. 33. After this: Del Vecchio, *Philosophie*.

[15]Maxime Rodinson, *Islam et capitalisme* (Paris: Seuil, 1966), Id., *Marxisme et monde musulman* (Paris: Seuil, 1972).

[16]Alphonse Gouilly, *L'Islam devant le monde moderne* (Paris: La Nouvelle Edition, 1945), 295

while others have clearly shown that international law in its essence is not foreign to Islam,[17] or else they have described the contribution of the Arab Muslim world* to the intellectual awakening of Europe.[18] On one level, it would be impossible to draw elements from these various analyses and to synthesize them. Such an attempt would necessitate reestablishment of the true historical perspective of a certain number of facts often neglected in general treatises dealing with the development of the law of nations. To treat the Muslim world in the manner it legitimately deserves, what must be done is to supplement, rather than to reject. In so doing, one civilization alone (and one which, at least in its initial phase, flourished in the Mediterranean basin) would be added to the traditions of Greco-Roman antiquity, Judaism, and Christianity. Of course, there were other civilizations which, in the course of their evolution, expressed their own original ideas concerning man, defined social structures, and established a system to govern relations with foreign peoples.[19]

The concept of international morality offers a vast perspective of principles, axioms and aspirations. This concept is linked to the momentous evolution of ideals which have aimed at protecting the fundamental rights of the individual ever since the dawn of civilization. According to circumstance, this same concept has taken on differing outer manifestations throughout history. Yet, its positive outcome – international public law – remains an embryo whose growth to maturity is constantly being stunted by the scope of its aims and the rapid changes inherent in those situations which need to be faced and solved. Thus, in no other field of judicial activity has the struggle for rights been so disjunct, fitful, and intermittent as on the level of international law.[20]

To the traditional terms of "law of nations" and "international law" "inter-

---

pages. After this: Gouilly, *l'Islam.* Jacques Austry, *L'Egypte et le destin économique de l'Islam* (Paris: Sociéte d'Edition d'Enseignement Supérieur, 1960).

[17]Mohammad T. Ghoneimi, *The Muslim Conception of International Law and the Western Approach* (The Hague: Nijhoff, 1968). After this: Ghoneimi, *The Muslim Conception.*

(*) Arab Muslim World is a cultural and not a racial entity which had in its folds all those Muslims who wrote and expressed themselves in Arabic. In other words, this was pax Islamica and not pax Arabica. — Tariq Quraishi (ed.)

[18]Sigrid Hunke, *Le soleil d'Allah brille sur l'Occident* – Notre héritage arabe. Translated from the German by Solange and Georges de Lalene (Paris: Albin Michel, 1963), 404 pages. After this: Hunke, *Le soleil d'Allah.*

[19]See various interesting articles in the *Revue internationale de la Croix-Rouge:* "Les lois de la guerre chez les anciens Hindous," 869 (1951); "L'esprit de bienfaisance impartiale dans les civilizations de l'Extrême-Orient," 670 (1952); "La naissance des idées humanitaires au Japon," 687 (1956); "Réalites du monde noir et droits de l'homme," 620, (1970), and "Un édit de Cyrus préfigurant la Charte des Droits de l'Homme," 633 (1971).

national morality" has been added. It is difficult, however, to define such a term.

The term could well designate a set of individual and collective feelings and beliefs, of good intentions and hopes, instead of a formal, structured system. The term "ideal law" has been rejected since it would have veiled a basic characteristic of the Muslim system: the coercive power of the law does not arise from some ill-defined autonomous pressure exerted upon human reasoning or conscience, as does the assertion of judicial imperative, but is derived directly from divine revelation. We have chosen these expressions for four reasons.

First of all, "law" in classical Islam is not synonymous with the object of Western juridical science,[21] a science which studies social phenomena by dealing with individual and collective behaviors in relation to a system of rules created by the needs of life, approved by the people, and often enforced by certain coercive procedures. For the Muslim, the rule of conduct is the divine will, expressed in the Qur'ān and made explicit by Muhammad's prophetic mission. It would be a grave error not to emphasize the eminently and fundamentally religious nature of those rules which determine the behavior of the Muslim. Two remarks are necessary here. First, Islam's "legal" attitudes, admittedly precise and indisputable, go far beyond the bounds of simple, strict dogmatic, positivism since they grow from *feelings* of brotherhood and justice. This explains why the law should not be seen as an abstraction which crushes the spirit of criticism, nor as an obligation imposed by an unquestionable system. The acceptance of duty is personal and is made individual by a certain emotional disposition, a state in which the individual surrenders himself not so much to pressure as to an attracting force.[22] Second, the original basis of the obligatory nature of judicial laws in a system governing relations between individuals and between various social groups is undoubtedly to be found in divine inspiration. Hence the moral force of such laws.

To the modern Western mind, the intimate relationship between faith and the law almost necessarily implies that the system concerned is "primitive." Since religion and divine will are being discussed, it is also imperative to depict the believer's idea of God, a factor which largely determines the law's

---

[20]Jean-Pierre Queneuduc, gen. ed., *Le Droit international positif*, by Louis Cavare, (Paris: Pedone, 1967, 1969), vol. 1: *Le Droit international positif*, by Louis Cavaré, pp. 12 f., 269 f. After this: Cavaré, *Le Droit*.

[21]Moreover, not very precise.

[22]Henri Bergson, *Les deux sources de la morale et de la religion*, 164th ed. (Paris: P.U.F., 1967), p. 46. After this: Bergson, *Les deux sources*.

substance. In Islam, the command is most certainly absolute and of a higher order; nevertheless, it is neither arbitrary nor irrational – how could it be, since God is first and foremost *the* Truth? Consequently, speculative thought geared toward the search for the truth should not oppose the demands made by faith. It is the divine will, inasmuch as it is the expression of the absolute truth, which imposes itself, and not the abstract order of some vaguely defined supreme authority. In the Islamic doctrine, no distinction is made between judicial obligation and pure ethical duty. This "automatic" separation of two very similar judgments of an act – a separation which has slowly formed in Western thought – perceives the moral character of an action within the subjective intimacy of the individual will, whereas the law sanctions only the outward, physical aspect of an act in the context of the objective social structure. This is impossible in Islam, for the law imposes certain formal demands and imperative duties on the Muslim which do not necessarily have the same implications for others. Conversely, certain rules of good conduct, which are nothing more than social ethics in Western philosophy, assume an actual judicial nature in Muslim thought. This intimate link between law and morality readily confirms the system's strength. In this regard, it gives us great pleasure to emphasize one point: in spite of the distinctions which Western philosophy has claimed to be able to make, a certain form of morality still exerts a constant influence not only upon judicial rules but also upon the positive improvement of those rules. For example, the trials of war criminals after the Second World War was entirely based upon this kind of morality. The law is less and less concerned with a simple accounting of a pure social fact but is becoming charged with a certain dynamic potentiality determined by the objectives in view. At this level, the relationship between Islam and the contemporary law of nations should not lead to erroneous conclusions or historical contradictions.

Our second reason for choosing the expression "international morality" reflects the belief that modern international law does not succeed in fully regulating social rapports in their political, economic, and psychological complexity, and that the law should evolve more rapidly so as to attain a more universal import on the level of the principles it sets forth. By refusing to focus our attention on an analysis of the existing normative structures or to discuss the technical regulations now in force, our study becomes more useful for it encompasses matters which go beyond purely judicial considerations and which evolve more quickly than law-related doctrines and institutions. If a system of morality is to be defined as a set of rules of conduct deriving their coercive force from a subjective belief concerning "good" and "evil," a dual problem arises: Can one even hope to arrive at a unanimous definition of "good" and "evil," or does their meaning differ from one culture to another? Also, if a rule is not always concretely and objectively expressed but rather appeals to the feelings of human beings, can it have any coercive force within a society or within a state which, by definition, represents an abstract organism? Can such a rule have any coercive reality whatever in a context which is, in the final analysis, fictitious?

True universality can be achieved only through the sublimation of a conscience which transcends external physical conditions. It would be naive to expect such an attitude on the part of a political entity, no matter how positive it may be. Nevertheless, the individual behavior of governments and citizens, as well as the ever-growing pressure exerted by public opinion, whether domestic or foreign, undoubtedly influences official attitudes. It is therefore possible to speak of a "public conscience" which represents a certain underlying gauge of that ethic which is supposed to teach men how to treat their fellow human beings. It is more than just a simple statement of social phenomena, being as it were perhaps an unattainable ideal, but one which directs political thought toward greater perfection. The more reprehensible the event appears to be, the more strongly the reaction is expressed. Even if the actual judicial systems of various countries are to remain profoundly different from one another, a progressive generalization of the concept of a "public conscience" backed by universal values seems possible by virtue of man's intrinsic value and because of the present-day possibilities of exchange and communication. This ideal of an international morality maintained on a practical and empirical basis would exert an influence upon positive law, but could not be codified in terms of norms, axioms, systems, or dogmas, for it would then risk losing its essential universal character. If one considers each nation to have its own morality at a particular moment of its history, it would in effect seem pernicious to impose new and foreign concepts which would threaten to disrupt its social life.

Future universalization of human values can be achieved only through reciprocal acceptance, not by artificial and forced harmonization. The diverse expressions of basic virtues originate in cultural traditions, in speculative metaphysical philosophies, in religious beliefs, or in all of them together. It is in this sense that an "international morality," both homogeneous and diversified, is conceived. The Muslim concept will therefore be presented in an identical perspective, without the system of international law being taken into account. Only that aspect will be presented which either directly or indirectly aims at protecting the individual as a concrete expression of the feelings of humanity and justice. Such aspects pertain to the foundations of the actual law which strive to guarantee peace through ensuring collective security, laws, and customs relevant during armed conflict, as well as those conventions relating to the protection of human rights. It is thus a question of what is commonly called "international humanitarian law,"[23] with which not all writers associate the "law of peace." The former expression seems to be inadequate, especially in its form, for the qualifier "humanitarian" is almost always unconsciously associated with the concept of "charity," whereas international morality is built upon a foundation of justice. As for the content, it is necessary to understand the concept in order to surpass the strictly formal aspect of the expression and not to overlook a possible law of nations which has not as yet been drawn up, the morality of which constitutes the substructures, and which perhaps represents the major part of a judicial reality to come. Even when certain states follow an "international" or "world" policy – oftentimes only to defend their selfish national interests – the day-to-day reality seems to confirm ever more clearly that their principles, which are not intelligibly differentiated and defined, lead to an unconscious synthesis of influences, the latter being of a diversified and mutually overlapping nature, emotive or rational, moralistic and parajudicial, philosophical, religious or ideological. Though they have not as yet assumed the imperative nature of law, these aspirations can easily be disclosed by the sanctions of public authority. They are sometimes absolutely opposed to established values. Some of them will be absorbed by future laws, others will be rejected for an indefinite period because they are a threat to the immediate security or, in truth, to the very existence of a society, whether national or international. Everyone, however, claims a certain sense of justice which is itself supposed to be rational and all-inclusive, encompassing most of those new values which it brings to fruition. It is thus an ideal reference for all social relations, be they individual, collective, or universal.

Positive law still expresses only a part of these demands, and, at times, does not fulfill even the minimal ethic required of it. If law is an essentially negative concept, one which forbids, then justice is a positive force which makes demands. The aims are different: whereas law aims at harmonizing individual and social interests, justice seeks the well-being of man as man. International law, of which attempts have been made to create a normative system, still remains an institution founded essentially upon pragmatism and compromise because of the absence of a higher authority which transcends the will of its subjects, as well as the absence of an actual executive power. Its basic foundations are those of rational necessity and moral conviction, both of which tend to gradually produce imperative claims.

The international community has undergone rapid and profound changes which purely judicial thought has not yet been able to assimilate. Positive

---

[23]Jean Pictet, *Les principes du Droit international humanitaire* (Geneva: C.I.C.R., 1966), 66 pages. After this: Pictet, *Les principes.*

law only adjusts gradually to the moral demands made by public opinion. The feeling of justice is imbued with overtones of absolute appeal as regards morality, and thus appears to be the perfect outcome of the law. Moreover, the influence it has on the law will be even more powerful since it appears both rational and fundamentally good, even if it were to lay to waste the existing structures. In the final analysis, international positive law, more than any other field of law, manifests an emotional state, a certain sentimental passion. That is precisely why its concrete expression is subject to a certain evolution which can temporarily attain great momentum in both progressive and regressive directions. These variations are an outcome not only of the general framework of international relations, but also of the development and originality of cultures. As a product of collective conscience, in accordance with the laws of reason, international law now has the capacity of once again becoming a "law of nations" in the true sense of the word – a corpus of laws common to all nations. It was in all likelihood the explosion of the first atomic bomb in 1945 which marked a major turning point in the history of mankind.[24]

In these pages, many varied aspects of the Islamic viewpoint will be dealt with: God; man; His creation; the Muslim community; and its relations with non-Muslim peoples. This choice is an outcome of the deep conviction – which has its origins in historical reality – that the task of maintaining international peace is indivisible in nature from that of maintaining respect for the individual within the confines of the state.[25] This idea is certainly not new,[26] but reappeared with greater force in the twentieth century, particularly after the Second World War, having been stifled for some time by the doctrine of voluntary positivism. This intimate relation corresponds to classical Muslim judicial thought. The broadened framework of "international morality" includes attitudes relative to the respect for and the protection of the rights of man without, however, drifting off into a so-called "confusionism" which has at times been rejected.[27] International morality, is in actual fact,

[24]Carl and Shelley Mydans, *Une paix violente*, translated by Marie-Alyx Revellat (Paris: Stock, 1968), p. 300. See also Karl Jaspers, *La bombe atomique et l'avenir de l'homme*, translated from the German by Edmond Saget (Paris: Buchet/Chastel, 1963), pp. 15 f.; also Jean-Claude Venezia, *Stratégie nucléaire et relations internationales* (Paris: Colin, 1971), 175 pages.
[25]Boris Mirkine-Guetzevitch, "L'O.N.U. et la doctrine moderne des Droits de l'Homme (Theorie – Technique – Critifque)," *Revue générale de Droit international public* 2, 1951):161-198, which again raises the idea, wrongly in our opinion, of the American and especially the French revolution. After this: Mirkine-Guetzevitch, *L'O.N.U.*. Also Charles de Visscher, *Théories et réalities en Droit international public* (Paris: Pedone, 4th Rev. ed., 1970), pp. 153 f. After this: de Visscher, *Théories*.
[26]Cruce mentions it in *Le nouveau Ciné*; Sully in his *Grand dessein*, in the seventeenth century; Rousseau and, above all, Kant in the eighteenth century. Refer to Graven, *Le difficile progrès*,

an indefinable collective feeling, and it has to remain such so as not to lose its universality through the postulation of axioms and dogmas whose validity could easily be refuted by concrete social reality. Its foundations are the ideals of justice, humanity, and reason, all compelling ideals which enforce a certain behavior within countries and which render social life acceptable on an individual, national, and international levels. This morality expresses neither precise norms nor technical rules but only a certain number of very general and abstract precepts. It is, moreover, dependent upon those actual laws which it transcends on its own authority, for it proclaims the highest values of the human conscience – in particular that of justice. It first of all unites nations, and though it may be supported by existing national systems, its demands may in certain cases surpass these national sovereignties.

On a universal level, observable positive law can still be characterized by the intervention of an authority which penalizes violations (and if needs be may sanction them even by force), whereas this international morality disposes of a destructive power that could cause the total disappearance of humanity. Is it not "realistic" and "progressive" to believe in the value of man, of his freedom, and of his will, as well as to propound a theory of law which would provide for the communion of all peoples? Islam will also make its contribution to this goal.

A thousand possibilities open up during this examination. Its formulation will be determined not only by its intellectual aim, but also by the fear of confusion and mental obstacles and reservations. The choices are all the more difficult owing to the subtlety of the arguments. It is probably a good idea at this point to mention a general conviction which will serve as a background to this illustration. The system governing contemporary international relations which, for historical reasons originated and evolved in Europe, is in urgent need of laying itself open to a greater universality in order to furnish tools suitable for the interdependence of nations and ensuring world peace. At the same time, it appears obvious that the institution of the law presently in force offers the only admissible framework for the foreseeable future despite the pernicious partitioning which arises from the exclusivism of national sovereignties. The superior principles of international morality could be enforced only through interstate channels, the general direction of which they could alter. Islam, among other civilizations, contains elements of the solution to present-day major problems. Still, it would be a great error to set the Muslim viewpoint in opposition to the established systems which are products of

pp. 74, 91, 123, and 125 respectively.
[27]Richard Sogno-Bezza, "La personnalité juridique du Comité international de la Croix-Rouge" (Ph.D. dissertation, Université de Paris, 1974), pp. 226 f.

Western thought. This constant wish to maintain a universal yet realistic scope necessitates the maintenance of a general view at the expense of detail. This could give rise to confusion.

Thus, the specific content of Islam will be set out in the unicity of its doctrine in order to discover the human attitudes it expresses, and to ascertain to what extent it is conducive to the flourishing of the Muslim's potentialities. It is not our aim to establish whether historic circumstances have more profoundly engraved the authoritarian or humanistic traits of Islam.

It is impossible to properly evaluate the specific concepts of humanity, justice, social order, and tolerance toward others without referring to the basic foundations of a civilization which assume a religious connotation, as is the case with Islam. Rules which appear surprising or even incomprehensible can be explained not by the interpretation of empirical and technical studies, but by seeing them as they appear in their natural environment, where they inspire moral and political thought. Such an approach allows man to define the understanding he has of himself, society, and the world – such concepts being both the reflection and the projection of an entire culture. The dual fact that Islam continues to impose a theocentric vision of the world while simultaneously asserting the intimate relationship between the spiritual and the secular necessitates an all-embracing presentation of the religion.

The study of Islam, in fact, leads us into a system of thought which is entirely different from Western canons. This complexity is all the more marked by the fact that a so-called "Eastern" religious system is placed side by side with a judicial or moral structure which claims to be universal, but which in reality remains an essentially European phenomenon. For the modern Western mind, reference to a God Whom we should obey, as well as the consideration of an ideally given social structure worthy of respect, are no longer "scientifically valid" aspects of the study of human relations. Limiting himself to a general examination of the dogmas of faith and of religious law (two tightly interwoven aspects), the exterior observer may partially borrow the highly convoluted and versatile terminology of the Muslim philosophers and "theologians." On the other hand, when he attempts to transfer them to social reality, he is forced to adapt his efforts to the unbending definitions of those concepts endorsed by international sociological and judicial practice. Vocabulary and terminology present a great problem, for the meanings of words and terms assume different values in the light of different cultural traditions and historical experiences. Thus, any semantic solutions remain inadequate when it comes to describing the psychological realities of two different civilizations – an Eastern theocentric culture and a Western rationalist one. It is essential that one raise the question, and then try to answer it objectively, whether expressions which differ on the outside may ultimately reflect similar concepts.

Objectivity does not mean indifference. On the contrary, it encourages the tolerant acceptance of differing and even opposing values, and it favors an open confrontation of ideas, a possible refutation of their interpretations, and an account of their consequences. One should at all costs avoid coming to the defense of any particular opinion, except in the case of attacking certain prejudices regarding Islam deeply ingrained in European thought.[28] Without too facile a polemic, one can reconstruct the picture of the society conceived by the Muslim doctrine, one which is still theoretically offered to all Muslims. It should be emphasized that the substructure of the Islamic system, being of a specifically religious nature, brought about a "state of being" which became so firmly rooted that it is ever-present and continues to spread.

For this reason, our study will be descriptive rather than analytical or critical. After all, is it not the very basis of a dialog to accept the values of others without necessarily seeking to justify or approve them, all the while remaining loyal to the set of beliefs with which one was raised?

It is Islam which will be studied, not the Muslim world. It is true that the sacred revelation did appear in the Middle East, the cradle of three expressions of monotheism. Following its expansion, this revelation then proved to be the heir of an extremely ancient cultural heritage; indeed, this revelation was perhaps the ultimate and most complete manifestation of civilization in this part of the world. The spread of ideas to Europe took place essentially in the Arabic language, across the Mediterranean and over the Pyrenees. Three factors in particular impose the choice of a global concept of Islam (as opposed to the consideration of the Arab-Muslim world). On one hand, it is indeed the religious phenomenon which allowed the development of a syncretic Islamic civilization. On the other hand, to attempt a definition of Islam in terms of its relationship or opposition to the Arabs and Arabism, would entail retracing the entire history of the Muslim world in all its details. And finally, "Arabic" Islam forms only a small part of the present-day Muslim world.

The study will be limited to an honest, straightforward description of a simple and logical religion. Specialists in the field could easily consider it an examination of a number of platitudes taken from secondary sources and

---

[28]On historic objectivity, see Adam Schaff, *Histoire et vérité*, a work on the objectivity of historical knowledge, translated from the Polish by Anna Kaminska and Claire Brendel (Paris: Anthropos, 1971), particularly the third part, chapter I, pp. 221 f. Also, Raymond Aron, *Introduction à la philosophie de l'histoire*, a work on the limits of historic objectivity (Paris: Gallimard – N.R.F., 1967) pp. 423 f.

never subjected to true critical evaluation. However, what the Muslims believe in is far more important than the manner in which Western orientalists
judge Islamic doctrine. Neither this doctrine nor the world pertaining to it
can be fully understood by some sort of fictitious idealization or concrete
reality. Rather, they can be grasped at an intermediate stage where these
shades of meaning blend with one another, a state which enables us to pass
unhindered from pure theory to the realm of those more "modernistic" interpretations which attempt to plaster the revealed message onto current issues. We have retained only those general principles of the religion which
constitute the subfoundations of an entire civilization and which still pervade
the Muslim soul, thus forming an ideological "continuity," and consequently
giving form to Islam's secular claims, despite actual contradictions and obstacles. It is also these principles which, during the post-colonial period, unify
and substantiate the diffuse aspiration of the Muslim peoples toward an identity, and thereby constructing a kind of mirror which perhaps reflects the intrinsically present image of a Muslim society to come. It is, in fact, a question of finding the present reality of Islam in the maze of its eternal, past
or future expressions.

It could seem somewhat strange that a non-Muslim European would undertake a study of this nature and scope. That is why we have limited ourselves
to a general description of the Islamic principles which bear testimony to our
mode of thought. We will not put forward any arguments not justified by the
compilation of sources, and we have made assertions only inasmuch as they
could be integrated into the logical framework of the Islamic system. Finally,
we have avoided as much as possible using an intuition which claims to be
rational, but which nevertheless remains a dangerous procedure to follow
when attempting to become familiar with the social and cultural phenomena
of Islam, the foundations of which are different from those of the West. Were
it not for the logic and simplicity of Islamic dogma, we would have considered our attempt rather presumptuous. Moreover, we have benefitted from
the friendship and kind cooperation of our Muslim associates. Their participation has proven to be of precious aid to us, in total conformity with the
prescriptions of the Holy Qur'ān:

> And do not discuss with the People of the Book except in the most
> gracious manner, except with those of them who are unjust.[29]

We sincerely hope that the pages which follow will do them no injustice.

---

[29]al-'Ankabut: 46 – translation by Denise Masson: *Le Coran*, Paris (N.R.F. "Pléiade"), 1976,
1087 pages.

Chapter 2

SUBMISSION IN HARMONY

> Whoever adds to the religion a
> dogma or a juridicial duty without
> the support of the Book of Allah or
> the sayings of the impeccable and
> infallible Prophet, is among those
> who "say about God that of which
> they know nothing" (Qur'ān 7:33).
>
> Muhammad 'Abdu

A Global Approach

At first glance, it could seem pointless to define Islam. Any attempt to explain the meaning of a current notion so that everybody can have an understanding of it runs the double risk of appearing too simplistic to the specialists and, at the same time, of being unnecessarily complex in the eyes of the uninitiated. However, it is certainly most appropriate to indicate the general scope of our study.

When considering religion[1] in the three etymological meanings of the word, we find that Islam presupposes on the one hand a voluntary preference, a free choice to surrender to a law and to moral and cultural rules; on the other hand, it implies the collection and preservation of a true human heritage. It especially and ultimately defines the position of the believer in relation to the absolute as well as relations of solidarity among men. It is in this way that Islam appears as a uniform social and political fact, as an observable historic phenomenon in short, as a civilization which has its own conception of man and his place in society and which has put forward certain axioms determining relations between peoples. Moreover, it has not only brought its own specific historic contribution to universal civilization, but also legitimately claims to provide solutions to the major individual, social, and international problems which disturb the modern world.

"Islam is the meeting between God as such and man as such,"[2] the introduction of the relative to the absolute. Islam's very essence is rendered by its name – in as much as a satisfactory translation is possible – a positive, active, and voluntary "surrender" to the divine will, neither resignation nor servitude. Etymologically, the word "Islam" is also akin to the Arabic word meaning "peace, serenity." It so happens that the two notions are related in the Muslim perspective. The pious acceptance, whether personal or collective, freely agreed upon, to observe the revealed law, reflects a permanent and dynamic attempt by the individual to find himself in a peaceful state of

---

[1]Henri Babel, *La Religion à l'aube d'une ère nouvelle* (Neuchâtel: Baconnière, 1969), pp. 16-17. We emphasize that we will consider here only the Western meaning of the term. For the Islamic understanding, "*din*" see pp. 47-48.
[2]Frithjof Schuon, *Comprendre l'Islam* (Paris: Gallimard – N.R.F., 1961), p. 13. After this: Schuon, *Comprendre*.

[21]

equilibrium with a singular and coherent world governed by divine decree. Based on the resolutely confirmed dogma of divine unicity, Islam developed a concept of a harmonious world ruled by a single, universal and unchanging law. In the name of existential unity, it intimately linked the temporal and spiritual domains and, claiming in addition to establish the "Kingdom of God on Earth," gave rise to a "nation," to a way of living, acting, and thinking — in short, to a civilization.[3] Apart from being a revealed religion, Islam also asserts itself as a historical and social phenomenon. It is, therefore, necessary to envisage it as an integral part of a coherent universal structure, and to bear in mind that, in its turn, it affects its followers' moral life and the community's institutional structures.[4] To briefly outline its essential teaching, it would perhaps have sufficed to emphasize its absolute and unbending monotheism, asserting itself in the unity of the world as well as the exclusiveness of the divine law which must control all — on an individual level, in the community and in the universe.

Islam is first and foremost, as a religion or an absolute ideal, a system of contemplation and action for both the individual and the group, which will occupy our thoughts. Both the revelation, definitive and unchanging, and the constitution of the original "Muslim city" took place in the seventh century of our era. These two facts will constitute the main source of our general information. Would it not be turning our back on evidence if we were to ignore the facts that Islam underwent a dogmatic evolution, that it asserted itself historically as a homogenous and unified political whole only for a relatively short period, and that, finally, Muslim political authorities have not always complied with the obligations of their religion? Similarly, could one speak abstractly of Christianity without mentioning that there is no analogy whatsoever between the message of Jesus and the fanaticism of the religious wars which tore the Christian world apart, not to speak of the atrocious and demented massacre of Jews in Hitler's Europe? Would it not be appropriate as well to emphasize, under the circumstances, the fact that in the West the expressions of one and the same faith have given rise to different social structures not only in time but also in terms of space? Does there exist at the present time any agreement or similarity between the southern Catholicism and northern Protestantism of the American continent, for example? In Islam, however, the problem does not assume the same gravity. Even if one agreed that religious factors are not the sole reasons behind various historical formations and social developments, it would nevertheless be necessary to state that, by virtue of its very specificity of faith, its imprints remained deeply

[3]Raymond Charles, *L'Ame musulmane* (Paris: Flammarion, 1958), 284 pages.
[4]Joseph Chelhod, *Islam d'hier et d'aujourd'hui*, vol. 12: *Introduction à la sociologie de l'Islam: de l'animisme à l'universalisme* (Paris: Besson-Chantemerle/Maisonneuve, 1958), pp. 1-2. After this: Chelhod, *Introduction*.

engraved in Muslim countries. The often-stated allegation that Muslim philosophy and the creative originality of its civilization are fossilized is erroneous and unjust. Islam asserts its political claim on an international level and actively pursues its religious expansion, especially in Subsaharan Africa. Considered in its entirety and in its unity, Islam is not a dead body engraved with the memory of a glorious past, but a very living reality.

In this context, we are bound to rapidly describe the principal characteristics of the three psychological attitudes of Islam with regard to modern political theories,[5] concentrating our attention essentially on the juridical aspects. The first reaction – a conservative one – holds religion to be the only superior and eternal expression of the law to be obeyed, an absolute normative system which rules over both the spiritual and the secular lives of the believers. It aims at rejecting all heterogeneous influences. The application of this attitude is found in certain states of the Arabian Peninsula. The second reaction aims at reconciling the twofold inspiration of traditional faith and modernistic influences. This is the philosophy of the great majority of Muslim countries of which Pakistan is perhaps the best known if not the most illustrative example. These states are simultaneously endowed with a modern constitution and honor Islam as the national religion. The dosage of this double influence can vary, and it is by no means sure that, in times to come, purely religious inspiration will not weigh through instead. Finally, the third reaction goes as far as the rejection of Islam, whether partial or total, in preference to foreign ideologies. The Turkey of Ataturk separated spiritual and secular, leaving religion to the individual conscience. Very few are the "progressive" Muslims who would dare suggest a secularization of individuals themselves. Such a project would in any case be absurd and unrealistic, for it would be flying directly in the face of the Muslims, the great majority of whom maintain a conservative religious attitude.

History reveals an absolute constant in Muslim civilization – its being centered on the divine from its very start up to the present time. This phenomenon, which often eludes modern Western thought and analysis, gives Islam its character of permanence. It was perhaps Descartes, whose philosophy nourished daily thought in Europe, who created one of the deepest fissures between East and West. By opting for rationality, he transformed European civilization from a "theocentric" to an "anthropocentric"[6] one. An identical debate arose in Islam during the eleventh century; al-Ghazzali put an end to

---

[5]H. Saab, "Modèles islamiques de modernisation au Moyen-Orient," (pp. 277-291), in *Renaissance du monde arabe*, ed. Anwar Abdel Malek, Abdel Aziz Belal, and Hassan Hanafi, (Gembloux: Duculot, 1972), pp. 282-285. After this: Saab, "Modèles islamiques.".
[6]Hassan Hanafi, "Théologie ou anthropologie," (pp. 233-264), in Abdel Malek, et al., *Renaissance du monde arabe*, pp. 234.

it by opting for faith,* and since then, the search within the framework of Muslim "theology," the supreme science to which all others lead, is in effect "carried out according to the law of Islam, and not according to reason, whether or not the latter is in agreement with Islam."[7] Thus, God remains the principal reference of Muslim thought, be it theological, judicial, or political. Not only does the Qur'ānic revelation guide, develop, and improve the Muslim, but it guarantees the ever-uncontested validity and permanence of Islam. This faith is kept in a "book," plain and complete, "an explanation of all things."[8] The word has remained the word. It indicates the path to be followed in order to be raised to perfection, the main and ultimate goal of humanity. This is the aim assigned to society by the divine law. The religion itself assumes the task of organizing the spiritual and temporal life of both the individual and the society, refusing the intermediary of a clergy which could maintain a religious monopoly. Islam is the absolute – divine and rational. Human reason has to comply with the revealed system. Faith is not an abstraction; on the contrary, it is a truly concrete phenomenon. It has to be grasped in its totality, as if beyond the bounds of time.

At this point, certain justifications must be made. In these pages, only "classical" Muslim juridical doctrine, which was codified in the eighth and ninth centuries of the Christian era, and which has undergone almost no change for the many centuries of Mongolian, Ottoman, then European domination, will be analyzed. We will make frequent mention of Prophet Muhammad who, along with his apostolic mission, led but a small political entity whose problems were to turn out far different from those which the modern Muslim world faces. We will quote the "traditions" [ahadith] ascribed to him, though their historical validity has been questioned by Western orientalists and historians. They nevertheless remain interesting, for in a certain sense, they crystallize the idea which Muslims have of Islam, and have furthermore helped in the formation of a certain moral attitude. We will deal with the assertion of the individual in Islam, even if a superficial outside view could lead us to believe that there is none, since the majority of Muslim countries are economically underdeveloped. The development of material civilization does indeed project a more honorable image of man. He is on a higher level and has more self-respect when he is not crushed by misery, when instruction

---

(*) Al-Ghazzali could not have put an end to this debate had Islam been anti-reason, or rationalism, as expressed by Greco-Roman thought, had not been vulnerable. That is why when al-Ghazzali, who had imbibed its dialectics, launched his offensive against rationalism, it fell apart.   Tariq Quraishi (ed)

[7]Abdurrahman Badawi, *Histoire de la philosophie en Islam*, vol. 1: *Les philosophes théologiens* (Paris: Vrin, 1972), p. 8.

[8]an-Nahl: 91, or again: "We have omitted nothing from the Book," al-An'am: 38 (Blachère).

is available to him, and when he enjoys leisure activities. Finally, we will develop the traditional Islamic conception of international relations, an eminently human and pacifist one, without taking into account that the Muslim nations, barely over their sometimes violent battle against European colonization, find themselves forced by circumstances into involvement in most of the recent conflicts: the Middle East, the Asian subcontinent, Cyprus, Kurdistan, Eritria, and the Philippines, among others. We have no fear that our study may appear to be anti-historical or "reactionary" in the true meaning of the term. It is by no means a matter of studying Muslim law in its particular present applications, nor of analyzing the attitude of individuals and states with regard to coercive norms. We refuse to "start a fashion" of or even to draw comparisons supported by specific attitudes in an attempt to show the possible incompatibility of classical judicial doctrine[9] or, on the contrary, to prove its agreement or its concordance[10] with the requirements of contemporary international morality. We will attempt, within the study's general perspective, to emphasize the humanistic or, on the contrary, the coercive aspects of Muslim dogma.

Let us note, in conclusion, that we have not endeavored to analyze how Muslims judge Western canons of international morality. The marvelous principles of European individualist liberalism must have appeared rather theoretical to certain populations oppressed by European colonialization. Such an inquiry would certainly not lack interest. However, we can well imagine that the illustrious English democratic revolution of the seventeenth century proved itself to be very theoretical and abstract for the Sudanese, the Palestinian, the Iraqi or the "Muslims in South Asia." The moving declarations of the French Revolution of "liberty, equality, and fraternity" must have rung false in the ears of the Algerian Liberation Army soldier.[11] The wounds of colonialism had barely healed when there appeared a new outbreak. In effect, Islam accuses the West of injustice because of its unilateral support of Israel.[12] The mistrust and the grievances, explicit or tacit, are not solely aimed at the free Western world. If some people do indeed see in Marxist socialism a conception of solidarity and social justice which is rather close to Islam, they generally reject the atheism of the former doctrine and do not forget that, despite

---

[9]Majid Khadduri, *War and Peace in the Law of Islam*, 3rd ed. (Baltimore: Hopkins, 1962), 312 pages. After this: Khadduri, *War*.
[10]Ghoneimi, *The Muslim Conception*, or again, in a most pronounced fashion, but on a specific subject: M. K. Ereksoussi, "Le Coran et les conventions humanitaires," *Revue internationale de la Croix-Rouge*, (1960):12 pages. After this: Ereksoussi, "Le Coran."
[11]F. al-Samir, "La pensée arabe face à la pensée occidentale," (pp. 295-308), in *Renaissance du monde arabe*, ed. Anwar Abdel Malek et al., p. 297.
[12]This is a lively feeling, above all – but not exclusively, in the Arab world.

the proclaimed principles of liberty and fraternity, Muslims living in the USSR are denigrated or even oppressed because of their religion.[13] It would perhaps have been appropriate to make mention at the end of this general introduction of that double reaction with respect to the two ideologies which divide the world. The conviction of the Muslims as to the present validity of Islamic laws will in all likelihood be the better understood of the two.

The Seal of the Prophets

A lot has already been written on the Prophet of Islam. His life was lived under the full light of history and his existence is known to us in detail. The image which Muhammad left of himself proves to be "scientific" to the extent that, being an integral part of the phenomenon of Islam, it discloses a certain manifestation of the religious concept and allows us to grasp his true greatness.[14] Depending on whether one wishes to portray (him) with respect and empathy[15] or with irony;[16] or whether one aims at elucidating the evolution of the sociological milieu in order to explain his coming onto the scene;[17] or, finally, whether one believes that Islam is the word of God, the presentation of its prophet will take on different shades of meaning. Muhammad, who is most certainly the object of emulation for the Muslims – an emulation which it would be dangerous to misinterpret – is exclusively the bearer of the external word and, in the eyes of the Muslims, does not have the same importance as Jesus Christ has for the Christians. It seems necessary, however, to know his life, because of the close tie that exists between the message and the messenger.[18] While emphasizing the strictly human nature of the Prophet, the Qur'ān nevertheless designates him as a "beautiful example" for the believers to follow.[19]

On the historical level, Muhammad was both an apostle and the founder of a political system which changed the course of history, and to a large extent influenced the subsequent development of the expansion of Islam. A

---

[13]Geoffrey Wheeler, *Racial Problems in Soviet Muslim Asia*, 2nd ed. (London: Oxford University Press, 1962), 67 pages, and Jean Prautois, "L'Islam et nationalisme en Asie dentrale soviétique," *Revue de Defense nationale*, (December 1971): 1842-1857.

[14]Roger Arnaldez, *Mahomet, ou la predication prophetique* (Paris: Seghers,, 1970), pp. 8 f.

[15]Tor Andrae, *Mahomet, sa vie et sa doctrine*, translated by Maurice Gaudefroy-Demombynes (Paris: Maisonneuve, 1945), 192 pages. After this: Andrae, *Mahomet*.

[16]Henri Lammens, *L'Islam, croyances et institutions*, 2nd Rev. ed. (Beirut: Imprimerie catholique, 1941), 334 pages. After this: Lammens, *L'Islam*.

[17]Chelhod, *Introduction*.

[18]Mohammed A. Draz, *Initiation au Coran* (Cairo: Al-Maaref, 1949), pp. 3 f. After this: Draz, *Initiation*.

[19]al-Ahzab: 21.

knowledge of the Prophet's life is necessary since the traditions which have been transmitted to us form an important part of Muslim law and morals. It is fitting, therefore, to describe the Prophet's personality according to the image he left of himself in the minds of the Muslims.[20]

Muhammad[21] was born about 570-571 AD, the son of a young widow who died a few years after his birth. Put in the care of his grandfather and then later in that of his uncle, he led the life of a young member of the Makkan oligarchy, coming from a family of good standing but of modest fortune. Tradition relates that even as an adolescent, he was distinguished by the trust placed in him by his fellow citizens, as well as by his constant concern to ensure intertribal peace and to guarantee justice. At the age of twenty-five, he married a rich widow fifteen years his senior. She was a relative who, having justly appreciated his noble qualities, proposed to him despite their age difference. This union brought him prosperity. Pained by the Arab population's moral degradation, he devoted the free time accorded him by his merchant activities to solitary meditation. Three years before the beginning of his mission, it was his custom to retire into a cave during the month of Ramadān, to offer prayers, and distribute food to the poor. As he was approaching the age of forty (610 AD), he received his first divine revelation. Three years later, the Archangel Gabriel instructed him to spread the message with which he had been entrusted. Henceforth, his role as a prophet was enhanced by that of a messenger. "The year 612 AD is the true point of departure of the activities of the Prophet of Islam, activities which the date of the *hijrah* was to divide into two periods of almost equal duration: ten years at his birthplace of Makkah, and ten more in Medinah, his new residence where he died"[22] in 632 AD at the age of a little more than sixty-one.

His mission was not to abolish the preceding revelations, but to confirm them while denouncing the violations perpetrated upon the previously revealed scriptures. It was his responsibility to purge any transgressions from the teachings of the prophets who came before him, to expand and add to them in such a way that they would be suitable for all humanity, regardless of the time and the place. By proclaiming the oneness of God, Muhammad became a political threat. From the outset, the small group of converts formed a

---

[20]D. Dinnet, and Sliman Ibrahim, *L'Orient vu de l'Occident* (Paris: Piazza-Geunthner, n.d.), 104 pages.

[21]Called thus by his grandfather and Ahmad by his mother, two names issue from the same Arab root meaning "praised" or "praiseworthy."

[22]Draz, *Initiation*, pp. 15-16. In fact, if one takes into account the first three years during which Muhammad had already received a certain number of revelations yet without an order to spread them, his prophetic vocation would have lasted thirteen years at Makkah and ten years at Medinah.

foreign body in the Makkan community. The proclamation of a monotheistic belief meant the rejection of traditional idol and ancestor worship, and thus posed a major religious threat to the society. The very natural and comprehensible opposition of the Makkan dignitaries to the new predication was therefore certainly not exclusively motivated by economic considerations, nor by the fear of losing the moral prestige brought by the pagan pilgrimage, as certain Western authors have claimed. There is nothing in the Qur'ān which would permit one to believe that. The hostility of the Arabs was expressed in essentially religious and political terms. Ideology which is national in character, even when little respected, becomes intolerant when abandoning it brings about the dissolution of that mystical tie which unites the members of the community. Religious opposition and its corollary, social conflict, were to degenerate into a struggle for power. Muhammad's adversaries "clearly understood that to adhere to his doctrine meant renouncing their national unity to a certain extent, and that to recognize his authority indicated a break with a former social order founded on custom and habit and concentrated in the hands of a few leaders ... This is what Muhammad's adversaries understood before him, with that clarity of vision stemming from hatred."[23]

Having a presentiment of the danger, Muhammad urged a small group of his adherents who were particularly vulnerable to flee to Abyssinia, and then organized the gradual exile of his faithful companions to the city which was to become Medinah.[24] The Makkans devised a plot to kill the Prophet. He got wind of it and managed to flee, almost miraculously, thanks to the brave complicity of his cousin 'Ali. Muhammad was received with enthusiasm at Medinah in July 622 AD.[25] This date marks the birth of the Islmaic era and the beginning of Muslim history. The term "hijrah" literally means emigration, exile, flight. The religion gives it a particular meaning corresponding to the breaking of ties with ignorance, the refusal of evil and the rejection of disbelief — in one word, to an act of faith.[26] It is interesting to point out that a "hijrah" is a "voluntary endistancing, although one determined by involuntary causes,"[27] a state continually being renewed when there is humiliation or oppression. The Muslim has to "emigrate" in order to struggle in the path of God, when this turns out to be necessary, until all injustice disappears.[28]

---

[23]Andrae, *Mahomet*, p. 124.
[24]It was called *Yathrib*, and later became *"Medinat un-Nabī"* the city of the Prophet.
[25]T. W. Arnold, *The Preaching of Islam: A History of the Propagation of the Muslim Faith* (Lahore: Ashraf, 1968), pp. 21 f. After this: Arnold, *The Preaching*.
[26]al-Anfal: 73.
[27]Draz, *Initiation*, p. 15.

The idea is often expressed that, during the first phase of his predication, Muhammad had announced the fundamental dogmatic ideas of Islam, and then in the second phase developed the ritual and liturgical stipulations, social and penal legislation, briefly, the corpus of Qur'ānic law upon which Islam survived in its early period. While being essentially Arab in Makkah, his teaching became universal in Medinah. On a strictly chronological level, this conjecture has been partially confirmed by historical criticism. The Muslim, however, interprets the facts in a different manner. For him, the Qur'ānic revelation does not assume a religious aspect on the one hand and a social and political aspect on the other. On the contrary, it appears as a whole, given in its totality. In the beginning, Islam used patience and persuasion. The legislative phase could not be realized until a solid community was formed. Quite logically then, this appeared after the eschatological predication.[29] At Makkah, Islam started out by forming the first Muslims who, constituting a small persecuted minority, were in need of a morality instead of a social legislation which they would not have been able to apply. Later, at Medinah, when the individuals were already molded by faith, Islam constructed an eqalitarian and mutualistic community endowed with divinely revealed laws. This chronology, which traces the birth of Muslim society, does not detract from but rather enhances the religion's universal nature.

With his settling in Medinah, the Prophet Muhammad's life becomes an integral part of Muslim history. His deeds and gestures have been transmitted to us in the most intricate detail. Muhammad the statesman never forgot his divine mission as a prophet and a messenger. He unceasingly displayed piety.[30] As a dynamic organizer, he was able to assert his combative spirit in defense of the rudimentary Muslim community and also to spread the message with which he had been entrusted. Combative yet magnanimous, he proved to be relentless toward the enemies of the faith. These three characteristics of the Prophet – piety, combativity and generosity[31] – seem to have shaped the growing Muslim community and to have foreshadowed the spiritual climate of classical Islam. The traditions constantly recount the generosity and humility of the Prophet, as well as his uprightness, his purity, his subtlety, and tolerance. A great captain, full of gentleness, heading the Muslim troops, he is equally portrayed by history as an honest, willing, and "democratic" statesman. A diplomat of finesse and integrity, he succeeded in

---

[28]Saal el-Dine Guizaoui, *En marge des études islamiques* (Cairo: Supreme Council of Islamic Affairs, 1967), pp. 82-89. After this: al-Guizaoui, *En marge*.

[29]Rouchdi Fakkar, *Réflexions sur l'Islam: Fondements de croyance et aspect social,* 2nd ed. (Paris: Maisonneuve, 1973), p. 91. After this: Fakkar, *Réflexions*.

[30]Maxime Rodinson, *Mahomet* (Paris: Seuil, 1968), pp. 25 f.

[31]Schuon, *Comprendre*, p. 117.

having the Muslim community legally recognized by treaty[32] while the fortune of arms began to smile upon him. Finally, on a psychological level, if one thinks of the fragility of an Arab leader's authority and the virtues demanded of him by the community, one can conclude that Muhammad, who managed to impose himself on such a vast scale, must really have been a superior man, a true prophet of God.

The Doctrine

Islam is not only a faith – it is a life to be lived in the present moment.[33] The Western term "religion" cannot but imperfectly and partially translate the meaning of the Muslim application, whose sense is vague and whose etymological origin is unknown. In Islam, "religion"[34] would seem to encompass truth, just behavior, and truthful attitude.[35] In its broad meaning, it represents the union of faith,[36] surrender to God,[37] and virtue.[38] In His message to mankind, God pointed out the truth, the law, and moral discipline : the first of these corresponding to intelligence,[39] the second to will, and the last to conscience. These three elements remain closely and inextricably linked. This is shown by enumerating the foundations of the "dogma": belief in God, His prophet, and in the revelation which he transmitted; belief in the prophets preceding him and in the scriptures they brought; and belief in the angels and in the Day of Judgment.[40] The juncture of the two terms, first and last, of the "credo" characterizes the exact nature of Islam, the "eschatological monotheism,"[41] and the unique nature of God being corroborated by His role as a judge. Indeed, the most moving passages of the Qur'ān deal with the unity of God, and on every page it refers to His majesty, His immateriality, and His compassion. The uncompromising monotheism of Islam gives it its most fundamental characteristic.

The intimate idea which the believer has of God is interesting and funda-

---

[32]Treaty of Hudaibiyyah with the Makkans.

[33]Syed Amir Ali, *The Spirit of Islam*: A History of the Evolution and Ideals of Islam, with a Life of the Prophet, 2nd Rev. ed. (London: Christophers, 1923), p. 178 f. After this: Amir Ali, *The Spirit*.

[34]"Din." See also chapter 6, p. 137.

[35]See the introduction by Omar A. Farrukh in ibn-Taimiyyah, *On Public and Private Law in Islam* (Beirut: Khayats, 1966), 202 pages. After this: ibn-Taimiyyah, *On Public and Private Law*.

[36]*Iman*.

[37]*Islam*.

[38]*Ihsan* means "beneficence" in the complete sense of the word: "to only do good, consciously and 'under the gaze of God.'"

[39]Schuon, *Comprendre*, pp. 13-14.

[40]an-Nisa': 136 and al-Baqarah: 285.

[41]Yohachim Moubarac, *L'Islam* (Paris: n.p. 1962), p. 57. After this: Moubarac, *L'Islam*.

mental, inasmuch as it determines his individual actions and, consequently, the social life of the community. Divine transcendency and omnipotence did not prevent the description of His attributes, the only possibility of relationship between the absolute and terrestrial human relativity which depends on it.

The Islamic concept of God is often misunderstood in the West, where He is represented as a merciless tyrant playing "with humanity as if on a chessboard."[42] On the contrary, His clemency and compassion are among the great themes of the Qur'ān. Numerous passages express in a moving manner divine care with regard to all beings.[43] God is eternal and omnipotent, extremely generous, a compassionate benefactor, but He is (also) the supreme judge. The Muslim's permanent surrender to the divine will creates an atmosphere of religiousness in which his life is bathed, and which represents the basic motivation of his moral life. In fact, the "remembrance of God"[44] who is invoked and called to mind a thousand times a day in expressions of current usage, should impose virtuous acts under all circumstances. This concept of God has also helped in creating a "style of action" in conformity with the religious dogma and with its spiritual perspectives. In this context, the fear of the Day of Judgment is in no way fear or anguish, but rather illustrates the essence of piety and awareness of the nobility of that responsibility entrusted to man.[45]

The belief in the preceding prophets and in the revelations which they brought constitutes two similar articles of faith. The Islamic concept is as follows: according to the various stages in mankind's evolution, God sent messages to enlighten and guide man. The Qur'ān is the final revelation, and Muhammad is the seal of the prophets, called to complete and correct the earlier scriptures. The Muslim must, therefore, admit and respect the preceding monotheistic revelations, all the while knowing that their meaning has been distorted and that he should reject all the falsifications which are contrary to the Islamic doctrine, especially those which violate the principle of divine unicity. Furthermore, the superiority of the Qur'ānic revelation is confirmed by the very fact of its chronological posteriority and of its character of being the ultimate divine message.[46] The association between faith and law is very in-

---

[42] Amir Ali, *The Spirit*, p. 150.

[43] We cite, for example: "We have created mankind ... We are closer to him than his jugular vein," Qaf: 16.

[44] See al-Baqarah: 16; and Schuon, *Comprendre*, pp. 180-182.

[45] Andrae, *Mahomet*, p. 73.

[46] Sheikh Mohammed 'Abdu, *Rissalat al-Tawhid*, an account of the Islamic religion; translated from the Arabic, with an introduction on the life and the ideas of Sheikh Mohammed 'Abdu, by B. Michel and Sheikh Moustapha Abdel Razik (Paris: Geuthner, 1925), pp. 112 f. After this:

timate not only for Islam but for all the religions which God, the unique guide and legislator, has sent to the world. He revealed His will through innumerable prophets,[47] certain of whom transmitted the scriptures. Islam, the final divine revelation, brings to man who has a need to believe and to know, a rule destined to guide him in each moment, as much in his personal behavior as in his relationship with God and his fellow men; a law, the respect for which represents the "necessary condition for ultimate salvation and eternal happiness."[48]

Belief in angels and demons expresses and illustrates the idea that God dominates the spiritual universe as well as the material world.[49] These angels and archangels reside in God's inner circle, passively obeying Him. Iblis (the Satan) was condemned for having refused to bow down before man, who had just been newly created;[50] he "was granted grace which will last until the Day of Judgment, of which he has taken advantage by leading men astray."[51] He is helped by demons, such as certain jinns to whom a certain number of misdeeds have been attributed.[52] Man was given two miraculous gifts by God: intelligence and freedom. The Qur'ānic revelation invites man to reject error and warns him that he will have to account for the actions he has performed during his lifetime. The evildoers will be subjected to infernal torments which are only barely mentioned in the Qur'ān, while those who are just will enter paradise, whose delights are described in picturesque terms. Together with the affirmation of divine unicity, the belief in happiness or in damnation in the eternal life constitutes the two basc tenets of faith.

Basically simple and logical, Islam never developed a sophisticated speculative theology. In effect, the Islamic doctrine is established in the Qur'ān. The theological development which derives from it has no other interest than that of leading to the mystery of God, such as God Himself suggests in the book in which the "word is deposited" – the Qur'ān. Being essentially reduced to the science of the unicity of God[53] and of the divine attributes, Muslim "theology" appears as a "poor" relative of the law. This affirmation needs to be qualified, since Islam does not really separate the two concepts. "Theolog-

'Abdu, *Rissalat*.

[47]"We have certainly sent to each community an apostle," an-Nahl: 36.

[48]Draz, *Initiation*, p. 66.

[49]Mohammed Bereketullah, *Le Kalifat* (Paris: Geuthner, 1924), p. 19. After this: Bereketullah, *Le kalifat*.

[50]See chapter 2 below. The Muslim authors do not agree on the "nature" of Iblis, whether he is an angel or a jinn.

[51]Henri Masse, *L'Islam* 9th ed. (Paris: Armand Colin, 1966), p. 107. After this: Masse, *L'Islam*.

[52]All jinns are not evil by nature; some of them are believers. See al-Jinn.

[53]*Tawhid*.

ical" speculation deals only with what must concern man: the attributes and not the nature of God. It was especially under the pressure of political and social contestations that dogmatic, scholastic theology[54] developed, in the course of the first two centuries of Muslim history, as a discipline separate from jurispurdence.[55] This theology was doomed at the very outset to a limited development. The sole major theme which fed the discussions dealt with man's free will. It also attempted to demonstrate the veracity and superiority of Islam in relation to the other two monotheistic religions. Raising Jesus to the level of divinity above all, as well as the rejection of Muhammad's prophetic mission, seemed illogical and heinous. On the other hand, since Islam brought a rule of life applicable to all daily actions, jurisprudence was to witness an immense development and to engender an innumerable amount of treatises. The latter developed continually in accordance with the expansion of the Muslim community and with the evolution of the social problems it encountered. So, although Islam took on the form of a "legalistic" religion, for the Muslim doctrine, knowledge regarding matters of faith nonetheless remained preferable to the study of law, which is but a corollary of faith, since it is the material actualization of faith. Faith represents the basis of a general and unique whole in which the concepts of faith and law are indivisible. Islam is not a religion with a rule, an orthodoxy with a judicial system, but a "juridical orthodoxy,"[56] the law of God.

The Law

The foundations of the law are the Qur'ān and the apostolic traditions which complement it. These two original sources are elucidated by human reasoning, collective consensus,[57] and individual analogous reasoning,[58] and are to a certain extent supplemented by some sort of auxiliary and vague sense of general welfare, or even by local custom, on the condition that these various contributions do not imply anything overtly contrary to the dogma. Together, they form the divine law[59] which indicates a "path to follow" — that is, not only what the faithful must believe, but especially the manner in which they are to act, guided by faith. The law determines the basic relations of man to God, with regard to his fellow men, and to himself. It has left nothing to chance, in a specific manner defining what is compulsory, recommended, legal, tolerated, or strictly prohibited. It embraces the body of duties

---

[54]*Kalam.*
[55]*Fiqh.*
[56]Schuon, *Comprendre*, pp. 13-14.
[57]*Ijma'.*
[58]*Qiyas.*
[59]*Shari'ah.*

imposed upon the Muslim "in his threefold capacity as believer, man, and citizen."[60] Surrender to the law and the desire to respect its conditions are derived from the acceptance of the faith which imposes a general conception of society and of its development.

Two elements are necessary for the definition of the sacred text in Islam: a divine book,[61] eternal and uncreated on the one hand, and a "recitation,"[62] the living word in the heart of the community on the other. For the believers, it is simultaneously a "food for the soul, a rule of conduct, a prayer book, the instrument of delivering sermons; it is their hymn and their history; it is their fundamental law and their code for all situations in life."[63]

For the Muslims, the Qur'ān is infinitely more important than any other sacred book is for its adherents. It is the "mediator" between God and humanity,[64] rendering any ecclesiastic organization redundant, since it asserts itself as the primordial reference,[65] the primary source of inspiration. Its mysterious dimension also stems from its literary presentation which, for the Muslims, is a true miracle proving the truthfulness of Islam.[66] It still remains in our day and age the inimitable and transcendent model of the Arabic letter. Not only does it represent the preeminent prototype of all literary work, but also the source of Arabic and Muslim literature which it creates, since the religion which it reveals is the "spring of a great number of intellectual procedures whereby writers are to illustrate their talent."[67] For Muslim orthodoxy, the Qur'ān is not a human production. It is rather the uncreated word of God, delivered in the Arabic language by the Archangel Gabriel to Muhammad. The various revelations appeared to the Prophet in innumerable fragments. As soon as they were revealed, they were transcribed here and there on the shoulder blades of animals, scraps of parchment, wooden tablets, palm leaves, or else on gazelle hides, for example. Little by little, they turned out to compose a unit, some passages of which developed without any relation to others, many verses being added and thus finding their place according to the explicit indications of Muhammad. Recent scientific discoveries have successfully determined the chronology of the various revelations with

---

[60]Lammens, L'Islam, p. 108.
[61]Kitab.
[62]Qur'ān
[63]Draz, Initiation, p. 18.
[64]Rondot, Islam p. 30.
[65]It is interesting to point out that in the everyday Arabic language the Qur'ān is often called "mashaf," a term which literally means a "compilation of leaves (of a book) and which can be assimilated with the French use of "code" to indicate a book of laws."
[66]Each prophet, Moses, Jesus, and Muhammad, had exceptional gifts for his age.
[67]André Miquel, La littérature arabe (Paris: n.p., 1969), p. 13.

apparent precision.

In 657 AD, twenty-five years after the death of the Prophet, the codification of the Qur'ān was completed, having been entrusted to those companions well known for their knowledge. The Caliph 'Uthman declared it the official book for all Muslims. Since then, it has been recognized as such by the entire Islamic world. In the eyes of the Muslims, the process by which the Qur'ān was "compiled" proves its miraculous and divine nature, bearing in mind the logical and literary unity of this book. Thus, it was to exist for all eternity. The verses, which were revealed separately and in no apparent chronological order, were to be laid one upon the other, according to a necessarily predetermined plan. "No other work, literary or other, was ever constructed under similar conditions, almost like separate numbered pieces of an old building which was simply to be constructed elsewhere in the same form as before."[68]

The prophetic traditions[69] consist of everything emanating from Muhammad when he was relieved of his divine apostolic mission.* Thus it is in no way the "word of God," but nevertheless assumes a legal significance of utmost priority. By reporting a saying[70] or relating an isolated incident, it encompasses all the advice and moral precepts of the Prophet, his practical daily actions, and finally his silence, indicating tacit approval of individual acts which he had witnessed or which had been reported to him. Built upon the personality of the Prophet, whose teachings it collected, it rapidly became a leading element in the Muslim legal structure, serving the purposes of explanation and interpretation. Initially orally transmitted, the "sayings" of the Prophet were systematically gathered by specialists performing a service of piety. In the ever-growing Muslim community, Qur'ānic attitudes in the strict sense were always further elucidated by the prophetic tradition, which thus participated in the establishment of ideal judicial norms.[71] This source rapidly became prolific, giving rise to several thousand traditions, some of which were illogical and anachronisms. Once Muslim orthodoxy was stabilized,[72]measures were taken to sort out and restrain the production of

---

[68]Draz, *Initiation*, p. 92.
[69]*Sunnah.*
(*) To say that the entire corpus of *āhādīth* is the repository of Muhammad's sayings "when he was relieved of his apostolic mission" is rather questionable. Prophethood by its very nature knows of no fragmentation as it is a lifelong mission. Nevertheless, there were occasions when the Prophet himself characterized some of his acts and opinions as personal, which he stressed were not to be followed. The *hadith* literature carries such distinctions. Tariq Quraishi (ed)
[70]*Hadith.*
[71]Georges H. Bousquet, *Le Droit musulman* (Paris: Armand Colin, 1963), pp. 25 f. After this: Bousquet, *Le Droit.*
[72]This was during the 9th century of the Christian era.

sayings. Verification and systematic classification led to the composition of official collections.[73] There developed a "science of traditions," whose effect was to ensure the validity of the prophetic tradition.

The reported tradition is presented in two parts: first of all, the chain of transmitters[74] or authorities, and then the dictum itself.[75] Muslim jurists, proceeding by a method which astounds the Western critical mind, were not so much concerned with the tradition's substance, since this went back to the Prophet who had become almost infallible, but scrupulously sought to establish the historical reality of the persons quoted, and to verify that they had truly the possibility of meeting one another, through successive relations going back to Muhammad and his companions. If the conditions to be met by the transmitters were not fulfilled, the saying was rejected. Though only the second source of law, the traditions exerted a considerable influence upon Muslim society. It imbued the Muslim judicial system with a remarkable degree of flexibility, and consequently played a significant role as an element of structure and support in the Islamic society.[76]

Reference must still be made to the obligations which form the "five pillars" or "cornerstones" of Islam, generally dealt with in the domain of the law, by being placed within the general perspective of Muslim monotheism. That is where their true nature is to be found. The link between faith, law, and ritualistic obligations is in fact coherent only in the framework of the absolute oneness of God Who revealed His will to man. On the level of superficial observance, the "five pillars of Islam," which derive their imperative force from Qur'ānic prescriptions, could seem to be a rigidly established ceremonial rite or a strictly mechanical execution. However, while respecting their form is a necessary condition for their validity, the clearly and openly declared[77] intention of the believer assumes a primary importance.

Of the "five pillars of Islam," the declaration of faith[78] is the most important and the most essentially Muslim. In truth, it represents the summit of the religious and juridical edifice. It demands the verbal confession of a sincere double belief, namely the unicity of God and the truth of the message

---

[73] The most celebrated are al-Bukhari and Muslim.
[74] *Isnad.*
[75] *Matn.*
[76] Caesar E. Farah, *Islam: Beliefs and Observances* (New York: Barron's, 1968), p. 163. After this: Farah, *Islam.*
[77] This is so except for voluntary charity so as not to humiliate the beneficiary because, for the obligatory charity (*zakah*), the beneficiary should not suffer any humiliation since his acceptance is, at the same time, a religious act and a legal right.
[78] *Shahadah.*

transmitted by Muhammad. It combines the abstract and the concrete, idealities and realities, spiritual and temporal experiences. The belief in Muhammad's prophetic mission is the evidence of discernment, and places itself between the relative and the absolute; it unites the world with God.[79]

A categorical affirmation of monotheism and an unreserved approval of the divine law, the declaration has at times permitted us to deduce that faith represented the preeminent theological virtue of Islam, whereas Christianity emphasizes charity, and Judaism casts a particular light upon hope. Such a statement might possibly shock Muslims, for they see Islam as the religion of all virtues developed to their highest level. Whatever the case may be, it would by no means be a question of exclusivity, but rather one of shades of meaning or degrees of intensity, in which case it remains obvious that neither hope[80] nor charity[81] are foreign to Islam, an eschatological religion. To the theological virtues of faith, hope, and charity correspond the paths of knowledge, action, and love.[82] These "paths" could partially explain the attitudes of the believers of any one of the three monotheistic religions with regard to their existential future as well as to their behavior in the framework of social reality.

Prayer, an expression of glorification and supplication,[83] whose ritual is very precisely determined, unites the Muslim with Islam and integrates man into the universal world. It confers upon him his dignity through a transcendental vision of his nature. As a result, it demands a humility emphasized by the physical aspect of the prayer since the most noble parts of the body must touch the ground. Ritual prayer[84] is not an invocation left to personal inspiration or some vague emotion, but an act which must be constantly nourished by the word of God. In "free prayer,"[85] on the other hand, the worshipper may either express himself spontaneously and in his mother tongue (if it is not Arabic), or recite Qur'ānic verses if he believes that his supplication could be better expressed by the latter.

Legal almsgiving[86] is quoted in thirty-two verses of the Qur'ān and is gen-

---

[79]Ahmed Hussein, *On Conviction and Islam* (Cairo: Supreme Council for Islamic Affairs, n.d.), pp. 176-177. After this: Hussein, *On Conviction.*
[80]"... Who despairs of the mercy of his Lord, but such as go astray," al-Hijr: 56. See also an-Nisa': 105 or again al-Baqarah: 218, and az-Zumar: 53.
[81]See, among numerous other verses, al-Baqarah: 177 and al-Qiyamah: 8.
[82]Schuon, *Comprendre*, note p. 74.
[83]Mohammad N. Ghali, *al-Salat* [The Prayers] (Cairo: Supreme Council of Islamic Affairs, 1961), 34 pages.
[84]*Salah.*
[85]*Du'ā'* is recommended for the night, especially during the month of Ramadān.
[86]Abdel Razzak Nofal, *az-Zakāh* [La part du Pauvre] (Cairo: Supreme Council of Islamic Affairs, 1961), 34 pages.

erally associated wth prayer. It purifies the giver by bestowing on him victory over selfishness and the moral satisfaction of participating in the creation of a more just society. It is not charity, but the obligation of the wealthy and the "right of the poor." As a contribution among "associates" of communal possessions, it achieves fraternity and solidarity. It is more than a social act; it is a religious duty whereby the believer voluntarily gives back to God a portion of his terrestrial property; in other words, he returns a portion of his divine benificence to avoid suffering in the life to come. The legal beneficiaries – though indirect on the level of religious metaphysics – are the poor, orphans, slaves wishing to buy their freedom, those in debt, prisoners, the newly converted, travelers in Islamic territories, and tax collectors.

According to the Muslim doctrine, fasting[87] enjoys a grace in the eyes of God which is beyond comparison with all other acts of piety and worship. It does not have the same character of penitence which Christianity has given it but is understood in Islam as an abstinence which imposes a certain restraint on the body. Fortifying the will, it frees man from his passions and purifies his spirituality through self-denial and deprivation. It therefore represents much more than just "an exercise like any other aiming at human equilibrium, be it physical and even psychological and spiritual ... It is essentially placing oneself at the disposal of God."[88]

The pilgrimage is the fifth obligation in Islam and is conditional on the financial and material possibilities for the believer to fulfill it, on his state of health, and on the obligation of having acquitted himself of all responsibilities toward his family. The ritual has strictly determined duties.[89] It has an obviously symbolic meaning which foreshadows "the interior journey to the ka'bah of the heart. It purifies the community just as the blood circulation, by passing through the heart, purifies the body." [90] It is the most explicit representation of the solidarity of the Muslim community which gathers as if in a "full assembly" once a year.

Among the basic duties of the believer, the *jihad* is sometimes mentioned, a word whose literal meaning is "effort." The translation "holy war" is, unfortunately, the most frequently used. In contrast to the others, this duty – "the exterior and collective manifestation of discernment between truth and

---

[87] al-Bahay al-Kholi, *Al-Siyam* [Fasting] (Cairo: Supreme Council of Islamic Affairs, 1961), 48 pages; and Ali A. Wafi, *Le Jeune et le sacrifice dans l'Islam et les religions anterieures à l'Islam* [Fasting and Sacrifice in Islam and Religions Anterior to Islam] (Cairo: Supreme Concil of Islamic Affairs, 1966), 79 pages.

[88] Moubarac, *L'Islam*, p. 64.

[89] Muhammad M. Merchant, *A Book of Qur'ānic Laws* (Lahore: Ashraf, 1971), pp. 71-98.

[90] Schuon, *Comprendre*, p. 48.

error"[91] – generally falls upon the community as a whole and simultaneously upon the individual.[92]

Morals

According to tradition, Ja'far ibn Abu Talib, leader of the first group of Muslims to flee, in answer to (Negus of Ethiopia who had offered them hospitality), defined Islam as follows: "The Prophet sent by God asked us to give up our idols and worship Allah, the only God. He commanded us to speak the truth, to remain true to our promise, to act benevolently toward our parents and neighbors, to avoid evil, not to spill the blood of the innocent, not to lie, not to lay hold of the belongings of orphans, and not to violate the honor of women. We believed in him; we were eager to make our lives conform to the precepts he taught." This definition clearly shows that, beyond faith and law, Islam contains a distinct element of asceticism. Did Muhammad himself not say that he had been sent to perfect the morals (of his people)? This seems, as a matter of fact, to have been his main concern at the beginning of his mission in Makkah. The Qur'ān confirms the distinguished and exemplary character of the Prophet.[93] Nevertheless, his "morality was the Qur'ān"[94]; in other words, his morality was not any particular "ethic," but covered the totality of daily actions by applying those precepts set out in the divine law.

Islam's unity has rendered it a religion difficult to describe by the traditional concepts of Western philosophy. This revealed law brought everything into order and did not ignore any act of the believer, guiding his personal conduct, his relations with others, and his behavior both within Muslim society and outside of it. The duty thus assumes a nature which is at once formal and ceremonial on one hand and ascetic or moral on the other. Muslim intellectual climate is characterized by the union of the spiritual and the temporal. What could appear as confusion to the West is a logical synthesis in Islam, the affirmation of a social adherence, the defense of the perfect unity of human nature. Specialized non-Muslim literature usually presents Islam under the double category of dogma and law. Since the division has already been made and has proved necessary for didactic purposes, it has seemed useful to open up yet a third supplementary category by examining the "Islamic system" not only in its sacred and institutional but also in its moral aspect.

---

[91]Ibid.
[92]See chapter 5.
[93]"In truth, you (Muhammad) are of an eminent moral condition," al-Qalam: 4 (Blachère).
[94]Ismail Kashmiri, *Prophet of Islam, Mohammed, and Some of His Traditions* (Cairo: Supreme Council of Islamic Affairs, n.d.), p. 12. After this: Kashmiri, *Prophet.*

This perspective does not distort since one of the three constituent elements of the religion is virtue. Beside the divine law, the "conscience" of the believer is also an authority which, at the bottom of his heart, calls him to account, and whose prime foundation – essentially religious – resides in the human soul and which never ceases to censure and to "criticize" as the Qur'ān indicates. Thus, faith and pious surrender do not cancel out the free judgment of the believer who has to assume the responsibility of his acts. Islam's imperative morality, which could be qualified as eschatological, is characteristic: the thought of the Day of Judgment urges the Muslim to respect the law, to abandon the ways of evil, and to preach virtuousness. As such, it brings in an element tending toward the morality of compensation, which it would be difficult for any religious doctrine to avoid. Besides, this perspective fits in perfectly with the general economy of Islam. In effect, the revelation appeals to the true nature of man, who carries in himself both good and evil and for whom the fear of retribution helps to impose an upright attitude. The religious ethic is nevertheless separate from this, since any social act must be performed only as an expression of inner faith, in the same way as external religious rituals. In Islam, the religion of certainty and intelligence, morality assumes a particular nuance in which kindness is not necessarily synonymous with sacrifice.

Although it is expressed in rather different terms, in its outer appearance Islam's moral system is fairly similar to the one known in the West, except that reasoning and discernment have priority over feeling and emotion. Indeed, "in the moral sense, the soul is simultaneously endowed with reasoning and intelligence. Failing this undying sense of good and evil, there always remains the idea of a universal duty and one which is universally recognized as such . The Qur'ān attempts to make us overcome our feelings of the moment by calling to its support the testimony of the sages and saints of all times. It is for this reason that one of the expressions most dear to the Qur'ānic revelation is to adhere firmly to those revelations which preceded it."[95] For the Muslim, none of the great moral precepts of the religions which preceded the Islamic revelation is foreign to his belief. If, on the other hand, a norm were to shock his reasoning or contradict the logical process of the law, the Muslim would be compelled to reject it as an error and to fight it as a heresy. Muhammad was a prophet, not a social reformer. The message which he conveyed brought about basic upheavals in the Arab society of that time, the reverberations of which are still echoing in the contemporary Islamic world. The divine law completed earlier revelations and definitively brought order to man's behavior. On the level of individual virtue,

---

[95]Draz, *Initiation*, p. 69.

the Qur'ān gives to its inherent justice and charity a true code of ethics and courtesy which molded Muslim civilization. Courtesy, along with good upbringing, good manners, and sincerity are the foundations of that sociability which were to make the community of believers a vast fraternity. From this angle, the individual's duty has precedence over his right. The establishment of a just and honest society is inherent to Islamic teachings. Virtues become obligations and precepts of faith. However, this does not mean that morality is dry jurisprudence, since the intention determines the quality of any action. In the final analysis, the virtue cultivated and the kindness distributed are nothing other than a humble and just offering of a negligible portion of that gratitude owed to Allah.

The essential social virtue, the basis of the Muslim's moral behavior, takes on a collective rather than an inter-individual aspect, a fundamental characteristic of the Islamic system. The Qur'ān, the traditions and classical doctrine all emphasize the necessity of consolidating and tightening the ties uniting the members of the community. "Thus the idea of universal virtue cast by the New Testament is further developed and takes shape, reaching into other areas of life. Is this to say that the Muslim community should slacken its internal bonds to lose itself in the ocean of humanity? On the contrary, two commandments were to remind it forcefully of its role as a distinct and more organic community."[96] These two particular commandments are, first, the constantly repeated injunction to the faithful to remain an indivisible entity, devoid of dissension or schism, and second, the moral duty to impose what is righteous and prevent what is evil. In this respect, it is proper to take into account the distinction that Islam makes between "man as such" and "collective man," bearing in mind, however, that "if there is a clear separation in Islam between man as such and collective man, these two realities are nonetheless profoundly linked together, given that the collectivity is an aspect of man – no man can be born without a family – and that, conversely, a society is a multiplication of individuals. It follows from this interdependence or reciprocity that anything done with a view to the community, such as the tithe for the poor or the holy war, has a spiritual value for the individual and conversely."[97] The concept of "man as such" will define for us man in relation to God, the "son of Adam," and collective man, the community of believers, the "Muslim city," in the perspective of its institutional organization and of its relations with the outside world.

Muslim morality[98] forms an integral part of the religion which, according

---

[96] Draz, *Initiation*, p. 81.
[97] Schuon, *Comprendre*, pp. 30-31.
[98] Mohammad A. Draz, *La morale du Coran*. This is a comparative study of the theoretical mor-

to tradition, is "the way to behave toward others." We will not judge to what extent it is applied and respected in our day. One great reformer of Islam has gone as far as saying that the lives of present-day Muslims has become "a manifestation which is contrary to their religion."[99] (He claims that) the decrepitude of and deviations from faith are such that it is actually the vices rather than the virtues taught by God and the Prophet Muhammad which characterize the Muslims: doctrinal corruption and intellectual ignorance, injustice and tyranny, treachery, falsehood and trickery, even when relating to God. Since the Islamic message is considered a coherent whole, the studies of Muslim authors on the foundations of morality, scanty as they are, must be sought for among a hodgepodge of publications in which jurisprudence, philosophy, history, and mysticism are all thrown together. Specialized publications are rare. Speculation in ethical matters is generally disapproved of since it risks damaging the moral equilibrium of the society and of the individuals who compose it by questioning or by even engendering a lack of respect for certain norms which are indispensable to the harmony of the community. The Qur'ān states this implicitly: "Most of the unbelievers follow naught but conjecture. Assuredly conjecture can by no means take the place of Truth."[100] The believer is nonetheless called upon to make an effort to understand the meaning and aim of the ethical code contained within the Qur'ān, so as to conscientiously put it into practice.

In essence, if not in expression, Muslim morality shows relatively fewer basic differences from Western precepts than one would initially think. To a large extent, the very nature of the divine revelation and the historical and sociological circumstances under which it appeared can explain the formal difference. The Christian revelation, which engendered a specific morality, is fixed and in a constant state of generation due to the theoretical possibility of imitating the life of Jesus. The Qur'ān is the permanent and definite word of God, bringing and representing the law which does not fail to appeal to the inner feelings of man, to his intelligence, and to his reasoning powers. Its observance requires a constant moral effort. The Qur'ānic references which appeal to man's innate consciousness of good and evil are numerous. To encourage the believer's rational efforts, to strengthen his will, and to make him transcend his emotions, the Qur'ān evokes the image and the life of those holy men who came before the revelation so that they may serve as evidence and examples. Thus, most of the precepts of universal morality are enumer-

---

ality of the Qur'ān, according to a classification of chosen verses, forming the complete code of practical morality. (Cairo: Al-Maaref, 1950), 715 pages. After this: Draz, *La morale.*
[99] Abdu, *Rissalat,* p. 136.
[100] Yunus: 36 (Masson).

ated and sometimes presented in a new light. The Qur'ānic revelation emphasizes its affiliation with and concordant attachment to the monotheistic religions which preceded it. Muhammad considered his mission as one to rectify the errors which had crept into Judaism and Christianity, to revitalize and supplement them.

Certain nuances are important, however. The narration of events and description of characters, which seek to illustrate ethical precepts, vary according to the Bible and the Qur'ān. The precision of a detail assumes its importance depending on the moral lesson derived from it. The story of Joseph serves as an illustration in this respect. For example, the Bible gives us a story of a failure and then revenge, whereas the Qur'ān gives a penetrating psychological description of the mechanisms of temptation. The Qur'ān points out that the story of Joseph is not "an imaginary story" but a "confirmation," a "lesson for men of understanding."[101] The differences in the accounts given of the lives of the prophets could well indicate delicate shades of appreciation of basic moral values. A comparative and interpretive study of the events mentoned in both holy books could perhaps bring out some important divergences between Muslim and Judeo-Christian morality.

Having at his disposition an entire revelation from which it is his duty to learn, the Muslim will attempt to improve his moral behavior not so much by searching for new truths, but rather by meditating upon the revealed values and observing them in practice, in imitation of the best of those who have preceded him or who live in his area.[102] In this respect, the relationship of the life of the Prophet and of his companions is particularly stimulating. Moreover, basing itself on the Qur'ān, the doctrine characterizes the believer as "he who orders good and forbids evil." Islam regards as evident the necessity of community life and of human solidarity. This results in specific duties which, even if they often assume a judicial formulation, appeal to the heart of hearts of the individual: respect for the person and the property of others, justice and honesty, respect for the given word, generosity, patience and a pacifist attitude, humility and courtesy. In the practice of moral norms, respect explicitly represents a necessary condition for eternal salvation.

Although it is a law for social interaction, Islam nevertheless offers more than a strictly social morality. Without a doubt, Muhammad was considered revolutionary, which he really was, inasmuch as every prophet is *ipso facto*, for he tries to transform the milieu in which he lives. However, the exclu-

---

[101]Yusuf: 111 (Masson). See also al-An'am: 84 and al-Mu'minoun: 34.
[102]Francois Bonjean, "Quelques causes d'incompréhension entre l'Islam et l'Occident," *L'Islam et l'Occident*, Paris (Cahier du Sud no. 9), 1947, 393 pages, pp. 33-51, p. 38. After this: Bonjean, *Islam et Occident*.

sively social aspect of Islam seems to have been overstated. It is true that many of the first converts were recruited from the humblest classes of Makkan society. In addition to this, Muhammad, like any magnanimous and noble personality, certainly showed compassion toward the unfortunate and unhappy. This is eloquently shown by the traditions. Above all, in its very substance and in the logic of its structure, Islam at once proved to be essentially egalitarian by its representation of God, the universe, and man. By attributing the unique source of all men to Adam, Qur'ānic teachings put an end to social stratification; the only superiority which an individual may possibly have over his fellow resides in his discernment, thus in his piety. However, if it is social, the Islamic doctrine does not appear to have to rouse humanitarian motivations in the believer such as could truly topple the established economic structure, for example. In effect, no true revolt is found against the fate of the poor, but rather prescriptions as to how to attempt to ease this situation. Still, it is necessary to explain the terms of this context. The solutions to the problems of poverty do not consist only of piety and fraternal generosity. By structuring society on the foundation of equity on the economic level, Islam strives to eradicate poverty. It prescribes the adequate fulfillment[103] of the essential daily needs of each Muslim. In the Islamic perspective therefore, legal almsgiving, a powerful instrument, is used to rehabilitate the poor and indigent.

In his moral life, the Muslim must respect the prescriptions of the divine law. It is not a question of a simple, mechanical automatism. The believer must feel himself deeply involved since it is incumbent upon him not only to do but also to "order" good, not only to avoid but also to "forbid" evil. It is this very characteristic which gives the Muslim society, even in our day and age, its foundation of tradition and conservatism. By the intimate union of the spiritual and the temporal, Islam necessarily makes the believer a morally committed being. Thus, despite the infinite transcendence of God, virtue is essentially a dynamic part of the will. The believer's commitment is indispensable. His attitude is guided by the Qur'ān and the life of Muhammad (as reported by the traditions), which is considered the ideal behavior of one attempting to live in conformity with the divine word. The law is divine, the obligation imperative, and the sanction eschatological. The foundation of moral life resides in faith and a sincere piety, which represents the most transcendent dynamic sentiment. The law, of an absolute nature, governs the practical activities of the believer at all moments of his life.

The general moral perspective varies according to the nature of the religion itself. A comparison is useful even if it separates concepts which in the Mus-

---

[103]*al-Ghina.*

lim perspective cannot be separated. If charity is in fact the main theological virtue of Christianity, in Islam it is faith which takes priority.[104] This implies that for the former, the path to salvation is sacrifice and generosity; for the latter, it is piety and respect for the law, and loyalty to the law bringing about the moral and spiritual elevation of the believer. The essential difference is probably the cause of the Western world's incomprehension of Muslim morality, which seems rather formalistic. Being an adherent of the religion of love and consequently of sacrifice, the Christian believes that in the Qur'ānic system of practical prescriptions, he distinguishes a limitation. The Muslim perspective is very different for he sees the foundation of his entire life not in individualistic effort,[105] but in the free and rational decision to respect the law. In short, the important question for the individual is to search for and to find where exactly he fits into the perfect order of the world. What constitutes good is equilibrium, whereas evil is found in disharmony. They are established and defined in the Qur'ān. They intend the protection of God's rights and those of man. Thus, each person ought to be able to find his due in personal and collective harmony. So, "this equilibrium, far from being an end in itself as is supposed by the Christian, who is accustomed to a more or less exclusive idealism of the will, is, in the final analysis, only a basis for escape in peace giving and liberating contemplation of the immutable, away from the uncertainties and turbulence of the ego."[106]

The Qur'ān does not bring a philosophy or an ethic to the believers. It confirms the innate moral sentiments of man and reveals to him the paths to follow. "The practice of virtue in reality demands the exact observance of the precepts contained in the revelation, whereas vice is essentially disobedience to, or revolt against, the divine law."[107] By extension, every human action has a religious value. The quasi-judicial aspect of Muslim morality reassures and stimulates the conscience of a believer who knows that any sin – which is not so much an expression of a perverted will as it is the consequence of his blindness – can be compensated for by the automatic dispositions of the law . The fault requires repentance and above all demands the sincere intention to return to the "straight path" and to remain firmly upon it."[108]

In the Qur'ān, more than fifty verses associate piety with good actions. Intention, truthfulness, and sincerity are the superior virtues of the moral life.

---

[104]We will return to this statement which, too abruptly advanced as it is here, could seem mistaken to Muslim readers (See chapter 3, pp. 117 f.).
[105]"God wants ease for you, He does not want for you difficulties," al-Baqarah: 185 (Masson).
[106]Schuon, *Comprendre*, p. 21.
[107]Denise Masson, *Le Coran et la révélation judéo-chrétienne: Etudes comarées* 2 vols. (Paris: Adrien – Maisonneuve, 1958), p. 674. After this: Masson, *Le coran*.
[108]The desire not to repeat the error committed is an integral part of "sincere repentance": "O

These qualities give to the revealed law – judicial in its formulation – an ethical aspect which logically fits into the legal system of Islam. The responsibility of the believer to respect what is forbidden and to fulfill what is compulsory is founded upon concepts which are eminently religious. Man, with his faith and intelligence, must think of himself as if he were living "under the gaze of God."

Nature provides man with a certain and tranquil fulfillment. The Qur'ān commands the believer to recognize and appreciate in nature obvious "signs" of the divine transcendancy and existence. The latter, however, is opposed to vulgarly material utilitarianism. Moderate pleasure leads to the equilibrium and peace of the pious man who, through discernment, is content with what existence brings him. Thus, this necessary moderation forms a barrier to unleashed self-centeredness and to extreme individualism. Put back into the context of the community, utilitarian morality then implies for the individual devotion and renunciation – in truth, sacrifice to collective utility and social solidarity. It is true that the Qur'ānic law offers him the material whereby he may assert his individual personality. It does not, however, authorize him to reconsider the evaluation of values or to sort through them and decide upon rejecting some of them since they have been imposed by divine revelation and because man on his own is incapable of determing an exact set of virtues. The law is external only in appearance; it requires the effort and commitment of the individual conscience as well as the maintenance and development of a harmonious and homogenous community for its implementation. This twofold aspect explains why the behavior of the Muslim often disconcerts the foreign observer; the contradiction between exacerbated individualism and collective, sometimes overwhelming, traditionalism seems to be permanent.

Intelligence and reasoning are found in the logical extension of nature, and they enable the universal order of things to be relocated; these faculties predispose one to wisdom. The believer, conscious of the precariousness of existence as compared to the absolute, will not have to torture himself about events exterior to him. He will consider the benefits of this world as being temporary and as a sign of the divine will even though such an attitude does not mean resignation. Thus, he will remain protected from a sensitivity which could lead him into error and excess in the framework of what is prescribed by the law. In fact, the law and spirit of the Qur'ān develop two currents: on the one hand, legalistic and ritualistic social organization, and on the other hand, a true surmounting of the inner life. The first aspect characterized Islam at the time of its expansion and the organization of its community. This aspect still seems to predominate since it is the easier of the two to systemat-

---

you who believe! Return to God with a sincere repentence ..." at-Tahrim: 8 (Masson).

ically classify.[109] Islamic morality, however, can be understood without one considering that the Qur'ān represents not only the law, but also a catalyst of thoughts guiding the behavior of the believer according to the only human finality: surrender to the divine will. Apparently dry and formalistic, Islamic "morality" is totally conditioned by the intention. Individual behavior is not imposed from the outside, but is "internalized" by faith. The believer's commitment arises from the choice he makes to obey. Thus, that very powerful attraction which sensitively exerts itself on most people is neither proscribed nor neglected. In this perspective, it is likely that the Muslim moralists did not fail to borrow certain ideas from Islamic mysticism, on the level of its content, even though they have often rejected its form.[110]

Contemplation upon the natural order of things, the appeal to reason, and the voluntary intention to observe the divine law collectively constitute the principle foundations of Islamic morality. It does not comfortably fit into any of the traditional frameworks of Western classification; in fact neither the sense of utilitarianism, nor reason, nor virtuous feeling would suffice with respect to moral rules. The Islamic revelation, because it reveals the absolute transcendence of God, is the necessary and sufficing parallel. Faith and law give men the power to effectively bridle their tendencies arising from passion and self-interest. They simultaneously represent the greatest existence-giving factor of moral life. The law presents the believer with a criterion for the appreciation of any specific situation and provides all concrete problems with a solution. Faith incites and vitalizes action. This concept is obvious when placed back into the theological economy of Islam in which faith is the essential theological virtue just as sincerity is the quality of grace. It is, primarily, the believer's commitment and, secondarily, the love of one's neighbor and hope in a better world to come which vitalize the action. By extension, it is not so much charity as the aspiration toward justice and a certain sense of equality which constitutes the external aspect of this action.

The Qur'ān explicitly confirms the fact that a wide latitude is left to the individual conscience, and it exhorts Muslims to "strive to do what is best, wherever they may be."[111] Furthermore, prophetic tradition reports that Muhammad defined moral life as: "Interrogate your heart. Virtue is that thing by which the soul is at rest and by which the heart can enjoy serenity. Sin

---

[109]Jean-Marie Abdel Jalil, *Aspects interieurs de l'Islam*, 2nd Rev. ed. (Paris: Seuil, 1962), pp. 34-35. After this: Abdel Jalil, *Aspects*.
[110]Abu Hamid M. al-Ghazali, *Deliverance from Error and Attachment to the Lord of Might and Majesty*, 4th ed., translated by W. Montgomery Watt (London: Allen and Unwin, 1970), p. 38. After this: al-Ghazali, *Deliverance*.
[111]al-Baqarah: 148. (Savary). *Le Coran*, Paris (Garnier), 1960. Blachère translated it as "Compete in good works."

is that thing which creates worry in the minds and torment in the hearts of
men..." The force of monotheism and the apparent exclusivity of Islamic law
have in all likelihood veiled the aesthetic and moral elements of Islam from
the rapid and superficial glance. It seemed useful to make mention of them
again.

Unity, Equilibrium, Harmony

The Western world, confronted by the concrete and perceptible problems
of material life and scientific progress, has to a large extent lost the sense
of the supernatural. It is astounding to it that the sacred should still provide
the premises of a valid intellectual process as well as the suggested foundation
of social organization. On the other hand, the concept of the holy, of the
invisible world, is far more immediate and real to those who live in non-
Western nations, for whom religion plays a particular role. It consists of the
belief in the absolute and in a unified and higher order of things. The world
is itself a moral system. The absolute is a kind of ideal basic value which
is indivisible and indecipherable: it is God Who, for the Muslims, revealed
Himself to men through His prophets. "The supreme virtue lies in adapting
harmoniously to this order."[112] Evil consists of any destruction of this harmony or unity. It is from this fundamental point of view that Islam appears
to be "the religion of certainty and equilibrium."[113] The only true reality,
divine unicity, necessarily brings about the balanced unity of man, of society,
and of the human race. Allah, as opposed to the concept of God according
to the Gospels, does not come down to man in a state of incarnation. Thus,
between Him and man there is neither intercessor, nor intermediary, nor
church or clergy. God is the absolute and unique point of reference, the beginning and end of the existential destiny of those who believe in Him and
in Muhammad. The individual is part of the community of believers, which
forms a fraternity whose only criterion for acceptance is faith. It is certitude
and the pride of possessing the truth which forms the foundations of Muslim
solidarity far more than the law or social structures. It is for this reason that,
if the Muslim world has not been able to maintain its political unity, Islam
has on the contrary shown a wonderful capactiy to preserve its religious cohesion, which has remained almost intact despite various schisms. The faith has
acted as a catalyst in the formation of a distinct entity which the vicissitudes
of history and contact with different civilizations have not managed to destroy. This very acute sense of belonging to an entity, and the vitalizing consciousness of possessing the truth have created a specific civilization, one

---

[112]Duncan B. MacDonald, *The Religious Attitude and Life in Islam* (Beirut: Khayats, 1965),
p. 1.
[113]Schuon, *Comprendre*, p. 17.

which affirms a particular definition of the individual, the state, and the world.

In Islam, all is unity. The ritual obligations express cohesion in an external and material manner. Five times a day, through prayer, Muslims prostrate themselves (at more or less the same time), in the same direction – toward the Ka'bah. Both the religious intention associated with the physical ritual and the prayer itself express man's spiritual and material unity. Moreover, worship is generally mentioned in the Qur'ān in conjunction with legal almsgiving, a religious obligation and reciprocal right which unites the nation of the faithful. In the same way, Ramadan symbolically unites all Muslims, for they must abstain from drinking and eating according to an identical schedule. It is, in addition, one of the foundations of Islamic egalitarianism, compelling both rich and poor alike to abstinence. As for almsgiving, it is a part of the conception of the Muslim community's unity and harmony. Compulsory charitable assistance enforces cooperation. The pilgrimage is the most perceptible manifestation of the unity of a community which shares the same faith. It is as much faith as it is a cultural practice uniting man directly with God, which constitutes the solidarity and unity of the Muslim community and, at the same time, leads to its universality. The concomitance – not metaphysical since we are dealing with a single but practical system – of the religious and the legalistic in Islam has the characteristics of the same unitary concept. The community of believers, formed by faith, has succeeded in outliving political disintegration, and the religious ties which transcend interstate boundaries have not been seriously affected.

The Qur'ānic message and the teachings of the Prophet have proven to be essentially progressive. These characteristics explain the extraordinarily fast development of Islam over the course of the first centuries of its history. Various factors enable us to partially understand why and how the immense and dynamic wave of reform and progress seems to have suddenly petrified. While the faith in its essence has not regressed, the Muslim world seems to have been immobile for almost seven centuries. The all-round character of the Islamic message and its impact on the conscience of the believers could both facilitate and obstruct a rebirth. This is a fact of which the Muslims are conscious, but one which does not question the validity of Islam.

A concourse of political, philosophical, and economic circumstances created a climate of uncertainty within the Musim world. On the political level, it was the advent of the numerous antagonistic dynasties, the crusades, the Mongolian invasion, the Tartars, and later on the Turkish intrusions which brought about the dislocation of the social body. On the economic level, the great discoveries of the European renaissance led to the deterioration of trade as the Muslims lost their naval supremacy mainly to the Portuguese. Social demands and uprisings also have shaken the community, especially in modern-day Iraq. Finally, on the philosophical level, the initial atmosphere of tolerance gave rise to intellectual, metaphysical, theological, and mystical fermentation. Islamic doctrine was exposed to the extremely violent assaults of the rationalists and philosophers. Imam al-Ghazzali tried to establish some sort of orthodoxy. Slowly, scholasticism asserted itself and then later triumphed. Soon, all research and efforts were stopped so as to preserve doctrinal unity. Religious cohesion and dogmatic coherence were safe and sound, but since then Islam has found itself on the defensive.[114] The Muslims realized the stagnation into which their brilliant civilization had fallen only when Europe displayed the superiority of its armed forces over the Ottomans, the dominant Islamic power of the day. Napoleon's invasion of Egypt produced a true shock in the Arab-Muslim world.[115] The basic dilemma which the contemporary Islamic world encounters is not so much to effect a "head-on" reform of its religion, which is rarely questioned, but rather to find the means of accomplishing a political and intellectual "renaissance" – all the more reason why this could not be done against, or without, Islam. Reformism seems to be opposed both to a vehement puritanism which would refuse to assimilate borrowings from Western civilization on one hand, and also to a pure and simple modernization of the religion on the other, which would then become exempt from Qur'ānic fidelity . It must be stated that the "modernistic" movement has not as yet found its just proportions.[116] A theoretical dilemma could be posed between quite simply returning to classical Islam or else moving toward a total secularization of Muslim institutions, faith being left to the individual in an isolated manner. Within the bounds of these theoretical limits, possible solutions are infinite.

Almost all Muslim reformers believe that Islam could be subject to a rationalization without the Qur'ānic authority or, to a lesser extent, the prophetic traditions suffering thereby. The modernistic Syrio-Egyptian school appears more traditional, even conservative, than the South Asian theologian-reformers. The two successive leaders, Jamal ed-Din al-Afghani and his disciple Muhammad 'Abdu, tried to bring about an Islamic reform without borrowing anything from the West, apart from modern technology.[117] The rebirth of the Muslim world ought to be made possible by returning to primordial Islam, cleansed of all doctrinal impurities. It would thus be more a question

---

[114]Farah, *Islam*, pp. 221 f.
[115]Khaldun S. al-Husry, *Three Reformers: A Study in Modern Arabic Political Thought* (Beirut: Khayats, 1966), pp. 5-6, which shades this statement. After this: al-Husry, *Three Reformers*.
[116]We will return to certain aspects of this question, below, in chapter 6.
[117]Hamilton A. R. Gibb, *Studies on the Civilization of Islam*, ed. Stanford J. Shaw and William R. Polk (London: Routledge and Kegan, 1962), pp. 320-335. After this: Gibb, *Studies*.

of a purification of the faith, freed from corrupted influences and practices, than a revision of orthodoxy. The Syrian Muhammad Rashid Reda has the merit, like his two masters, of recognizing the power of modern ideas as well as that of stigmatizing modern Islam's doctrinal sterility.[118] In his opinion, history has shown that Islam was able to accept and assimilate all secular progress. He rejects the prohibition of speculative effort and research, and he refuses to admit that modern life may be paralyzed by a legislative system which was developed in the first three centuries of Muslim history.[119] The Egyptian reformers preach a return to pure Islam and express a very marked suspicion with regard to certain reformers, especially toward the Kemalist Turks. Their intellectual procedures remain bound by orthodoxy. It lays a special claim to a clearer and more logical distinction between what is essential and what is secondary.

The South Asian reformers seem to go even further. Sayyed Ahmed Khan proposed a modernized Islam through adaptation of Western knowledge. Muhammad Iqbal[120] demanded a revitalization of the faith by the adaptation of a historical method of interpretation in the context of discussion and communal consensus,[121] where certain passages of the Qur'ān could be reevaluated and reconsidered in an allegorical perspective. Amir Ali[122] went even further still and "proved" that Islam is able to adapt to those demands of modern civilization which are truly useful and have a real value for the progress of humanity, the condition being a return to the unadulterated texts of the prophetic traditions and the Qur'ān.

The reformist movement does not yet seem to have brought many solutions. It nonetheless expresses the present vitality of Islam, which too many non-Muslim authors choose to consider as an obsolete and fossilized system. Thus, the question of modernization perhaps presents more problems than it solves. On a purely religious level, moreover, despite the atrophy of the systems of the Muslim world, the faith still exerts an invigorating attraction thanks to the simplicity of its dogma and its theological logic, its religious force, and its capacities of cultural adaptation. Islam is spreading, particularly in Africa, faster than any other religion. That is why it still represents a governing force in the modern world, despite the technological backwardness of

---

[118]J. Jomier, *Islam d'hier et d'aujourd'hui*, vol. 11: *Le commentaire coranique du Manar: Tendances modernes de l'exégès coranique en Egypte* (Paris: Maisonneuve, 1954), 363 pages. After this: Jomier, *Le Commentaire coranique*.

[119]Lammens, *L'Islam*, pp. 271-274.

[120]Muhammad Iqbal, *The Reconstruction of Religious Thought in Islam* (Lahore: Ashraf, 1958), 205 pages. After this: Iqbal, *The Reconstruction*.

[121]Muhammad A. Ahmed, *Iqbal and the Recent Exposition of Islamic Thought*, 2nd ed. (Lahore: Ashraf, 1965), 64 pages. After this: Ahmed, *Iqbal*.

[122]*The Spirit*.

the Islamic community. It has succeeded in rejecting two of the modern ideologies which were posing a threat to it: atheist communism and secular materialism. However, the Muslim peoples have not been fully capable of withstanding the onslaught of nationalism during recent times. The reinterpretation of doctrine, so denied by modern reformists, is done in an almost anguished climate since it apparently presents a great danger. It runs the risk of opening the door to a maze of theological debates which could lead to anarchy all the more easily since no ecclesiastic institution really exists to guide or put an end to the problems. It would be the end of the unity and mystical cohesion of the Muslim community. The political and social transformation necessary to adapt to the modern world seem to remain largely dependent on a religious rebirth since orthodox Islam refuses to separate the spiritual from the temporal. Thus, the evolution of dogma could well prove to serve as a non-religious factor.

Toward a True Dialogue

It is necessary to briefly allude to the incomprehension which seems to have almost constantly marked the relations between Islam and Christianity. The opposition – in truth, hostility – was almost immediate. The passage of time, meetings, and exchanges do not yet seem to have eliminated all the prejudices, even if modern historical research has proven the falsity of traditional accusations.

Being chronologically posterior, Islam was seen to be superior by the Muslims and, at the same time, as heinous and erroneous by established Christian societies. In Byzantium, the Arab armies were from the outset the incarnation of the invasion, being an expression of God's wrath against Christian sinners. They saw in these forces either divine retribution or a "Jewish plot."[123] Through weakness and ignorance, the Christians pronounced judgment upon Islam by assimilating it with anterior revelations and existing religions. They saw it as a heresy and held Muhammad to be an impostor. Propaganda and ignorant fear soon gave credit to the ideas which were to persist even though political experience was to belie them. Ideas such as war and pillage were branded as dogmas of Islam, as was the fallacy that Muslims were guaranteed entry into paradise if they killed Christians. Certain authors, intending to attack the faith by discrediting its Prophet, drew a naive and simplistic parallel between Christianity and "Mohammedanism," a deformed image of Muhammad – a blood-thirsty heretic and womanizer. This prejudice, as well as the

---

[123]Alain Ducellier, *Le miroir de l'Islam: Musulmans et Chretiens d'Orient au Moyen Age* (Paris: Juillard, 1971), pp. 31 f. After this: Ducellier, *Le miroir.*

aversion toward the "non-believer," nourished by infantile figments of fiction, dominated Western thought during the entire Middle Ages. These ideas were even reinforced in Europe, if not on the battlefield, during the crusades. The Muslim world then fell under the political domination of the West. Vulgar information described Islam in preremptory terms as an outdated and fatalistic ideology which had caused considerable material backwardness for its followers. The colonialists did not believe that they could receive anything of value from an exchange with the subjugated Muslims.[124]

"Islamology" and "orientalism" have progressively proven to be honest scientific disciplines whose motivations were not, however, always without self-interest. The study of Islam progressively became an element of the colonial question.[125] The intellectuals of the Middle Ages, liberated from mysticism and the reigning obscurantism, cherised a secret admiration for the Arab-Muslim civilization. During the renaissance and the following century, political and scientific concerns remained mainly centered around Europe. Even when Western intellectual methods were founded upon the legacy of Islam, which had been overthrown especially in Spain and Sicily, the Europeans refused to admit the cultural influence of the "infidel." The eighteenth century brought about a rather favorable judgment of Islam. The rationalist philosophers in particular exalted Muslim wisdom and tolerance in order to attack all the more violently the church and the absolutism of the period. A certain taste for exoticism was probably not entirely foreign to this benevolent attitude. In the nineteenth century, romanticism permitted a more sympathetic acceptance and a sometimes naive understanding of Islam in Europe.[126] Finally, in our present age, authors are making an attempt to explain the Muslim doctrine scientifically and generally without prejudice. This doctrine nonetheless seems to remain misunderstood by the Western public, not so much through the lack of information as through an excess of erudite publications difficult to grasp by unitiated readers. Those old prejudices concerning the "false prophet" or the "infidels" against whom Europe led crusades[127] are still alive. This incomprehension is perhaps "deeper and can be summarized as follows: it is between relatives that there is the least understand-

---

[124]Louis Massignon, "Le respect de la personne humaine en Islam, et la priorité du droit d'asile sur le devoir de guèrre juste, *Revue internationale de la Croix-Rouge* 402 (June 1952): 448-468, especially 460. After this: Massignon, "Le respect."

[125]Jean-Jacques Waardenburg, *L'Islam dans le miroir de l'Occident*, 3rd ed. (Paris: Mouton, 1969), 381 pages. Gouilly, *L'Islam*. See also, to a certain degree, Henri Masse, "Avertissement de la première édition," *L'Islam* (Paris: Armand Colin, 1930).

[126]Ahmed A. Galwash, *The Religion of Islam*, 4th ed. (Cairo: Standard Press, 1956), pp. 27 f. After this: Galwash, *The Religion.*

[127]This is a prejudice certainly revived by recent history, which has seen opposition between Europe and the Islamic world, with the latter fighting the former for its independence.

ing. In Islam, the Christian finds things which remind him of his own religion ... articles of faith and ideas which are extremely close to his own ... he is so familiar with this that he bypasses it with that absent-minded indifference which we have toward those things we think we know too well but which we do not know sufficiently so as to understand them better."[128]

As to the Muslim's attitude toward Christianity, it is tolerant up to a certain point and then becomes unbending. The existence of one unique God without a partner, implies the existence of a single general and exclusive law. On different occasions God sent to humanity His various prophets to transmit part of His will, depending on humanity's practical needs and spiritual level. The Prophet Muhammad received the law which confirmed and completed all the preceding messages. The earlier revelations, if not approved by the Qur'ān, must of necessity be violently rejected as being the product of error or malpractice. From this point of view, Western academic research has sometimes appeared offensive and frankly doubtful (in the eyes of Muslim scholars). Orientalism has even been associated with imperialism.[129]

A more fraternal dialogue seems to have opened up in recent times. The study of universal moral values provides a healthier basis for the debates serving as "steppingstones" between Islam and the West.[130] We have undertaken our study in this perspective. The historian must re-place the facts and ideas into their concrete reality. We wish to show Islam's past contribution and its possible future concurrence with regard to the development of a universal morality. That is where our ambition ends, without exclusivity toward other civilizations, nor an attempt to go beyond the framework of a historical, judicial study. We cannot, however, hide the feelings which have guided us at times. In effect, "if it is true that men are thus divided and opposed to one another – Orientals and Westerners – is it not absolutely desirable that a union of hearts be established between them?"[131]

---

[128]Andrae, *Mahomet*, p. 9.
[129]Tewfik M. al-Roueni, *L'influence de la législation islamique sur l'unité arabe* (Cairo: Supreme Council of Islamic Affairs, 1966), pp. 56 f. After this: al-Roueni, *L'influence*.
[130]J. Scelles-Millie, *Pierres d'attente entre le Christianisme et l'Islam* (Paris: Maisonneuve, 1961), 32 pages. See also the message of president Anwar as-Sadat to the Islamic-Christian congress of Cordoue, *al-Ahram*, September 12, 1974.
[131]Daniel Robs, his letter to *Messages d'Orient*, 2 (Alexandria: n.p., 1926), 266 pages.

Chapter 3

CHILDREN OF ADAM

...Whoever kills a human being for
other than manslaughter or corruption in
the earth, it shall be as if he had killed
all mankind, and whoever saves the life
of one, it shall be as if he had saved the
life of all mankind.

Qur'ān, 5:32

Man as Such

The manner in which an organized society conceives of man with regard to his essential reality and to his position and role within the group determines an evaluation of the values of a civilization. Any comparative judgment of systems, whether cultural or philosophical, always ultimately refers to the conception of the human being in a given group. Three approaches in particular are taken by those who tackle the question of man's existential condition and his destiny.[1] One can, in effect, intend to deal with man in his pure essential reality. That is the role of the philosopher. Attention could also be concentrated upon the ideological and spiritual principles which regulate man's behavior and help fashion his personality. This is the task of moralists and sociologists. Last of all, it is possible to define a concept of man in the light of ethical and judicial institutions established in the course of historic and social experience, institutions which are respected since they protect the individual and society by defining mutual rights and obligations. This study belongs to both the jurist and the historian. In this perspective, man will first of all be considered on an individual level and then on a collective level, by which we do not mean the order/disposition of human relations but the organization of the community.

In the Muslim mode of thought, centered around God and the revealed book, man's intrinsic value is determined by his relation with the absolute and with regard to his immediate or eternal destiny. The Islamic view encompasses the human condition in its entirety. The revelation presents itself as a global entity. It is so rich in detail that an overnuanced account could lead to confusion. If oversimplified, it could on the other hand give an erroneous idea of the essential concepts.

Any "ideology" immediately clarifies, whether tacitly or explicitly, the nature of the individual as well as the place he is assigned within the group, in accordance with the social objective in mind. For an eschatological religion such as Islam, God is the primordial and unique point of reference since He is at once the origin and the finality of human destiny. It is therefore important to know what idea

---

[1]Ali I. Othman, *The Concept of Man in Islam in the Writings of al-Ghazali* (Cairo:Dar al-M'āref, 1960), 213 pages. After this: Othman, *The Concept.*

Muslim thought has forged of God so that this image should, by deduction or contrast, allow us to understand the concept of the essence of man.

The Qur'ān was revealed so as to make God known to man, not to explain human nature to mankind. Providing a comprehensive law which closely associates the spiritual and the temporal, it represents a rule of action which indicates moral virtues but does not present a list of elements peculiar to man's intrinsic nature. Islam is the religion of faith and discernment. The persuasive power of its teaching results from the fact that it discloses the reality of the absolute and points out creation's harmonious unicity which depends on this absolute. God is therefore absolute and omnipotent, representing the primary force and power. "He is at the summit of abstraction; He is distinct from all things."[2] This conception of the infinite divine transcendence, so often repeated, and whose presence completely surrounds Muslim life, means neither incommunicability nor inaccessibility. It is true that Muslim theologians agree that God is without condition and unknowable. However, what is incomprehensible to the intelligence on its own becomes clear through the revelations. By revealing the Qur'ān, as with all preceding revelations, God entered into communication with man. The absolute allowed itself to be grasped by that which is relative, owing to a mysterious divine intervention in human destiny. Islam's "concept" of God, and consequently its image of man, are essentially different from those of Christianity. The Christian, "son of God" through baptism, may attempt to participate in the divine life itself because of the new existence which he develops within. As for the Muslim, he does not dare to envisage any participation in the divine life since he is too conscious of the transcendence of Allah.[3] By the mystery of incarnation, the Christian can hope to attain eternal bliss through association with love and divine holiness – through assimilation with God Himself. For the Muslim, there is no such thing.[4] Nevertheless, he too experiences the eternal, but in a different way and through different sources: by meditating upon the Qur'ān. The expression of God's attributes could be important, showing how the faithful have attempted to grasp a certain "concept" of God. Muslim theology, however, was constantly careful to avoid placing too much emphasis on this speculation, fearing that this may be detrimental to the concept of divine unicity and transcendence, and that it may even lead to some form of anthropomorphism or polytheism. Muslims do not believe that they can truly know

---

[2]Osman E. Chahine, *L'originalité créatrice de la philosophie musulmane* (Paris: Maisonneuve, 1972), p. 158.

[3]Masson, *Le Coran*, p. 39. The qualificative noun of "Father" in relation to God has been excluded in Islam because of the meaning which it has taken on in Christianity. Also see Ameer Ali, *The Spirit*, p. 142. Nevertheless, in order to illustrate the infinite bounty of God, Islam chose to compare it to maternal love, more generous and more disinterested. In fact, Muhammad said: "Toward His servants, Allah is more tender than a mother."

[4]The one exception, perhaps, is that of the "Sufi" (mystics) whom we will not discuss.

God. The Prophet advised them not to contemplate His being, but to meditate upon His attributes of which there are ninety-nine, called the "Most Beautiful Names of God." They give to Allah all the qualities in an infinite and inaccessible degree, in such a manner that there is nothing similar to God, neither in His being nor in His perfection.

In the Muslim concept, however, God's transcendence does not exclude His mercy or His benevolence toward man. God's generosity makes Him "accessible" to humanity. The Qur'ān alludes to this on numerous occasions, teaching us that "all that are in the heavens and the earth entreat Him. Every day He exercises universal power."[5]

"The God of Islam, unique in His essence, attributes and acts, is an all-powerful God, the judge of the universe and lord of the Day of Judgment. Into the bosom of His mercy will He call those creatures who did not oppose the voice of the guide with sarcasm and contempt, but who raised themselves to the feeling of dependence on their creator, from the pride of their power founded upon earthly possessions. The divine inspiration of the oldest of the Qur'ānic suras is expressed in eschatological images. Woe unto those who do not repent and who do not surrender themselves to God. A terrible and painful punishment awaits them. Woe to the nations who dared to oppose and despise the exhortations of the prophets who were sent to them. God destroys them. It is He Who knows all, understands all. He is the creator of the heavens and the earth, of life and death. He is the lord of the throne. His wisdom is perfect, His will absolute, His power cannot be resisted; such are His qualities revealed through His creation itself. While all things depend on Him, He is independent of all which is not Him. None of His creatures resemble Him. With them He has only one relationship; He is their creator, they belong unto Him and unto Him will they return. But this all-powerful God is just. He cannot be conceived of as unjust. He knows even an atom's worth of good performed by His servant and does not suffer him to lose the benefit thereof; He cannot bring any unto the slightest injustice, not even as small as the fiber of a date kernel."[6]

However, divine infinite mercy cannot be understood independently of divine omnipotence.[7] This is a very basic concept in Islam. Thus, the first trait in the portrait of man according to the Muslim conception is brought into light : human nature acquires intrinsic value only through the immense generosity of Allah,

---

[5]ar-Rahmān: 29 (Reda).
[6]Laura V. Vaglieri, "Apologie de l'Islamisme," translated from Italian by Maxime Formont, (typewritten), p. 14.
[7]"And were it not for the grace and mercy of God upon you, not one of you would ever have known purity of soul. Nevertheless, God purifies whom He pleases" an-Nur: 21 (Abbasi).

Who "created [man] weak."[8]

The question arises as to whether or not man enjoys free will with regard to God's omnipotence. The problem of predestination, inherent in the logical structure of any monotheistic religion, is certainly not peculiar to Islam. There would be no particular sense in listing the Qur'ānic passages which emphasize man's full responsibility and freedom, or in listing those which on the contrary assert the determinism of man's temporal and external lot. As to a judgment based on the superficial observation of the daily lives of present-day Muslims, this could lead to erroneous conclusions.

From a religious point of view, the concept of predestination, which at the outset appears absurd to our reason, constitutes the fundamental essence of piety. Thus it was emphasized with particular insistence perhaps in Islam.[9] Despite the Prophet's verbal recommendation, not to discuss destiny, as reported in the traditions, predestination was abundantly discussed during the first centuries of Islam. However, these discussions were not always divorced from matters of political timeliness: certain caliphs attempted to ostracize and even eliminate the rationalist philosophers with the sole aim of better establishing their authoritarian powers. The last gasp of the rationalist doctrine, that of Imam al-Ghazzali, would perhaps have succeeded in triumphing had it not been for the Mongol invasions. The latter imposed an often savage tyranny by means of the sword, justifying their despotism by the immutability of divine decrees.[10] To develop upon the various theological arguments deployed in favor of or in opposition to a certain concept would necessitate a comprehensive study of the theology and hence of the entire intellectual life of the Muslims.[11] Historical circumstances can to some extent explain why the Muslim community sometimes seems to have been crushed by the divine omnipotence, and how the idea of "Muslim fatalism" became so deeply rooted in the minds of Westerners, who appear to have forgotten Islam's historically grandiose cultural and material achievements.

According to contemporary Muslim orthodoxy, the Muslim must believe and proclaim that God has decreed all things. Nothing can happen on this earth which has not been written on the divine tablets. God commands man to have faith, obedience, and to perform good deeds. He has equally decreed evil, disobedience, and disbelief, not by virtue of His pleasure or through His salutory guidance, but through the ways of temptation. One who believes that God is not outraged

---

[8]an-Nisa': 28.
[9]Andrae, *Mahomet*, p. 67.
[10].Amir Ali, *The Spirit*, pp. 412-454.
[11]Franz Rosenthal, *The Muslim Concept of Freedom, Prior to the Nineteenth Century* (Leiden: Brill, 1960), p. vii. After this: Rosenthal, *Freedom*.

by evil and disbelief is most certainly a nonbeliever.[12] In fact, to claim that God
– Who in no way foresees, but who sees all in one eternal gaze – does not know
everything "in advance" and that He does not know the precise course of events
of this existence would mean to deny His omnipotence and, in so doing, to reject
His divinity. On the other hand, the perspective of the Day of Judgment, on
which the Qur'ān constantly insists, inevitably implies the idea of man's responsibility, which could only be just if man were free to choose between good and
evil, as so many verses of the Qur'ān indicate. Thus, he is free. By denying
this liberty, one would tacitly be inferring that God was unjust by condemning
or rewarding man for his deeds which he would not have been free to choose,
and for which he could consequently not bear any responsibility. One of the
most fundamental of Allah's attributes is His justice. If God had wished to
impose His will on man's behavior, He would not have allowed anybody to go
astray.[13] Predestination is irrefutable to reason if divine unicity implies the
existence of a natural, higher order. God shows man the way by appealing to
his sense and reason, thus making him responsible for what he becomes. Man's
freedom resides in his intelligent choice to respect the revealed law and to
recognize the divine decrees. It is not a question of a mechanical determination
but of conscious choice. The personal responsibility which will be taken into
account on the Day of Judgment[14] implies that man is endowed with discernment
of choice and with freedom. This is his eminent dignity. It is in this way that
the idea of predestination, so sharply pronounced in Islam, does not contradict
the notion of human freedom.[15]

"God alone is absolute liberty. Human liberty, despite its relativity,...is however nothing other than liberty, just as a weak light is nothing other than a
light."[16] Since man does not know the future life in store for him, his actions
derive from a decision of his will and of his intelligence. He is thus free and
responsible for his choice. "Such a choice contrasts violently with the mechanical
determinism which exists in the physical world."[17] The individual's very ignorance of his fate should stimulate his will. Were he to know beforehand that he
was destined for salvation or condemned to perdition, he would make no effort
to try and progress. Thus, the belief in predestination could mean neither resignation nor abnegation, but on the contrary represents an assertion of man, freed

[12]Galwash, *The Religion*, pp. 238 f., and Farah, *Islam*, pp. 120 f.
[13]"We have tried them with both prosperity and adversity in order that they might return to the
straight path by abandoning their errors," al-A'rāf: 168.
[14]"O you unbelievers! Make no excuses this day! You are only being requited for all that you
did" al-A'rāf: 66 (Masson).
[15]Omnia Rida, *Le libre arbitre dans l'Islam* (Alexandria: n.p., 1969).
[16]Schuon, *Comprendre*, p. 14.
[17]Galwash, *The Religion*, p. 243.

from anguish, once he has "finally admitted the eternal order of things and accepted his total dependency."[18] The belief in predestination, understood from this angle, is not a "fatalism" which paralyzes any effort of free will. "It gives man a new strength, a new forcefulness of will; it makes the difficulties of this world seem insignificant to him; it gives him the courage to hope for and to dare (to attain) what is impossible."[19]

Islam combines the assertion of the divine will governing the universe with the recognition of human responsibility based on intelligence and liberty. In this respect, the conclusion can be left to popular wisdom. The two notions of destiny and initiative have been tied together. They are, it is said, the two pouches of a carry pack hanging over each side of a pack animal. If one of the pouches contains more objects than the other, it will slide off and the whole load will fall to the ground. Else, if the pack remains on the animal's back, the beast's fatigue will increase and the journey will become difficult. If, on the contrary, both pouches contain an equally heavy load, the journey is made without fatigue, success is total, and the aim is achieved."[20]

Free and responsible, man is not a puppet in the hands of an all-powerful, arbitrary deity. Liberty in his choice of actions and the resulting responsibility give him his eminent dignity and are the foundations of his moral life. Man's greatness thus comes from the fact that he has freely chosen to be obedient. Because the believer is directly connected with God, without any mediator or intercessor, without a church or saint cult, his responsibility is individualized and strictly personal.[21] As a monotheistic religion, Islam gives man a doubly universal dimension, associating him on the one hand with divine moral order and on the other promising him an eternal future. No subject is more frequently mentioned than man.[22] The existence of an immortal, immaterial soul destined for bliss is essential, in the full meaning of the term. The soul, in truth, represents the essence of man in the perspective of his eschatological destiny. It has to be considered an acquired reality, incomprehensible, and inexplicable.[23]

Muslim theology has not been greatly preoccupied with theoretical abstractions

---

[18]Emile Dermenghem, "Témoignage de l'Islam," in *l'Islam et l'Occident*, Paris (Cahier du Sud, no. 9), 1947, 393 pages, pp. 372-387, p. 381. After this: Dermenghem, "Témoignage."

[19]Andrae, *Mahomet*, p. 62.

[20]Rene R. Khawam, *Propos des Arabs sur la vie en soiété*, (Paris: Albin Michel, 1964), p. 101.

[21]"No bearer of burdens can bear the burden of another. Man can have nothing but what he strives for," an-Najm: 38-39 (Masson).

[22]Ibrahim Madkour, "The Concept of Man in Islamic Thought" in *The Concept of Man: A Study in Comparative Philosophy*, 2nd ed., ed. S. Radhakrishnan and P. T. Raju (London: Allen and Unwin, 1966), pp. 452-475. After this: Madkour, "The Concept."

[23]"[The unbelievers] question you about the Spirit. Respond: 'The Spirit proceeds from the order of my Lord and it has communicated to you but little of knowledge,'" al-Isra': 85.

but has rather discussed the psychological nature of man, using the vocabulary of the revealed book. Man was created both "weak"[24] and "of the best stature"[25] so that he may maintain his (honored) place and fulfill his function in the universal order (of things). Indications and deductions from the account of the creation of Adam, the father of humanity, allow us to gain a better understanding of man's nature. Issuing directly from the hands of the creator, man was made of clay and was animated by the spirit which God breathed into him.[26] In this allegory, the notion of human autonomy can be perceived, man being divided between his transcendental spiritual nature aspiring to plentitude and his eminently weak material nature succumbing to temptation. God honored the "sons of Adam."[27] He gave them knowledge superior to that of the angels,[28] but He created them from clay, a fact which ought to protect him from [a feeling of] false grandeur or excessive pride.[29]

The error of Adam's disobedience figures in the Qur'ān,[30] although the description and interpretation of the facts differ greatly from the Biblical version.[31] It is because they disobeyed a strict order that Adam and Eve were punished, not because that they attempted to taste knowledge. God is in no way opposed to man's desire to learn; on the contrary, He encourages it. They were thereafter excluded from paradise and had to enter a world characterized by enmity. God forgave them their error and promised to reveal unto them a law which they may obey and hence be saved.[32] Islam thus rejects the idea of a "fall of man" – of original sin – whose consequences were to be transmitted to all of mankind. This difference implies a fundamental contrast with Judaism and especially with Christianity as regards the concept of man and the foundation of his moral life. In fact, in Islam man is "envisaged, not as a fallen creature in need of a miraculous saviour, but as a creature...endowded with an intelligence capable of conceiving the absolute, and of a will capable of choosing that which guides it."[33]

---

[24]an-Nisa': 28.

[25]at-Tin: 4.

[26]Sad: 71-72.

[27]al-Isra': 70.

[28]al-Baqarah: 31-33.

[29]Madkour, "The Concept," p. 454.

[30]al-Baqarah: 35-36.

[31]Ali M. Muhajir, *Lessons from the Stories of the Qur'an*, 2nd ed. (Lahore: Ashraf, 1969), pp. 1-30.

[32]"Assuredly, there will come to you from Me a guidance. Whoever follows My guidance, on them shall be no fear, nor shall they grieve," al-Baqarah: 36-38 (Blachère).

[33]Schuon, *Comprendre*, p. 13. We have omitted from the citation the qualificative of "deified" because it shocks Muslims. According to them, this adjective really cannot be used in the Qur'ānic context, for nothing exists in all of creation which could resemble the Creator as attested by al-Ikhlas: 4.

Therefore, on an exclusively personal level man is responsible for his universal destiny according to his attitude toward the divine law. Thus it appears that the concept of human nature could be considered more on a juridical than a philosophical level; this is reasonable in the context of the Islamic system's logical construction. Traditional Islam is satisfied with what the Qur'ān teaches about human nature. The foundations of political and social speculation assume a concrete nature, without necessarily referring to man's intrinsic essence.

In Islam, as in the other monotheistic revelations, man appears as the privileged creature of God, who has made him His representative in the universe,[34] and has endowed him with power and particular abilities. In his primordial and superior state, says the Qur'ān,[35] the human being is a marvelous sign of divine omnipotence and mercy. The Prophet is reputed to have said that God was a hidden treasure who wished to be known. To this end, He created man so that He could be perceived. Muslim mystics have extensively developed this idea which has never been contested by the keepers of orthodoxy. Perfect man is thus the "microcosm which reflects the perfection of the macrocosm and hence deserves to be God's representative on earth."[36] His existence, as a sign and proof of divine existence, endows man with his superior state. It is here that the Muslim doctrine's specific approach is to be found: man cannot aspire to be associated with God by means of love and sacrifice, contrary to the Christian perspective, but remains the distant sign and visible symbol of the indecipherable. Man is therefore reduced to "the individual witness ... through ritual internalization, 'unifying' the personality with the image of Abraham's One God, whom he acknowledges and serves through his ritual practices"[37] and through all his daily deeds.

The Qur'ānic revelation is meant to reform humanity on the model of a better man. The knowledge it imparts of God Almighty, the laws it imposes, and the admonishments of reprobation which it utters only serve to increase the believer's dignity. The fear of God is actually something entirely different from anguish, something far greater than it. It illustrates and elucidates the nobility of the responsibility incumbent upon man. Following this train of thought, the very terror of hell is linked with the greatness of man who is responsible and endowed with discernment. Islam attempts to combine those two concepts which have provided the material for abundant discussions among philosophers: the meaning of eminent human dignity and man's fundamentally weak nature. By freely accepting to submit to the requirements of the revealed law, man acquires his dignity. Evil is essentially disobedience toward the law. Man places himself in

---

[34]al-Baqarah: 30.
[35]Fusselat: 53.
[36]Madkour, "The Concept," p. 475.
[37]Massignon, "Le respect," p. 453.

a state of disequilibrium by not wishing to be what God has made him for by such an action he rejects his eminent dignity. This fault represents a lack of self-respect and hence a lack of respect for the value of the human being. Man enjoys great dignity for God created him as an end unto himself, assigning him an eternal destiny and admonishing him with the Day of Judgment. Thus, the Muslim concept corresponds to that of the other eschatological religions. The outward expression is different, however, because the Muslim is specifically placed within the framework of his relations with God. In this respect, it would suffice to mention that human dignity and the respect of others are clearly defined and greatly encouraged in the teachings of Islam. They are clearly brought into focus by the astonishing commandment of God which required the angels to bow down before Adam,[38] whom God had honored by revealing to him the names of things, thereby glorifying knowledge and conferring man's dignity upon him through intelligence. The angel[39] Iblis, having refused to obey because of pride, is driven from paradise. He then becomes Satan[40] and eventually becomes the incarnation of evil. Because of his disobedience and through having refused to acknowledge man's superior dignity, Iblis was severed from divine grace. He became rebel toward God's will and the enemy of men. Is not such an allegory striking because of what it seems to imply: the lack of respect for the individual is the essence of evil?[41]

In Islam, the concept of man is "ideal, based on a precise message with a precise aim."[42] It is in this perspective that the following divine word can be better understood, all the more since the Qur'ān repeatedly stresses the individual nature of human responsibility and since Islamic law has made the personalization of the rule a fundamental norm: "Whoever kills a human being for other than manslaughter or corruption in the earth, it shall be as if he has killed all mankind, and whoever saves the life of one, it is as if he has saved the life of all mankind."[43]

Human Rights

In a collective society, an individual's rights[44] are determined and guaranteed by the duties of the other members, both individually and collectively. According to the traditional Western concept, the definition of rights and duties can be

---

[38]al-Baqarah: 34 and al-A'rāf: 11.
[39]Some of them think that Iblis is not an angel but a jinn.
[40]This comes from the Semitic root "the one who opposes himself to someone."
[41]We unreservedly take into account this interpretation, for it is ours and we have found no confirmation of it in our Islamic sources.
[42]Madkour, "The Concept," p. 475.
[43]al-Ma'idah: 32 (Masson).
[44]We use the phrase "rights of man" in its modern international understanding.

provided by criteria which are imperative or subjective, traditional or periodic, varying with social evolution and conditions. The obligation to respect individual's rights within the bounds of what is considered common property, draws its coercive force especially from sociological reasons, which could be confused with morality, since the latter is the emblem of cultural traditions, psychological aspirations, and ideological certainties. The guarantee of individual rights is also given by the automatic and oftentimes violent reaction on the part of a society or of individuals in the face of an upset balance between man's privileges and the collective imperative.[45]

In Islam, rights and duties, prohibitions and restrictions are of a religious nature. At first sight, reciprocal relations must be clearly defined since the revealed law is supposed to arbitrate under all circumstances. However, Muslim law conceives of man on the individual and collective levels, in two senses which, though not different, are dissimilar. Thus, the swing of the pendulum between individual rights and the necessity of common property is not absent but will be present in a particularly Islamic perspective, and should consequently find its equilibrium through the exact application of the revealed law.

The Qur'ānic principles of human justice, honesty, and solidarity create duties for each member of the Muslim society. They generate a certain atmosphere of mutual courtesy and good will, a practice of civility which has religious foundations and significance. In the same way, the order to "require good and prevent evil" gives the Islamic society an almost paternalistic character of routines and practices. It remains true, however, that the historical foundation of Islam's philosophical essence is the autonomy of the individual – that is, the assertion of "human rights" extended within the community. As in any "political system," Islam certainly puts communal interests "before those of the individual, if needs be, on the condition that it does not dehumanize the latter, and that it does not cause the loss of his liberty and dignity."[46]

In Islam, the triumph of the person-oriented thrust is manifested and enhanced only through the religion.[47] The emergence of the individual represented the very nature of early Islam, and consequently explains its success in seventh-century Arabia by virtue of the great change which it brought about in the notions of man and society. From a historical point of view, Muhammad's mission contributed in particular to a rapid social and spiritual edification in Arabia. Man

---

[45]This reaction could take the form of vengeance in primitive societies while that of judicial procedure – even of "terrorist" resistance or of political repression in the modern community.
[46]Madkour, "The Concept," p. 460.
[47]Anouar Hatem, *L'Islam et les Droits de l'Homme* (Geneva: Association suisse-arabe, 1974), 32 pages.

then became aware of his personality, of himself, and of his duties. Islam basically represented the affirmation, the liberation, and the prosperity of man. By extension, and not in opposition, the elementary differentiation between the person and the individual was enhanced, on the level of social organization, by the establishment of a strongly unified community of religious inspiration. Man no longer projected himself within a traditional group, the tribe or clan, but asserted both his individual and collective personality in reference to God, the fundamental, transcendent, and absolute norm. In reality, "it is the balance between transcendence and imminence which allows for personal and social equilibrium; it is metaphysical affirmation which allows for liberty in the city of man. To say 'God is the greatest' is to close the door upon all servitude. It means declaring and asserting oneself to be essentially free."[48]

The more transcendent and absolute God is, the freer man is in relation to all others. Freedom in servitude to God determines personal value. In this way, "human rights" or man's "dignity" are only indirectly derived from his basic value. Man's superior quality is his freedom in equality. God's omnipotence leads to man's freedom from man. His exclusive adoration, direct and without intermediary, asserts the believer's greatness and guarantees his dignity. He understands, in effect, that he need not fear being the slave of any but God . Nothing can befall him which God has not ordained for him. This very acute awareness of the absolute puts all which is relative into its true perspective. A deeply felt sense of equality dictates the Muslim's duties toward man and society as well as points out his rights. This is very clearly a notion fundamentally different from that of Western civilization. From the Islamic point of view, man was not defiled by an original sin and then uplifted by a divine incarnation. The Qur'ān does not suggest, it gives orders. As such, man's dignity does not arise from some vague metaphysical notion, but from his choice to freely serve God. He is respected all the more as he submits to the prescriptions of the revealed law, thus finding his place in a world of harmony.[49] His only duty is that of being an earthly creature who, because of his intellect, is capable of choosing obedience to the divine will.

By indicating that man is capable of distinguishing between good and evil, and by the admonishment of the Day of Judgment, the Qur'ān thereby defines an image and concept of human nature. It is particularly difficult to express the originality of Islam, so resolutely different from the traditional Western perspective. Man is first and foremost respectable in his capacity as a believer. However, since the Qur'ān was revealed to all humanity originating

---

[48]Dermenghem, "Témoignage," p. 381.
[49]"The most honorable among you, in the eyes of God, is the most pious," declared Muhammad at the time of his last pilgrimage.

from the first human couple, Islam does not make any exceptions.[50] Hence, any value judgment should be made on two different levels. On a "religious" level, the value of man is identical for all divine creatures. On the "judicial" level, the value of the believer is in a certain sense superior by the very fact of his having chosen to follow the Qur'ānic revelation.

As a respectable being, can man claim "rights"? On an abstract level, certainly not. Dependent on absolute divine transcendence, man, as the servant of God, has no independent value of his own,[51] but he is at the same time far more valuable, since he exists by virtue of the external intervention of God, who unilaterally conferred a title upon humanity. This kind of convention gives a certain stability and determines each person's juridical status. The title is enhanced and supplemented by the Qur'ānic revelation which indicates the rights and the law to be followed, on both the individual and collective levels. The individual's "rights" result from the obligations prescribed for others by the religion. The primary value resulting from the way the believer conceives of God as well as the relationship which he must maintain with Him makes him aware of a sense of absolute equality which could seem negative since it is the corollary or the consequence of man's vacuity in the light of God's absoluteness. The ideas of the human being, of his liberty, and of his dignity are, as values, at stake only in a secondary stage, but always in the light of divine transcendence. On the practical level of society, this essential quality which Islam accords all believers generates a "sense of community" based on justice. When the sense of equality is projected on a collective scale and reciprocated among the members of the society, it succeeds in creating the ultimate sense of human dignity on the level of moral principles.

Respect for the personality of others is explicitly prescribed, going as far as to prohibit mockery and sarcasm toward them.[52] At the same time, the very strongly marked notion of man's responsibility implies, for him, the duty to respect, preserve, and assert his own dignity. It is in this twofold perspective, personal and interindividual, that the Muslim conceives the dignity of man.

The principle of equality determines the notion of man and thus represents the cornerstone upon which the structure of the social system rests. This is

---

[50]The expression "children of Adam," very current in the popular language, is mentioned seven times in the Qur'ān. See, Masson, *Le Coran*, p. 598.

[51]However, the believer can hope to receive divine assistance: "... delivering the believers is an obligation for us," Yunus: 103, or again ar-Rum: 107 (Masson).

[52]"O you who believe! Let not some men among you laugh at others; it may be that the (latter) are better than the (former)," al-Hujurat: 11 (Blachère).

a particularly Islamic sentiment; no religion or ideology prior to Islam ever asserted it with as much force. It does not seem superfluous to briefly elaborate upon this concept, taking into account some of the various expressions which Western speculation has retained.

On a metaphysical level, men are basically equal because of an equivalent servitude to God. The quality of being a believer perhaps confers additional dignity. In its ethical usage, the concept of equality is very badly defined. On the level of formal or external equality, the Islamic juridical notion of equality corresponds in essence to the present Western acceptation: the legal prescriptions and sanctions are the same for all citizens. One nuance must be emphasized, however. Since "citizenship" is determined by the acceptance of Islam, certain prohibitions[53] or obligations[54] are not enforced with regard to non-Muslims who may, according to circumstances, be subject to the legal sanctions provided for by their own religious legislation. This is one of the basic traits of Muslim tolerance.

The notion of political equality is even more difficult to define and has moreover greatly varied during the history of the Muslim empire. Since the death of the Prophet, the question has been raised, sometimes violently. In essence, Islam appears fundamentally "democratic." Nevertheless, the law is divine, given. No legislating body seems necessary or possible. The concept of "political rights" would hence not have any meaning, and in this context, it would be more a question of "political duties." The development of rules of practical application was the subject of great debates. Muslim "law" was always made more clear by the "community consensus."[55] It can for this reason be considered that political equality was guaranteed since, theoretically, nothing prevented a Muslim from opposing the acceptance of a new term. On a historical level, such a procedure does not seem to have been pursued for long periods of time. However, it would have corresponded perfectly to the example brought to us by Muhammad's never-failing practice to consult with his companions on all important decisions. The non-Muslims were of course excluded from these privileges. Since man's juridical status is determined by the law which God revealed, he who rejects the revelation places himself "out of the law" and consequently deprives himself of enjoying these privileges by virtue of his very refusal. On the other hand, he is not required to respect certain dispositions of Islamic law, provided that these exceptions do not interfere with the social order of the Muslim community. If the law determines the juridical status of the individual, the dignity of man as such

---

[53]As example of this is the consumption of certain foods or alcohol.
[54]The *jihad* is illustrative of this, just as all pillars of the faith are.
[55]*Ijma'*.

or, more exactly, the equality of all human creatures is no more diminished by his refusal to embrace Islam. The Qur'ān condemns all sorts of social divisions or stratifications[56] as being contrary to the nature of men, who are, according to the *hadith*, "as equal as the teeth of a comb."

Finally, on the level of "real" or material equality, Islam is uncontestably opposed to this notion.[57] The Muslim, attached to the essential, should not allow himself to become enslaved by material needs. The Qur'ān acknowledges differences of fortune and protects private property. In a society which has remained eminently theocentric, based on a philosophy of the absolute, the very concept of material possessions is of a religious nature: wealth and poverty are decided by God.[58] In the final analysis, all possessions belong to God alone. Man only has the privilege of usufruct on earth. The only juridical limitation on private property is that it must have been acquired honestly. One who enjoys its privileges must avoid excess and wastage. The basic principle of justice, which regulates relations between members of the community, serves as a restraining force, and the compulsory almsgiving results in a certain redistribution of wealth.

It is important to note that, historically, few other religions or ideologies have caused such a powerful movement of social leveling. The essential equality of men, as well as the duty to materially help the less fortunate members of the community, not in the capacity of privileges but in that of obligations, was to lessen material differences if not to practically eliminate social stratification.[59] Even though Islam recognizes and protects individual property, when the latter is acquired honestly and used intelligently, stipulations (concerning this property) are nonetheless very strict. Islamic jurisprudence actually stipulates that the destitute or starving have the right to share the meal of one who is satiated. The Muslim has a right to the food of the table of another Muslim who has enough to eat, whether the latter likes it or not. In the face of possible refusal, the hungered person is authorized to

---

[56] "Truly Pharaoh behaved with arrogance in the land (of Egypt) and he divided its inhabitants into castes ... he opened it to corruption," al-Qasas: 4. This translation emphasizes that the verb *asfada* is equivalent to the French: corrompre, pervertir; and rendre mauvais, inefficace or inapte à fonctionner; or even désorganiser, vicier, muire, and so on. The remark is very interesting. It illustrates the difficulty of finding the correct French word for its Arabic counterpart. In addition, the translator indicates the analogy between social disorder and tyranny as between the latter and the division of society into classes.

[57] "Allah has bestowed His gifts of sustenance more freely on some of you than on others," an-Nahl: 71 (Blachère).

[58] "Allah dispenses and measures His sustenance to whomever He pleases," ar-Ra'd: 26 (Blachère).

[59] Mirza M. Hussain, *Islam versus Socialism* 2nd ed. (Lahore: Ashraf, 1970), 170 pages. After this: Hussain, *Islam*.

use force, and should he perish during his struggle, he will die as a "martyr."[60] His murderer is held guilty. If, on the other hand, the hungered one were to kill his adversary, no punishment would be inflicted upon him since he had been fighting for his legitimate right.[61] Such an assertion of social rights assumes a force which has not been manifested anywhere in history, even in those systems which condemn private property.

Considered from the Western point of view, which played a major role in the development of the "Universal Declaration of Human Rights," the Islamic doctrine concerning "human rights" is rather specific and could appear ambiguous. In effect, on the metaphysical level, the believer enjoys total liberty with his fellows by their common servitude to God. The revealed law is a code of formal obligations for the believer. The latter has no "right" with regard to God, but only duties.

The cornerstone of the social system is equality. It is essentially through this principle that, throughout the course of its teachings, Islam has repeatedly asserted (the importance of) the human being, often in opposition to society and existing institutions when they were not applying the divine laws. At the present time, the Muslim citizen still displays remarkable freedom and individualism in a society which has lost its original dynamism and which often finds itself stultified by tradition. This opposition, whether tacit or active, individual or collective, is never directed against the law but against its application. Even nowadays it is maintained by the cultural tradition and ancestral psychology of Islam. The individual succeeds in maintaining a kind of mental detachment, drawing upon what remains most essential in the Muslim doctrine: all comes from and returns to God. It can thus be considered that the great "merit of the Muslims is that they have placed above all things the matter of submitting in one way or another to a discipline of supernatural inspiration. [This fact places them] ... at the pole opposite that of modern Western constitutions, whose primary and atrociously coarse and vulgar aim is 'collective happiness,' as it is proclaimed in the first article of the Declaration of Human Rights, or that of the state, or the race."[62]

The Qur'ān recognizes human dignity, for God preferred man "to many other creatures."[63] Accepting this principle is not only a moral concept but implies obligatory consequences, namely the respect of one's fellow man. The

---

[60]Promised eternal salvation, then death in the "path of God."

[61]Ahmed Chalaby, *Islam: foi – législation – morale* (Cairo: Supreme Council of Islamic Affairs, 1969), p. 127. After this: Chalaby, *Islam*.

[62]Philippe Guiberteau, "Islam, Occident, Chrétienté," in *L'Islam et l'Occident*, Paris (Les Cahiers du Sud, no. 10), 1947, 393 pages, pp. 165-173.

[63]al-Isra': 70.

respect of one's own dignity is proven by his sense of responsibility. Man
is respectable and worthy because he is responsible. This responsibility sup-
poses the liberty of choice. The circle is closed; all the premises of Islamic
morality come together and are fulfilled. Man's superiority above all other
creatures is thus "theologically" proven. Here we mean man, not the believer,
as has sometimes been claimed by some. The Qur'ān[64] is in any case clear
on this point: Iblis was condemned for refusing to bow down before Adam,
the father of all men (who were not stained by Adam's original sin). Their
eternal salvation depends on them alone, a dignity which stems of course
from divine mercy, but which is supported by total and terrifying individual
responsibility.[65] If man has only duties with regard to the divine legislator,
his rights are nonetheless guaranteed by the very limits which the law places
upon the liberty of others. This reciprocal definition will no longer be subject
to the changing will of men. Thus, the recognition of God's absolute transcendence and of the vacuity of all earthly things in no manner restrains the
essence of Muslim humanism. Finally, if the status of the believer enhances
the dignity of the human being by virtue of the double fact that he chooses
to submit to the prescriptions of the revealed law and that he becomes a
member of the Muslim community, the non-Muslim also maintains his dignity. Equal to the Muslim in his immense inferiority to God, he excludes
himself by refusing the superior quality offered by the law. In this way, he
is different, he is a "stranger," subject to his own laws. The Muslim is obligated to respect him as such.

Equality and the Status of Women

In the framework of the essential equality of all human creatures, the current status of women, and in particular the problem of polygamy and divorce,
leaves much to be desired. In fact, the abuse and distortions of Muslim
thought concerning both the status of women as well as slavery seem to have
arisen simultaneously in the 'Abbasid period. The brilliant society which then
reigned in Baghdad, as a result of the influence of recently converted Muslims, brought about moral depravation. The stories from the "Thousand and
One Nights" give one a rather precise idea in this respect. At the same time,
however, it is clear that in the Umayyad caliphate of Spain, women enjoyed
respect and liberty. They participated totally in the social and cultural life of
the period. The man submits to the "lady" in order to win her favors. Fur-

---

[64]al-Hijr: 28-46.
[65]"... We did indeed offer the faith to the heavens, to the earth, to the mountains. They refused
to undertake it. They were afraid of it. Only man undertook it ..." al-Ahzab: 72. We emphasize
here that, in the Islamic view, the "trust of the faith" should be understood as the "charge of
responsibility."

thermore, it is delightful to observe that it was the influence of the Muslim poets which, via Spain, taught European Christians respect for women and the gallant love which the troubadours transmitted through their songs into the very heart of Europe.

The teachings of the Qur'ān and the example of the Prophet were aimed at a primitive people whose ancient traditions could not be suppressed all at once. Through the written word and intellectual means, Qur'ānic legislation brought about considerable improvement in the status of the women of pre-Islamic Arabia. Polygamy most certainly received explicit recognition, and the practice of divorce was ratified, but certain terms were imposed in order to limit its scope. Historical evolution brought about notorious abuse based on a purely literal interpretation of the Qur'ān which, on the whole, was done to support male selfishness. In modern times, women in Muslim society have a shocking status, according to the canons of contemporary Western civilization. Among the most violently polemic of all debates between the West and the Muslim world, as well as those within the latter itself is the one concerning the status of women. They led to more misunderstanding than comprehension because their starting points were fundamentally diverging premises. It is thus important to paint a picture, though necessarily a limited one, of "women's rights" in Islam. We will not, however, take the present-day situation into account, for at this time Muslim woman does not benefit from the position which should be hers.[66] It must also be kept in mind that the Qur'ān was by no means meant to reform the morals of pre-Islamic Arabia (alone), but that it brought, on the contrary, a perfect and eternal law applicable to human realities and social necessities of all times. We will therefore successively consider the nature of woman, then the Muslim idea of marriage, and finally its two corollaries – polygamy and divorce.

Islam addresses both men and women and treats them in an "almost equal"[67] fashion. Islamic law in general aims at a characteristically protective goal. As far as women are concerned, legislation provides precise definitions of their rights and shows an intense preoccupation with the guarantee of these rights. The Qur'ān and prophetic traditions demand that the woman be treated with justice, kindness, and benevolence; they introduced a great moral concept of marriage and aimed at improving the conditions of women by granting her a certain number of judicial rights.[68] The rights of women, which are "sacred" according to one of the dictums of the Prophet, are: equality before the law, personal private property, and inheritance rights.

---

[66]Muhammed M. Pickthall, *The Cultural Side of Islam*, 3rd ed. (Lahore: Ashraf, 1969), p. 141. After this: Pickthall, *The Cultural Side*.

[67]Madkour, "The Concept," p. 456.

[68]Andrae, *Mahomet*, p. 190.

The fact that the male heir receives a double portion is not considered by Muslim jurists to be a discriminatory measure, but rather an advantage which is obvious and logical because only the man has the duty of providing entirely for the needs of the family, whereas the woman disposes of a personal management of her property. The respect of feminine prerogatives appeared so basic that one of the main Muslim jurists[69] decreed that in every Islamic town a woman should be appointed as a judge, officially responsible for keeping a check on the respect of women's rights.[70]

Western literature generally seems to give credit to the idea that the rights of women are only theoretical or imaginary in a system which permits polygamy and apparently unilateral divorce. The observation of contemporary Muslim society reinforces this opinion. Thus, at this point, it is necessary to emphasize three peculiarities of the Islamic notion. First of all, marriage, which is most decidedly an intimate union and a "solemn alliance,"[71] is a strictly juridical act – a contract. It does not have any character of a definitive sacramental union. In all likelihood, the latter concept still unconsciously impregnates Western thought whose aversion to polygamy expresses itself in a semireligious manner, rather more emotive than rational. If polygamy appears degrading for the woman, certain Muslims on the contrary believe that monogamy, springing from the Christian notion of marriage as a sacrament, still bears the imprint of contempt for the woman, the prohibited being of eminently sinful nature, who could be permanently possessed by a man only through a "mystical union of souls."[72] Interestingly enough, a novel which recently appeared in France, describing a fictitious society governed by women, imagines the suppression of the traditional institution of marriage and preaches a kind of free "polygamy" as the expression of a new feminine liberty.[73]

Islam's second characteristic arises from the fact that the law claims to legislate realistically and not in an idealistically, taking into account man's true nature. Finally, Islamic morality imposes decency which, on a sexual level, can only become a concrete reality through marriage. In the light of these three elements taken together, Islam, which most certainly did not introduce either polygamy or divorce (these having existed in all civilizations at a given moment of their development), acknowledged but also limited their legitimacy. In general, the terms are as follows: a man is permitted to take

---

[69]Abu Hanifah, see below, chapter 5, pp. 235.
[70]Pickthall, *The Cultural Side of Islam*, more specifically on p. 142, thinks that "Muhammad has raised the status of woman to a point, after which she can only go (higher) in theory."
[71]an-Nisa': 21.
[72]Pickthall, *The Cultural Side*, pp. 160-163.
[73]Robert Merle, *Les hommes protégés* (Paris: Gallimard, 1974), 378 pages.

up to four wives on the condition that he can provide for them all equitably.[74] While polygamy is allowed, an honest monogamous union is the desired objective. It remains an ideal and one which is perhaps incompatible with the true nature of man. A legitimate polygamy should ensure a more decent family life than an unrespected monogamy under which naturally lies adultery, defamation, lying, and which causes forced celibacy for certain women as well as deprivation of children for many couples.[75] "Modern" interpretations of Qur'ānic attitudes claim that the latter must necessarily lead to the abolition of polygamy. Not only does the law determine a fixed limit to the number of simultaneous marriages, but it also imposes the condition of treating the possible wives in an absolutely equal manner. Man, who is not capable of treating several wives equally on both a material and an emotional level, will therefore marry only one. As for the Arab feminist movement, it demands the abolition of polygamy in order to ensure a woman's "personality, dignity, and stability, as well as the happiness of her family."[76]

The same pragmatic spirit seems to have prevailed in Islamic stipulations concerning divorce, the latter occupying a very important place in the Qur'ān. Here again, the Islamic conception refuses to recognize human nature to be more virtuous than it really is. At the same time, in the Islamic perspective, man must in no way deprive himself of the benefits and pleasures which God sends to him. Since marriage is essentially a contract, it can be annulled if the clauses thereof are not fulfilled. The motives, though, must not be spurious, for the Qur'ān never ceases to enjoin a conscientious respect for commitments made. The permission to divorce is evident, but it must be done according to a determined framework; a form of reconciliation is moreover provided. The woman is entitled to ask for divorce only under certain conditions. Since she is thus placed at a disadvantage, she has the right to material compensation. The correct procedure is spelled out in all its details in the Qur'ān. An entire chapter[77] is devoted to divorce and many verses (of other chapters) make further reference to it. Divorce is most certainly a social scourge. Muslim doctrine considers it as such, but also recognizes that its regulated authorization may be preferable for some, as opposed to its absolute prohibition which sometimes generates, in the case of those long-since mar-

---

[74]an-Nisa': 3. We note that this is the only mention made in the Qur'ān concerning the precise number of spouses. Robert Roberts, *The Social Laws of the Qur'ān*, 2nd ed. (London: Curzon, 1971), p. 7. After this: Roberts, *The Social Laws*.

[75]Ahmed M. al-Hofy, *La tolérance de l'Islam* (Cairo: Supreme Council of Islamic Affairs, 1969), pp. 14-18. After this: al-Hofy, *La tolérance*.

[76]Resolution of the Congress of Arab Women, held in May 1971 in Tunis. See *al-Ahram*, June 2, 1971, p.???

[77]at-Talaq.

ried, forced celibacy,[78] and which opens the way to adultery and concubinage.

According to the Qur'ān, woman is of the same substance as man. She was not created from one of his ribs, but represents "his twin half" according to a dictum of the Prophet. The Qur'ān stipulates that God "created pairs" of all things.[79] The revelation rejects the idea that woman married man to commit the original sin. Thus, Muslim doctrine has never used (such) irreverent terms as did some of the Church fathers who, for a long time, considered women as "the agents of the devil." On the contrary, the Qur'ān grants the gift of perfection to two women.[80] 'Asiyah, the wife of Pharaoh, and Mary, "daughter of Imran" and mother of Jesus. The prophetic tradition added Khadijah, wife of Muhammad, and Fatimah, his daughter.[81]

In their capacity as believers, women are subject to obligations identical with those of men. Being of the same substance as men, they are thus equal to man but nonetheless remain different. It is true that men have a kind of preeminence[82] over women. For Muslims, as it is for science and common sense, the couple are equal on spiritual and intellectual levels but differ from each other physically. Furthermore, the preminence of the man is affirmed only in the mutual relations of the couple, as a distinction of functions.[83] There is nothing Islamic about wearing the veil which materially illustrates the inferiority of the Muslim woman. Muhammad recommended only that they behave in a modest fashion and that they cover their hair and necks with a scarf. It was apparently in Persia and the Near East that Islam encountered this custom in the cities. The Muslims adopted it for psychological and social reasons, since in those days a woman who showed her face had the reputation of loose morals.[84] This practice was maintained for a long time under the pressure of tradition, not through any religious obligation. The degradation of the feminine condition is moreover a characteristic peculiar to the Mediterranean world.[85]

The aim of the present document is not to judge an institution but to describe it objectively, by providing elements obtained from Muslm sources, so

---

[78]al-Hofy, *La tolerance*, p. 22.
[79]adh-Dhariyyat: 49.
[80]at-Tahrim: 11-12.
[81]Masse, *L'Islam*, p. 134.
[82]al-Baqarah: 238. This applies, above all, on the economic level since only the man is legally responsible for satisfying the needs of the couple. The wife must therefore conform to the material level which her husband is honestly capable of offering her.
[83]Pickthall, *The Cultural Side*, pp. 152-153, 158.
[84]Pickthall, *The Cultural Side*, p. 142.
[85]Germaine Tillion, *Le Harem et les cousins* (Paris: Seuil, 1966), 218 pages.

as to respond to the usual objections raised by outside observers. It appears therefore that it is not so much the legal disposition as it is the application on the part of the Muslims which is condemnable. Nothing in the teachings of the Qur'ān justifies the present situation of women in the Islamic world. Only ignorance, and in particular the ignorance of the Muslim woman herself with regard to her rights, can explain it. In effect, "placing ourselves in the absolute perspective of the religion, together with those who are rigorous and unshakable, accepting the situation created for the Muslim woman, if we then compare it to that of the pre-Islamic woman, we observe that great ammendments were brought to her by the new religion; in the latter case, we note that (Muslim) men have strayed far from the liberal spirit of the religion, only to adhere to a soulless formalism, thereby committing, in the name of Islam, abuses severely censured by the very same religion which they follow so literally."[86]

"Paradise lies at the foot of the mother," or again "The best among you is the one who is best toward his wife," said the Prophet. Such assertions could never have issued from a society which had no respect for the woman as such. Her present relative inferiority as compared to the man is the direct outcome of the general social and economic conditions of Islamic society. Besides, this has been well understood by feminists who base their claim on the usual two pillars of the awakening of the Muslim conscience: the political and religious aspects. In this respect, their battle runs the risk of being both easier and much more difficult than that of Western women. They will, in effect, have to make up a far more considerable time lapse. On the other hand, their task will be facilitated by the fact that they will not have to struggle against a legislation established primarily by men who are in a position to accept or refuse to grant them "privileges" which would diminish the severity of the civil code. The Muslim woman has an already acquired right to social equality, private personal property, respect and security in marriage, compensation in the case of divorce, and the enjoyment of purely feminine interests. This right is granted to them by the divine law itself. They will have to obtain its practical application on the part of men precisely by evoking Islam itself.

Liberty and Slavery

The principle of equality is the cornerstone of the Islamic social edifice; it has fashioned the construction thereof. History clearly shows that Islam managed to develop a homogenous and integrated society without classes, in

---

[86]H. H. Benabed, "Les conditions de la femme musulmane," in *l'Islam et l'Occident*, Paris (Cahiers du Sud, no. 9), 1947, 393 pages, pp. 211-219. See also Emile Dermenghem, *Mahomet et la tradition islamique* (Paris: Seuil, 1963), pp. 77 f. After this: Dermenghem, *Mahomet.*

which the claim of "liberty, equality, and fraternity" (the main motivations of the revolts of the West) could not have stirred up true feelings since it did not fulfill a real need. The basic principle of the absolute equality of all men brings into focus the other two terms of the slogan – fraternity and liberty – by encompassing or, more exactly, transcending them.

In this context, liberty is an affirmed natural and given fact, a general characteristic of man, an essential principle of life. Simultaneously, fraternity appears as the basis of Islamic society. It is for this reason that only a very minimal part of the abundant Islamic juridical literature is devoted to the discussion of liberty and is even then limited to the strictly legal and technical aspects of the problem.[87] References to equality, however, are very numerous, in the Qur'ān, prophetic traditions, and in scholarly publications. Liberty, seen as a corollary of equality, is expressed by the feeling or vague pride of being independent. Here the free man is contrasted with the slave. It has been claimed that freedom in the Muslim perspective is not the "kind for which one dies."[88] This statement is too abstract to be accepted without nuances. It is true that the sense of "human liberty," which can thus correspond to the feeling of equality, remains vivid in the Islamic conscience, where it ends up progressively representing the expression of all that is noble and superior in man, thereby contributing to the preservation of that term's dignity.[89]

As for the concept of "civic liberty," which is more of a metaphysical ideal than it is a political reality, it did not develop simultaneously for the twofold reason that man was its deputy and that the believers did not claim to be able to transform the divine law. Thus, on the metaphysicial or religious level, liberty does not represent any particular theoretical problem in an ideally egalitarian system. On a social level, it was to assume a purely judicial aspect, contrasting the free man with the slave. Hence, the appeal to individual liberty had no reason whatever to arouse emotional outbursts such as it kindled in the West against social oppression. Naturally, it did not create any political force capable of transforming the greatly integrated Muslim society. In the same way, it was far more the feelings of dignity and human equality, as well as the aspiration to collective freedom in the sense of independence, which pushed the Muslims to struggle against European colonization.

There is no doubt that the Qur'ān recognizes slavery, an institution which at that time existed universally. It deals with slavery in order to limit its abuse

---

[87]Rosenthal, *Freedom*, pp. 333-34.
[88]Louis Gardet, *La Cité musulmane: Vie sociale et politique*, (Paris Vrin, 1961), 417 pages. After this: Gardet, *La Cité*.
[89]Rosenthal, *Freedom*, p. 121.

and to gradually bring about its disappearance through the moral and religious conviction of the natural equality of all men before God and His law. It is most certainly one of Islam's great merits that it ceased to consider the status of slavery as a natural fact, but saw it rather as an accidental exception, injurious to the liberty which forms the principal subfoundation of the community of men. Moreover, Muslim moralists are unanimous in declaring that the Qur'ān and Muhammad placed themselves as adversaries of slavery and aimed at eliminating it by means of the juridical and moral decrees which they enacted. At the time of the revelation, the stipulations of the law addressed a backward and patriarchal society. For psychological and economic reasons, the Qur'ān could not blot out this institution in one stroke. Slavery has existed in all nations at some stage of their development[90] and has disappeared with the improvement of the conditions of economic production, " the progress of human thought and the increase in the sense of justice among all humanity."[91] It was one of the pre-Islamic traditions destined to be abolished in the long run by a system of gradual emancipation.

The originality of Islamic thought concerning slavery arises from the idea of man in society. Liberty is above all a judicial notion which in no way places man's dignity or greatness at stake. Liberty is not founded upon human nature but on a positive decree of God. This does not in any way mean that slavery is the necessary and lasting destiny of a certain category of people who are inferior in their very essence to others. On the contrary, it could only be accidental and temporary. Thus, the Muslim slave has never been the "thing" of Roman law. No discredit soiled his status. Contrary to medieval Christianity, Muslim doctrine, strongly impregnated by Qur'ānic prescriptions, was not influenced by the theories from Greek antiquity, especially those of Aristotle, concerning slavery.[92] Instead of suddenly abolishing slavery, for objective and realistic reasons Islam enunciated the terms of its gradual suppression and at the same time attempted to diminish the hardships of this institution. The system has a double characteristic: reduction of access to servitude and expansion of the way toward liberty.

On the level of restrictions, the Qur'ān aimed at limiting the reasons for slavery: only those captured during a legitimate war and hereditary descendents were retained.[93] Historical practice admitted the purchase of slaves, of

[90]See, for example, Eugene E. Genovese, *Economie politique de l'esclavage: Essais sur l'economie et la societe du Sud esclavagiste*, translated by Nicole Barbier (Paris: Maspero, 1968), 263 pages.
[91]Amir Ali, *The Spirit*, p. 258.
[92]Rosenthal, *Freedom*, p. 30.
[93]Furthermore by jurisprudence (*fiqh*) alone, in apparent contradiction with the Qur'ānic provisions.

which the Qur'ān does not make any mention – it does not seem to have existed during the time of Prophet Muhammad and his four immediate successors.[94] It appeared only under the reign of the Umayyads. All other motives authorizing slavery, retained by pre-Islamic Arab traditions and the former codes of other civilizations, were rejected. On the economic level, moreover, there are many reasons for freeing slaves regardless of their religion. Emancipating slaves is an obligation for the believer who would otherwise be guilty of involuntary homicide,[95] intentional perjury,[96] or else illegitimate divorce.[97] The *hadith* orders the liberation of one slave by a person who has not been able to keep the fast of Ramadan. Ill-treatment also constitutes sufficient and obligatory cause for liberation. Muhammad said: "One who has inflicted excessive hardship (corrective measures) upon his slave or who has laid a hand upon him, may expiate his fault by setting him free." An injured slave is to be set free. A female slave who gives birth becomes free upon the death of her master. Her children are legitimate and enjoy the same rights as those of free women.

Apart from these strictly imperative terms, the Qur'ān also appeals to the Muslims to release slaves so that they may thereby accomplish meritorious acts for which they will be rewarded.[98] It provides to this end the allocation of a certain portion of the compulsory legal tax.[99] Finally, there exists a decree which, though less well-known, is of considerable importance, whereby the master is obliged to grant an act of emancipation to the slave who wishes to buy his freedom: "And such of your slaves as seek a writing of emancipation, write it for them if you are aware of any good in them, and bestow upon them of the wealth of Allah which He has bestowed upon you."[100] Muslims emphasize the wisdom of this injunction: the duty to materially help the slave in the process of emancipation ensures him a true liberation. History has shown, in the United States of America for example, that slaves emancipated without any financial support experienced difficulties in truly freeing themselves. Destitute and unemployed, they would usually return to their former masters. These different procedures which we have enumerated led to the gradual abolition of slavery without upsetting the balance of the community's economic structure.

Simultaneously, Islam guaranteed various safeguards and the personal sec-

[94]Roberts, *The Social Laws*, p. 54.
[95]an-Nisa': 92.
[96]al-Ma'idah: 89.
[97]al-Mujādilah: 30.
[98]al-Balad: 13.
[99]*Zakah* – al-Baqarah: 117.
[100]an-Nur: 33.

Humanism in Islam

urity of the slave, all the while trying to improve his treatment at the hands of his master.[101] Numerous examples illustrate that slaves not only had the benefit of humanitarian treatment but also enjoyed respect. Zayd, emancipated by Muhammad, often led Muslim troops in battle. His son Usamah was at the head of the Syrian campaign. Bilal, named governor of Medinah, as well as Qutb ad-Din Aybak, founder of the Islamic empire in South Asia, had been slaves.[102] Without a doubt, slaves enjoyed (the privilege of) a juridical personality and could also play a certain social role. As believers, they could ensure the security of a stranger (to the region) just as free men could do.

Beyond the facts given by Islamic tradition, Qur'ānic legal attitudes and decrees historically bore basic and fundamental consequences. Slavery in effect seems to have initially appeared when early warriors saved the lives of the vanquished enemy and decided to use them for nonrenumerated labor, as a practical and concrete expression of the victor's right. Through the assurance of the personal integrity of slaves, equal to all men, upon whom their owners no longer had the right of life and death, and by means of granting rights and judicial claims, a system of protecting prisoners of war was formed. This is most certainly the most original and progressive contribution made by Muslim thought of that time.

As far as treatment (of slaves) itself is concerned, the belief in the natural equality of men gave a particular status to the Muslims' slaves. Muhammad, according to the *ahadith*, forbade referring to them by the term "slave," since all men are the slaves of God alone; he recommended that they be called "brother" or "child." On many occasions, the Prophet reminded the Muslims that the "slaves were their 'likeness' whom God had placed under their control."[103]

The present section would have been superfluous if its aim had been only to describe a situation which is now abolished. The aim is to show that, even though Islam tacitly permitted and explicitly recognized slavery, it took measures for its gradual elimination. Besides, it is indispensible to consider the question in a specifically Islamic perspective: human liberty derives from a divine decree, not from the decision of man. The judicial status which God decreed and which – within the confines of what is allowed according to the Qur'ān – places one man under obedience to another, does not strip him of

---

[101]an-Nisa': 36.
[102]The first three named had previously been set free. The "slave" sultans of Delhi and the Mamelukes of Egypt raise an interesting juridical problem: their status necessarily had to be that of free men since they were Muslims.
[103]In particular at the time of the "Farewell Sermon of Muhammad," during his last pilgrimage. See Roberts, *The Social Laws*, p. 57 and al-Hofy, *La tolérance*, pp. 164-165.

his personal rights. The institution of slavery, common to all pre-modern societies, corresponds to specific conditions of (economic) production. Both were to disappear simultaneously. Europe in the eighteenth and nineteenth centuries had attained a stage of economic development which rendered the abolition of slavery possible. That is how Europe appeared as the champion of anti-slavery. History furthermore shows that the attitude of each of the Western countries differed according to its material resources far more than according to its actual spiritual aspirations. Slavery was gradually replaced by serfdom in the countryside and then by renumerated labor. Would it be incongruous, in this respect, to project Qur'ānic terms onto contemporary Muslim society, bearing in mind the now forced relations within the economic system, and to see whether those injunctions concerning slaves and servants could constitute the framework of social legislation or of a work ethic in conformity with the general spirit of Islam? Thus, the well-known recommendation of Muhammad would become: "Your subordinates (slaves) are your brothers whom God has placed under your control. May he who employs a worker (who possesses a slave) not impose upon him any task which is beyond his powers; should he have to do this, he must come to his aid. If the employee (slave) commits an error, he must pardon him or dismiss him (he should exchange him), but let him not illtreat (torture) him at all."[104] Such an extrapolation or projection is not necessarily absurd if one considers that, in the true Islamic perspective, and contrary to all others, the status of the slave is strictly juridical and by no manner of means casts a slur upon his intrinsic value as a human being.

Justice and Charity

In the context of "international morality," spiritual motivations arising from traditional civilization, and therefore also from religion, determine certain individual or collective attitudes. The Christian sense of "charity" brought about several great movements of human solidarity, which in their turn induced a humanization of positive international law. It seems interesting to consider the approach of Islam, which considers justice as "the act closest to piety."[105]

---

[104]This interpretation is our own. We agree to substitute "repeal" for "exchange," taking into account the historical tracings. We present it reservedly, even though a suitable explanation was found in Haroon K. Sherwani, *Studies in Muslim Political Thought and Administration*, 4th ed. (Lahore: Ashraf, 1968), p. 256. After this: Sherwani, *Studies*.

[105]al-Ma'idah: 8 or still: "O you who believe! Practice justice constantly by giving proof of faith fulness to God, even as against yourselves, or your parents, or your kin, and whether it be (against) rich or poor, for God has priority over both. Do not follow passions to the detriment of fairness lest you swerve or you turn away; verily, God is well-acquainted with all that you do," an-Nisa': 135.

This venture has to be undertaken with great caution since the use of terminology runs the risk of leading to confusing or blurring fine distinctions, but it is nonetheless useful since it allows us to discern a specifically Islamic concept which exerts an influence upon social relations and, in rather a direct manner, defines the spirit of international relations.

The eminent state of the equality of men and of their individual responsibilities, which derive from a very strongly asserted belief in and consciousness of divine transcendence, could imply the establishment of an extremely individualistic society, going as far as "the refusal of solidarity in the Christian sense, of restorative compassion."[106] So, the question arises as to whether submission to an all-powerful divine will and obedience to the laws ruling a society where justice and order should reign have pushed aside the compassion and charity of inter-individual relations. In its modern moral acceptation, the term "charity" is sometimes opposed to justice. Are the two terms really opposed, or do they overlap while dealing with the same basic moral principles? Are they of similar inspiration, or do they proceed, in one case, from emotion and, in the other, from reason? The debate is situated on a metaphysical level and figures in these pages only because the Islamic notion is quite different from the Western concept. Furthermore, it seems that this problem lies "at the very heart of the preoccupations" dealing with the definition of human law,[107] and consequently, of international morality.

Justice weighs and distributes reward or punishment according to deeds; charity gives according to needs, without calculations or accounting. The former is a blindfolded woman holding a scale; the latter could be her sister, not seeing much more, with her arms stretched wide open. Charity could represent the primary of all justices, and, conversely, justice should be the fruit of true charity. Does each concept represent not so much the basis of moral conduct as rather two foundations of distinct principles from which arise two systems of differing moralities; or, finally, are these two concepts on the contrary reconcilable on a transcendental level? This is the debate which stirs up Western civilization, the latter divided between Christian idealism and intellectual rationalism.

This problem has to be tackled from a particular point of view, which does not oppose two terms or concepts but two world views. It is these world views which, by means of the image they give of the social and spiritual objectives of man and of the community, determine the "political" conception of a collectivity. For Islam, the paradox between justice and charity does not arise for justice constitutes the pivot around which all basic moral values

[106]Massignon, "Le respect," p. 451.
[107] Pictet, *Les principes*, p. 18.

gravitate. Thus, it would be wrong to think, as do many Western authors, that Islam preaches charity, but that for historical reasons the latter atrophied or lost its vigor and gradually came to represent no more than a mechanical and external duty. Conversely, it would also be a mistake to imagine a Muslim justice which was strict to the point of lacking equity and ignoring tolerance.

In the present context, it is necessary to situate the Islamic revelation in its historic perspective. In effect, Muslim writers,[108] when dealing with the evolution of the message sent by God to man,[109] according to their mental and sociological development, explicitly assert the originality of Islam. In the first period, God revealed a religion which first of all appealed to the senses, for humanity was at that stage incapable of understanding any teaching which would have surpassed this framework. In the second phase, since humanity had been enriched by experience and had had its emotions refined, God revealed a religion which preached asceticism, purity, and love. However, society, following the course of its evolution, could no longer live in purity and altruism; discord replaced generosity and dispute gained precedence over charity. At the ultimate stage of development, God then revealed the Islamic religion which, taking feelings and necessities (the heart of reason) into consideration, was called upon to govern all human relations and to organize earthly society while at the same time pointing the way to eternal happiness . This account of the parallel progression between the assumed evolution of humanity and the succession of divine messages is interesting since it shows how reason is supposed to have gradually taken precedence over love, legal organization over altruism and generosity, and hence justice over charity. By way of illustration, the Prophet said: "If the nations become closer to God through all sorts of good deeds, you (the Islamic peoples) will approach Him through the intelligence which you will have acquired."

It would perhaps be appropriate to define our terms at this stage. First, charity. In the purest sense of the word, it means neither beneficence nor generosity, humanity, altruism or kindness; even less, pity, benevolence, mercy, or compassion. It is far more than that. These virtues have only their antithesis in common: selfishness. Selfless, spontaneous, and unreasoning love of one's neighbor is not synonymous with charity, or better still, is not charity itself other than inasmuch as the agent looks upon "men 'per oculos Dei,' so as to justify the infinite giving of oneself, in order to exalt God as man."[110] In this sense, the concept of charity is eminently religious and es-

[108]Abdu, *Rissalat*, pp. 112 f.
[109]al-Isra': 107.
[110]André Lalande, *Vocabulaire technique et critique de la philosophie*, 10th ed. (Paris: P.U.F., 1968), p. 41.

sentially Christian. As for the Qur'ān, it qualifies as good men those who, among other meritorious acts, give "good – for the love of God – to the poor, the orphan, and the captive."[111] A truly religious conception of charity is thus not unknown to Islam, but it never acquired the same importance which it has in Christian morality. Modern vocabulary took hold of the term and made it lose a great portion of its expressive power by rendering it almost synonymous with beneficence. Almost synonymous only, for it has retained from its theological origin an additional meaning which makes the concept very difficult to define. The idea of charity most certainly fashioned Christian morality and today still remains an underlying presence, even in a de Christianized society.

The definition of "charity" was purposely chosen in its Christian specificity since these pages are especially addressed to Western readers: "... the infinite giving of oneself, in order to exalt God as man ..." This latter expression is not acceptable in the Qur'ānic context. On the other hand, the "infinite giving of oneself" is distinctly marked in Islam since the revelation exhorts Muslims to fight, at the expense of their own lives, to defend "women and weak children."

Certain explanations are also necessary so as not to give rise to misunderstanding and render an injustice to Islam. It is also necessary to point out that the Muslims appear very sensitive to the Western writers' practice of contrasting the concepts of justice and charity for they view these two concepts as remain inseparable and complimentary. The Qur'ān never presents them in a situation of paradox. In the practice of charity, the opposition of charity / justice does not exist for the Muslim. To illustrate this point from the point of view of the Qur'ān, excusing an evildoer constitutes a non-charitable and antisocial act, for not only would one be failing to neutralize the harmfulness of the guilty one upon society, but one would moreover be allowing him to continue his pursuit of evil ways. Punishment is active charity, required for the protection of the community and also to prevent the misguided one from straying even further away from God. The Qur'ān addresses man in his unity: his deep sentiments – good or bad – and his daily activity in a perspective which could be called "applied psychology." Therefore, charity in Islam constitutes an essential human value, one of the basic virtues of those who claim to be "Muslims." Nevertheless, the Qur'ān claims that it should be active, collective, and universal. In this light, it affirms itself as specifically Islamic. It does not represent an idealized and perhaps unattainable norm, but, on the contrary, an effective rule which should cement any society aspiring to permanence.

---

[111]ad-Dahr: 8.

Given that during the course of time an immense majority of men have proven themselves incapable of regulating their behavior according to the demands of perfect charity, justice becomes the principal pillar upon which a healthy and integrated society can establish itself. Since man was created essentially weak, the revelation indicates a "path" for him and imposes social structures. For the Muslims, who consider Islam the complete and perfect religion, this fact does not in any way restrain the expression of the great universal virtues, such as the love of one's neighbor and generosity, since the Qur'ān tells us in effect that divine mercy "has encompassed all things." The application of the revealed law – a norm of perfect justice – stimulates the intellectual and moral evolution of human beings toward a more elevated level of altruism which subsequently has to allow the ideal of love to become the governing reality in human matters. The Qur'ānic teaching stipulates this superior objective: "...they find in their breasts no need for that which has been given to the fugitives, but prefer them above themselves though poverty become their (own) lot ... Such are they who are successful."[112]

Is justice itself nothing more than a system of negative formal restrictions, absolute obligations, or the possibility of demanding reciprocity, or is it rather the impartial separation between what is allowed and what is forbidden? According to the Islamic system, whatever is legal, upright, and in conformity with the revealed divine law, is just. In its turn, the concept is of religious nature. In the Islamic vision of a balanced world governed by divine decree, justice is soundness since God carries out His law which He has communicated to man through the Qur'ān. It is the theological character of justice which most emphatically distinguishes it from all other virtues, just as the Christian religious sentiment makes much more of charity – the simple philanthropy. The very term for "justice" in Arabic[113] etymologically means "equal" and "equitable."

The principle of equality, moderation, and proportionality leads to beauty in nature[114] and goodness in man. According to Muslim doctrine, justice represents both the foundation and the ultimate aim of all divine revelations. It is thus expressed on two levels: God's justice toward His creatures and the justice of men among themselves. Muhammad was expressly instructed to bring equity among men.[115] The Qur'ānic concept is considered superior to the corpus of meanings and systems developed by men since it reaches into the inner core of the believer, all of whose deeds, motives, and intentions

---

[112]al-Hashr: 9.
[113]'*Adl*.
[114]Asaf Fyzee, *A Modern Approach to Islam* (Bombay: Asia Publishing House, 1963), p. 17.
[115]ash-Shura: 15.

are known to God.[116]

The Islamic system rests on certain norms of equilibrium. The very conception of Allah is midway between power and severity on one hand, and compassion and mercy on the other. The Muslim community consists of the "people of the middle," to use a Qur'ānic expression which refers to far more than a simple geographic notion. The demands of morality are equidistant from the extremities, in both directions. Virtue is a middle point, the "happy medium." "This average, this equality" is justice, the fundamental virtue – a justice without excess, from which all feelings of hatred and revenge are banished, a justice which in essence takes all proportions into account. Put back into this context, the Muslim concept of justice appears to have been still better defined by the term of equity, in the sense in which the West generally understands it.

This very strongly asserted principle of justice plunges its roots into religion, which shows the believer the true scope of the concept, through the threat of the Day of Judgment and the "burning faith in God the judge, in His incomparable majesty, in His absolute right to punish..."[117] and in His immeasurable justice. However, the adjectives which the Qur'ān uses to define the divine attributes, as well as their variety and abundance, denote the importance also attached to the goodness, benevolence, and mercy of God. Here, the Islamic notion is in accordance with the Jewish and Christian concepts in which God is necessarily merciful because He is perfectly just. Far from weakening it, clemency gives justice a kind of plenitude. Mercy appears to be not only complimentary but even an integral part of equity. This concordance implies that moral prescriptions or formal commandments, such as loving and helping one's neighbor and supporting one's relatives, the poor and strangers, are definitely found in Islam. Certain verses of the Qur'ān explicitly command this. That is where the similarity ends, however. The Muslim is not required to pray for those who persecute him, nor to love his enemies.[118] The Christian injunction appears absurd to him, shocking to reason, and contrary to nature. In fact, the enemies of Islam are essentially the enemies of God and are therefore eminently heinous. They must be opposed. If need be, violence against those who disturb order and disrupt harmony becomes a legitimate action, "one of the functions of 'justice' in its

---

[116]Anwar A. Qadri, *Justice in Historical Islam* (Lahore: Ashraf, 1968), p. 1.
[117]Andrae, *Mahomet*, p. 59.
[118]It may prove better to be merciful in a case like this; after all, "A good action does not resemble a bad one. Repel evil with what is better: the one who is separated from you by hostility will become your intimate friend," Fusselat: 34 (Masson).

broader sense."[119] The Muslim will not turn his cheek to the one who struck him but will fight against evil in the best possible manner without forgetting that the ultimate goal is reconciliation and peace.

Mercy and benevolence are rules deserving of particular respect but are not abstract and idealized notions. Order is equivalent to equilibrium and harmony, to unity and justice. It is in this context that these notions must be placed since religion furnishes both individual moral precepts and the foundations of social institutions. The individual obligation of justice, backed by mercy and generosity, is expressed on a collective level by the altruism which is derived from the concept of solidarity and is according to Islamic doctrine, indispensible to the community of men. It is an outreaching gesture which is opposed to selfishness, without necessarily eliminating individualism or utilitarianism. In Islam, justice is the essential religious force, and altruism the principal moral of social order.

The resemblance between certain social and external practices, the identical nature of spontaneous human reactions, as well as the similarity of insufficient vocabulary, can lead to confusion since they rarely circumscribe the same concepts from one religion to another, or from one civilization to another. Muslim "charity" does not correspond to what Christian theology and the general Western meaning imply but, on the contrary, to a "profound fraternity under the direction of God."[120] This fraternity could most definitely attain great heights and cannot be seen as simply the mechanical execution of the law. In this respect, the legal "poor due," one of the "five pillars of the religion," is a pregnant illustration of Muslim thought. It is perhaps not superfluous in this context to outline this concept with greater precision and with regard to its implications for the believer himself.

The obligatory nature of giving (the poor due) could erroneously lead one to believe that the feeling of generosity and charity are "diseased," having been rendered somewhat mechanical by Islamic legalism. It seems that almsgiving was exclusively voluntary at the outset. It became compulsory with the birth of the Muslim state, both to help the growing number of needy believers and to help the indigent families among those who were fighting under the banner of Islam. Thus, it became a "tax" with its proceeds going to very specific humanitarian goals. If, in time, it assumed more marked legal connotations, it maintained its character as a religious obligation, an act of piety, and also that of a charitable action in the moral meaning of the word.

---

[119]René Guenon, "Sayful Islam" in *L'Islam et l'Occident*, Paris (Cahiers du Sud, no. 9), 1947, 393 pages, pp. 59-64, p. 59.
[120]Gaston Zananiri, *L'Eglise et l'Islam* (Paris: Spes, 1969), p. 42. After this: Zananiri, *L'Eglise*.

Actually, its legalistic appearance does not in any way limit generosity to the material domain: "A kind word with forgiveness is better than almsgiving followed by injury," stipulates the Qur'ān.[121] Almsgiving is practiced for the love of God and not so much for the love of one's neighbor. In reality, within the Islamic perspective, everything belongs to God; no man has any exclusive property whatever. Thus, almsgiving represents a spiritual exercise closely corresponding to the general philosophy of the religion which encourages each Muslim, on a personal basis, to rise above material preoccupations, which takes him from selfishness to altruism, from individualism to collectivity.

In giving the legal poor due, a Muslim does not have the impression of being dispossessed of a portion of his property but of giving back to God a minute fraction of His immense generosity. The intention of thus paying homage to the creator of all things truly gives the poor due its character of being a pious deed. It moreover assumes a purifying character,[122] and it guarantees the legality of the property from which it has been taken. The two Arabic terms which are translated as "almsgiving" in English etymologically express the ideas of "purification" and "assertion of the truth."[123] Thus, the gesture of generosity does not lose its spontaneity since it is based on religious conviction. Furthermore, the one who turns to the believer for "God's goods for the love of God" maintains all his human dignity. "Charity" thus conceived and legalized loses the humiliating aspect which it sometimes assumes with regard to the beneficiary. It is not a gift left to the discretion of the wealthy but the "right of the poor"[124] legally due and, in the case of "apparent possession," can be demanded by force if necessary. It fulfills the absolute obligation of justice. Religious intuition is basic and essential because it determines the positive enforcement of the law, putting relations between men in order. Fraternal love, benevolence, mercy, and generosity thus no longer appear as moral virtues but mainly as precepts of faith. Alsmgiving is very characteristic in this respect since it expresses both religious purification and the practice of justice. In addition to this, the law prescribes the spirit and manner in which the believer should give alms. That which is given must represent what is best and exclude what is base.[125] Intention is essential. The prophetic tradition tells us that Muhammad explained the meaning of intention in his first sermon in Medinah: "He who is able to save his face from

---

[121]al-Baqarah: 264 (Blachère).

[122]"Take alms from their goods in order to purify them and make them spotless," at-Taubah: 103.

[123]Respectively, *zakah* and *sadaqah*; see Roberts, *The Social Laws*, pp. 70-71, and Masson, *Le Coran*, p. 587.

[124]al-Ma'arij: 24-25.

[125]"O you who believe! Give [in charity] of the good things which you possess ... Do not turn toward that which is vile with the purpose of dispensing of it," al-Baqarah: 267 (Blachère).

the Fire (of Hell), even if it is by the simple means (of the giving of one poor person to another) of a morsel of date, should do so, and he who possesses nothing (not even that much, should protect himself from Hellfire) by a good word toward a neighbor. For the reward of a good action is increased from ten to seven hundred times."

Following the same line of thought, the Qur'ānic concept of punishment is equally interesting since it gives Islamic justice its true dimension. It should also give a better understanding of the Muslim approach to justice. The institution of vengeance by blood, so harmful in pre-Islamic Arabia, was almost totally abolished by Islam. However, the Qur'ān does not totally exclude justice tainted with the idea of retaliation. God will not punish "those who take revenge on injustice but those who oppress others; after all, the important matter is that of being patient and forgiving."[126] Thus the law of retaliation, rejected by Christianity, is taken up again and integrated into Islamic law in a considerably altered form.[127]

In the framework of general Muslim philosophy which preaches moderation and the "happy medium," clemency and forgiveness complement and embellish justice. Benevolence toward the good man and forbearance toward the misguided whom one attempts to guide back to the correct way are higher expressions of reason and discernment. True piety entails faith and deeds. The object of faith is Allah and the Day of Judgment; deeds are primarily deeds of compassion. Generosity should characterize all actions of the believer, even extending to everyday politeness. This spiritual beauty, this beneficence, too hastily called "charity," covers a wide range of human actions. In this respect, the Prophet is reported to have said: "Every good deed is charity. Your smiling at your brother is charity; an exhortation directed at your neighbor to perform virtuous deeds is the equivalent of giving alms. Putting one who has wandered away back on the right path is charity; helping a blind man is charity; removing stones, thorns, and obstacles from the road is charity..."[128]

Taken separately, the logics of the Islamic system are well structured and solid. Charity and justice are the two poles within which morality necessarily has to oscillate; they are limits beyond which this morality cannot go; they represent a double point of reference, and morality cannot arbitrarily choose one to the exclusion of the other. Put on the level of personal ethics, this

[126]Dermenghen, "Témoignage," p. 373.

[127]"If you chastise then, chastise as you have been chastised. But if you show patience, that is indeed the best ..." an-Nahl: 126 (Masson). "Be patient" is interpreted by the Muslims in the sense of "pardon."

[128] Amir Ali, *The Spirit,* pp. 54-55.

nuance is similar to the movement between individual rights and duties. It would therefore be clearer and correcter to show that in theory, as in practice, the pivot upon which moral choices are balanced is different in Islam from that of the Western concept influenced by Christianity. In Islam, the pivot point is justice, and mercy constitutes a limit which prevents too strict a legal "vengeance." For Christianity, the pivot point is charity, and justice becomes the obstacle which prevents an excessive generosity from leading to unfairness. Thus, the bases of morality in each system are essentially divergent, even though the external practical manifestations seem almost the same. The reason for this difference is, above all, religious.[129]

On the other hand, the conception of Allah is fundamentally different from the image which the Christians have of God. Most certainly compassionate and generous, Allah, by virtue of His unicity, His omnipotence and His role as the supreme judge, represents the absolute. He did not make Himself "relative" by becoming human through His son, sacrificed because of His love for humanity. On the other hand, the very expression of the reciprocal revelations differs. Both are intended to improve man and humanity. The one, however, is in a constant state of evolution; the other, by way of contrast, is the divine law, given and immutable. As we have already seen, the predominant theological virtues are chairty for the former and faith for the latter. The conception of man and of the world derives from the essential message of the two religions. In opposition to Christianity which proposes felicity in the hereafter, Islam suggests and indicates the happiness of the virtuous man – on earth also – within a society structured according to the divine will. On the level of morality, Muslim law addresses both the individual and society, while Christian law is more personal. The Qur'ān shows the way to follow in order to achieve the perfect human community. However, the disbelief of men stains it, thereby upsetting its unity and harmony. Although it is taken from the very source of the revelations, the image of man is basically different. The Muslim has the law which he is moved to respect by his discernment. In the pride of his faith, he is fully responsible and exposes himself to punishment if he breaks the rules, an infringement considered as religious disobedience. For the Christian, man is above all a sinner; he must exercise sacrifice and seek abnegation in the love for others in order to follow the teachings of his faith. This aspect of the lack of basic responsibility, accompanied by the faith which motivates him to do good, implies on an ideal collective level that he may expect similar charity from his neighbor. The Mus-

---

[129]It is logical to think that the religious aspects are not exclusive. However, as our research deals with Islam, we will not consider the question of whether Christianity influenced the moral conduct of individuals and political decisions of states. We have chosen a theoretical view – a stereotyped image which is perhaps obsolete.

lim, on the contrary, limits the expression of his sentiments to justice along with mercy. He does not expect a more favorable reciprocity. The concept of human nature and the attitude of the Muslim thus prove to be different and are determined by his religion, as it is this religion which has cast the foundations of the civilization to which he belongs. An individual's spontaneous decision or his practical behavior may seem to be an indivisible part of his being. On the contrary, the expression of the moral rule runs the risk of drawing an even greater contrast, in reality, a violent opposition. If Leibniz's famous dictum "Justice is the charity of the wise" is perfectly acceptable to the Muslim, the precept "Love your enemy," on the other hand, shocks his understanding. To him it appears contrary to reason and order, a gross injustice.

A "Profile"

We have chosen certain aspects which ought to enable us to illustrate the manner in which man is represented in Islamic doctrine, and also to explain, by extension, the economy of presiding over the organization of the "Muslim City" and over the management of foreign relations.

The conception which man has of God is of fundamental importance in a theocentric society. For any global view or ideology, the perception or definition of the absolute or, as the case may be, of the objective in mind, determines the nature of the human person, situating this person within the organized group, defining the priorities which are preestablished for him, just as they establish the rules which are to govern reciprocal relations. In Islam, God is absolutely transcendent, but neither isolated nor inaccessible. However, contrary to the believers of the other two great monotheistic religions which have fashioned traditional Western philosophy, the Muslim has neither the impression of being the recipient of a particular advantage, inasmuch as he is a divinely chosen individual, nor the feeling of having been given exceptional dignity by virtue of the belief that God became man. It is from this point of view that the difference is most perceptible, not so much in divine transcendence as in the ways which God chose to make Himself known. The Muslim can acquire a certain experience of the eternal and have a limited divine knowledge through studies and practical respect of the Qur'ānic revelation. He does not expect the fulfillment of a divine promise made specifically to him, nor does he deem himself authorized to expect particular respect for his human dignity. Since God is unique and addressed the whole of humanity, all men are essentially equal, in a communal and total submission to the divine will.

After equality, liberty represents the second basic principle for the assertion of the human being and the expansion of his personality. God most certainly and necessarily knows the destiny of each individual since His omniscience encompasses eternity. As for man, not knowing his future fate, he is free to choose obedience and effort in the framework of universal harmony or else disbelief and abdication. He asserts his liberty by chosing to obey. God's unicity and omnipotence therefore guarantee the equality and liberty of men, consequently asserting their great stature. Nobody can feel enslaved to any of the slaves of this God Who has provided everything for humanity. As the privileged creature of God, Who has made him His deputy on earth as well as the token of His universal mercy, man in essence enjoys eminent dignity since he has been promised an eternal destiny. The Qur'ān does not explicitly define human nature, and traditional Islam has not advanced very far in speculative research as to his intrinsic value, the latter having assumed a primarily juridical aspect. In the revelation, the only explicit indications are descriptions of exemplary and morally eminent personalities: "And all that We relate to you of the story of the messengers is in order that thereby We may make firm your heart. And herein has come unto you the Truth and an exhortation and reminder for believers."[130]

Eternal salvation depends on man alone, on his individual involvement, and on his personal effort. This immeasurable responsibility illustrates the immense confidence which God has placed in man and consequently determines his greatness. Reciprocally, the respect for the revelation ensures and guarantees man's rights. The prescriptions of the law indicate both what is permissible and what is exactable since it is forbidden unto others. God's absolute power and His extraordinary transcendence free man from man and constitute the very basis of the total equality of all individuals. This is one of the most specific contributions of the Muslim religion to universal civilization. It is on the basis of this concept that Islam developed its philosophy and its legislation regarding human rights. The system's economy proves to be logical. Stripped of all rights with regard to God and the law, man can on the other hand demand, both from other individuals and from the community, his rights which are guaranteed by the revelation. These are asserted with such vigor that they permit insubordination and revolt against political or social injustice.

Although dynamic in its origin and in the course of its expansion, while establishing and stabilizing itself, the Muslim system apparently became set in a rather static attitude. It even allowed oppression and tyranny in the course of its history. The Muslims see the reason for this in the disrespect for Islamic norms. Thus for them, Islam remains by nature and in its character the religion of the assertion of the human being, of his prosperity, and of liberty in equality. In this light, Islam, contrary to an idea deeply rooted

---

[130]Hud: 120 (Masson).

in the Western conscience, brought an original system which was to lead to the suppression of slavery. Even more than the solutions which it offered, the terms in which it presented the problem in fact were the most original contributions of Islam. The essentially judicial conception of liberty was to help in putting an end to the earlier conviction that slavery was a necessity of natural law. In addition, the teachings of the Qur'ān and of the Prophet Muhammad prove to be in ardent defense of the rights of women. Their status, however, gradually declined in the course of history. The modern Muslim woman faces a long struggle to recover her rights, but she may call upon the Islamic legislative system itself to help her in this task.

God's unicity and His ordering the world into a harmonious and balanced entity define the fundamental and so inherent Islamic virtue of justice. Moreover, the divine omnipotence constantly prevalent in Islamic philosophy reminds us of the vacuity of all things and stands in permanent opposition to self-centeredness. Finally, God's attributes evoke mercy, generosity, and clemency for the believer. The logics of the Islamic system and its simplicity bring out its hierarchy of values and make it easy to understand. Based on reason and emotions, the Qur'ānic revelation has provided for all situations and wishes to order everything. Nevertheless, it appeals to the noblest sentiments of man in order to regulate his conduct. The example of the legal poor due is particularly illustrative in this respect. Although it is an obligatory action, almsgiving does not become legalistic or mechanical since its motivation remains deep down religious. For one who practices it, it is a deed of purification; for the recipient thereof, it is a gift from God.

Since Islam presents itself as a law with an aptitude of directing all aspects of the believer's life, it is by nature a code of formal and compulsory laws. Its manifestation concerns individual and community phenomena as well as those which are social and political. It draws its coercive power from its religious nature. Through the conception which it gives of God and man respectively, Islam immediately proves to be egalitarian. The Muslim can live his religion in a complete way only "under the gaze of God." The refusal to separate spiritual from temporal matters imposes a respect for the moral law on the Muslim, a respect which is neither external nor mechanical but based on the free choice which is supposed to have led him to embrace the Muslim faith. Thus, Islam is affirmed as a perfect religion and a total system – as far more than an ideology – a true transcendent humanism which generated a specific and particular society and gave birth to a mentality as well as a moral conduct difficult to place within the confines of Western philosophy. This humanism which, without excluding an absolute monotheism, surpasses the Western philosophy and definitively gives man his true greatness while simultaneously allowing him to develop his own potentialities. Islam recommends that man grant supremacy to the spiritual, and that he take advantage, decently but fully, of the earthly privileges which God has granted him as a token of His mercy.[131] Asserting the value of the human person, Islam at the same time imposes upon him specific limits and duties which are very demanding, deemed crucial for personal and communal equilibrium. Even on the individual level, the Muslim ethic can be understood only in terms of the Qur'ān which is its essence and forms a pair with its sentiments.

Islamic doctrine refers above all to man's judicial nature alone. Moreover, the fusion of the spiritual and the temporal is such a constantly asserted factor that, from what precedes, one can understand the nature of man by deduction from Islam's juridical and moral laws. The basic duty is obedience and righteousness with regard to God. In respect to man, the range is wide and varies from justice to honesty in transactions; from sincerity, fidelity, loyalty to commitment, to respect for and amiability toward others – in particular toward parents and relatives; from humility and equality to the respect and protection of the weak, especially widows and orphans. The Qur'ān is the keystone of the Muslim ethic. It does not describe man in his metaphysical conception since the spirit (or soul) is a thing which concerns God alone, but it orders him to follow a certain conduct. All moral values are hence identified with piety.

The assertion of man with regard to man and the reminder of his nothingness with regard to God generate the development of a balanced humanism[132] which could lead neither to an abusive cult of the individual, an established end in itself, nor to a blind and unconditional devotion to the existing political structures. It was the great force of Islam which was to succeed in guaranteeing human rights and in protecting the community against two ideologies which divide the world and could have posed a threat to it: frenzied liberalism and tyrannical materialism.

---

[131]"O you who believe, eat of the excellent (foods) which have been given to you by Us," al-Baqarah: 167. See Hussein, *On Conviction*, pp. 173-174.
[132]Madkour, "The Concept," p. 475.

Chapter 4

THE MUSLIM CITY

You are the best community
which has been chosen as an example to mankind; you enjoin the good
and forbid the evil and you believe
in God.

Qur'ān 3:110

Collective Man

Islam appeared as a movement asserting the priority of the social with regard to the collective and, consequently, the free and responsible human being as opposed to the individual, bound to a traditional group. Within a very short time, the society which Islam formed became aware of its separate entity, differentiating itself from the outside world by a common ideal of mutual rights and obligations. This phenomenon is not, of course, specifically Islamic. Still, the notion of group, or "community" – an *ummah* is peculiar to Islam because it professes witness exclusively centered upon the divine, immutable, and eternal word – the Qur'ān.

This group was to assert itself not by exclusivity, but by remaining open as much as possible since integration of new members is provided for on the basis of specific criteria and general conditions such as adhesion to the faith. Islam thus brought a new and very generous concept of "nationality." The link which united members of society became both religious and political, if one must use Western terminology.[1] For the Muslim, faith means submission to God and obedience to His law. Hence, Islam imparts to the community a character which is specific as well as compelling by virtue of three of its fundamental aspects.

On the one hand, the revelation spells out the believer's obligations in all aspects of his life and defines his duties to God and society. The obligation of helping to maintain and expand the community is expressly imposed upon him – even if prevailing circumstances call for the sacrifice of his life to achieve these goals. On the other hand, the rituals of worship serve to give him, by the very precision with which they were determined, a very strong sense of belonging to an organized group. Finally, the Qur'anic concept of the world, presenting the creation as a harmonious and balanced whole under the driving force of God, contributes to the strengthening of the communal edifice, the gathering of the believers becoming an order in which each one

---

[1] *Din* seems to be used, in the text drafted at the time of the Prophet, to designate, indistinctly, the "religion" or the "government." See Muhammad Hamidullah, *The First Written Constitution in the World: An Important Document of the Time of the Holy Prophet*, 2nd rev. ed. (Lahore: Ashraf, 1968), p. 37. After this: Hamidullah, *First Constitution*.

finds his true place.

The identification of the individual and the flowering of his nature is asserted insofar as it is an integral part of the "community" which represents "a cathedral and not the sum of its stones."[2] Islam defines the concept of "collective man" as man as such. Man and communal man represent two separate entities, each with a place corresponding to its own nature within the global vision of creation. Single man, with regard to society, is not a concept which needs to be defined, for Islam does not distinguish between one man and several men but rather between the individual and the community. This differentiation is essential as it allows one to understand Islamic social ethics, which organize collective rather than inter-individual ties, as well as the concept of the Islamic city and its relations with the outside world. However, "if there is, in Islam, a clear separation between man as such and collective man, these two realities are no less profoundly interdependent, given that collectivity is an aspect of man ... and that, conversely, society is a multiplication of individuals. It follows from this independence or this reciprocity that all which is accomplished with a view to collectivity ... has a spiritual value for the individual, and vice versa."[3] The believer thus fulfills his obligations to the other members of the social group to the extent which, considering the individual or collective level, he observes the revealed law. Since organized collectivity is the only social form possible to the Muslim, Islamic virtue proves itself to be essentially collective and not inter-individual.

The teaching of universal values and the strongly proselytic character of Islam in no way relaxes the sacred communal bond. On the contrary, two provisions command the believers to maintain a distinct organic community. The Muslims are, in fact, pledged to assert themselves as a united and indivisible community around their ideal and behind their leader. In addition, they are obliged to prevent the triumph of evil in their midst and to teach and cultivate the good. This moral order causes their community to distinguish itself from others by it moral virtues.[4]

The doctrine of existential unity results from the principle that the divine unicity places each thing on its level and in a perspective of global universal order. The unity of mankind is necessarily a part of global harmony. Considered in this way, the community as a whole also constitutes a unity. In his eternal destiny, man at last, being part of the much larger whole represented by the community, sets the same goals for himself as those deter-

---

[2]Dermenghen, "Témoignage," p. 374.
[3]Schoun, *Comprendre*, pp. 30-31.
[4]Draz, *Initiation*, pp. 81-83.

mined by God. Individually, he has a multiplicity of purposes in his relation to the other parties within a diversified community, by acting or reacting upon them and undergoing repercussions, directly, on the various levels of higher entities of which he is a part. The least original image but the most illustrative is that of concentric circles which are formed by successive ripples on the surface of disturbed water. It is therefore probable – and not because of the possible influences of the pre-Islamic nomadic Arabs with whom the Western authors have dealt abundantly – that this explains one of the fundamental characteristics of the Muslim, who remains individualistic while simultaneously attached to the community. Fully understanding the doctrine of the unity of existence in the universal order raises the apparent contradiction between the affirmation of the individual and his supposed subjection to the whole. In this general perspective, one can also grasp the behavior of the individual, the social and moral rules, the organization of the community and its philosophy of ties with the outside world.

Islam believes that grouping people into a community is indispensible because their nature renders them incapable of living alone. The makeup of society is the inevitable result of this inability. The necessity of grouping together is in reality twofold.[5] On the one hand, man's innate desire for domination and aggression can lead him to irrational acts of self-destruction. Authority and power alone can constrain his envy, arrogance, suspicion, and individual conceits, thus mutually protecting all members of the group. On the other hand, man does not enjoy the right to satisfy his multiple individual needs. Cooperation and mutual aid become obligatory upon man if he wants to survive. Life in society brings out its coercive force *sui generis* because, through its role as a go-between, man procures the nourishment needed for his survival and the weapons needed for self-defense. At the same time, he receives the guarantee of security and the benefits of social mutual aid.

In fashioning man, God made social grouping a necessity. The society therefore satisfies the doctrine of existential unity. Furthermore, according to the Qur'ān, man is by nature weak and subject to temptation. When he succumbs to it, he is rendered aggressive and evil. Society forces him to dominate his inclinations. Since man is free, the makeup of a community presupposes a mutual agreement. However, the foundation of being party to this "social contract," which stipulates duties and guarantees rights for each person, does not express itself by the sole agreement of free wills of an undefined choice but responds to a necessity proceeding from the nature of man. The agreement of wills remains subordinated to a higher norm: the actual will of God. In this perspective, it immediately becomes obvious that the refusal

---

[5]Mohammed A. Lahbabi, *ibn-Khaldun* (Paris: Seghers, 1968), pp. 125-136.

of participation in a group could appear as condemnable, reprehensible dissidence.

It is difficult to find the exact term with which to describe the Islamic "community" because it must take into account the close association of the spiritual and the temporal as well as all the moral and juridical regulations abounding in the Qur'ān. One can approach such a definition with the expression "a life style,"⁶ or an "organized ideological community," if one uses the term ideology in its proper meaning of a global vision of the world and of its inception. Islam asserted itself in this manner at the time of its revelation. Muhammad impressed the worshipping of one god upon the tribes of the Arabian Peninsula and to form a coherent and fraternal entity. Religion was the impetus which led to the formation of such a solid, specific society that the various forces which sought to tear it apart throughout its history never succeeded in doing so. Even in our day, nationalistic tendencies notwithstanding, the believers' sense of belonging to a community which has differentiated itself from others remains strong. Islam is so influential in all aspects of a Muslim's life that his behavior, his way of doing things, and even his intellectual bearing can only be understood in terms of religion. Therefore, Islam not only imposes a quality of being, a virtuous attitude, but equally implies a respect for rules of morality and action.

The imprint of the spiritual upon the temporal or the influence of religious law over all daily activities is all the more noticeable since Islam calls for communal solidarity in order to enforce the divine regulations. In fact, the Qur'ān orders⁷ that the Muslim community form a society whose members, individually or collectively, command the good and forbid the evil.⁸ The application of religious values implies a transformation of man, of society, and of the world. Being a religion and culture, Islam asserts itself as an active and dynamic expression of a collective will. The solidarity between the members of the Muslim community is very strongly affirmed and specifically legalized by Qur'ānic law. It is understood as an inescapable feeling of mutual dependence and collective mutual aid. Its motivation is at once reasoned and altruistic, then charitable or sentimental. It asserts itself as a quasi-juridical obligation engaging the responsibility of each person. This interdependence therefore takes on the form of common moral responsibility with regard to the observance of Islamic laws and of social cooperation for the development of the community.

---

⁶Othman, *Concept,* p. 195.
⁷"Let there arise out of you a band of people inviting to all that is good, enjoining what is right, and forbidding what is wrong." āl-'Imran: 104 (Blachère). "Right" is an unsatisfactory translation of "*ma'rouf,*" signifying "that which is known" by the revelation, for the good of mankind.

The accompanying regulations are not formulated in the name of moral principles or of natural right; they are imposed as a positive social legislation in the name of that which is due as an imperative duty of the believers. The analysis worked out here has an exclusively social perspective. On the religious level, spontaneous feeling is certainly not opposed to deliberate action because spiritual conviction facilitates rational obedience. Intention and action complement each other in order to form an indissoluble whole in the framework of divine relation. This view reinforces the image of the "collective man." This legalized and imperative duty of solidarity is much more obligatory in Islam than in any other organic community. Since the believer is responsible, directly and individually for his worldly actions only to God, the question arises as to what is his responsibility to his society, its members, and its institutions.

To begin with, there seems to be a contradiction between the affirmation of the human individual, of his fundamental equality and his exclusive responsibility on the one hand, and the religious and practical necessity of grouping together in a community on the other. The particular nature of obligatory Muslim solidarity holds each Muslim personally responsible for not violating the law. Islam itself enjoins personal intervention in order to impede transgression and to bring about the good. It has thus created an immense obligatory fraternity and, accepting responsibility for the organization of secular matters, has given birth to a society marked by the spirit of the revelation as much in its institutional aspect as in its cultural aspects. Natural factors of "Muslim mentality," such as the sense of belonging to a community, the importance attached to social virtues, a certain inclination to live as a group, harmony or conformity, did not delay the appearance of characteristics unique to Muslim culture, since it was imbued with a religious influence integrated in a collective rhythm of life.[9]

It is interesting to note to what degree a certain idea of the world and belief in a universal destiny for man colors the daily behavior of millions of beings. No other modern ideology can claim to compete with Islam in this respect. Yet, its organized political body, which historically controlled the application of the law, no longer exists. For the non-Muslim observer, this institution, centered exclusively on a book, a tradition, and its juridical interpretation from which it draws its solidity is very astonishing! It is a religion without

---

[8]About this tradition it is reported that the Prophet Muhammad said one day: "Help your Muslim brother, whether he be oppressed or is an oppressor." Some people asked him: "I will help my oppressed brother, but how can I help the oppressor?" The Prophet replied: "By preventing him from doing evil."

[9]Gardet, *Cité*, p. 23; and Grouilly, *Islam*, p. 26.

priests creating a social and political community whose leader derives his power from the faith, even though, he is not a religious authority. This political master who has no legislative power and only limited executive power has as his only task the assurance of the just application of the law, and of maintaining the community's cohesion and encouraging its expansion. The idealized Muslim state, finally, is guided and directed by a sense of the sacred which "goes so far as to transform it into an organism placed at the service of religion."[10] It would perhaps be useful to briefly describe, in this perspective, the institutional wheels of the theoretical Muslim city in order to best determine the dimensions and limits of the rights accorded to believers and non-Muslims.

A Theocentric Brotherhood

There is a strong tendency to categorize the institutional system of Islam according to the West's political science label. This practice gives a "scientific" character to the undertaking and allows one to avoid emphasizing, without negating, the absolute binding of the spiritual and the temporal, of ethics and the juridical sphere. This proclivity to systemization has not spared Muslim authors either, for some of them have tried, in order to achieve a specific objective, to assimilate Islam with some of the grand categories established by international political theory: theocracy, monarchy, republic, democracy, socialism, and so on. The vocation of religion is immense, unlimited. Law moreover happens to be objective, "positive," and not only a spiritual ideal. As practical experience has varied greatly during the fourteen centuries of Muslim history, one can advance very diverse yet specific arguments, see contradictions, and arrive at some outwardly logical conclusions which are nevertheless fundamentally opposed to the letter or the spirit of the revelation. The confusion is maintained by an interpretation whose tools are the techniques, terminology, and ideas of the West.[11]

The Islamic system refuses to separate the diverse elements of individual and collective life: multiplicity of objectives is unknown to it.[12] The sole and ultimate end of man, as well as that of society, is to serve God,[13] to obey His will, and to live by His law. The Islamic conception of a theoretical state is difficult to describe since there is no demarcation between properly political and other kinds of institutions. To go beyond the simple enumeration of

---

[10]Ghelhold Introduction, p. 159.
[11]Ahmed, Iqbal, pp. 41-42.
[12]Sherwani, Studies, p. 253.
[13]"My prayer, my offering and my devotion [the consecration of my person], my life and my death are [all] for God ..." al-An'am: 162. Translation proposed by Mme. A. de Zayas Abbasi.

generalities which cannot reproduce the true image of the ideal Muslim city commonly reflected by the actual political understanding of the believers, it is convenient to refer, in the first place, to the policy of the Prophet and in the second place, to show, from the foundation of the Qur'ānic revelation, the specificity of Islamic organization by demonstating why it does not correspond to any of the grand categories characteristic of Western political thought.

The treaty signed by Muhammad, upon his arrival in Medinah, among twelve Arab tribes and ten Jewish tribes, is a document of the highest interest in that it is considered as the "first written constitution of the world."[14] This clearly juridical agreement is made up of two distinct parts, probably drafted at different times.[15] The first part confirmed the Muslim community and created a distinct political entity composed of the twelve Arab tribes of Medinah and the refugees of Makkah. The second part consisted of a "military alliance" with the ten Jewish tribes of the area. The main provisions of the "constitution," which united a heterogeneous population and created the embryonic Muslim state, were the following: the tribal communities remained but became interdependent in order to create a single political organism. Accepting Islam conferred "nationality" to all members of the community, who were thereafter equal among themselves and devoted to mutual assistance. This solidarity was fraternal on the inside, but it established itself as an affirmation – in truth a claim – on the outside.[16] Muhammad represented the central government, the essential privileges of which were to declare war or to secure peace, and to have the final say on any juridical matter. Obligatory military service was instituted and, at the same time, "private" intertribal wars were forbidden. The members of the community no longer had the right to carry out justice by their own hands but now had to refer the matter to the federation's authority or to the Prophet's central government as the final resort. The latter has the privilege of "ordering the good and forbidding the evil," of making sure that one person cannot oppress another, and of assuring social justice by the redistribution of communal wealth. Muhammad was not, however, an autocrat since God is the sole source of authority for both the leader and for the members of the community.

The Jews and the unbelievers of Medinah were accepted on the condition that they end all ties with the enemies of Islam. The Jews could keep their religion and enjoy individual rights equal to those of the Muslims. They ac-

---

[14]Hamidullah, *First Constitution*, which has inspired us a great deal in the pages which follow.
[15]Sherwani, *Studies*, p. 254 confirms the hypothesis of Hamidullah, *First Constitution*, pp. 30 f.
[16]Gouilly, *Islam*, p. 26, has revealed it, in the twentieth century; this seems indicate that this is a case of a permanent characteristic.

cepted the authority of Muhammad and recognized his exclusive military command as well as his role as a judge, using Biblical law, in settling those of their disputes which they could not settle themselves. They had to cooperate in meeting war expenses but could only participate in combat with the express permission of the Prophet. In modern terms, they were autonomous on the level of internal affairs but had no international powers. The Medinan legislation, established on a contractual basis and being of a transcendental origin, marked a perceivable difference with the former traditions since all new citizens were allowed into the bosom of the state on the basis of faith, which introduced some elements of morality into the law. The objective of the state remained the material and spiritual well-being of the community in a spirit of service and fraternity. The divine law indicated the "good" and stigmatized the "bad." Obedience to worldly authority, in the framework of the Qur'ānic law, was an imperative for the conduct of public affairs, nothing more.

The system established by Muhammad and maintained for the most part by his four immediate successors appears as an ideal, simple, realistic, and applicable system. According to the Muslims, it was mankind's and the world's imperfections which caused such a system to breakdown. It was respected, in fact, for only thirty years. A schism rapidly appeared between constitutional theory and governmental practice. A distinction arose between Arabs and neo-converts, resulting in a kind of social stratification fundamentally opposed to Muslim egalitarianism. The idea of fraternity was no longer imposed with so much vigor in the individual sphere. The first symptoms of disintegration of communal solidarity took form when the Umayyad "monarchy" was born. Its founder, Mu'awiyyah, was inspired by the Byzantine Empire's luxury and pomp, which the companions of the Prophet had always rejected. He became an absolute autocrat, while Muhammad had only wanted to be a man among his brothers. Power tempted him to attach more importance to worldly affairs than spiritual preoccupations. The ideal and exemplary Muslim city had vanished.[17] The dynastic system installed in the seventh century lasted with various ups and downs until 1924, and all of it now belongs to history. It is, however, undeniable that the principles upheld by the Prophet still inspire the philosophical thought of present-day Muslims. Politics, in Islam, cannot be considered as being outside religion. It is convenient, from this time on, to hem in the outline of the ideal "Muslim city" and, first of all, to define its localization and sovereignty.

---

[17]Sherwani, *Studies*, p. 258; Bereketullah, *Le Khalifat*, pp. 55 and 57; Husseini, *Constitution*, pp. 3 and 7; see the introduction by S. Khuda Bakhsh in Joseph Hell, *The Arab Civilization*, 2nd ed. (Lahore: Ashraf, 1969), 200 pages, Idem, *Politics in Islam* (Lahore: Ashraf, 1967), p. vii.

According to Western terminology, sovereignty implies a singular power which has no superior and which gathers together the diverse tendencies or forces in society. According to the Islamic doctrine, this superior source is God.[18] The expression of His will resides in the Qur'ān. The Prophet, his successors, and the political leaders have power only through delegation. Each believer is a viceroy of God on earth for the law is imposed upon all. "Those [who] are vested with authority,"[19] both spiritual and temporal, do not have absolute power but are at the service of the community in order to carry out the terms of the law. They cannot claim any kind of infallibility in the interpretation of the divine directives, for that resides in the unanimous agreement of the community,[20] and therefore could not claim an unlimited temporal power. In reality, as neither the Qur'ān nor Muhammad has established a particular form of government, the Muslims are used to choosing which structure they want, on the condition that it allows the application of the divine orders. In the proper sense of the term, this state, whatever it may be, cannot represent a "theocracy" – even if it is intrinsically founded upon a revealed law having a sacred character, defining the good and injustice. This is for two reasons. On the first hand, the divine will is imperative not only for the Muslim state to construct its "national" legislation form, but is also for the entire human race. On the other hand, the political leader neither decrees nor legislates but only oversees the correct application of the immutable law.

The Islamic community has never constituted, either in theory or in practice, a theocracy as is often very improperly claimed in the West.[21] The term is paradoxical as the caliph is not a religious chief, and moreover a priestly caste has never governed Muslim society since the church is an institution foreign to Islam. No person or organ is entitled to modify, amend, or complete the revealed divine law.

Can one, on the other hand, actually talk about "democracy," in its generally understood sense?[22] One can trace, the heritage of the Bedouin and Arab democratic conditions in the first Muslim institutions. The "democratic"

---

[18]"The dominion of the heavens and the earth belongs to God" āl-'Imran: 189 (Masson). See also al-Jathiyyah: 27 and al-Hadid: 5 "To Him belongs the dominion of the heavens and the earth; and all affairs are referred back to God" (Masson).
[19]an-Nisa': 59.
[20]*Ijma'*. This idea has led certain Muslim authors to conclude that sovereignty belongs to the people.
[21]Some even perceive it as "derision" on the part of Westerners. Sherwani, *Studies*, pp. 270-271. The reaction seems, however, excessive since the Muslim authors also employ this locution. See Pickthall, *Cultural Side*, p. 177.
[22]Democracy here is defined as a political state in which the sovereignty belongs to the totality of the citizens, without distinction of birth, fortune, or ability." Lalande, *Vocabulaire*, p. 214.

character was historically reinforced by the fact that, during its expansion, Islam liberated individuals from religious tyranny and governmental intolerance. Some people have seen the Islamic city as a sort of republican system whose fundamental law, the "constitution," would be immutable. The Qur'ān recommends consultation between the leader and the members of the community. Some nuances deserve to be emphasized.

To begin with, the leader of the Muslim community draws his power from this community which, by choosing him, gives him a sort of contract of allegience. However, the designation of leader is not made by means of the assembly of all believers deciding by majority vote. Instead, a college of electorates which is recognized for its wisdom and piety decides and the mass of citizens can only disapprove of or ratify the choice.[23] The authority of the leader, elected for an unlimited period of time, is then absolute as long as he does not try to surpass the divine law. If such a case were to arise, he would be deposed. Theoretically, he could not become a dictator since he has been deprived of any legislative power. The rule is laid down in a definitive fashion in order to assure the freedom of both the government and the governed.

It would be useful here to mention a fundamental difference, as much in their mutual source as in their final objectives, between Islamic law and modern European legislation. In Western democracy, according to the current understanding, the source of the law is the sovereign will of the people; its objective is internal order and justice. In Islam, the law is decreed by God; the prime objective of the believer is, therefore, to attain divine proximity through respect for and observation of the revelation. The law thus establishes itself as a code of duties and obligations.[24] The Muslims should join their efforts to attain, within the framework of the community, the goals which the Qur'ān has imposed upon them. Each one, while adhering to Islam, agrees to an imaginary contract. Thus, there are no laws binding on God, and law and social morality base the right on the duty which is imposed upon all believers, without distinction. Its respect reciprocally guarantees the rights of all members of the community. Each adherent to Islam consents to an imaginary contract. Thus, he has no right with regard to God. The law and social morality therefore base the rights upon duty which is incumbent upon all believers without exception. One again encounters justice as the cornerstone of the entire Muslim moral and legal system. Islam is a rule of life. Respect for its laws and institutions should lead a homogenous society, by transforming the life of each individual, to form from the whole a single organism, a "col-

[23]Pickthall, *Cultural Side*, pp. 177-179.
[24]Fyzee, *Modern Approach*, pp. 28 f.

Humanism in Islam

lective me."[25]

Historic experience has shown that the Islamic world, like other systems of government, knew tyranny, oppression, and injustice. The spirit and the letter of the Qur'ān, as well as the example of Muhammad, offered absolute guarantees for the protection of each individual's rights. Insubordination, both on the practical and the social level, is formally possible. The Qur'ān proclaims that "God does not love the oppressors." It recommends the avenging of injustice and the showing of an inflexible resistance toward unjust force which God will punish. The believer therefore has the right to oppose it and to remove his government, should the occasion arise. Abu Bakr, succeeding Muhammad, clearly proclaimed: "Obey me, ... according to the traditions, just as I obey Allah and His Prophet. If I disobey, you owe me no obedience."

As sovereignty belongs only to God, the right to disobey is readily understood to have certain limits. The Prophet says: "He who disobeys his Lord deserves no obedience at all." Thus, insubordination became more than a right for the Muslims; it became a duty for the believers who were obliged to order the good and forbid the evil. Traditions also report that Muhammad declared: "If the people realize that their leader is an oppressor, and they let him be so, God will punish them." The revolt against injustice and oppression thus assumes an obligatory character. This duty, of course, is understood in the framework established by the revealed law which includes everything: "O you who believe! Give your response to God and His Apostle when He calls you to that which will give you life."[26] By the very nature of the Muslim city, abandoning the faith is a detestable decision: apostasy is unacceptable. The individual who does so actually places himself "outside the law," and the group which proclaims it places itself in a situation of secession. According to the Qur'ān, apostasy (*irtidad*) will be punished by God in the Hereafter: "Those who repudiate God after having believed ... he who, deliberately, opens his heart to unbelief, the wrath of God is upon him and a terrible punishment will befall him."[27] It should be noted that such an action is not punishable by death, for this would contradict the spirit of Islam which forbids force in the matter of religion. According to the prophetic traditions, only those apostates who ally themselves with the unbelievers to fight against Islam should be pursued and put to death as enemies because they are traitors who endanger the security of the Muslim community. In this particular case,

---

[25]Ahmed, *Iqbal*, pp. 48-49. We find here the concept that we have explained above by the term "collective man."
[26]al-Anfal: 24 (Masson).
[27]an-Nahl: 106 (Masson).

an individual or collective revolt should be checked by the person in authority, by force if necessary.[28]

The affirmation of divine unicity and transcendence, repeated at least five times a day, liberates man. The profession of Islam creates an almost emotional conviction which urges sincerity and loyalty toward God, the religion, the believers, and the government. Solidarity in this manner surpasses the strict rational or material interdependence in order to give birth to a fraternal community under the guidance of God, a "theocentric brotherhood." The Muslim conception of social justice is illustrative in this regard. It overflows the framework of simple economic justice and is to be realized only by collective integrity, interdependent equality, supervised freedom, and the "right of self-respect and self-love."[29] There are numerous appeals for fraternal cooperation and for mutual respect in the Qur'ān. By binding the spiritual and the temporal, the law orients the individual toward the righteous road of equilibrium between private interests and communal necessities.[30] As for political sovereignty, the wealth and the ownership of all goods return to God. Man only enjoys their usufruct. Private ownership is thus recognized in a direct fashion, but it represents only a social function of which the sane utilization aims at the well-being of the community as a whole.

Islam cannot be assimilated by either of the two ideologies which have divided the world, for it has distinguished itself from them in certain domains. If, for example, private property and individual initiative are recognized as opposed to collectivist communism, they are strictly limited, which is contrary to Western liberalism. Acquisition is only possible by work, gift, or inheritance. It is invalid if it is the result of aggression, dishonesty, usury, or gambling. More than that, its keeping is conditional. It should not be opposed to the communal good or the equality of opportunity for all citizens, and it should not favor the exploitation of the weak. It may be abolished, should it lead to the monopolization of essential public resources or give voice to the greed which destroys the society's equilibrium while creating an artificial social stratification. The institution of legal alms which, according to tradi-

---

[28]Muhammad Ali, *The Religion of Islam*: A Comprehensive Discussion of the Sources, Principles and Practices of Islam (Cairo: National Publication, n.d.), pp. 591 f. After this: Muhammad Ali, *Religion*. El-Hofy, *Tolerance*, p. 118, claims the contrary, while basing himself nevertheless only on jurisprudence.

[29]Mahmoud Abd-al-Meguid, *Le socialisme arabe à la lumière de l'Islam et le fait arabe* [Arab Socialism As Put in Light with Islam and the Arab Cause] (Cairo: Supreme Council of Islamic Affairs, 1966), p. 23. After this: Abd-al-Meguid, *Le Socialisme arabe*.

[30]Hussain, *Islam*, p. 161; and Ibrahim M. Ismail, *L'Islam et les doctrines économiques contemporaines* [Islam and Contemporary Economic] (Caire: Supreme Council of Islamic Affairs, 1965), pp. 78-79. After this: Ismail, *L'Islam*.

tion, consists of "taking from the wealth of the rich to return to the poor,"[31] and to a lesser degree, the endowment *(waqf)* assumes an internal redistribution of the Muslim community's wealth. Egoism should be compensated for by solidarity; greed by legal tax; personal interest by faith in God Who, according to the words of Muhammad, "... will throw out of His thoughts the population of a city in which one of its inhabitants is found hungry."[32] Respect for the Islamic revelation should lead to a balanced society, without stratification or class struggle – an ideal social order founded not on human reason but on divine will – one which will assure without antagonism the affirmation of liberty and equality, the two principal rights of man, in social justice.

The *Khilāfah*

The fraternal solidarity of the Muslim community is a humanitarian concern, strengthened by a feeling of necessary interdependence shared by the believers united in a common observance of the divine law. The sense of fraternity previously expressed, among others by Christianity, is in Islam the aim of a principle and a juridical act.[33] The double dependence in regard to God, to man as such, and to the Muslim city cemented the solidarity of its members in all aspects of daily life, spiritual as well as material. Thus, from his establishment in Medinah, Muhammad seems to have fulfilled the functions of a prophet and, at the same time, assumed the responsibilities of a chief-of-state. It is fair to emphasize that, as much by his words as by his deeds, he consistently showed that he was, first and foremost, a divine messenger.

At his death, no particular method or arrangement had been outlined for the community to follow while electing their new leader. This issue caused very lively discussions, religious schisms, and the most bloody political secessions in Muslim history. The lack of precise directions for the organization of the *ummah* is both surprising and logical: surprising in the perspective of Islam's social philosophy, according to which the association of men under a coercive authority is a reasonable fact; considering the social philosophy of Islam, for which the grouping of men under a collective authority is a clear proof; logical in the Muslim political spirit which grants the temporal power the sole authority to oversee the just and full application of the law.

---

[31]Raihan M. Sharif, *Islamic Social Framework*, 2nd rev. ed. (Lahore: Ashraf, 1970), pp. 150 f. After this: Sharif, *Social Framework*.

[32]Or again: "He does not belong in the midst of us, he who sleeps on a full stomach while his neighbor is starving."

[33]Pickthall, *Cultural Side*, p. 155.

Because of the disputes and struggles which were aimed first at persons, then at clans, and finally at dynasties, it took about three centuries after the death of the Prophet before an attempt was made to produce an institutional definition of Muslim power. At this time, Islam had reached the end of its first great wave of territorial expansion, and the need for stabilizing its domains was strongly felt. If, since the beginning, no proposition was ever unanimously accepted by the community, the opponents had equally never dealt with the necessary character of the institution, but rather with the person of the caliph or, in a more subtle way, with the methods of his election.

Born as a logical emanation of the "system of Islam," caliphate is not considered by Muslims as one of the pillars of Islam. Its institutional aims, in the first place, are the general well-being and respect for the law, then the cohesion and expansion of the community. If it had been one of Islam's essential pillars, the Qur'ān doubtlessly would have legislated its organization in great detail, and Muhammad would not have failed to point out the directives concerning the succession. Before his death, he designated Abu Bakr to lead the collective prayer. It is interesting to point out the mental bearing of the companions of the Prophet who chose this same person for caliph, by making an analogy between the *imam* leading the communal prayer and the leader conducting the political affairs of the society. The nature of his task was thus immediately determined: the state and the religious community formed a single whole.

Observance of the law and the rituals of worship impose on the believer at the individual level and on the community at the general level certain objective conditions leading, theoretically, to the need for an organized Muslim state of which all Muslims would be natural citizens. The importance of the community's leader did not so much reside in his abilities or the powers which were attributed him as in his role of representing the law and succeeding the prophet, with the exception, of course, of the entire apostolic mission. This is the image which the believer respected in him.

Systematic accounts of the organizational structure and its working are very rare. The best known is that of the tenth to eleventh century jurist al-Mawardi. According to him, the principal task of the caliph is to maintain the internal cohesion of the community, to guarantee its defence, and to assure its external expansion. The caliph possesses, in order to do this, a certain number of political powers which are enumerated at great length. On the international level, he must protect the Muslim faith, defend the state, and struggle against all forms of tyranny. He enjoys the right to declare a "holy war" and to gather troops for the security of the border regions. Internally, the caliph must make justice reign and impose the truth. State institutions are essentially intended to separate the good from the evil, to forbid the blameworthy, and to impose what the revelation defines as obligatory. In short, he has to keep the community on the "right way." He oversees the correct funtioning of the government and levies the taxes. Besides, he is supposed to arbitrate juridical disputes by punishing those who transgress the law and by preventing all oppression. He can sanction, by formal decrees, answers given by the doctors at law to doctrinal and legal questions. Still, he cannot claim any doctrinal authority or real juridical competence since legislative power resides in the revealed law. Possessing limited executive power, he exercises a centralizing function to the extent that he appears as the representative of the law and the guarantor of communal unity. In practice, these privileges were not reserved exclusively for him, and over the course of history they progressively diminished.

Theoretically, the caliph could be nominated either by communal consensus, as with Abu Bakr, or by his predecessor's designation, as with 'Umar. In the case of elections, the decision is limited to a college of believers "knowing how to distinguish the good from the bad" – in other words, experts in "religious" affairs. Once appointed, the caliph is obligated to loyally carry out, the task with which he has been entrusted. His responsibilities as leader and his duties as sovereign are supposed to far surpass his privileges.[34] He is confirmed in his post by a type of understood plebiscite or declaration of allegiance (*bai'ah*) from the people or their qualified representatives.

Even with opinions differing on the possible necessity of a particular familial or ethnic extraction for the caliph, most authors agree upon the definition of his task and the limit of his powers. Historically, it is necessary to recall that the definition of the function and the determination of its privileges took place in the third century of the *hijrah*, at a time when the caliphate had already asserted itself, several decades before, as a *de facto* monarchy. At the same time the bases, from that moment on unchangeable, of Islamic legislation were worked out. The main collections of the apostolic tradition also became one of the regulators of daily life. The judgments and juridical schools of Orthodox Islam formed a new base of obligation reference, after the Qur'ān and the traditions. This simultaneous, double guidance provided, consequently, a certain formalism which transformed the sociopolitical philosophy of the community. The caliphate became an institution subordinate to a rigid legalism of the faith and an organ placed at the service of the religion when the holders of political power found it in their interests to do so. The social system took the shape of an absolute monarchy and sometimes established itself as "theocratic," contrary to the transcendent spirit of Islam. Those who had the authority and competence to call upon the divine teaching

---

[34]Farah, *Islam*, p. 30; and Amir Ali, *The Spirit*, p. 287.

thus, indirectly, governed. This historical evolution makes it even more difficult to understand a system to which traditional Western ideas are not very applicable.

Soon the authority of the doctors at law, jurist or casuist, came to assert itself on the political level. For example, the sermon preceding the collective prayer on Friday (*khutbah*) quickly assumed the aspect of a manifestation of political loyalty. If divine blessings were invoked on the sovereign, it meant that his authority was recognized; if this was not done, it would be the equivalent of declaring his downfall. As the successor to Prophet Muhammad, and much later, "Prince of the Believers," the caliph led a community in which social and religious affairs were tightly united. Refusal to obey him became disobedience to God. Nevertheless, he enjoyed no spiritual authority and quickly lost doctrinal powers to the doctors at law, who pronounced judgment on the basis of a formalized and codified body of law. On the political level, his privileges of execution were progressively diminished, being seized by those local governors or quasiautonomous sovereigns who used the immensity of the empire to their advantage. Finally, under the influence of the conquered and newly Islamized populations, the caliph ceased to be a leader of the Arab type – a first among equals – and eventually became a true absolute monarch, living in the middle of a splendid court with extraordinary pomp. He continued to be a powerful symbol working for the unity and cohesion of Islam. Meanwhile, a groundswell was in motion which undermined and went on to destroy his religious prestige and, above all, his political authority. These vicissitudes are the domain of history.

The "classical" doctrine of the caliphate worked out by the authors depicted the Muslim state not as they saw it, but as an abstract ideal, outside of time, which at that instance already belonged to history. Rejecting all exterior influences, they referred to the Qur'ān above all and, to a lesser degree, to the history of Arabia at the time of the Prophet and of his immediate successors.[35] This particular approach, more theoretical than realistic, is an asset to a better comprehension of Islamic "political philosophy" and of the constitutional foundations of the Muslim state.

We must also be aware of mistakenly likening the caliphate to the papacy. This error has often been denounced but persists in Western schools of international history. The orientalists have perhaps contributed to the acceptance of this idea by unreservedly, and without sufficient explanation of nuances, stating that the Islamic institutional system is "theocratic." If the caliph "represents" the revealed law and symbolizes communal centralization, he cer-

---

[35]Sherwani, *Studies*, pp. 110 f., which deal with al-Mawardi.

tainly cannot be likened to the pontiff of a religion which has an ecclesiastical structure or a sacerdotal hierarchy. This double authority which the Ottoman sultan supposedly possessed was invented much latter by the European powers, despite logic and Islamic doctrine, as the appropriate way to help them achieve their imperial objectives.

Although mistaken, this idea found practical acceptance.[36] Catherine II requested the right to protect the Orthodox Christian minorities living in Muslim lands, and the Turks granted it to her on the condition that they would have the same right for the Muslim minorities in the Russian empire. The idea of endowing the Ottoman caliph with a type of spiritual jurisdiction over global Islam proved to be a clever political move by Russia, who afterward anticipated being able to detach certain European provinces from the sultanate. The Turks, for their own political ends, also tried to exploit the fiction of the sultan being the "Protector of the Muslim Religion," particularly at the end of the nineteenth century when their strength was weakened by the double blows of Europe's resistance and internal disputes. They apparently intended to compensate for the decline of their political power on the spiritual level. This claim of protecting Muslim minorities under Christian rule seems, in fact, to be a reaction to similar European claims over Christians living in Muslim lands. The foundation of this premise was, however, based on a mistaken understanding of the Islamic system, which defines the status of "protected" non-Muslims and will be dealt with later on. Finally, the alleged holiness of the caliphate and the idea of its right of jurisdiction over global Islam were used as a weapon in the conflict of the Western imperialists themselves. Guillaume II made it the foundation of the pan-Islamic politics of imperial Germany.[37] The likening of the Ottoman caliph to a sovereign religious pontiff was thus a political fiction imposed by Europe and sometimes used by the Turkish sultan himself when it was in his interest to do so. The First World War put an end to this.

The fortunes of the caliphate were intimately bound with the history of Turkey, rich in internal and external intrigues. During the last part of the nineteenth century, the Ottoman Empire saw liberal generals opposed to despotic sultans. With the stroke of a pen, the Kemalist revolutionaries abolished the institution by forcing, under the threat of violence, the vote of the national Grand Assembly which consecrated its abolition. The Muslim community was from that time on deprived of its centralizing organ, at the

---

[36]The first success was the signing, in 1774, of the Treaty of Koutchouk Kainardji between the Tsarist Empire and the Ottoman Empire.

[37]This latter has, since 1908, even posed as the "protector" of the Chinese Muslims. See Francis Borrey, "Les musulmans chinois," *Messages d'Orient* (Alexandria: n.p., 1926), pp. 57-68, 65.

very time when particularist and nationalist tendencies were developing with a new vigor within the bosom of Islam. The Arabs joined their forces with the European armies in order to *liberate themselves* from the Ottoman yoke. The weakness of the Muslim reaction to the disappearance of the caliphate should, however, not be attributed to false deductions. Of course, the prestige which the institution enjoyed while fighting externally against the West and internally against liberal demands had greatly decreased. The [idea of the] nation gained priority over that of the fraternity, probably for good, from the political point of view. The various attempts to reestablish the caliphate had no results. The secularization imposed in Turkey did not start a genuine trend. The present situation is ambiguous and unstable. Nevertheless, Islam remains a political reality. The spiritual still tends to influence the social thought and temporal organization of the Muslim world, and perhaps in a progressively increasing fashion. Its impact grows apace with those nations formed from the wreckage of the Ottoman Empire and leaving the fold of European colonialism and taking better charge of their destiny. The feeling of brotherhood remains strong in the believers' conscience and transcends political borders. Nostalgia for the ideal Muslim city lives on.

The opinions of modern Muslim authors diverge. Some – very clearly a minority – believe that Islam offers only a religious truth, an ideal of spiritual life and an example of moral discipline, and they contend it does not lay down any code for the conduct of political affairs. The very absence of rules outlining the correct method of electing a successor could prove that the Islamic revelation was not at all destined to form a state, and, indeed, both the Qur'ān and the traditions do not mention it. The most radical theory in this sense[38] tries to show that the revealed law should be completely detached from the institutional organization of the community. The caliphate would essentially be a secular creation thriving on the confusion ushered in by the doctors at law and maintained by the suppression of freedom of thought, which had formerly been the strength of Muslim civilization.

This debate, which sets the most brilliant minds of the Muslim world against each other, remains largely theoretical since it no longer represents a current problem for the Islamic community. History shows that Muhammad from the time of his installment in Medinah, simultaneously fulfilled the functions of a prophet and chief-of-state, consequently leading and "legislating." By a classic sociological process, the believers as a whole asserted themselves as a homogenized entity opposed to the pre-Islamic society whose laws and

---

[38]Ali Abdel Razek, "L'Islam et les principes du gouvernement," trans. Yegen Foulad, in *Messages d'Orient* (city: publisher, date), pp. 119-144, condemned by al-Azhar.

taboos it rejected. Furthermore, the abolition followed by the nonexistence of the caliphal institution at the present time does not justify ignoring the evidence that Islam represents more than a rule of faith and a moral discipline. Islam has the resolute ambition of establishing rules of conduct for the daily activity of its adherents. Of course, no Qur'ānic injunction defines any political organization. It did, however, emerge as a natural outgrowth of the spiritual and temporal provisions of the Muslim doctrine, which are obligatory for each believer. Finally, the global harmony of the faith, in its conception of the world and the existential unity of all the constituent bodies, represents a strongly centrifugal force inside the community, in spite of the opposition of clans, theories, or individuals. Nevertheless, it still remains true that the elimination of the [later-day] caliphate, because of the fixed formalism and its reactionary nature, put an end to the medieval conception of a Cesaro-Papist state which was *Islamic* only in name. Consequently, this allowed the Muslim community to participate, although in a disorded fashion, in the international community as it is presently organized.

The brutal suppression of an institution which had lasted for more than thirteen hundred years did not cause any perceptible repercussions on the Muslim world. This phenomenon corresponds perfectly to an essential characteristic of Islam, which is a religion without a church or a world ideology possessing no centralizing body which could be powerful and oppressive. The dismemberment of the Muslim city's constitutional organs did not at all cause the believers to lose their feeling of belonging to a specific community based on the word of God and the tradition of His prophet. In fact, despite the ideological differences and political tendencies of various contemporary Muslim states, the believer retains a strong sense of belonging to a very widespread community directed by the sacred. It is in this perspective that Islam will always be called upon to furnish answers to problems posed by the organization of Muslim states and, also to exercise an increasing influence on future international relations.

UNIVERSALISM

One could question or, on the contrary, insist on the universalist character of Islam. An intellectual aproach to this notion is hampered by the ambiguity of the concepts used and, moreover, is largely determined by the observer's point of view. The meaning which one attributes to words, as if they must have an exclusive meaning, is often the one which is given the highest subjective importance or which serves to better demonstrate a particular proposition. One must, therefore, attempt to unravel the tangle of concepts involved!

Being simultaneously a religion and a social system, as far as universalism is concerned, Islam can display four different aspects from four possible points of view: metaphysical, religious, sociological, and political. The four views certainly could not produce fundamentally divergent concepts for they are derived from a single source. However, the expression of a concept will logically vary as a reaction to a specific situation. The belief in absolute monotheism and in the divine oneness, expressed with a conviction and a vigor going beyond that of all other religions, makes Islam, on the metaphysical level, a universal ideology in the most complete sense of the word. On the one hand, the individual is not an end in himself in addition to enjoying a transcendent destiny, but an element of the whole. On the other hand, the universe is governed by divine decrees, and the "Muslim" is the one who submits himself to this transcendental will. Humanity is one. Mankind not only has evolved from the same man, but from a sole creative will – that of the one God.[39] Monotheism thus implies by its very nature the existence of a single and global order. Eternal law is universal. Besides this fundamental aspect, the idea of man contributes to the universalist character of Islam. In fact, he is considered man as such because he is free and responsible and yet not isolated since he is simultaneously a collective or social man destined for final salvation. This double conception of the individual on the metaphysical level corresponds to the idea of universalism generally accepted by modern Western philosophy.[40]

Islam also strongly advocates the universality of moral principles. While the social ethics brought by Christianity are essentially inter-individual, Muslim morality, by consolidating community ties, unites feelings, based on universal virtue and the obligatory regulations, which are indispensible to collective life.[41] Undoubtedly, the universalist character of Islamic morality partially explains the speed with which Islam penetrated the most diverse geographic regions and cultural environments, instead of remaining in the Arabian peninsula. This religious phenomenon is equalled only by Christianity, as the other African or Asian religions hardly surpassed the limits of the traditional context in which they originated. Thus, the question could be asked if a universal and tolerant religion such as Islam could perhaps be used by mankind to put an end to imperialism and domination when the principle of universality is supported by a politically homogeneous and militarily strong community. Furthermore, the universalism of the faith could imply a certain type of latent exclusivism since the way to eternal salvation is outlined by divine law. Before deriving a conclusion from this study of Muslim universalism in a general perspective, it should be approached on a strictly religious level. There

---

[39]"It is He who produced you to be born from a single person ..." al-An'am: 98, and also al-A'raf: 189 (Blachère).

[40]Lalande, *Vocabulaire*, pp. 1168-1172.

[41]Draz, *Introduction*, p. 81.

is no need to state that this division is to a large degree arbitrary, and in truth opposed to the global spirit of Islam.

Western authors have devised an explanation which shocks the Muslims, based on the chronology of the revelation of various verses. According to them, the Prophet Muhammad was originally raised as the apostle of his nation. Initially, his mission was to furnish a book and a guide, in a language which would be clear to the Arabs, the only people who had not yet received one. This would mean that it was only during the second period of his preaching, at Medinah, that the universalism of Islam was declared, which led the Muslims to form a separate entity at the moment of the rupture with the Jews. Islam imposed itself from that time on as a pure revelation, as opposed to the distorted or falsified scriptures of the Jews and, to a lesser extent, of the Christians.

The Muslims reject this alleged explanation, considering it to be a pernicious attempt on the part of the orientalists to hurt Islam. To begin with, as the Prophet only transmitted the eternal and immutable divine word, he played no active role in the composition of the revelation in terms of material circumstances or of his own will. The nature of the divine message indeed could not depend upon its human messenger. Accepting a chronological explanation would deny the authenticity of the revelation which must be accepted as a coherent whole – the Qur'ān, in its complete and definitive presentation. Moreover, this history is falsified since the revelation is directly addressed to all men: "This is but a calling addressed to the world."[42]

This conviction does not convey a radical exclusivism. If one refers to the essential concept of the unity of mankind under divine direction for what it is, one could deduce that God has authorized diverse beliefs. Being the truth, the revelation is one, but it could have laid down various ritual or legal forms out of respect for monotheism. Each revealed religion is thus true in essence; no group has a monopoly on the truth.[43] The divine government is unlimited; God commands the entire universe. The Islamic community represents only a part of the whole. From His immeasureable Will, God has endowed certain societies with better or more complete directives than others.[44]

Initially, mankind formed a single race and one nation,[45] then God decided

[42]Sad: 84 (Masson), verse revealed at Makkah. See the commentary of Blachère, *Coran*, pp. 482 f., who is, properly speaking (lit: précisement), the initiator of the chronological explanation.
[43]Fyzee, *Modern Approach*, pp. 23 f.
[44]Othman, *Concept*, pp. 188 f.
[45]al-Baqarah: 213, and Yunus: 19.

to separate them into families, tribes, and nations[46] so that they could attain mutual understanding. The single criterion of superiority resides in the fear of God, thus in the submission to His Will. No man is excluded *a priori* from eternal salvation; on the contrary, God desires redemption of each person. The universalist aspect is so obvious that it does not require any further development. In the Muslim point of view and on the social level at least, "pluralism confirms unity; diversity is a principle of harmony, not of confusion."[47] This concept of particular revelations destined for various peoples guarantees religious tolerance. The universalist premise of Islam is not contradicted if the various revelations are seen as being successive. The truth has not been brought to the knowledge of all of mankind just one time. Each divine message is valid until the following revelation confirms, absorbs, and deepens it. As the final expression of the will of God, the Qur'ān guarantees the authenticity and truth of the former messeges, but no longer their validity which has been partially outdated by the advent of Islam. A perfect and complete religion, it surpasses all the others: "O you to whom the Book has been given! Believe in what We have revealed to you, confirming that which you possessed before ..."[48] Therefore, on the religious level, Islam gives proof of possessing an incontestable universalism by the doctrine of absolute monotheism and the principle of the unity of the world. Besides, each man, without distinction, is invited to participate in a simple dogma and to enter thereby into a homogenous community by the easiest initiation there is: the profession of the faith (*shahadah*). If he refuses to embrace Islam, "God is prompt in His reckonings."[49] Socially, however, the individual is accepted and enjoys all rights, except that of harming the community of believers.

The question of universalism can be placed on the social level, a perspective which merits some slight differences in approach. Since the revelation legislates for both spiritual and temporal affairs (areas which are completely interdependent) to an equal degree Islam appears to demonstrate a certain exclusivism on the social organization level, which overlaps into its doctrinal universalism and, by the same variable, could diminish it.[50] The Muslims reject this idea and express it differently, namely that the nonbeliever excludes himself from the community established on the foundation of the Qur'ānic revelation by refusing to embrace the faith. A particular status was worked out in order to regulate the situation of these individuals separated from the social body united by the sacred tie of its religion and respect for the revealed law.

---

[46]al-Hujurat: 13.
[47]Dermenghem, "Témoignage," p. 375.
[48]an-Nisa': 47 (Masson).
[49]āl-'Imran: 19 (Masson).
[50]Chelhod, *Introduction*, p. 162.

The exclusion of nonbelievers from certain rights in the Muslim city is a logical consequence of the community's institutional nature. For some time it was speculated that the oratorical utterance "O man" used in the suras revealed at Makkah was replaced by "O believers" at a later date, when the Prophet settled in Medinah.[51] This dispute is mistaken and should not be vested with the importance that is sometimes attached to it in the West. In fact, it is not necessary to consider this utterance independently of its global context. "O man" or "O people" is used when the call is adressed to all of humanity: "O you people! I am, in truth, sent to all of you, as the Prophet of the One to Whom belong the skies and the earth."[52] On the other hand, "O believers" is used when the instruction, more precise and specific, is addressed to the Muslims themselves: "O you who believe! Incline, prostrate, adore your Lord, do good .. fight for God ... Who has given you the name 'Muslims' ... Perform, therefore, the prayer, give alms. Hold fast to God; He is your protecting friend. A blessed Patron and a blessed Helper."[53] Therefore, the importance given to the chronology is not really significant, all the more so because the Qur'ān in its current presentation, laid down according to the instructions of the Prophet, constitutes an indivisible and universal whole. The divine revelation is addressed to all men in order to invite them to embrace the faith and, on a different level, to indicate to the believers in particular the regulations to follow. Thus, the makeup of a separate community naturally breaks away from the Qur'ānic teaching, without restricting the universality of the divine call in any way.

Adhering to the doctrine preached by Muhammad meant, for the first believers, a rupture with the former tribal social order and becoming a distinct entity. The Muslim nation was born by rejecting custom and tradition. The community, however, kept a universal ideal since it did not reject the truth of the juridical and moral rules contained in the previous revelations. It asserted itself only against the pagan Arabs. Besides, it remained largely open to all on the social level but involved the rejection of certain beliefs. In an essentially theocentric society, it was normal to demand the professing of monotheism. It is mistaken to compare the legalized solidarity of the Muslim community and its corollary aspect of exclusivity with that of primitive societies due to their common denominator of respect for tradition. Even on the social level, the grouping of believers remains open without any restrictions. The universality of Islam is all-encompassing because the cement of society is not, as it was in ancient cities, a matter of race, origin, or birth, but

---

[51]Lammens, *Islam*, p. 61, which seems to ignore that the oratorical utterance "O man" or better "O peoples" is frequently encountered in the Makkan suras.
[52]al-A'raf: 158 (Masson).
[53]al-Hajj: 77-78 (Masson).

the profession of monotheistic faith. From the advent of Islam, and later in variable degrees during its establishment outside the Arabian Peninsula, the assertion of the unity of the world under the guidance of a single God marked the decline of national religions or of local beliefs in favor of universalism, which also triggered the emancipation of the individual. Adherence to the faith gave the individual the right to fully integrate himself in the social, political, and fiscal spheres of the community. Thus, the supposedly exclusivist aspect of Islam on the social level appears as such only when seen from the exterior. The unbeliever is actually invited to participate in the community without restrictions, but he excludes himself by refusing to embrace the faith and analogously to abide by the law. As a monotheist, he remains obedient to the rules of his own religion. The phenomenon is inherent in the theoretical Islamic society, totally centered on the divine revelation which legislates for the affairs of the world.

Finally, the last level of Muslim universalism to be presented – that of politics – must be dealt with in two aspects: external universality which corresponds with religious proselytism, although not totally covering it, and internal universality in that which the law imposes upon the members of the community. A review of these would be useful here. The appearance of Islam produced in Arab society a resistance which necessarily had to degenerate into a political struggle. The Muslim community, having scarcely emerged, immediately formed a distinct entity. The expression of this self awareness took on a "national" aspect since it rejected the traditional norms used in determining who belonged to a certain tribal group. It is a case of a classic sociological process. Political Islam was born by turning in the direction of Makkah during the prayer. This decision did not impart much of an "Arab" character to the community since the Ka'bah was considered to be a temple of Abraham, father of all the believers.[54] It is wrong for the reader to assume that Muhammad, in making this choice while establishing an independent monotheistic religion separate from the other religious communities, would have attempted to isolate his community for the sole purpose of not sacrificing its "nationality." On the contrary, the very specificity of the Islamic doctrine paradoxically imposes universalism. The Islamic idea of the world and of society can only be understood in its religious essence. The principles of unity and universal order necessarily give rise to a united and well-ordered human society. Each individual group forms a homogeneous entity, an integrated part of the universal society, inside of which reciprocal possibilities and needs generate cooperation. The necessity of working together emerges from the interdependence of nations which, geographically speaking, do not have

[54]Muhammad Ali, *Religion*, pp. 510 f.

enough natural resources to attain economic self-sufficiency. The difference between the organized communities – like the natural dissimilarity between individuals – has been willed by God for the benefit of humanity.

The religious unity of Islam, reinforced by the worship rituals and the generality of the law, leads to political homogeneity. Besides, the assurance of having the true revelation encourages Muslims to reject all other allegiances and to recognize no citizenship other than that of Islam. In reality, the struggles for influence and dissidence from a traditional or local nature surfaced very quickly. They were sometimes based on a cultural reaction and a political demand of the newly converted populations. The disintegration of the political community could, however, issue from a confrontation of military dynasties. The nationalist bent of the contemporary politics of certain Muslim states is a recent phenomenon. It appears to be both the sequel to colonial division as well as the consequence of a political opportunism which drove the various peoples of the Muslim community to work for their independence on an often particularist level. This present state of affairs is probably a permanent political reality. Religious proselytism continues – an individual preoccupation of each Muslim – but the universalist political claim is no longer the same. As the community of believers has been divided into national states, a tendency to separate the spiritual and the temporal has progressively been imposed. The Muslim's quasi-mystical collective feeling of belonging to a fraternal entity transcending borders is still alive. It will probably never stop influencing the political conduct of Islamic governments.

Finally, the strictly human element should be the sole point of anchorage of all analyses concerning Muslim universalism. Its religious preaching is universalist because it sees for man an eternal, transcendental future. Likewise, belief in a single and universal God brings about the dissolution of all ethnic principles or national feelings. Finally, the conception of the world as a constellation of diverse communities, each of which is grouped around a divine messenger, leads to the respect and tolerance of other peoples. The doctrine of necessary collaboration among nations, by the very fact of their respective differences, and the prohibition of force in religious matters could prevent proselytism of the faith from making room for political imperialism. The guardrail here is the strict observance of the divine law. On the internal level of the Muslim world considered in its entirety, history has shown that religious solidarity asserts itself more solidly than political ties. The universality of the revelation surely indicates the generality of the faith but stops short of requiring, in theory, uniform political structures. This brief review should help us to better understand the internal political organization of the Islamic community, the status of non-Muslim minorities, and the arrangement of ties with the outside world.

The Foreigner

The foreigner's status is easier to define if one speaks of it in the negative, namely that it is the complete nonparticipation of a homogenous group. It is a case of ties which – whether two individuals or two collectives who are identical in some respects and different in others – enter into a relationship or oppose each other with a sort of intensity which represents the very negation of its identity. The first character is conditioned acceptance; the second is outright rejection. The ties and mortar of social cohesion can be, for example, sociological, political, economic, or juridical. On the level of social or personal reaction, the foreigner is perceived as a danger and seen as an internal or external enemy when his number, attitude, or position of power call into question the very structures of the group.

In the Muslim city, the spiritual is not separated from the temporal, and the law forms an integral part of religion. The Islamic community, however, could not be absorbed by the organization of any other primitive collectivity[55] whose cohesion is founded upon its religion, precisely because – being universalist and cosmopolitan – Islam recognizes and accepts difference to a certain degree. This attitude is at first seen in the Islamic conception of man.[56]

Amid the numerous examples reported by the prophetic tradition, one in particular will suffice since it is very illustrative in its formulation. Seeing a funeral procession passing by, we are told that Muhammad stood up. His companions imitated him, but they told him that it was only a Jew. "Is this not a soul?" he responded to them, thus affirming the fundamental equality of all men as divine creatures. In this context more than in any other, a precise terminological definition proves to be necessary.

The Islamic understanding of "community" (*ummah*) has no equivalent in either Western thought or historical experience. Gathering the believers together by a tie simultaneously political and religious, the Muslim "community" centered on the sacred word of God and united by the pride of following the final and true revelation, corresponds neither to the "people" of medieval Christianity nor to the Western "nation" of the eighteenth century. It is still

---

[55]Antoine Fattal, *Le statut légal des non-musulmans en pays d'Islam* (Beirut: Institut de Lettres Orientales, 1958), p. 10, which is the fruit of extremely serious research; an excellent source of technical and historical juridical information. We have been inspired by it especially on the factual level. After this: Fattal, *Le statut.*

[56]Mohammed al-Harkan, et al., *Le dogme musulman et les droits de l'homme en Islam* Beirut: Dar al-kitab al-lubnani, 1974). The previous was presented at conferences in Riyadh, Paris, the Vatican, Geneva, and Strasbourg, between eminent Saudi Arabian and European jurists and intellectuals. In particular: "La conception de l'homme en Islam et l'aspiration des hommes vers la paix," pp. 147 f. After this: al-Harkan, *Le dogme musulman.*

the concept of a human individual which causes difficulty in understanding. In Western thought, man participates in a hierarchical social life by his external and concrete action. The Muslim, on the contrary, is integrated into the egalitarian collectivity through his individual "testimony," the interiorization of his will, and the qualities proper for a believer.[57] Declared intention and verbal profession of the faith are the conditions for communal acceptance. Likewise, obedience to the divine will defines the social structure. The fundamental rules of the collective are thus determined by the worship which is due to God.

A special status must be reserved for nonbelievers in a society with an essentially religious base. However, his status is not comparable to that of antiquity's *hostis*. The originality of the Islamic system, when compared with antiquity's, is the universalism of its revelation and its expansion. Islam is superior to Judaism and Christianity in this regard, for it accepts the prior monotheistic religions which it simultaneously authenticates and surpasses, thereby affirming the fundamental unity of the divine religions. Through this fundamental affirmation of the divine law's universality, relativity is an allowable rule in the juridical domain.[58] Here is one of the most remarkable contributions of Islam to the formation of a modern universal conception: tolerance, a religious obligation and a juridical imperative. The Qur'ān indicates it explicitly: "We have revealed to you the Book and the Truth in order to confirm that which existed of the Book and is a guardian over it, thereby judge between them by what Allah has revealed, and do not follow their desires away from the Truth which has come to you. For each we have appointed a divine law and a determined way. Had Allah willed He could have made you one community. But He has wished to try you by that which He has given you. So vie with one another in good deeds."[59]

In the general framework, three categories of non-Muslims are outlined. The first is the pagan who is unreservedly convinced to embrace the new faith. When he takes a position as an enemy of Islam or of the Muslims, theoretically he has no choice other than conversion or struggle until death. Next, the follower of a monotheistic religion who lives outside the Muslim world (*harbi*), but who might temporarily reside in it by a very simple process. This later appears closest to the concept of "foreigner" in modern doctrine. The third is the monotheist[60] "protected" by the Islamic community. By

---

[57]Massignon, "Respect," pp. 450-451.
[58]Joseph Chelhod, *Islam d'hier et d'aujourd'hui*, vol. 13: *Les structures du sacre chez les Arabes* (Paris: Besson-Chantemerle/Maisonneuve, 1958), p. 258. After this: Chelhod, *Les structures*.
[59]al-Ma'idah: 48 (Masson).
[60]Jews and Christians. History shows that Islam had extended, by analogy, the status of "pro-

a too simplistic extrapolation, Western literature has often held that this "protected person" is a "second-class citizen." In fact, these people were foreigners who obeyed their own laws and who were "protected" in the true sense of the term because, geographically speaking, they lived in the political and cultural domain ruled by Islam. They formed homogenous religious minorities whose status was guaranteed by juridical provisions obligatory upon Muslims and part of the Qur'ānic revelation

By recognizing the truth of the previously revealed divine message given to certain peoples, and by placing itself in a common relationship with the Jews and Christians by way of Abraham, Islam opened the door to ethnic and social coexistence. At the same time, by attaching the Qur'ānic revelation to the Bible and by stripping the doctrine of everything considered contrary to strict monotheism, Islam seems to deny the possibility of theological dialogue. The logical rigor of its teaching, the simplicity of its doctrine, and its inherent tolerance offer conquered people a religious liberty quite superior to that accorded by the Christian states themselves, particularly in the eastern part of the Mediterranean area where heresies, often taking the form of a national claim, were in conflict. Thus, the "Muslim community" does not overlap with the concept of the "world of Islam" (*dar al-Islam*). The first assumes a religious meaning; the second implies a structure both political and religious, including non-Muslims on the basis of an established procedure.

Monotheism accords each person the honor of integrating himself into the human species – without any special or particular consideration. The unity of the revealed messages involves respecting the followers of previous scriptures at a time when, in a parallel manner, conversion to Islam afforded the individual the possibility of attaining the maximum degree of perfection by integrating himself into the community of believers. The profession of faith, "There is no God but Allah; Muhammad is His messenger," by which the individual integrates himself and participates fully in the Muslim *ummah*, is in fact a double recognition: that of the oneness of God and of the role of the Prophet Muhammad as His messenger. The intrinsic value of all men as such remains identical. Objectively speaking, however, the vocation of the Muslim is superior to all others since he follows the divine order: "O mankind! We created you from a single (pair), and made you into nations and tribes that you might know each other. Verily the most honored of you, in the sight of God, is the most pious among you. God is He Who has full knowledge and is well acquainted (with all things)."[61]

---

tected" persons to the Zoroastrians, Sabians, and other religious communities living inside the Islamic world.
[61]al-Hujurat: 13 (Masson).

On the purely religious level, it is interesting to point out that the attitude of the three great monotheistic religions toward nonbelievers is, to a large degree, determined by their fundamental choice. Here we find Islam's originality which integrates the three common theological virtues with a certain particular intensity for the faith. Judaism quickly withdrew into itself: the hope of seeing the fulfillment of the covenant's promises seems to be the exclusive privilege of a clan. Out of charity, Christianity is expansive, desiring that all men should benefit from the grace which the Christians have received, without offering formal rules for individual conduct or for public affairs. Finally, by the faith and respect it commands for the divine revelation which is considered to be global, Islam instructs each Muslim to spread his beliefs while respecting those of others.

On the individual level, what distinguishes a Muslim from a nonbeliever is an above all moral – almost psychological – element. His awareness of the absolute and his religious makeup urge him to conduct himself with a certain "purity" which gives him that air of dignity, of superiority.[62] On the collective level, this "purity" expresses itself by the intention to establish on earth an ideal community which seeks the good and struggles against the evil. Although it is a society open to all who want to join it, the collective cannot admit those who have not accepted its fundamental premise, namely Islam. However, nothing prevents Muslims from maintaining amicable relations with non-Muslims, as long as those ties do not endanger the community.[63] Those non-Muslim monotheists who live in the Islamic world can live there in peace and practice their faith, being governed by their own institutions under the authority of their religious leader who is reponsible to the Muslim authorities. Some specific "nations" have been organized and centralized, remaining obedient to their own religious order yet integrated into the social superstructure of the Islamic community which protects them.

According to dictionaries of the Arabic language, *dhimmah* "protection" means faith, pact, contract.[64] It is therefore a contract by which the Islamic community authorizes the conquered monotheistic populations to retain their faith, under the guarantee of Islam, in exchange for payment of a compensatory tax and respect for certain strictly defined legal obligations. The principle of capitation tax finds its juridical foundation in the Qur'ān.[65] The

---

[62]Abdel Jalil, *Aspect*, p. 169.
[63]"Allah does not forbid you to be nice and fair toward those who have not taken up arms against you and have not expelled you from your homes because of your religion. Allah loves those who are just," al-Mumtahanah: 8 (Blachère).
[64]See Fattal, *Le statut*, p. 18.
[65]at-Taubah: 29.

methods of its application were determined at a later date, especially during the period of conquest.

The juridical character of the treaty of protection can neither be compared nor likened to the current concepts of Western juridical doctrine.[66] This institution moreover evolved with the history of the Islamic Empire, under the influence of external contributions, and likewise with the movement of the Islamic world's structures toward a kind of secularization. It suffices to take note of the general principles of the system – of a complicated jumble of historical events, juridical opinions, and incidental contacts – with the aim of showing how Islam has, since the seventh century of our era, tried to furnish an original response to the question of minorities. Juridical-historical parallels are dangerous because the ancient institutions are the fruit of conceptions often far removed from our modern aspirations or realizations.

The protection of non-Muslims in Islamic territory deserves to be analyzed because it asserted itself as an original way at the very moment when the West emerged from the Middle Ages and was aware of the necessity of determining the regulations governing relations between foreigners.

On the level of juridical definition, one can regard the protection treaty as a covenant by which the monotheistic inhabitants of a conquered territory obtain from the Muslims the security of their persons and their possessions, just as the recognition of their civil and public rights is an exchange for their payment of a compensatory financial tax and agreeing to block any undertaking which might be launched against the security of the community of believers. It constitutes a bilateral agreement subject to the usual conditions as regards its form and validity.[67] Briefly, this means that it should in no way infringe upon or alter the precepts of Islam, that it should reflect complete agreement between the signatories and stipulate clearly and concisely the rights and duties of each person. The conquered people accepts the authority of the Muslim state, without however renouncing its faith and its religiously derived social laws. At the same time, Islam promises to protect this community from all internal or external attacks. The treaty of protection has a permanent character; it is guaranteed by the imam who is the only person entitled to decide whether its provisions are applicable or not. By means of the personali-

---

[66]One can compare the related idea of the *deditio* of Roman law, by which the vanquished became a client of the Empire on the basis of a relation of reciprocal faith. See Fattal, *Le statut*, p. 75. The parallel is, however, unacceptable, for it does not take into account the overlapping of the spiritual and the temporal in Islam.

[67]Mohammed A. Bêchebichy, *Les relations internationales islamiques*, [Islamic International Relations] (Cairo: Supreme Council of Islamic Affairs, 1966), pp. 38-39. After this: Bêchebichy, *Les relations*.

zation of the law, peculiar to the Muslim conception, the covenant of protection is obligatory not only for the state, but also for each believer and each protected person individually. Thus, it has the power of law. The "political" authorities must oversee its application by punishing the believer who interferes with the protected person's rights. In a like manner, the violation of an obligation by a protected person is his responsibility alone and, therefore, does not cancel the assured benefits of the minority community to which he belongs.

Claiming that the conquered population, by accepting to pay tribute to the Muslim authority which guarantees it protection, "gives up its external sovereignty and the major part of its internal sovereignty"[68] is certainly a mistake of anti-historical deduction and identifies the institution of the capitation tax with a modern juridical procedure, such as a colony or a protectorate. On the contrary, this is an original and autonomous act which is as different from the pure and simple law as it is from an international treaty. It is the political expression of Islamic tolerance which allows those citizens living in the Islamic world to enjoy a particular status. The rights and guarantees collectively given to minorities living in the bosom of Islam are inalienable and permanent, regardless of the state of relations between the Islamic world and the external co-religionists of the minority populations. These particular and obligatory provisions have probably "provoked, in Islam, the birth of an embryonic form of public international law among its primary canonists even before Grotius took care of this for Christianity."[69]

Certain Western authors[70] consider the institution as a sharing of sacralized hospitality and of the right to asylum. Others want to see it as the result of the supposed permanent state of hostility between Islam and the external world,[71] or else a refined form of imperialism,[72] which makes second-class citizens of the nonbelievers living in the Muslim world. In reality, the procedure rests upon three specifically Islamic considerations: justice, respect of the individual by respecting the foreign guest,[73] and the personalization of jurisdiction. These are the true foundations of the institution, whatever the

---

[68]Fattal, *Le statut*, p. 75.
[69]Massignon, "Respect," p. 450.
[70]For the use of the formulation, see ibn-Khaldoun, *Les textes sociologiques et économiques de la Mouqaddima*, translated and annotated by Georges H. Bousquet (Paris: Rivière, 1965), pp. 69 f. After this: ibn-Khaldoun, *Mouqaddima*.
[71]Khadduri, *War*, pp. 175.
[72]Fattal, *Le statut*, p. 76.
[73]The Islamic tradition takes pleasure in insisting upon the Prophet's attentiveness and friendliness toward protected persons, such as accepting their invitations, visiting their sick, assisting with their funerals, and so on. Chalaby, *l'Islam*, p. 31.

subsequent juridical interpretations or political and social uses it may have known during the course of Muslim history. In fact, if the capitation tax had only been a subtle method of expansion, Islam's tolerance of the conquered peoples' religion would be a paradox, for the Qur'ānic teaching does not separate the spiritual and the temporal. Besides, the protection of minorities would have ceased upon the renewal of armed hostilities between Islam and the external world, to all intent and purpose in a permanent state of war. Furthermore, on the strictly social level, the protected persons do not belong to some inferior category. Slaves, even Muslims, occupy a subordinate place in the societal hierarchy. There is no need to recall that a number of the "People of the Book" have played an important political role in Islamic history.

Even if religion effectively gave nationality to Islam, it certainly did not determine the level of citizenship. Of course, the personalization of the law divides the inhabitants of the same state into different communities. The members of a minority group obey their own laws and are not obliged, except for certain provisions protecting public security, to observe the Islamic regulations to the same degree as the Muslims. Tolerance is, therefore, acceptance. It was to allow for the establishment of a system which guarantees the person and the goods of minorities by ensuring the respect of their religion, mores, and institutions.

The capitation tax treaties draw their juridical foundation from the Qur'ān, while the methods of application were decided by past covenants and later doctrine. One can separate the main fundamental ideas without necessarily making a systematic critique of the sources. The prophetic tradition, in as much as it is accredited and considered as obligatory, furnishes a valuable contribution for the comprehension of the system. The number of treaties, real or supposed, signed by the Prophet or his successors, is fairly large and is presented in a sufficiently coherent fashion to permit the extraction of a general rule. The first known treaty is the one between Muhammad and the inhabitants of Medinah.[74] This treaty has often been considered as the charter of the Muslim "theocratic" state. In order to benefit from the divine revelation, the Jews were for all intents and purposes considered as members entirely separate from the community of believers. The charter guaranteed their protection and assured their rights, freedom, and security, which were identical to those of the Muslims. It made them a party to the defence of the city. Since they recognized the authority of the Prophet, they were for the most part admitted into the Muslim community, all the while maintaining a separate religious status. A type of confederation of Arab Muslim and Jewish

[74] In the year 623 of our era. See Hamidullah, *First Constitution*, 2nd part.

tribes was established, which went on to form the embryo of a new state, having broken with the narrow tribal loyalties and choosing a new social superstructure. This charter was abrogated by the course of events and due to the treason of the Jewish tribes. In 626, after three violent confrontations, two Jewish tribes were expelled, and the third one was put to death for having allied itself with the enemies of the new faith. Since then, the "Islamic city" grouped together only Muslims and its foundations became even more religiously based.

During the following years, the Muslims conquered various populations. Muhammad assured them of a safe life, and they retained their goods in exchange for a financial or material compensation the importance of which varied according to the need.[75] The Prophet might have granted, at this time, a very liberal covenant to the monks of the St. Catherine monastery in the Sinai. A critical analysis of the chronology seems to prove, however, that this document is a fake, probably completely forged by a Nestorian monk. Nevertheless, the fact that a number of Muslim authors[76] did mention it could indicate that, regardless of whether it is authentic or not, this covenant corresponded in its letter and spirit to the Islamic legislation which deals with protected minorities.

In 630, Muhammad signed a final covenant with the Christians of Najran. Muslim jurists came to regard this treaty as the example of which provisions were applicable to conquered populations. While a delegation was visiting, the Prophet issued a decree bearing a pledge to protect the population of the city and that of the surrounding area, to guarantee their person and their goods,[77] and assured them that they remained free to follow their creed and their form of worship, in exchange for their acceptance of a sort of political suzerainty under Islam. In return, the persons thus protected agreed to deliver a certain fixed amount of uniforms, to furnish on loan armor, lances, camels and horses if the Muslim troops launched military expeditions against Yemen, and to offer hospitality to envoys of the Prophet for a period of one month. The protection and the guarantee extended to the entire population while the responsibility for violations remained individual; no protected person could be punished for the offense of another.

From a strictly legal point of view, the population of Najran lost practically

---

[75] Among these various populations were: a Jewish tribe of Khaibar in 628, Magian and Jewish populations of Bahrain whose leader embraced Islam in the year 629, the population of Northern Arabia in 630, Christians at Dumat and Alia, and Jews at Abruh and Makua. Fattal, *Le statut*, pp. 18 f.

[76] Amir Ali, *The Spirit*, pp. 84-85; and Galwash, *The Religion*, p. 70, for example.

[77] Louis Massignon, *Parole donnée* (Paris: Union générale d'éditions, 1970), pp. 155 f.

none of its rights, were it not for the prohibition placed upon usury. Specific provisions forbade the humiliation of protected persons, all forms of oppression, and the unwarranted interference of Islamic power in the Christian ecclesiastical apparatus This covenant became known as the "Edict of Muhammad Concerning the Christians," and later the "Edict of Muhammad Concerning Mankind." The fact that Islamic tradition accepted it as accurate and the experts on jurisprudence have recorded it as such made it the prime source of law concerning the status of non-Muslims residing in Islamic territory. These legal provisions rapidly assumed an inspired and permanent character. The treaties subsequently concluded by the caliphs were often only repetitions of the accord signed between Muhammad and the Najranites.

The terms left by the Prophet were soon unable to cope with the numerous new situations produced by the territorial expansion of Islam. The caliphs created new legislative regulations, often inspired by Qur'ānic teachings, by the example reported from the Prophet, and also by the prevailing customs in the conquered territories. Some, at least during the period of Islam's expansion, were guided by their personal intuition. Based on these various practices, some regulations were developed and imposed. The reference text was a letter of the Syrian Christians to Caliph 'Umar. Numerous clues have proven that it certainly was written at a later date. It was, nevertheless, considered as the definitive law, regulating the contacts between the protected minorities and Islam, because the jurists of the classical era held it to be true and codified it as such. The fact, however, that the document which supposedly determined the general rule might really have come after Caliph 'Umar seems to show, on the one hand, that any defined doctrine – outside of the prophetic tradition – did not exist until the grand undertaking of juridical codification in the ninth century of our era, and, on the other hand, allows one to assume that the protected persons' liberties were the object of various regulations progressively marked by restrictions and limitations.[78] This codification, known as the "Covenant of 'Umar," is imprinted with a certain spirit of intolerance. The apocryphal character of the document, which is presented in the form of a request coming from the conquered populations, could be a late invention of new converts desiring not to be confused with their former co-religionists and who themselves inspired some of the restrictive provisions under which they had suffered before the Islamic conquest. Perhaps it represents the fruit of a scholastic exercise carried out by some later jurists who attempted to deposit, in a single text, the successive limitations imposed on the protected peoples – without taking into account the

---

[78]The new character which the Islamic state assumed at this time under the Abbassids must also be emphasized.

times, places, or circumstances under which they were introduced. Most of these limitations rapidly fell into disuse and were strictly imposed only intermittently, as was called for by the circumstances or persons overseeing the destinies of the Muslim empire.

The treaty of protection imposes certain obligations on the conquered populations and concurrently guarantees most of their freedoms. Their principal obligation was to pay the tax. This did not represent a penalty but a form of compensation. It would actually appear illogical that the Muslims, with their universal ambition and their enthusiasm for the true faith, would have accepted the maintenance of unbelief in exchange for a material contribution. This tax, on the contrary, was the amount determined for the privilege of being able to stay in Islamic territory without in any way having to join in the effort of defending or expanding it. In principle, it does not represent a humiliation but rather a contribution to offset the public burden instead of physically participating in its wars. The Arabic term for this tax[79] in itself signifies "compensation." Thus, only those men who are old enough and physically able to carry arms have to do so. Besides, the armed contingents of the protected populations who participate directly in the war effort on the side of the Muslim troops[80] do not have to pay it. The compensatory character of the tax stands out even better in a certain event reported by Islamic history. Having taken Homs in Syria, the Muslim troops considered retiring as they faced a counteroffensive which foretold a concentration of Byzantine troops. The Muslims proposed to the Christian population a reimbursement of the tax whose payment was pending, but they asked the Muslims to stay and then joined with them to defend the city. After jointly repulsing the Greek attack, the inhabitants of Homs were exempted from the compensatory tax.[81]

The compensation tax, as its name indicates, is a tax based on a head count. The early doctrine had not formally determined the form which the payment should assume: tribute, a contribution in kind, or a financial tax. It constituted a personal tax according to very well-defined categories of the taxpayers and corresponded exactly to a compensation for the non-bearing of arms. Women, children, and the handicapped were exempted from it. Moreover, the charge was, as for military enrollment, proportional to one's wealth: twelve dirhams for an economically weak and protected person, his corresponding Muslim of this social category having to serve as an infantryman; twenty-four dirhams for a member of the middle class, his correspond-

---

[79]*Jizyah*, synonym of *jaza*, etymologically means retribution, renumeration, compensation. See Fattah, *Le statut*, p. 266.
[80]The Armenians form a good example in the initial period of the Muslim expansion.
[81]Chalaby, *l'Islam*, p. 173.

ing Muslim having to serve as a cavalryman; forty-eight dirhams for the rich among the "People of the Book," while their Muslim equivalents would have to equip a retinue and serve as a cavalrymen.[82] The leader of the protected community was generally responsible for collecting the funds, the total amount of which would be fixed in accordance with the last obtained census count of the subjugated inhabitants. The capitation tax thus rapidly assumed the form of tribute. With the growing rhythm of conversions to Islam, the tax became heavier for each non-Muslim individual and it even assumed, at certain times, a character of humiliation for those who had to pay it. Nevertheless, it is a case of historical incidents or of events and not of any fundamental changes in the concept of the capitation tax. Besides this financial charge, the protected persons were expected to abstain from attacking the Muslims and were to respect Prophet Muhammad. They were compelled to carry out certain obligations relevant to military security: prohibiting the lodging of spies, or simulating by their attitude the bearing and behavior of Muslim soldiers. They had to furnish guides, house the Muslims passing through, and repair roads and bridges, should the occasion arise. They were also required to abstain from disturbing public order. In short, the charges imposed on the protected minorities appear – even by modern standards – moderated and equitable: payment of a tax in compensation for the non-bearing of arms; respect for the religion and, above all, the political and social institutions of the conquered state; indirect participation in the protection of the community; and, finally, respect for public security.

In exchange, the Muslims allowed the protected populations to stay in the Islamic territories, to keep their religious convictions while shielded from internal or external dangers, granted them security of their person and goods, and guaranteed their fundamental liberties. Even though subject to restrictions initially imposed for reasons of strict security, these liberties principally included the freedoms of conscience and worship, physical or individual; of personal, political, economic, property, and mercantile status; of work; of assembly; and of inheritance, as well as respect for their own institutions. As a matter of fact, the protected people kept the use of their laws and of their courts, with the possibility of having access to Islamic jurisdiction if they themselves deemed it necessary.

On the purely metaphysical level, one could provide a long epilog to the concept of equality and the way it was applied within the social structure. All men are equal in a common servitude to a transcendent and universal God. On the juridical level, equality will only be established among the believers. The non-Muslims see themselves as being guaranteed limited rights

---

[82]Fattal, *Le statut*, p. 266.

because they refuse to follow the Qur'ānic revelation, but they likewise enjoy all which is accorded to them because of the respect due their revealed book. Finally, on the economic and social level, the "People of the Book" could be the equal to the Muslims. Tradition reports that Caliph 'Umar al-Khattab gave alms to an elderly Jew and then instructed the Muslim treasury to take care of "this man and those like him, for it would be unjust on our part if we let them die of hunger in their old age, seeing that they also paid the capitation tax during their youth."[83]

The ecclesiastic and administrative structure of the protected communities remained operative. The patriarchs, bishops, and rabbis were generally elected according to the traditional procedure and enjoyed a certain status as officials. Their jurisdiction, as well as their spiritual and temporal authority, was recognized by the state and sanctioned by the caliph. By paying capitation tax, the "People of the Book" obtained a guarantee of inviolability of their person and their goods and, consequently, took on some of the juridical personality of the believers themselves. Objectively, they had no reason to fear being victimized by governmental or private arbitrariness. Moreover, tradition reports that Muhammad said: "One who kills a protected person will not smell the aroma of Paradise."[84] 'Ali declared that the Islamic state granted protection to the conquered populations, and they agreed to pay the capitation tax in order to make their blood equal to that of the Muslims.[85] This understanding is fundamental, for it clarifies the Qur'ānic regulation[86] suppressing any legal difference between a Muslim and a protected person. It evidently implies the principles of equality, of punishment and the guarantee of inviolability and individual liberty. A certain objection is often raised, in this context, toward Islamic institutions about the fact that the testimony of a protected person cannot be considered as proof when a dispute between him and a Muslim arises. From the Islamic perspective, this limitation is understandable since the believer who makes false claims would be violating not only a covenant whose provisions his religion demands that he respect, but also an obligatory rule which draws its very force from the Qur'ān itself. This should represent a sufficient guarantee.[87]

---

[83]Bêchebichy, *Les relations*, p. 19; and El-Hofy, *Tolérance*, p. 51.

[84]Or again: "One who oppresses a person bound to him by a promise or violates his rights, or imposes upon him a task which is beyond his ability [to perform], or extorts something from him, 1 will be his adversary on the Final Judgment." El-Hofy, *Tolérance*, p. 41.

[85]Fattal, *Le statut*, p. 117.

[86]"O you who believe! The law of equality is prescribed to you in cases of murder: the free for the free, the slave, the woman for the woman," an-Nisa': 178 (Masson).

[87]In practice, it has certainly been abused; the condemned protected person could, if he is involved in a case against a co-religionist, annul any unfavorability by converting to Islam.

Some limitations and abrogations of these rights have appeared during the course of Muslim history. These were at first the deeds of men. The restrictive interpretation of the law seems to find its driving force in the desire to humiliate the protected persons, perhaps under the influence of the thought of antiquity which considered the personal tax as a mark of servitude. Later Muslim jurists have exaggerated its character. Those who conquered in the name of Islam had, in reality, no reason to scorn the conquered populations who had generally greeted them as liberators. In this spirit, the institution was considered more as a friendly invitation to non-Mulsims who, living among the believers, should have been able to convince themselves to embrace Islam because of its message's truth and its institutions' perfection. Almost all of the restrictions placed on their liberties were the result of an exaggerated application of some of the provisions having a strictly military character. A certain intolerance secreted these particular measures and was nourished by them in return. The spirit of the law was diverted by the arrogance of men; these violations were accepted, then sanctioned by the juridical doctrine of a certain time. Among the very rare cases in which the restrictive provisions were being applied, some of them were doubtlessly justified by objective historical considerations.

The first prohibition sought to prevent the protected populations from gathering with the Muslims and copying their habits and general attitudes. At the time of the conquest, the conquered population dressed differently than the Arabs. The main preoccupation of the Muslims was how to distinguish combatants from the protected civilians. For reasons of strict security, the latter were not allowed to imitated the Arabs who simply wanted to prevent foreign populations from wearing their "uniform." From this legitimate decision was born a series of distinctly discriminatory measures aimed at the protected populations: wearing imposed clothing and distinctive badges,[88] a prohibition against bearing arms and riding on saddles, an obligation to wear around the waist a certain colored sash, and shaving the forehead. These practices were imposed intermittently and with a rigor depending more or less on the prevailing circumstances. In addition, the conquered populations were obliged, understandably, not to furnish any information of a military nature to the enemies of Islam, and not to harbor their spies or to provide them with guides.

The conquering troops took care to build their buildings as high as possible for military observation. This measure was later on exploited in a vexatious spirit. Under the pretext that "Islam dominates and cannot be dominated," the

---

[88]This was probably a practice in the conquered territories which had known similar discriminations since the time of the Byzantines.

minority populations were told not to build a church or synagogue higher than a mosque, or houses higher than those of the Muslims. For identical motives of security internal in nature, the conquerors were obliged to make specific arrangement in order to prevent eventual mass demonstrations which would not have failed to group themselves under the banner of religion, in view of the social structure of the time. These considerations of strict public order were, also, in time exploited to humiliating ends. The protected populations were not allowed to publicly display any of their religious rituals, and to raise their voices in churches, in the presence of Muslims, in the market, or in public places.

It is irrelevent to mention – in attempting to explain them – the limitations historically experienced by the institutions which protected minorities in Muslim territory because theoretically the system offered an original and very tolerant solution to the problem of "foreigners." The historical acts and opinions of legislators[89] differ considerably on some of the most interesting issues. Neither has practice always corresponded to officially recognized doctrine. The number and repetition of certain humiliating decrees aimed at the non-Muslims prove, with their regularity itself, that these restrictions were never really accepted by, or applied to, the population. Whatever excesses might have taken place in some rare reactions or discriminatory tendencies of certain juridical interpretations, the law guaranteed the protection and inviolability of the conquered populations. The respect for difference was the most gracious expression of Islamic tolerance. It would be mistaken and unjust to denounce the zealousness of Islam by considering certain of the less numerous abuses which have occasionally marked the history of the Islamic state.[90] The Islamic law brought, on the contrary, new and generous solutions at a time when "intolerance, in the modern sense of the term, was universally considered by the feudal world as a state virtue."[91]

The application of the protective system to conquered populations has varied in accordance with the geographical, psychological, political, and economic transformations of the Islamic state: from the initially limited community of believers grouped around Muhammad to an immense empire which politically and culturally dominated the largest area history has ever known. Establishing himself at Medinah, the Prophet assumed power in behalf of the new state. The necessities of public organization immediately gave rise to is-

---

[89]This difference was often, in "Islamic law" as elsewhere, due to the doctrinal fixation of existing politics, at the given moment.
[90]Basile Homsy, *Les capitulations et la protection des chrétiens au Proche-Orient, aux XVIIe, XVIIe et XVIIIe siècles (Beirut: Harissa, 1956), 420 pages. After this: Homsy, Capitulations.*
[91]Fattal, *Le statut,* p. 161.

sues of integration between the faithful who had emigrated from Makkah, the Medinans who had accepted them, and the Jews and pagans who both were important minorities at that time. The first community did not exclude the nonbelievers who in so far as they were monotheists and retained their religion and their institutions. The treaties of guarantee signed between Muhammad and the inhabitants of Medinah, then with certain populations of the Arab Peninsula, one of them being the Christian community of Najran, were to serve as a political guideline for his successors. This institution was, however, quickly swallowed up by events when put into practice. The Prophet himself had to drive the Jews out of Medinah because they had attempted political suicide through intelligence contacts with the enemy. Caliph 'Umar banished the Christians of Najran who practiced usury which was a violation of the provisions of their treaty with Muhammad. If, later on, the general principles of the system were not always applied in their spirit, it must still be stated that the Jews and the Christians were not harassed in the practice of their worship, and they were neither systematically discriminated against nor forced to abandon their faith to adopt Islam. Actions which may now seem violent were in all levels based upon more for decided reasons of state rather than due to religious intolerance.

Such a guarantee was never fundamentally challenged, for it emerged from a sacred contract which each Muslim was obligated to respect. The methods of carrying it out have varied. Even in the worst occurrences, they never reached the dimension of systematic persecution.[92] Since the codification of the provisions regulating the status of the tributary populations, a narrow-minded chief executive could find a pretext in the body of detailed and minute instructions just to limit the liberties granted to non-Muslims and to force the latter into a state of effective servitude. These cases were exceptionally rare and temporary.

To the Western authors who claim that a number of Christians or Jews embraced Islam in order to avoid bad treatment and the payment of the financial tax, Muslims respond that the large number of conversions is on the contrary explained by the admiration which the protected populations had for the tolerance of the caliphs and for Islamic justice.

The more strongly Islam asserts itself the more tolerance it seems to show on both internal and external levels. Even the wording of the Qur'ānic verses prohibiting forced conversion[93] show a quiet assurance. The strength of the

---

[92]We will raise a single very well-known exception: the persecutions of Jews and Christians during the reign of the Fatamid Caliph Hakim bi Amrillah in Egypt at the beginning of the eleventh century. They were the result of a mental illness.
[93]al-Baqarah: 256.

ummah allows the believers to fear neither the Jew nor the Christian and, therefore, to respect their person and religious institutions. At the time of the first wave of expansion, the Muslim community was largely inspired by the very liberal provisions granted by the Prophet and his immediate successors. The restrictions, gradually brought in, fell for the most part into disuse and were systematically reapplied only in the course of specific circumstances.

History proves that the system of capitation tax was an admirable type of tolerance when applied with foresight and intelligence. Furthermore, it must be pointed out that when the climate of intolerance reached its height, those Muslims holding diverse religious and philosophical tendencies suffered just as much as the protected peoples,[94] if not more so. Tradition reports, for example, that a Muslim who came into contact with a group holding opposing ideas could save his life only by falsely claiming to be a protected person.

After the great disasters which befell the empire at the hands of the nomadic invasions[95] and the brutal contact with the West during the crusades, the nature of the guarantees of protection changed in tandem with the transformations made in the very structure of Islamic power by the arrival of the Ottomans. A true persecution, supported by popular fervor, swooped down upon certain non-Muslim minorities who had lent support to the enemies of Islam, thereby menacing its very survival. The Christian communities of Armenia were its best-known victims.[96]

On the juridical level, the provisions related to the tributary minorities seem not to have undergone any abrupt change.[97] The system was transformed following a slow maturation in the general structure of the community. The Ottomans grouped the "People of the Book" into three strongly centralized categories: Monophysite Christians, Duophysite Christians, and Jews. The patriarchs and rabbis kept their accrued privileges, for the sultan could in that manner exercise a stricter control over the minorities through their leaders.[98] The tributary populations appeared as almost autonomous "nations" within the

---

[94]O. Houdas, *L'Islamisme*, new ed. (Paris: Ernest Leroux, 1908), p. 222. After this: Houdas, *Islamisme*.

[95]These were the Seljuks and, above all, the Mongols.

[96]It is, however, convenient to point out that the Armenians had given assistance to all of the foreign invaders, beginning with the French crusaders and then – above all – the Mongols in whom they thought they recognized Nestorian Christians.

[97]At the time of the taking of Byzantium in 1453, Muhammad II had declared to the newly nominated patriarch, Genmadius Scolarius, of Constantinople: "May you be a Patriarch of peace and may the heavens protect you; may we be friendly in all circumstances where it would be necessary for you and may you enjoy all the privileges which your predecessors enjoyed." See Fattal, *le statut*, p. 366.

[98]Zananiri, *l'Eglise*, p. 233.

empire, "under the shadow of justice," or again "under the Sultan's wing of protection."[99]

European intervention in the internal affairs of the Muslim empire – Ottoman at that time – used the pretext of "protecting" the tributary minorities. It would take a long time to detail the whole plot. In brief, the Italian and French Provencal merchants obtained directly from the Egyptian Mamelukes or Turkish sultan some privileges and guarantees for their trade in the Levant. Wishing to ally France with the Sublime Porte in order to neutralize German strength, Francois I and Sultan Sulaiman II signed a treaty, known under the name of "Capitulation," in 1535. This unilateral concession – for it granted no corresponding concessions to the Muslims living in Christian territories – gave a certain number of privileges to French nationals residing in the Ottoman Empire. This treaty served as an example to other, later and similar ones decreed between Istanbul and the European powers.

Since the seventeenth century, the West[100] has demanded the right to protect not only all Europeans in Islamic territories, but also all Eastern Christians, in a sort of continuity of the spirit of the crusades. The initiative did not have any real consequences for it only took the form of a unilateral declaration. Nevertheless, "with time and the weakening of Turkey, this protection would succeed in obtaining, as foreseen, certain religious and even political goals."[101] Its actual results were essentially political. From the end of the eighteenth century and afterward, the Europeans came to use the alleged persecution of Christians to realize their imperialist ambitions. The caliph, from that time on, became curiously likened to a supreme pontiff of the religion. The French claim engendered others which were identical yet from other European states. Catherine II of Russia demanded and obtained, in 1774, the right to protect the Orthodox minorities.

On the basis of the capitulations which allowed the West to arrogate to itself a real say in the affairs of the Ottoman Empire, and under the pressure of Europe – particularly of France, then Austria – which correctly saw this as a means of penetration, the status of non-Muslim minorities was likened, in fact if not in law, to that of a foreigner from the first half of the nineteenth century on.[102] The privileges of foreigners became so great that numerous protected persons sought naturalization in order to enjoy attendant benefits. It is useless to recall the scandalous abuses which such consular jurisdiction engendered. This system was maintained by the political might of Europe until

---

[99]Homsy, *Capitulations*, p. 46.
[100]This petition was led by Louis XIII of France.
[101]Homsy, *Capitulations*, p. 246.
[102]Fattal, *Le statut*, pp. 366-367.

the Treaty of Montreux in 1929.

The original and generous Islamic provisions for the protection of the non-Muslim populations, applied with a varying level of wisdom but generally in a manner respecting the letter and spirit of the Qur'ānic law, were thus used as a means of European intervention into and domination over Islamic lands. Historical changes of fortunes and subsequent political interpretations have disfigured the image of Islam. It is evident that it would be difficult to reestablish this system in the modern Muslim world. In our day, moreover, the Orthodox reformers seek to cover by correct Islamic juridical guarantees the right of full citizenry accorded to all Jewish or Christian minority populations. This is nothing less than the solution Islam proposed since the seventh century to the problem of minorities, and constitutes a remarkable innovation.

Man and Believer in the City

The Qur'ānic revelation, which imposed itself at once as a spiritual guide, a moral code and a temporal law, rapidly organized a conscious political entity around itself. The community of believers established itself as a precise and logical structure in which each Muslim could truly find his place and participate. It was in this communal integration and out of respect for the revealed law that the believer discovers his identity. The collective organization imposed by Islam is balanced by an individualism (inscribed) in an eschatological framework, seeing that the personal actions of each are to be weighed at the final judgment.[103] The sense of the absolute, the affirmation of the divine oneness, and the assurance of having the exclusive truth will result in a solid, strongly theoretical society in which the believer is personalized as an integral part of an entity which surpasses him. Social cohesion is the result of the evident inability of man to live outside the group, and it is therefore to agree to a kind of "social contract" which is not at all the result of his free will, but a demand of God accepted by man.

By refusing to separate the spiritual from the temporal, the Qur'ānic revelation asserts itself as both a religion and a social system. It would be betraying Islam to describe it only as being timeless[104] or envisaging it only as sociopolitical. On the contrary, one must take into account these two intimately linked aspects without ever wanting to estimate if one among them has, historically speaking, proven more successful than the other.[105] Although

---

[103]For the development of this idea in a reverse sense, see Montgomery W. Watt, "Islam and the Integration of Society" (London: Routledge and Kegan, 1961), pp. 157 f.

[104]Louis Gardet, *L'Islam: religion et communauté* (paris: Desclée de Brouwer, 1960), p. 272. After this: Gardet, *Islam*.

[105]As is the case in and also the fact in for example, Stanley Lane-Poole, *Studies in a Mosque*

Islam and its political system have not been absolutely concomitant, it is evident that the revelation and how it was used have profoundly marked the society. The expression of fundamental liberties has varied with doctrinal evolution. Throughout the course of history, however, two fundamental pillars seem to have remained standing despite all opposition: justice and equality – values which are essentially Islamic. Islam recognizes only a single aristocracy, that of piety. If, with the development of the empire, an inevitable social differentiation involving the classification, on the material level, of the Arab warriors from the conquered and newly converted populations, of the landowners from their "clients," of the educated from the workers of the land, is apparent, such stratification has never been institutionalized or even less legalized. The feudal landowners, the aristocracy of blood, or the bourgeoisie of money hold ideas foreign to Muslim political philosophy. This is probably the reason why some newly converted populations – such as the Iranians, for example – were able to impose systems of government and administration upon those whom they assumed and maintained leadership over and, perhaps also, why foreign slaves succeeded in establishing strong and brilliant dynasties.

On the other hand, Islamic solidarity put certain limitations on individual liberties. Here, one is faced with the dilemma of figuring out how to balance the organization of a homogenous society maintained by a mystical tie and founded upon the concept of collective justice, with the guarantee of freedoms of conscience. Accepting Islam involves a person's total integration into the community. Therefore, as the believer becomes an integral part of a spiritual unity, abjuration or apostasy is inconceivable. Whoever does such a thing would place himself "outside the law": he would exclude himself from society. While the Qur'ānic and the prophetic traditions foresaw for him a punishment in the other world, jurisprudence saw him as being subject to death if his treason was active and endangered the community's security.

History shows that the Islamic world has, at times, experienced a certain intolerance, especially during the period of its decline. Even at that, it has remained, as a general rule, less intransigent than all other religions or ideologies. Abu Bakr, named successor by the Prophet, addressed himself to the faithful as follows: "I have been delegated to be your emir. This does not mean that I am the best among you. If I am just, help me. If I commit an error, show me the right path. Loyalty demands sincerity. Lying is treachery. I shall defend the right of the weak, and the oppressed will be stronger than his oppressor ... Obey me as much as I obey Allah and His

(Beirut: Khayats Oriental Reprints, 1966), p. 101. After this: Lane-Poole, *Studies*.

apostle. If I transgress their commands, you are no longer obliged to obey me." This declaration is interesting in that it defines and limits that which could be called "political guarantees." It authorizes a conditional opposition to the community's leader when his orders contradict the revealed law but, to an equal degree, prohibits insubordination to the revealed law itself. This duality is understood by the fact that the political leader of the Islamic community has no doctrinal authority.

Juridical elaboration stopped with the death of Muhammad. The community designated a successor, the caliph, whose sole task was to oversee the just application of the Qur'ānic regulations and to maintain and expand the Islamic community. As the guarantor of Islamic unity, he exercised only a centralizing function since he had no juridical or legislative power. Theoretically, he was only the agent and the representative of the law which even he had to obey.[106] He had no real spiritual power even though he was the Prophet's successor. He was elected indirectly by the people, and while this mandate gave him authority, it equally imposed the constitution upon him. The Islamic state is not a "theocracy"[107] because, in the final run, the power belongs to God. The caliph secures the "lieutenancy" of the political leader. With the establishment of dynasties and the blessing of Islamic doctrinal research, the caliphal power gave itself a pontifical character, put at the service of religion. The influence of the newly converted is certainly part of this solution. The institution, rapidly emptied of all political prerogatives, maintained itself over the years because both the Ottoman sultans and the European imperialists saw it as a way to achieve their political objectives. The brutal suppression of the caliphate after World War I brought about only weak protests. To consider that its abolition mark "the ruin of Islam as a temporal community would be to completely misunderstand the very nature of its unity."[108]

Rare indeed are those contemporary Muslim political leaders who fail to search for a type of legitimacy by evoking Islamic principles. Numerous states, born out of the wreckage of the Ottoman Empire or the casting off of European colonization, have formally adopted Islam as their institutional base. In addition to the political institutions, the fundamental Islamic concepts of the rights of man and his role in society are still alive, grafted with varying levels of success from the European democracies. They at least remain deep

---

[106]Reuben Levy, *The Social Structure of Islam*, 2nd ed. 1st printing: *The Sociology of Islam*. (Cambridge: Cambridge University Press, 1969), 536 pages.

[107]And this is so even if one qualifies it as "laic and egalitarian." See Gardet, *Islam*, p. 286. We refer here to the usual belief of Western theory that "theocracy" is, in reality, a "sacredocracy."

[108]Gardet, *Islam*, p. 285.

in the popular conscience. The legalized and obligatory moral precepts which they contain are more positive and dynamic than in any other system, for they are not a passive expression of a generous sentiment but rather an active personal commitment. Morality does not fail to appeal to the individual's conscience and intelligence, but compulsory, altruistic action undoubtedly takes precedence over strictly charitable humanitarian feeling. This form of committed morality resounds with remarkable overtones of equity. The Islamic community presents itself as a balanced social entity in which the individual is not only an end in himself but also part of a society which forms a coherent whole.

By the eternal destiny which it assigns to man and by its conception of a single God ordering the ways of the world, Islam strongly confirms itself as a universalist religion. The divine oneness implies one world, one truth, and one law. Adhesion to the community is open to all, without restriction. The confirmation and acceptance of prior monotheistic revelations offer to their followers a certain recognition. In historical retrospect, the virulent attitude toward polytheists seems to have been aimed only at the pagans of Arabia, who showed themselves to be particularly aggressive in their opposition to the newly born Islamic community.

Modern doctrine takes pleasure in recognizing that the diversity of peoples corresponds to the divine will and does not contradict the principle of existential unity since all of the different communities find themselves – because of their natural need for interdependence – in a universal homogeneous entity. Islam, collectively, and the believer, personally, should therefore be not only "tolerant," but also respectful of the multiplicity of nations, as it is an expression of divine wisdom: "Say: 'O you who do not believe! ... You have your religion; I have my religion.'"[109] Only God will judge unbelief.

Even the expression of "tolerance" can assume a pejorative character when it appears in the moral and political language of a Europe as it was emerging from the wars of religion. The adversary or heretic was "tolerated" for the essential reason that he could not be suppressed. In modern semantics, tolerance corresponds to a disposition of the spirit in which a rule of consistent behavior forbids itself to take any coercive measures against those who do not share identical convictions. It is not indifference in which one would preclude manifesting ideas or defending them with violence. It also expresses respect for an idea which it nevertheless rejects, by considering it as a contribution to the whole truth. In this sense, one must acknowledge that Islam has been religiously tolerant and has even gone beyond this, for it respects

---

[109]al-Kafirun: 6 (Masson).

and protects those who still follow the former divine revelations. Finally, in a politico-historical view, and notwithstanding economic imperatives and administrative necessities, the Islamic state has shown a remarkable consideration for the "People of the Book" by allowing them to live in its bosom. It has allowed the existence of their administrative, ecclesiastical, and juridical institutions, even though they do not correspond to Qur'ānic law, and has not imposed upon them those prohibitions which it considers to be divine orders. Islamic tolerance is consideration for the non-Muslim, justice, and the Divine Will. Its obligatory character gives it a particular dimension which allows it to join things together in the broadest sense of the term. It inspires respect for a person who defends an idea of which it does not approve; it is not acceptance of an idea which must be rejected. The Qur'ān which does not fail to denounce the errors and falsifications which the "People of the Book" have introduced into their revelations nevertheless prohibits the believers from insulting the "the polytheists."[110] The respect is aimed at the man, not his opinion.

At a time when exclusivism and intolerance were virtues of the state – and would remain so for several centuries – in the Christian West, the Islamic empire had already accepted large communities of non-Muslims protected by inviolable treaties. This meeting of Muslims, Christians, and Jews created among them an atmosphere of indulgence which the Mediterranean world had never previously known. The politico-juridical originality of the system derives from the specific character of Islam. By refusing to recognize the prophetic role of Muhammad, the monotheistic populations excluded themselves from the Islamic city. The principle of the personalization of the law allowed them, on the other hand, to keep their institutions as long as they did not harm the Muslims' interests and security. The system's harmony progressively disintegrated with the institutional and structural transformations of Islamic power and under the pressure of imperialist Europe. The status of protected persons disappeared with the advent of modern times. It is not certain that it was replaced by a more favorable one. Modern ideas of pluralist democracy – often utopian – satisfy the understanding more and respond more precisely to new ethical conceptions. Nevertheless in a completely realistic view, it is necessary to state that the different systems proposing to ensure respect for minorities offer few effective guarantees. Recent history unfortunately proves this!

The specifically Islamic characteristics of the system and the distance which separates modern times from the time when it was applied in letter and spirit

---

[110]"Do not insult those whom they call upon besides Allah," al-An'am: 108 (Blachère).

prevents its classification into any of the categories used by modern juridical theory and prohibits making any value judgments based on the regulations of contemporary international morality, which is a Western emanation. The Islamic solution to the problem of minorities does not appear "medieval" or "ancient." The acceptance and protection guaranteed to an individual who by his own free will cannot be fully integrated into communal and state structures as well as the respect for that person and tolerance for his concivtion seem to be modern ideas – an eternal ideal. They certainly did not fail to influence the development of universal conscience and to make their own contribution to the elaboration of international law.

In spite of all the vicissitudes of history, the Qur'ān has imposed a tolerance which, even in our day, is respected in few sociopolitical systems. Since the seventh century, it has cast light on the irrevocable fact that even those individuals who do not participate in the mystic and juridical community ties are after all still human and worthy of treatment as such. As a contrast, one can point out that the contemporary doctrine of internal law is still seeking an exact definition of what "minimum status" means when dealing with foreigners!

The expression of norms claiming to be eternal, along with the theoretical description of institutions which have not assumed form other than doctrinal speculation, almost necessarily assumes an archaic and faded appearance to the eyes of the badly informed foreign observer. For the Muslim, on the contrary, the axioms coming from the Qur'ān remain eternally valid, for there could not possibly be "modern" or "old" ideas in the divine revelation, only absolutely just and true principles. Our desire was not to judge, but rather to show by some brief references that probably before any other civilization or religion, Islam most magistrally asserted for the human person and sought an egalitarian society, wedded to the ideals of the best justice possible under the direction of a law considered to be transcendental. The values expressed by the Qur'ān remain undoubtedly intact and can participate in the construction of a more humane world, even in our present age.

Chapter 5

THE UNIVERSE AND THE WORLDS

> This right which makes that victory leaves to the vanquished people these great things: life, freedom, laws, goods, and always religion...
>
> Montesquieu

The Division of the World

As a total divine truth and perfect spiritual ideal, constituting a particular political entity and social organization, Islam is a universal creed based on a profound consciousness of monotheism. While it is the religion of certainty, which directs the conscious energy and will of the believers toward the organization of the earthly world, Islam seems to have revealed the facets of both internationalism and exclusivity. In its turn, the image of the world projected by the religion determines a specific theory of international relations: of either the organization of peace or the state of war. In the final analysis, it also defines rules pertaining to the waging of aggression.

The Qur'ānic revelation and the civilization that it engendered gave rise to a specific view of man and society and contributed in forming a system of rules pertaining to relations between nations. This was done through the new laws it brought and through the transmission of ancient principles which the expanding Muslim world adopted and communicated. These rules and principles have to be put into the specific context of international relations such as Islam conceives them. For the purposes of an essentially theoretical demonstration and as a starting point, we will consider the ideal of a unified, integrated, and uniform Muslim world without taking the historical or contemporary political reality into account.

A question immediately arises: can one abstractly speak of an "international Islamic law"? Islamic law is a rule of action; law is the classification of acts and the evaluation of their consequences. Law is universal since it has in mind all human actions. Thus, one cannot conceive of an "international law" separate from the global Islamic law, founded upon different sources and maintained by particular sanctions. Nonetheless, a specific discipline by the name of *siyar* developed rapidly.[1] Its sources lie primarily in the Qur'ān and traditions. Judicial doctrine did not evolve a general theory of international law as a particular branch of the judicial sciences but rather developed a

---

[1] That is to say "movement" or "behavior." The meaning of the term acquires the restrictive sense of the "conduct" of the Prophet in his wars and, still later, of the conduct of Islamic governments in international affairs. See Muhammad Hamidullah, *Muslim Conduct of State*, 5 rev. ed. (Lahore: Ashraf, 1968), pp. 10-12. After this: Hamidullah, *Muslim Conduct*.

theoretical structure which offered solutions for each analyzed case. In the classical concept, elements of a political or sociological nature were not supposed to play any decisive role. The foundations of the Islamic law of nations are the eternal truth and justice revealed by God. Neither the custom nor the actual practice of political and diplomatic relations constitutes a formal source of the law. This concept is thus quite different from the modern understanding of law in which various international nations establish the future content of the rules, to a large extent determining their meaning.

It is difficult to give a systematic presentation of the Islamic system. This is because, apart from a few exceptions, its sources and documents are to be found scattered in general treatises.[2] Moreover, the distinction between private and public law, as understood by European doctrines, does not exist because of the law's unicity.

In its positive modern conception, international law presupposes the recognition of independent entities with which relations are established on the basis of respect for sovereignty and equality. If the ultimate goal of Islam was to indefinitely extend its geographical boundaries and the application of its judicial rule, then "Islamic international law" would seem eminently temporary. The close ties between the spiritual and the temporal, supported by the claim of universality, would have excluded the coexistence of the Muslim state with other political systems, even though Islam tolerates Christianity and Judaism on a religious level. Similarly, it would seem impossible to accept different Islamic sovereignties as legal entities. The notion of "nationality" would be absent since Islam first of all represents a community of believers rather than an assembly of citizens. Thus, the non-Muslim would turn out to be not so much an enemy as a potential object of submission to the Qur'ānic law. If the non-Muslim notion of state was foreign to Islamic law,[3] then a conclusion could be made that "Muslim international law" does not exist.

The Islamic representation of the universe is simple and strictly logical. The principle of divine unicity and the general conception of universal order both

---

[2]Generally under the chapter of the "holy war" or of "penalties." With the aim of giving an idea of the complexity of the research, we note, for example, that ibn-Taimiyyah, *On Public and Private Law*, pp. 135 f., in explaining the "holy war," successively deals with war, rebellion, prayer, transactions, loyalty to and confidence in God, goodwill toward others, patience, alms, charity and gentleness, pardon, the joy of life, good intentions, and compensation. From there, he proceeds to forbid finding oneself alone with a woman, advises women not to travel alone for a time span of two days or longer, and he prohibits the libertine of having elegant and beardless servants, etc.

[3]Louis Milliot, *Introduction a l'étude du Droit musulman* (Paris: Sirey, 1953), pp. 779 f. After this: Milliot, *Introduction*; and Majid Khadduri, "The Islamic Theory of International Relations and its Contemporary Relevance" J. Harris Proctor, *Islam and International Relations*, ed. (London: Pall Mall, 1965), pp. 24-39. After this: Khadduri, "The Islamic Theory."

imply the existential unity of the world. The Qur'ān teaches that God in His omnipotence decided that for the good of humanity the unity of society should be broken: "O mankind! We created you from a single (pair) of a male and a female, and made you into nations and tribes, that you may know each other."[4] Thus, the universe constitutes a unique entity, though from the inside it appears pluralistic, as a collection of diverse communities, in submission to varying laws revealed by God through chosen prophets: "Unto each people is given a guide."[5] In spite of many warnings, the nations have not always respected the law which has been prescribed for them. Muhammad, the seal of the prophets, brought the final message in order to correct the errors or malpractices which had appeared in preceding messages and to complete the transmission of the divine law. This conception is important in the context of international relations because of its threefold consequence. Theoretically speaking, pagans or polytheists did not receive any benefit from the rules which determined relations between peoples unless they showed aggression to Islam. The nations who could justify the source of their beliefs as coming from a book of divine origin were accepted. This recognition is moreover all-encompassing since "there exists no community which has not been visited by a messenger (of God)."[6] Finally, the third and most important consequence from the point of view of inter-community relations was that since Islam claimed to bring the definitive laws and restore universal order, it stood as a world ideology.

The Muslim world, ruled by a formal divine law[7] of universal vocation,[8] had to define the kinds of relations which it was able to maintain with neighboring nations. As a highly structured state and the propagating mechanism of a total conception of the world, it was necessarily going to collide head-on with Christianity, which is also a social and political entity having its own universal and imperialistic claims, despite its internal divisions. This phenomenon is the domain of history.

According to classical Muslim doctrine, the earth is divided into two "worlds": the "world of Islam" and the "world of war." There is nothing unusual about this bipolar conception which does not have any particular importance in itself. In fact, the notion of states as sovereign political entities had not been defined at that time. In theory, a non-Muslim society did not claim judicial equality or even the formal recognition of its existence before attaining a certain level of civilization. This meant being won over to the idea

---

[4]al-Hujurat: 13 (Masson).
[5]ar-Ra'd: 7 (Masson).
[6]Fātir: 24 (Masson).
[7]As in Judaism.
[8]As in Christianity.

of divine unicity and to have ceased representing a potential danger for the Muslim community. This conception is in no way an extravagant one. The principle of excluding from society peoples of such nations who still have to attain an adequate level of development according to the norms of a certain civilization[9] is fully alive in the twentieth century. Whereas the criteria of evaluation were material in the West, in the Muslim perspective they happen to be spiritual. However, the theoretical aspects pertaining to the apparent makeup of the two "worlds," as well as the principles governing their mutual relationships, make it possible to define the foundations of the Islamic concept of international relations.

In opposition to the "house of Islam"[10] stands the "house of war."[11] In their literal meaning, these names could at first sight lead us to believe that the world is [in the Islamic concept] clearly and irrevocably divided into the Muslim community and the mass of non-believers. In addition to this, they also seem to suggest mutual relations necessarily based on violence. This impression is further reinforced by the subsequent definition of a third division, the "house of reconciliation."[12] This latter division is the specific designation for those non-Muslim states which maintain peaceful relations with Islam, or better still, the territories of protected populations and tributaries of Islam. In order to have a clear understanding of these concepts, it is necessary to give a precise definition which would remove the confusion so often caused by the use of terminology.

In the "house of Islam," Muslim laws and traditions are established and respected. The great majority of the community's members have embraced the faith, and all monotheistic minorities, having accepted the capitation tax, enjoy consequent protection. Since the divine law is applied, all individuals in the "house of Islam," both Muslim and *dhimmi*, are guaranteed security. Thus, the "house of Islam" is also the "house of peace"[13] or the "house of justice."[14] This is the realm of law, order, and harmony. The religious connotation obviously arises from the fact that the Qur'ānic revelation simultane-

---

[9]See Ghoneimi, *The Muslim Conception*, pp. 129-130 f. This author states that the classic Islamic theory of demanding the acceptance of monotheism without insisting upon the adoption of Islam shows itself to be more tolerant than the former doctrine of the West, of which the exclusive criterion of recognition was belonging to Christianity.

[10]*Dar al-Islam*. We prefer the phrase "world of Islam" to the generally used phrases of "house," "abode," or "domain of Islam" because they correspond more exactly to the literal translation of *dar* by reproducing less precisely its political meaning.

[11]*Dar al-Harb*

[12]*Dar al-Sulh*.

[13]*Dar as-Salam*.

[14]*Dar al-'Adl*.

ously offers the faith and the law, respect for which necessarily implies peace and justice. This is the world of Islam. Hence, the primary reality upon which the definition is based is not the religion of the population but the existence of specific institutions and the application of particular rules. The definition's corresponding criterion is the security enjoyed by the inhabitants. The house of Islam, as opposed to the house of war, is thus characterized by the laws which the individual applies and the resulting security which he experiences. A country can be called Islamic if, first of all, the laws it applies are Islamic, and if, secondly, the Muslims and protected minorities enjoy security and the liberty to practice their religion, whether individually or collectively.[15] In the opposing case, the country is considered hostile, belonging to the "house of war," even if it claims to be Muslim and regardless of what the religion of its inhabitants may be. This double condition provides an interesting definition since it reveals the underlying concept of war in Islam. Furthermore, it corresponds to the deeper spirit of the religion, even though certain Muslim jurists or certain Western Islamologists have refuted it, and even though it has been belied by historical events.

The concept of the "houses" is essentially theoretical and primarily juridical. The geographical definition of the "realm of Islam" and its internal divisions seems to be of no real importance, all the more so since the law of rights is "personalized" and not territorial in Islam. A concise description will thus suffice. For most Muslim authors, the sanctified territory surrounding Makkah[16] is reserved exclusively for believers; the Hijaz represents a second division into which non-Muslim monotheists are permitted to go without, however, being allowed to live there permanently. The remainder of the "house of Islam," the largest geographical category, is open without restriction to the "People of the Book" who are allowed to live there as protected persons, or to travel there as foreigners in possession of a travel permit. Since they were first and foremost the product of doctrinal elaboration and the result of historical events or of psychological considerations, these mental geographical divisions were in no way detrimental to the definition of the "world of Islam," nor did they influence international relations.

The "world of war" is not supposed to group all non-Muslim states together. Under certain conditions these states may on the contrary by right and in reality enjoy legitimate existence and total independence. The world of war

[15]Ghoneimi, *The Muslim Conception*, p. 156; and Majid Khadduri, *The Islamic Law of Nations*, translation of Shaybani's Siyar (Baltimore: Johns Hopkins, 1966), pp. 218-219. After this: Khadduri, *The Islamic Law*, which is the introduction pp. 1-74 and Shaybani's Siyar, for the translation pp. 75-292.
[16]*Haram*.

is characterized by the absence of institutions whose function it is to establish peace and justice and also by the nonobservance of the Qur'ānic rule and spirit. It is the reign of violence, ignorance, and tyranny, and is thus identified with the "world of injustice."[17] In the generally accepted term, the word "war"[18] itself takes on a specific meaning. It refers to a situation held to be objective, under the elucidation of Islam's religious and juridical canons. Considered from within, it means war in the genre of anarchy, tension, and disharmony. The "world of war" is opposed to the "world of Islam" by its own institutions, but nothing implies *a priori* that the Muslim should necessarily declare war against this world in order to impose Islam. This bipolar division of the world expresses a struggle between two systems which are opposed by nature – a struggle between justice and injustice, good and evil. In the "world of war," the law applied authorizes oppression, violence, tyranny, and religious coercion. It also permits usury, gambling, alcoholic drinks and any other activity considered to be reprehensible by Muslim morality. Such a state is identified with the "world of war" even if its leaders claim to be Muslims.

The quality of the laws governing a society constitutes the first criterion of the definition. The second deals with the safety of the believers. Those territories in which the Muslim cannot outwardly practice his religion belong to the "world of war." In this respect, Islam guarantees the security of the monotheistic minorities under its protection. The formal recognition of Islam, implying the guaranteed freedom of any person to embrace the faith and to observe its ritual obligations, excludes a country from the "world of war," even if the governmental authority is non-Muslim.

The third and final definition touches upon a more concretely definable reality, geographical in essence. In effect, any neighboring and contiguous territories of the "world of Islam" into which entry is forbidden to Muslims and from which military attacks could at any moment be launched[19] are considered to be a part of the "world of war."

At this stage, we should emphasize three important characteristics. On one hand, the definition of the "world of war" is singularly restrictive since the conditions of evaluation and classification are only cumulatively valid. If one of the conditions is absent, the territory under consideration could not be taken to be an enemy. Furthermore, the basic values of appreciation, the quality of the laws applied, and the security of the believer show that the division

---

[17]*Dar al-Zawr.*
[18]*Harb* as opposed to *Jihad.*
[19]Mohammad Abu Zahra, *La Conception de la guerre dans l'Islam* [The concept of war in Islam] (Cairo: Supreme Council of Islamic Affairs, n.d.), pp. 41 f. After this: Abu Zahra, *La Conception.*

of the world in the Islamic concept is not geographical, as has often been claimed in the West.[20] It is true that some Muslim political leaders seized the opportunity so as to justify their desire for expansion, thus helping to give credence to this idea. It is still true, though, that the geographical distinctions and juridical definition do not coincide. In effect, "Islam recognizes two large divisions of humanity: the one branch comprises those who are the true servants of God and champions of the truth, while the other includes those who pursue evil and are champions of error. Islam declares itself in a state of war against all those who constitute the latter category."[21] Since the "world of war" is thus considered because of the iniquity of its institutions and because of the persecution of believers, there immediately appear great possibilities of adaptation and harmony. As a last resort, peaceful coexistence is determined by the very evolution of the "world of war." The hostility of the "world of Islam" ceases when injustice and persecution cease. Of course, the superiority of the Qur'ānic law is never questioned any more than Islam's claim to universality has ceased. However, a non-Muslim country which does not threaten the community of believers and which possesses institutions enforcing the respect of justice and guaranteeing freedom of worship, would be considered as not belonging to the "world of war." Consequently, pacific relations based on integrity and mutual recognition should be able to evolve. Interpretation has greatly varied with the course of history, and such variations often happened during fluctuations in the military and political strength of the Muslims. Still, they were always the deeds of men.

From this point of view, it could seem superfluous to mention the third section of the divided world: the "world of reconciliation"[22] or of "alliance."[23] In effect, it seems hard to understand how a third category could be logically fitted into the bipartite division of the universe. Again, the definition of this latter "world" does not appear very clearly.[24] It is, moreover, a later contribution and seems to be the bequest of a single school of law.[25] However, it is of twofold interest to analyze this category since, first, this could give a better understanding of the bipolar Muslim conception of the world and, second because it shows the possibility for Islam to establish relations with non-Muslim states, devoid of subjection and hostility.

[20]Lammens, *L'Islam*, pp. 82-83, among others.
[21]Abul Hassan A. Nadawi, *Islam and the World*, translated from the Arabic by M. Asif Kidwai, 2nd ed. (Lahore: Ashraf, 1967), p. 142. After this: Nadawi, *Islam*.
[22]*Dar al-Sulh*.
[23]*Dar al-Ahd*.
[24]Did the "People of the Book" understand that they had signed a pact of allegiance and accepted the capitation tax or is it rather a case in which the territories or states voluntarily maintained peaceful ties with Islam, or does the term cover both instances?
[25]The Shafi'i school.

Since it is possible to envisage a "world of neutrality,"[26] it would be of interest within the context of the system as a whole to enumerate its legal foundations and historical causes. Muslim legal theory recognizes three kinds of neutrality which are confirmed in political practice: Ethiopia, Nubia, and Cyprus.[27] The particular status granted these three countries has its origins respectively in the benevolent attitude of the Ethiopian king toward the Prophet Muhammad and his first companions; in military considerations, such as the inaccessibility of Nubia; and in international rivalry in the case of Cyprus. It is thus undeniable that psychological, practical, military, or diplomatic reasons have played their role. Nonetheless, the basic legal principles seem to have been respected.

Ethiopia was saved from Islamic hostility because first of all it opposed the persecution of believers from the very earliest days, offering asylum to the Muslims who had fled Makkah. Second, the Ethiopian king had recognized the legitimacy of the Qur'ānic law and Muhammad's prophethood. The treaty between Nubia and the Muslim state primarily aimed at putting an end to constant mutual hostility. It appears as a document concluded between two states which reciprocally recognized each other's neutrality, and whose clauses took on an essentially commercial form. However, one of the main clauses deserves special mention since it concerned freedom of conscience and religion.[28] As for Cyprus, it was never a part of either of the "worlds," but was simultaneously subjected to a double allegiance to both Byzantium and Islam. The Cypriots recognized the legitimacy of Muslim law and for a time paid a tax to the Umayyads.

These three examples illustrate and strengthen the theory which claims that the bipartite division of the world and the virtual hostility which it seems to imply are not based on geographical criteria but are determined by the conditions mentioned above: justice, security, and freedom of conscience for the Muslims. There is a certain kind of specialized literature[29] which tries to give credit to the idea that neutrality is a concept foreign to Islam. This assertion represents the conclusion of an analysis which is primarily based on the idea of unyielding antagonism between the Muslim community and the rest of the world. However, neutrality ought to be the normal state of relations if one keeps to the classical definitions of the "worlds" of Islam and of war.

---

[26]*Dar al-Hiyad.*
[27]Khadduri, *War*, pp. 252-267. Again, was it that the countries which enjoyed the status of neutrality directed no aggression against Islam? This seems, unfortunately, no longer to be the case with Ethiopia.
[28]It stipulates, besides, that the Nubians were authorized to build a mosque in their capital.
[29]See, above all, Khadduri, *War*.

Moreover, the Qur'ān considers this case.[30] It is true that the traditional doctrine offers little information and does not give a systematic description of
the rights and duties emanating from the status of neutrality whose legal conception, in any event, appeared only recently. A specifically Islamic theory
has yet to be codified, based upon scanty doctrinal references and pertaining
especially to practice.[31]

The matter of relations between Islam and non-Muslim peoples has been
the object of numerous contradictory discussions which have more than mere
theoretical value since they determine the possible legitimacy of armed conflict and thus, indirectly, the rules pertaining to the conduct of aggression.
The division of the world is an incontestably yet not exclusively Islamic concept. More recently, it has been claimed[32] that it was the product of reflections of certain jurists who based their arguments on Muhammad's order to
the first believers to leave Makkah, the "land of war," in order to make for
Medinah, the "land of Islam." The division of the world, according to them,
is not advocated either by the Qur'ān or the traditions, and the emigration
of the first believers nullifies distinctions and dissipates all contempt.

Such a point of view of course does not correlate with the true spirit of
Islam and disregards the near absoluteness of Muslim doctrine on this matter.
The question presents itself in a different perspective, which is in fact practical and ultimately more interesting. Do relations between the "world of
Islam" and the "world of war" necessarily have to be governed by permanent
hostility, marked by armed conflicts interspersed with temporary truces,[33] or
can they, on the contrary, remain pacific, thanks to the concept of the existential unity and order of the world as well as to the recognition and respect
of the revelations preceding Islam? This question will be the object of discussion of the following section.

Patience

The revelation creates for the believers a spiritual, psychological, and legal
bond of a religious nature. According to the jurists of classical Islam, it

---

[30]Particularly an-Nisa': 90: "Except for this law those who would have sought refuge with your
allies and those who march against you, sad at heart of having to fight against you or against
their own people. If God had wanted, had it pleased Him, He could have given them power
over you, and they would have fought you. If these people withdraw from you, if they do not
fight against you, if they offer you peace, God does not allow any act of hostility against them,"
(Reda).
[31]Hamidullah, *Muslim Conduct*, on pp. 283 f. blazes some interesting trails in this direction.
[32]Bêchebichy, *Les relations*, p. 20.
[33]Lammens, *l'Islam*, pp. 82-83 and Khadduri, *War*, whose idea is the very thesis of the book.

moreover implies the necessity of establishing a solid and autonomous Muslim state as a body which applies the divine laws, subjecting both society as a whole and the individual: believers or protected "People of the Book." The imperative existence of a state, based on a faith both universalist and proselitic, engendered a certain philosophy of relations with the outside world which was theoretically maintained until the abolition of the caliphate in 1924.

For Islam as for any other state or system, the organization and quality of relations with neighboring peoples were largely conditioned in practice by its geographical position and its military power which evolved with the course of history. The foundations of "foreign policy" could be found in the Qur'ānic revelation itself. As an "intermediate nation"[34] on the geographical and cultural levels, the Islamic community was obliged to maintain the most cordial relations possible with contiguous states. The idea of "intermediate" goes beyond the strictly geographical notion, assuming a moral, individual, and collective meaning – that is, connotations of prudence, equilibrium, and moderation.[35] Nonetheless, the question arises as to whether the universal calling of Islam, implemented by a state symbolizing a tool for spreading the faith, allows for coexistence with neighboring nations, and especially with those systems which also have claims to internationalism. On a religious level, it was by accepting the preceding divine revelations that Islam appeared to acknowledge the legitimate existence of foreign states on a political level and in accordance with the community concept of that period. The Qur'ān, in essence, cast the foundations of a pacific system of relations on an almost planetary scale when it asserted that each nation had received its own divine "warning."[36]

Even though the Qur'ān at times violently attacks the Jews and, to a lesser degree, the Christians, accusing them of falsifying the scriptures, it does not in any way pronounce a judgment of exclusion upon them. On the contrary, it seems to explicitly guarantee the legitimacy and rights of various societies to exist.[37] Thus, the principles governing international relations must have been immediately very liberal since they admitted the existence of "foreign entities" in a large universal community of nations. The prophetic traditions report many examples confirming Qur'ānic instructions. For example, when

---

[34]al-Baqarah: 143.

[35]Nation "stretched to the extremes" according to the translation of Blachère.

[36]Muhammad Ali, *The Prophet of Arabia* (Beirut: Khayats, n.d.), see the last page.

[37]"Among His signs are the creation of the heavens and the earth, and the variations in your languages and your colors. Verily, there are signs here for those who know," ar-Rum: 22 (Masson). The term "sign" is here understood in the sense of "proof."

he received the representatives of the Christian community of Najran, Muhammad reproached them for claiming that Christ was divine and invited them to become Muslims. However, he did not exert any pressures on them whatsoever but, on the contrary, placed his mosque in Medinah at their disposal so that they could pray there according to their faith. He concluded a treaty with them, three points of which deserve mention. First, the agreement had no time limit. Second, the allowances offered and requested by the young Muslim state seemed equitable: that the Najranites furnish clothing, arms, and mounting horses in the event of a foray into the Yemen, and that they receive and put up any Muslim emissary for the period of one month. In return, Muhammad guaranteed the protection – at no expense of military service or tithe – of the state, the persons, possessions, and religion of the Najranites. Finally, the negotiations had taken place between two powers which mutually considered each other as equals: one, Najran, artisans; the other, Medinah, military.[38]

On the legal level, there are numerous and oftentimes violent debates as to the possibility of formal recognition of foreign states by Islam. Some non-Muslim writers claim that the countries constituting the "world of war" lack the legal means of truly being subjects of Muslim international law; they could only be the objects thereof, owing to certain humanitarian attitudes. On the contrary, modern Muslim authors believe that Islam – which most definitely did not invent anything new in the realm of international relations – was nevertheless the first coherent legal system to assert the notion of a total acknowledgment of exterior political entities[39] and which, on the basis of a sacred duty, guaranteed rights to foreign peoples in times of war as in times of peace.

Modern terminology is not compatible with the terms of the divine revelation and thus renders any comparative analysis difficult. Since the contemporary international system is founded upon the theoretical concepts of equality and reciprocity, the question arises as to whether these conditions can be fulfilled by traditional Islamic legislation which aims at universality. Muslims reply in the affirmative, arguing that the rule of divine law should most certainly be established throughout the entire world and by any means, especially by peaceful methods[40] since the religion could not be imposed by force.[41] In

---

[38]Massignon, *Parole donnée*, p. 159 which is cited besides in this regard an author less favorable to Islam than Lammens.
[39]Hamidullah, *Muslim Conduct*, p. 68. The problem of establishing diplomatic relations is different, as, for example, the position of Saudi Arabia vis-à-vis the Soviet Union.
[40]al-'Ankabut: 46.
[41]al-Baqarah: 256.

their opinion, the Qur'ānic revelation confirms the principle of nationalities,[42]preaches peace, and demands scrupulous respect of treaties. On the level of doctrine, international law was established so as to define the rights and duties of foreign states since the founders of the system considered the Muslim community as a unique whole.[43] Different forms of mediation, arbitration, and negotiation were recognized and practices systematized.

The manner in which the Prophet and his successors addressed the kings and leaders of non-Muslim peoples shows that they treated them as equals. The minutely elaborate procedure regulating the status of ambassadors and envoys is another expression of this behavior, over and above the immunities and tax exemptions, on the condition that there be reciprocity. It was on an identical basis of reciprocity that an Islamic commercial international law was founded. These premises, selected from among others, constitute convincing arguments, especially if one emphasizes the fact that the myth of the legal equality of states is a recent concept which had not been defined by any of the ancient systems of law. History shows that the Muslim authorities, without renouncing the universality of Islam, were bound by a certain number of specific legal obligations in their dealings with foreign nations. By contrast, it was not until the middle of the nineteenth century that the Ottoman Empire was acknowledged by the West, out of respect for the law of nations, and with several reservations due to the "barbaric humanity" of this empire!

Embassies were already established in the time of the Prophet immediately after the creation of the Islamic community at Medinah. Sometimes their specific aims were to conclude an armistice, peace, or negotiations for the exchange of prisoners. Many of these missions also aimed at inviting the outside world to embrace Islam and could thus have assumed the character of a notification of aggression[44] leading either to an armed conflict or to the signing of a treaty of capitulation. The time span of history, ignorance of the true facts, and the evolution of the minds of men should nevertheless not lead to erroneous conclusions. The enthusiastic energy of the first Muslims and the consequent hostility of the tribes of the Arabian peninsula produced conflicts which could be considered as attempts at "discussion" or as legitimate defense. Of course, one particular Muslim faction, the Kharijites, claimed that force rather than persuasive discussion should be used in order to impose upon nonbelievers the true faith and law capable of routing evil and estab-

---

[42]al-Baqarah: 62 and al-Hujurat: 13.
[43]Hamidullah, *Muslim Conduct*, pp. 72-73.
[44]Khadduri, *War*, p. 245. We specify that the call became a notification of hostilities if the foreigner showed himself hostile to Islam since there is "no compulsion in religion," al-Baqarah: 256.

lishing justice. In this respect, it was not difficult for them to quote Qur'ānic verses taken out of context. The disappearance of this party as a political force and the extinction of the ideas it propagated, at a time when the Muslim state was rapidly expanding and becoming a great military force, prove that Islam opposed fanaticism in its own cradle. At the present time, numerous Muslim authors[45] explain that, in the true spirit of Islam, the basis of relations between Muslims and other peoples is peace. Qur'ānic quotations,[46] legal interpretations, and historical illustrations abound in their writing.

Two examples – one individual, the other collective – may serve to illustrate Islam's "recognition" of foreign political entities: the safeguard guaranteed all foreigners and the procedure regulating the conclusion of treaties.

The original system of protection granted to non-Muslims traveling in Islamic territory openly proves that Islamic doctrine never preached the extermination of nonbelievers. This principle was legally formulated from the time of the revelation itself; its spirit has remained in Islamic political morals. European travelers were highly impressed by this, as is indicated in their reports, particularly in the eighteenth century. The "foreigner" is the nonbeliever. Since he is a member of a country not ruled by Islamic law, and hence of the "world of war," he has a special status. He is not considered as an enemy since, according to the Muslim notion, war is against governments and not against peoples. Even in a period of hostilities between Islam and the territory from which he comes, it is always possible for him and his family to enter, travel, and temporarily reside in the Muslim world without danger or any harrassment. The safeguard granted to him makes him the beneficiary[47] of a recognition of his personality and guarantees the security of his person and property. His treatment is regulated in strict accordance with the Qur'ānic faith or else, should such a case be necessary, according to the clauses of a possible treaty uniting Islam and the individual's country of origin. The judicial basis of this institution is not without a prosyletic spirit: "If one among the pagans ask you for asylum, grant it to him, so that he may hear the word of God; and then escort him to where he can be secure. That

[45]Abu Zahra, *La Conception*; Bêchebichy, *Les relations*; Amir Ali, *The Spirit*; Katirjoglou, *La Sagesse*, for only a limited number of citations.

[46]"If they [the non-Muslim] incline toward peace, incline toward them ..." al-Anfal: 61 (Blachère). Or again: "O you who believe! When you engage yourselves in the cause of God, investigate carefully, and do not say to anyone who offers you a salutation: (you are not a believer!) coveting the goods of the life of this world. The spoils are abundant with God! Not long ago you also were in the same situation, but God conferred on you His favor. Therefore, carefully investigate before you condemn. God is well aware of all that you do," an-Nisa': 94 (Reda).

[47]*Mustamin.*

is because they are men without knowledge."[48] On the level of practice, the rights granted to a foreigner who enjoys the privilege of security depend on the kind of relationship which he has established with the Muslim world – that is, temporary and occasional. Other than the protection of his person and property, he enjoys the right to practice his religion, to remain subordinate to his own national legislation, and to indulge in trade within the confines of the law. He conversely has the duty of respecting the Islamic religion and the person of its Prophet, of not causing public disturbance, and to leave the territory upon the expiration of his permit. Should he violate any laws of conduct – that is, if he commits a penal error, the protection remains valid but does not acquit him of whatever punishment the law has provided. Reciprocally, if he were to be the victim of a Muslim, the latter would be punished by the leader of the community or his representative since the safeguard engages the responsibility of both the community and of all the believers individually.

The formalities according to which the permit is granted are reduced to their simplest expression. If the intention of the nonbeliever is clear, a greeting or even a simple gesture are sufficient. The safety of the foreigner who thus enters into Islamic territory is absolutely guaranteed since the institution draws its force from the divine law. It could not be subject to the ever possible fluctuations in the legislation of man. The foreigner becomes a sanctified guest. If for some imperative reason the safeguard were to be broken, the beneficiary enjoys the absolute right of being re-escorted without violence to the boundaries of the state from which he comes. This institution, considered to be the living expression of Islamic tolerance and sanctified hospitality, is in fact much more. In a certain sense, the right of anybody to offer asylum on behalf of the society as a whole is a sort of individual manifestation against the authority of the leader and against the mystical community bond.[49] It thus illustrates above all else the intrinsic respect which Islam shows for the individual.

Upon expiration of the permit, which cannot exceed a year, the foreigner returns home or else remains in Muslim territories. In such a case, he is permitted to live indefinitely in the "world of Islam," thus becoming a "protected person,"[50] subject to tax, integrated into the community of those whose faith he shares and subordinate to its social laws. By virtue of these terms which

---

[48]at-Taubah: 6 (Abbasi).
[49]One could equally make the opposite deduction, namely that it is a case of an individual manifestation of the collective responsibility, by which the leader himself is obligated to and reinforces the communal mystic tie.
[50]*Dhimmi.*

facilitate the permanent settling of foreigners wishing to leave their country
for one reason or another, the Muslim community soon appeared as a virtual
place of asylum and refuge. From this point of view, it seems obvious first
of all that Islam "grants" rights to individuals coming from foreign countries
and, second, that the prohibition for Muslims to form friendships with Jews
and Christians[51] can be understood only insofar as such a relationship could
threaten the faith of the believer or bring harm to the community. The Qur'ān
in any case clearly indicates this: "O you who believe! Take not for friends
and protectors those who take your religion for a mockery or sport, whether
among those who received the Scripture before you, or among those who reject faith..."[52] Not only do the prophetic traditions show this while history
proves it, but the Qur'ān orders it. The Muslim must in fact be generous toward a foreigner who is not hostile toward him. Thus, fruitful and permanent
ties were established on the levels of both commercial relations and cultural
exchange. Whatever the international situation may have been, the doors of
the Islamic world remained wide open to non-Muslim travelers, refugees, and
merchants.

However, this institution did not only have proselytizing aims. Wishing to
escape isolation and ignorance, the believers drew from the most diverse
sources of knowledge. By soliciting amicable relationships, the Muslims contributed to the development of their community and at the same time brought
about an immense stirring of peoples and ideas. Thus, they contributed to the
rise of a brilliant civilization which developed in subsequent centuries, spreading into three continents. In this context, numerous were those who, right
from the beginnings of Islam, traveled to foreign countries: merchants for
business, scholars seeking documents to translate, travelers in pursuit of their
own pleasure, missionaries to convey the Qur'ānic message, and so on. The
laws to which they still submitted showed that Islam recognizes the validity
of foreign legislatures. Having left the "realm of Islam," Muslims were obliged both by legal doctrine and by their religious ethics to abide by the laws
of the country where they were stationed and to fully observe the conditions
of the permit which they had been granted. Of course, this was the case inasmuch as they would not have to violate the principles of their faith in order
to do so. Moreover, they remained bound by the contracts they had concluded
with the foreigners before leaving Muslim territory.

---

[51]"O you who believe, do not make ties of friendship with the Jews and the Christians. They
are friends, protectors of each other (against you) ..." al-Ma'idah: 51 (Abbasi). The translator
states that this verse was revealed after the year 5 A.H., after the Jews and the Christians had
together shown themselves hostile to Islam.
[52]al-Ma'idah: 57 (Masson).

Of course, the institution of safeguard existed before Islam. At all times, nations have felt the need to maintain nonbelligerent relations with their neighbors. The Muslims, however, were to make this a principle which would be enforced throughout the state, giving it a sacred value, facilitating and extending the field of its application. This development attained such a point that the safeguard is sometimes considered to be an original Islamic institution. Historically, it has played an important role by making temporary though frequent individual contacts between the world of Islam and the outside world. It also allowed for an extensive pacific exchange of people and ideas, techniques and products. Finally, by providing security to foreign envoys on assignment (in the world of Islam), it laid the foundations of diplomatic activities which soon became established between the Islamic state and its neighboring countries.

The treaties provide the second concrete example which illustrates the Islamic practice of international relations. The treaty of Hudaibiyah was the first "interstate" pact which the Muslims concluded with the Makkan aristocracy. It consecrated the birth of the Islamic state under the direction of Muhammad, simultaneously recognizing Islam as the official religion professed by this authority. Henceforth, the community of believers was going to have to define the policy of its relations with the outside world.

The process was identical to that which, at all times and in different parts of the world, brought about the beginnings of international communities. The proximity of different institutions, as well as the necessity of the coexistence of oftentimes hostile societies, create obligations which over time crystallized into legal norms. The motivations behind such a situation may be material interest, ethical considerations, or the fear of retaliation. The principles behind the application of the rules may vary according to political or social evolution, both in the country under consideration and in the neighboring entities, or these principles may vary in accordance with the equality or disparity in military forces and with the evolution of public and private consciousness. It is therefore extremely hazardous to venture historical parallels since comparisons become meaningless when too great a time span separates the facts under consideration. On the other hand, the basic norms which hold the system together are bound to remain, and it is from this point of view that the Muslim political philosophy concerning treaties and conventions should be analyzed.

The quality of a treaty depends on the theoretical concept of international relations, and on the consideration given to the negotiating party, and to the legal terms enforcing respect for these clauses. Islamic legislation distinguishes three types of treaties according to their aim: the peace treaty, the treaty of protection, and the treaty of ransom. The conventions of peace and armistice derive their legality from Qur'ānic terms and attitudes as well as from the prophetic traditions.

There are three conditions of validity binding on the treaties. First of all, the clauses may not violate the precepts of Islam nor may they harm the Muslim community. Second, the terms of the agreement must be formulated concisely and with care and must formally define the rights and duties of the contracting parties.[53] The treaties concluded by the Prophet constituted a kind of example or archetype. Even though their content changed over the course of Muslim history,[54] their form remained perceptibly similar. Finally, the third condition of validity is that the treaty express the perfect accord of the signing parties. Here we have an essential order which proves that the contractual spirit of Islam in no way means the unilateral imposition of Muslim claims over an opposing party. The Qur'ān moreover explicitly accords the "immunity of Allah and His Apostle" to non-Muslims with whom the believers have concluded a treaty. It requires that the Muslims be just toward their partners as long as the latter remain just toward the Muslims.[55]

It is not without value in this context to quote several verses of a single *surah* to show the extent to which the respect of the promise and of signed treaties are sacred in the Qur'ānic teachings:

Fulfill the covenant of God when you have entered into it, and break not your oaths after you have confirmed them; indeed, you have made God your surety for God knows all that you do.

And be not like a woman who breaks into untwisted strands the yarn which she has spun, after it has become strong. Nor take your oaths to practise deception between yourselves, lest one party should be more numerous than another: for God will test you by this; and on the Day of Judgment, He will certainly make clear to you (the truth of) that wherein you disagree.

And take not your oaths to practise deception between yourselves, with the result that someone's foot may slip after it was firmly planted, and you may have to taste the evil (conse-

---

[53]"And take not your oaths to practice deception between yourselves," an-Nahl: 94 (Blachère). See also al-Ahzab: 70.

[54]There is an evolution of the initially essentially religious aspect to the more political considerations after the establishment of the Islamic empire.

[55]at-Taubah: 1, 4, and 7; see also, for example, al-Anfal: 58, or al-Mumtahanah: 8-9.

quences) of having hindered (men) from the path of God, and
a mighty wrath descend on you.

Nor sell the covenant of God for a miserable price: for with God
is (a prize) far better for you, if you only knew."[56]

The opinions of Muslim authors differ over the duration of these treaties'
validity. All of them, according to the jurists, seem to claim that peace should
necessarily assume a temporary nature ranging from two to ten years. This
time limit[57] helped to give credit to the idea that Islam could only view its
relations with the outside world in terms of permanent hostility. One should,
however, take into consideration the fact that first of all, the contracts were
indefinitely renewable and that, second, ten years represented a reasonable
time period at an era of profound change in the Arab world which led to the
formation of new political entities. There is no doubt that Muslim jurists saw
in this limitation an opportunity of extending the domination of Islam; a
means which the political leaders could have exploited if the need arose.
However, even if classical legal doctrine seems to be unanimous on the limitation of the treaties' validity, the Qur'ānic revelation makes no mention of
it, nor the traditions of the Prophet indicate any limitation.[58] It is thus in all
likelihood a question of primarily academic value which has ceased to matter
in the practice of states in our day and age.

On the level of conventional practice, those agreements formally limited in
duration[59] seem less numerous and less important than those of unlimited duration. The second international pact concluded by the Islamic community[60]
was in no way limited, nor were any of the many treaties signed in the course
of history until the official end of the caliphate.[61] Naturally, diplomatic relations gradually developed and concurrently the number of treaties increased.
The two main reasons for this most likely lay in the increasing contacts with
the Christian West and the fragmentation of the Islamic state, which brought
about agreements and alliances determined by political expedience. Such ag-

---

[56]an-Nahl: 91-92, 94-95 (Masson).
[57]This is based on the precedent of Hudaibiyyah.
[58]It should say: "The Byzantines have a sure peace with you, Muslims."
[59]Truce for ten years and ten months accorded by the Mameluke Sultan Baibars, in April 1272,
with the Franks and the crusade detachments of England, besieging Saint-Jean d'Acre for example. See René Brousset, *L'épopée des croisades* (Paris: n.p., 1957), pp. 428-429.
[60]Treaty of Najran.
[61]By way of examples: the Peace of 1180 between Saladin and the leper king of Jerusalem
Baudouin IV, the Treaty of Commerce of 1535 between the Sublime Porte and the king of France, the Treaty of Paris between the Ottoman Empire and the European powers, the adhesion
of the Ottoman Turks to the Conventions of Geneva, and so on.

reements could, however, not have been concluded without time limits if it had been a matter of some formal and basic condition of Qur'ānic law: the validity of a treaty in time has no influence whatsoever on its value.

Over and above the treaties of capitation with the monotheistic peoples contained within the Islamic state, treaties which oblige the Muslim community as a whole but which engage the responsibility of the individual for protected persons, thereby assuming the character of constitutional guarantees, there is yet a third category of agreements which had in mind more specific objectives such as the ransom of prisoners,[62] the establishment of a temporary truce, and the capitulation and evacuation of strongholds. Others aimed at humanitarian objectives such as the evacuation of the wounded and the guarantee of free passage for religious pilgrimage. This type of treaty naturally was of a temporary nature.

The authority to conclude treaties of international status belonged to the Prophet and then to his successors, the caliphs; with regard to treaties of capitation, such contractual authority was given to the imams since these required a profound knowledge of the precepts of the faith.[63] Nevertheless, executive power was often delegated to military commanders in the field or to the imam's representatives. It was only after ratification, however, that they engaged the responsibility of the Muslim community. An agreement which did not correspond to the basic precepts of the religion could be annulled, on the formal condition that the opposing party was notified and that there be a reasonable period of time before the contract finally ceased to be valid.

The obligating power of the treaties is founded upon a religious constraint which guarantees strict observance of the treaty. Any violation would cause a sanction all the more severe since the duty is sacred, deriving from the Muslim conception of the divine message. The foundation of all moral values lies in fact in God's "covenant" with man: the successive revelations and the Qur'ān, descended through Muhammad. Thus, the first virtue of the believer and the community should be to one's promise. The firm intention to fulfil any obligations made, loyalty, and good faith represent the principles underlying Muslim conduct as well as the basis of the state's political philosophy. According to the Qur'ān, God Himself is "faithful to His promises."

Depending on their aims, the treaties could be either permanent with defeated and subjugated peoples, or else temporary military truces, or specific agreements. Their supposedly temporary character seems to be a conclusion

---

[62]The systematization and the development of which were to have important consequences on the formation of the law of modern war.
[63]Bêchebichy, *Les relations*, pp. 39 f.

of classical juridical speculation for there is nothing which formally stipulates it in the Qur'ān. On the contrary, the example of the Prophet shows that the Pact of Medinah, the first international pact of collective security and the first assertion of the principle of religious freedom, had no time limit. Whatever the case may be, the restrictions in doctrine seem to be the result of a twofold consideration. On the one hand, Islam recommends that treaties be concluded with great caution, proportional to the magnitude of the agreement.[64] On the other hand, the reservation is due to the very idea which Islam held of the outside world, as being potentially dangerous and aggressive in essence. According to classical doctrine, to attribute a permanent value to the treaties would be to contradict the basic principle of the opposition between Islam and the "world of war." In fact, the duration of a treaty of undefined duration depends on how loyal the Muslims are to the conditions of the agreement since the believers are required by their religion to adhere scrupulously to the agreement for as long as their contractual partner does the same. However, if one admits that neither the bipolar division of the world nor the constant hostility between ideological systems is more than a historical or factual statement and in no way a legal justification, then the notion of the precarious nature of treaties collapses because of its lack of notion support. We should finally point out that Islam most probably gave a new dimension to the concept of compulsory respect for treaties by making the terms of such treaties legally binding on a truly religious basis. Since God is in effect considered as a third party in the agreement,[65] any violation, whether individual or collective, implies the distortion of an obligation contracted toward Him.

Islam, hardly less than any other religion or ideological system, has naturally known violence and war. Its political expansion was also to a certain extent achieved by the sword. Man – and not the faith – was the main culprit. Islam should be the religion of justice and compassion.[66] However, this compassion is of a particular nature and is distinct from the principles of Western ethics impregnated by Christianity. Muslim compassion is as much individual as it is collective: it is active rather than passive. It is a communal thing since it not only appears as mercy or charity toward one single individual but is equally expressed in favor of society and particularly toward those who are just. It is active because it allows the use of force to establish fraternity and

---

[64]One could, moreover, make a case here of the fact that modern international law also advances restrictions, through the clause "rebus sic stantibus." Besides, it would be easy to speak ironically on the sort of "perpetual" treaties or alliances which recent history has known.

[65]"Remain loyal to the covenant of God when you have entered into it! Do not violate the oaths after you have solemnly confirmed them and have taken Allah as a guarantor against you!" an-Nahl: 91 (Blachère).

[66]"We sent you [Prophet] only as a [sign of] mercy for the world," al-Anbiyya': 107 (Blachère).

mutual concord, to do away with evil and to curb injustice. Under its Muslim meaning, virtue is above all engaged and dynamic, having both direction and compulsion.

Effort

The traditional Western prejudice which portrays Islam as a belligerent religion gave rise to a derogatory and permanent definition of the Muslim "holy war." The term leads us to believe that Muslims are supposedly encouraged to take up arms in order to impose the faith by force, annihilating those who reject it.[67] The generic term of *jihad* means "effort," perhaps a violent one, but in no way specifically a military one. Still, in the noninformed public opinion in the West, it seems to have retained only its meaning of war. It is true that this can be explained by psychological and historical reasons. Furthermore, a certain tendency toward demagogy has incited certain contemporary Muslim political leaders to make reference to the "holy war" in its exclusively military meaning, precisely in order to hide their intellectual and administrative bankruptcy.

The exact meaning of *jihad* cannot be explained unless it is put back into the context of Islam as well as into the Islamic philosophy of international relations. The "holy war" is in effect that instrument which, if needs be, must impose the reign of Islam – in other words, peace and justice under the protection of the revealed law – upon a recalcitrant and aggressive "world of war." The Muslim community, in submission to the revealed divine law, is necessarily hostile toward error and injustice. This firm opposition must be concretely manifested in terms of varying efforts, determined and conditioned by the nature of the unbalance to be corrected: personal struggle against one's inner erroneous tendencies; moral combat for the respect of Qur'ānic orders; effort made to spread the religion through a pacific missionary calling[68]; armed aggression in a just war, in the "path of Allah"[69] so as to protect the community and to free isolated believers from persecution. Under such conditions, the "holy war" is in reality an instrument used to impose the "world of Islam," understood as harmony, order and peace, which are both spiritual and material, individual and collective. Yet, this "war" does not have the aim of imposing the religion by force. On the contrary, it demands of the believers that they overcome their inner passions. The "passionate ardor for the

---

[67]See, in particular, Lammens, *L'Islam*, pp. 82 f., as well as Khadduri, *War*, where the idea is even more nuanced.

[68]"... but strive against them [the unbelievers] with the utmost strenuousness, with the Qur'ān," al-Furqān: 52 (Blachère).

[69]al-Baqarah: 190.

cause of Allah"[70] should be no more than the effort to live according to His law and the struggle to have His justice reign.

The effort – a violent one if needs be – to impose order and equity[71] is considered by Islamic legislation to be a fundamental duty. As an obligation of solidarity, as opposed to the "Five Pillars of the Faith" considered to be personal duties, it is seen as one of the principal duties of the community's leader. This collective character corresponds to the religious definition of the Muslim community which "orders good and forbids evil," as well as to its political conception of international relations. On the individual level, the believer is engaged in a permanent "holy war," attempting to check his self-centeredness and follow the prescriptions of the divine revelation. This is a spiritual obligation between him and God. The duty of holy war becomes personal, crystalized on a physical and material plain, when the imam calls upon the believers for the defense of Islam. Only in this perspective does the specifically military aspect of *jihad* appear.

Muslim jurists distinguish four types of "holy war": the war waged by the heart, the tongue, the hand, and the sword.[72] The first of these, the "war of the heart," is the internal spiritual and moral struggle which should lead to man's victory over his ego. This is the most important, the most necessary, and the most meritorious. The "war of the tongue" or of gesture is the effort of calm preaching and of setting edifying moral examples for non-Muslims. Within the society it commits the believer to intervene and struggle in an effort to correct error and enforce good conduct. It contributes to collective stability and moral solidarity. Finally, the "*jihad* of the sword" corresponds exactly to armed conflict with the enemies of the Islamic community and foreign leaders who either persecute the believers or restrict the freedom of conscience of their subjects. It results from the rejection of oppression and from the dynamic conception of justice and mercy.

Muslim doctrine established a hierarchic ordering of values. In effect, the most meritorious *jihad* is the one which we "wage against ourselves," according to the prophetic traditions.[73] This personal effort made to overcome the

---

[70]For the use of the formulation, see ibn-Khaldoun, *Les textes sociologiques et économiques de la Mouqaddima*, translated and annotated by Georges H. Bousquet (Paris: Rivière, 1965), pp. 69 f. After this: ibn-Khaldoun, *Mouqaddima*.

[71]This is the essential theme of the sura entitled *at-Taubah*.

[72]Khadduri, *War*, pp. 56-57.

[73]The Prophet, returning from a military expedition against some neighboring enemies, moreover declared: "We are returning from the small holy war to the grand holy war."

self is considered to be "the greatest holy war."[74] Thus, an armed holy war is relatively secondary, representing no more than the most concrete manifestation of effort. Yet, it is only this expression of the *jihad* which has ever stuck the Western mind. It is also the only form which discretely enters into the context of the present discussion.

In the limited area of the armed holy war, Muslims not only have the right but the duty to engage defensively in hostilities of six different types: against the enemies of God, for the defense of frontiers,[75] against apostates, and against secessionists,[76] against groups who disturb public security, and against monotheists who refuse to pay the capitation tax. We shall briefly discuss each category.[77]

The enemies of God are those who threaten the existence of the Islamic community, those who persecute Muslims and, finally, polytheists. Islam and polytheism, which stands as the enemy of Muslims, cannot coexist. Pagans have to chose between faith or the sword. In reality, however, history has shown that, beside the Jews and the Christians, Islam has tolerated the presence of many other religious communities which have claimed to have a "book," when these fell under its domination and later when the Muslim troops reached the Ganges. Open, armed aggression against the polytheists ultimately seems to have been directed toward the hostility of narrow and barbaric paganism having no conception of a superior divinity. In practice, it was limited to the pagans of the Arabian Peninsula at the time of the Prophet.

The guarding of frontiers is a "holy war" by definition since its aim is to protect the Muslim community and to drive back enemy attacks. This particular form was of importance during the European counteroffensive.

Holy war against collective apostasy appears primarily as a scholastic, juridical exercise. Only one major historical example is known to us: the effort of a "prophet," Musailimah, immediately after the death of Muhammad, to gain the support of some of the recently Islamized tribes. Abu Bakr, the first successor, reestablished the unity of the peninsula. Collective apostasy is in fact secession. Muslim jurists agree in thinking that the treatment of the conquered should be of the severest type because they rejected the religion. The leader of the community, the imam, may call a *jihad* against groups of dissident believers. This is one of the most difficult and controversial aspects of Islamic doctrine. Islam asserts the believers' right on the basis of justice.

---

[74] *al-Jihad al-Akbar.*
[75] *Ribat.*
[76] *Baghi.*
[77] We are inspired in this above all by Khadduri, *War,* pp. 74 f.

Individuals who are victims of injustice arising out of real or imagined nonapplication of the Qur'ānic law enjoy the right to revolt. Moreover, the Qur'ān recommends that the Muslims remain a unified community. Violent contestations or dissidence should be checked. Between disorder and injustice, it appears that the doctrine gradually gravitated toward the second type of alternative. On a practical level, history shows that the Muslim armies were far more occupied with waging internal wars than with hostilities against the outside. Ultimately, it was the war of the conqueror which was "holy!"

The *jihad* against deserters and highway robbers corresponds to the traditional role assigned to armed forces of ensuring public security and internal law and order.

The holy war against monotheists is an awkward matter to describe since the image which was left of this institution, by history to a certain extent and by legal doctrine to a large extent, does not exactly coincide with the spirit of the Islamic revelation. Theoretically, the "People of the Book" who showed hostility toward Islam and the Muslims would have a choice of the following alternatives: faith, capitation tax, or war. This triple option is understandable only in reference to the basic Muslim conception of war and only by distinguishing between the individual and society. In reality, war is not waged against peoples but against states. At this level, Islam demands from authorities the possibility of openly spreading its religious message as well as freedom of conscience for such citizens who may wish to become Muslims. A refusal would lead to war. On the individual level, once military force has been imposed, Islam offers the option of adhering to the faith on payment of a personal and not a collective tax. Thus the ultimatum has to be made in this twofold perspective. If this is not the case, the war would be neither holy nor just since the Qru'ān itself formally forbids aggression and explicitly prohibits compulsion in religious matters.

Apart from the preceding conjectures, violence is forbidden and war is unjust. All believers participate in the "holy war," virtuous women and children included. On the other hand, only mature males who are independent and in good health participate in its military manifestation. Beyond loyalty and obedience toward his leader, the combatant must be motivated by good intentions. In this way he participates in a double holy war: on the battlefield where he presents himself in order to defend the cause of the religion and not in search of booty, and in the second coinciding form of *jihad* in his heart where he checks anger and greed so as to fight against his enemies with clemency and honesty.

Thus, in its widest sense, "holy war" does not mean active hostilities, even though antagonism between the Muslim community and the "world of war" is supposed to be permanent. If it assumes the form of active combat, the *jihad* would necessarily have to be a just war in its cause, its aim and in the manner in which it is waged. In the Qur'ān and prophetic tradition the references to the "holy war" in its broader meaning of effort are numerous. Classical Muslim literature does not cease to praise its merits. On the particular level of hostilities as such, the obligation is collective if Islam initiates the attack while individual if Muslim troops are engaged in the defense of the community. Holy war, therefore, can be both offensive and defensive.[78] When it is of a defensive nature, it presents no doctrinal problems since it corresponds to the essential right of self-preservation.

On the other hand, the aggressive *jihad* has been the subject of judicial and religious controversy, for neither the Qur'ān nor the prophetic tradition appear to prescribe it in any precise manner. Classical authors who wished to reconcile their points of view with the terms of the sacred law imagined a progressive succession of divine commandments. At first, patience and forgiveness were recommended to the Muslims after which they were allowed to fight against the aggressors. Then, in a third phase, the community was granted permission to initiate the combat at certain times of the year and, finally, to wage war without restrictions of time or place.[79] Even as an offensive operation, the "holy war" is supposed to remain a sanction against those who disobey God, opposing the establishment of the revealed law. To combat nonbelievers who prevent their fellows from embracing and following the paths of God became a meritorious virtue. This point of view qualifies the adjective "offensive."

Open hostility, as hostility in action, though it may be undeclared, makes it legitimate to use all means necessary for the defense of Islam. It is possible to imagine that the aim of the "holy war" is expressed in an alternate and opposing manner. In fact, does it aim more to subjugate than to convert the nonbelievers? Subjugating them should subsequently allow the population of conquered territories to freely choose the Islamic faith. The war would then be a sanction against governments which prevented the population from professing Islam. If, on the other hand, the main objective of violence was religious conversion, the holy war would then be punishment of nonbelief itself. Though this be a fundamental principle, the opinions of classical authors are divergent.[80] At the present time, the point of view of Muslim specialists is

---

[78]ibn-Taimiyyah, *On Public and Private Law*, pp. 135 f.

[79]Ghoneimi, *The Muslim Conception*, pp. 140 f.

[80]Abu Hanifah leans toward the first solution by fixing as a definition of the criteria of "domain of war" the security which the believers enjoy, whereas ash-Shafi'i advances the second idea which evidently gives a more aggressive aspect to the Islamic theory of international relations.

ialists is unanimous. On the one hand, it is not for man but for God alone to judge and punish disbelief. On the other hand, the theory of international relations could not be based on anything but Qur'ānic principles. Since compulsion in religious matters is formally forbidden, the aim of the war of force can therefore not be the conversion of non-Muslims.

When looking back at the events of the remote past, one can largely succeed in understanding how the usage of the "holy war" became distorted in Christian public opinion and also perhaps in the Islamic consciousness. By sacrificing himself for the defense of the religion and the cause of God, the believer was making the greatest and ultimate profession of his faith. He, the martyr, was promised the bliss of paradise. This religious zeal of the warriors doubtlessly stands as one of the reasons for the rapid geographical and political expansion of Islam. This, however, had never been one of the primary objectives of the holy war. Islam in no way seeks political dominion of the world or submission to the faith[81] but, on the contrary, condemns destruction and unnecessary violence. Since it aims at the harmony of the world and peace among men, it authorizes resorting to force in order to right evil and to curb iniquity. The prime objective of violence is not war as such, nor territorial expansion of the community, nor even religious proselytism, but the establishment of peace in justice.

The explanation for the rapidity of Islamic expansion can be found in political science. Conquests followed the traditional paths of migration and may be analyzed just like any historical phenomenon. The great strength of the warriors' faith provided them with a zeal and spirit which most certainly directly influenced their military victories and, indirectly, the subsequent Islamization of the conquered peoples. Thus, religion seems to have played no more than a purely psychological role in the conquest. The deformation of ideas can be explained by the coincidence of the two phenomena. However, the aggression and violence shown by the Muslim troops at times had no direct connection with the religious doctrine. One can gain some idea of the pure spirit of Islam by considering the manner in which the Prophet and his first successors treated the civil populations subjected to their rule in newly conquered territories. They were highly aware of the fact that they had no right other than the application of justice. Subsequently, however, if the political domination of the Muslim empire was spread mainly by arms, the Islamic faith was essentially spread by pacific ways. The fact that certain later Muslim leaders violated basic Qur'ānic rules in no way diminishes *jihad*'s divine and eternal value. This statement could seem incongruous in appearance,

---

[81]"If Allah would have willed, He would have made you one community," an-Nahl: 93 (Blachère).

especially since Muslim law – which is normative and idealized – is not the result of a codification of existing practices. It nevertheless shows that one should practice great caution in analyzing historical facts and events which contradict the Qur'ānic revelation.

There are two mental attitudes – the one objective and the other subjective – which deserve mention, for they also contributed to the degradation of the concept of the "holy war." Islam had hardly attained stability when it appeared as the torch of civilization, being permeated with basic Qur'ānic moral principles and benefiting from the refined culture of certain conquered peoples. The believers were most probably tempted to transmit their ideology to the neighboring populations crushed by the despotic feudal system and oppressed by the tyranny of ecclesiastic hierarchies. History repeats itself. The example of aggression undertaken in order to "liberate" peoples from injustice and servitude is not unique! Moreover, the fact that the Qur'ān forbids aggression as well as opening hostilities without valid reasons was to encourage Muslim leaders to enumerate the reasons for the just war which they were waging. The procedure soon gave the conflicts the character of reciprocity. The religious element of the Muslim holy war asserted itself especially during the European counterattacks of the tenth and eleventh centuries which hid behind Christianity to reconquer Spain and brandished the sword so as to reclaim the holy places of Palestine. For both Christianity and Islam, respect for religion served as a pretext and motivation for a war of conquest.

As a result of the confrontation between Christianity and Islam, there remained only a somewhat truncated version of the concept of holy war, retaining only a specifically military characteristic. In the West, as much as in the Muslim world (if not more so), political and religious matters were inextricably linked at that time. The Christian in those days sought his salvation in his struggle against the Muslim. Even before the sword of the Crusades, the sovereign-pontiff Alexander II in 1063 granted the absolution of sins to believers fighting to expel the Muslims from the Iberian Peninsula. Islam, like Christianity, offered eternal salvation for all soldiers who fell in the "holy war." It is possible to establish certain illustrative similarities between the two religions as a result of their first great political confrontation from the eleventh century in spite of the tragic, bloody events which took place all over, as well as of the periods of understanding and near-fraternity which existed for some time.

On the individual level, the crusader set out to massacre the nonbeliever upon the oftentimes repeated call of Urbain II: "God wills it." As to the Muslim warrior, his was the moral obligation of being motivated by good intentions and to be in a state of "greater holy war," – that is, of restraining his anger and passion in order to treat his enemy magnanimously. Moreover, Islam had an institutional safeguard for the monotheistic minorities which had come under its political control. In general, these minorities suffered no particular persecution. On the other hand, the Spanish "Reconquest" ended in none other than the expulsion of the last "Moriscos" from the Iberian Peninsula. They were largely autochthons descended from converts.

In Palestine, the crusader kings rallied the Christians of the Levant into one state, without attempting to organize a special institution for the Muslim minorities nor even giving any thought to a true coexistence. Finally, on the judicial level, the Qur'ān safeguards the clergy,[82] declaring that God protects non-Muslim places of worship: "Did not God check one set of people by means of another, there would surely have been pulled down monasteries, churches, synagogues, and mosques, in which the name of God is commemorated in abundant measure."[83] This prohibition is corroborated and elucidated by the prophetic tradition which forbids soldiers to do harm to any religious persons, whereas they could logically have been the primary targets if the motive of the "holy war" had been religious. Without putting Western civilization on trial, we should nevertheless mention by way of contrast that several centuries later, the founders of international law in Europe excluded the Muslim "infidels" from the benefits of the law of wars. Yet, the concept of "holy war" remains branded as the expression of the Muslims' religious fanaticism. How ineradicable are the prejudices!

Islam is the return to primordial unity. All effort, violence, and war are necessary to combat those who, by opposing divine plans, are hostile to justice and peace. The enemy is disorder, disharmony, and evil in all its forms. Man carries these elements in himself; they are all his tendencies and temptations which oppose his personal unity. By becoming interiorized, the holy war sought to encourage the Muslim to wage a constant battle against himself, against the inertia and distortions of his cultural and social milieu, thereby preparing himself for "the task of material, intellectual, and moral regeneration which justifies the efficient demand for a better earthly existence"[84] for him, his community, and all of mankind. Through his personal struggle, the believer declares his quality of manhood and, by simultaneously taming his selfishness and restraining his passions, he asserts the rights and duties of all individuals living in a society governed by order and righteousness.

The holy war is permanent, without interruption or end. The Muslims are convinced of this. The Qur'ān explicitly indicates it: "And strive in His cause as you ought to strive (with sincerity and under discipline). He has chosen

---

[82]al-Baqarah: 191.
[83]al-Hajj: 40 (Masson).
[84]Abdel Jalil, *Aspects*, p. 75.

you...It is He Who has named you Muslims."[85] Good is in constant conflict with evil; such is the will of God. The world of Islam, understood as the reign of unity and equilibrium, is in constant confrontation with the world of war which is considered as disorder and excess. The believer is obliged to take part in the *jihad*, both in its inner moral expression as in its concrete, visceral manifestation. The specifically military aspect of the "holy war" is, however, secondary and intermittent. The paths leading to the total Islamization of the world are numerous. They do not stem from the wish of the believers but rather from the divine will.[86] In all eternity, there is only one true reality: the existence of God alone. The Qur'ān does not bring a new message to humanity. It affirms itself as the continuation and culminating fruit of the monotheistic revelation. All men are free to embrace the faith; the believer would be lacking in humility and would consequently be disobeying God if he attempted to impose his faith by force. If his convictions make him pugnacious, his respect for the law restrains his zeal. Thus, the holy war is "surpassed and transfigured by peace in God, by consciousness of the absolute."[87]

The notion of holy war is always topical in Islam. The Prophet after all said: "*Jihad* will last until the Day of Judgment." This is obvious, for in human society there will always be progress to be made, injustice to combat, and oppression to abolish. If the contemporary Muslim world participates – albeit in scattered groups – in the life of international society, one should not see this only as a reconciliation between the "Dar al-Islam" and the "Dar al-Harb."[88] Good and evil cannot be reconciled; order and injustice cannot coexist. On the contrary, it could be first and foremost a case of a certain transformation in the "world of war." In reality, the Islamic states as such are no longer threatened because of their religious doctrine, and all things considered, rare indeed are those Muslims who are persecuted because they proclaim "Our Lord is Allah." The military expression of the holy war would thus no longer have any reason to exist. The *jihad* of the heart, tongue, and hand remain necessary for the preservation of Islam's humanitarian values, and are indispensable for the task of the social and economic development of the Muslim world. The allegory of armed effort, magnified by Muslim literature, will most certainly persist but will be taken in its strictly literal sense. As a matter of fact, the sword "above all symbolizes the power of the word, a thing which should moreover be rather self-evident, especially since it is one of the meanings generally attributed to the sword, and which is not

[85]al-Hajj: 78 (Masson).
[86]Yunus: 99-100 and al-Kahf: 29.
[87]Schuon, *Comprendre*, p. 69.
[88]As well as Khadduri's claim in the epilogue to *War*, pp. 268 f.

foreign to Christianity either."[89]

Violence

Violence is permanent and inevitable. All kinds of antagonism have increasingly torn the world apart ever since God created man. Islam's sociological doctrine[90] sees several reasons for this. It resides as much in human nature – the tendency toward aggression, love of power and fortune, jealousy and rivalry of interests – as in the makeup of society: contestation and defense of central authority. Nevertheless, truth must triumph over error, good must vanquish evil, and justice crush injustice. Antagonism between individuals, groups, and nations is unavoidable: "If your Lord had so willed, He could have made mankind one people: but they will not cease to dispute."[91] God explicitly indicates that human beings "are enemies to each other."[92] Here, it is interesting to be reminded of the fact that, if the fall of Adam bore no consequences for the intrinsic nature of man, it did have a consequence for the mechanism of social relations. War not only represents an inevitability but also a fundamental necessity for the harmonization of the world, by means of mutually neutralizing men.[93]

More than being legalistic in essence, Islam is a revelation which resolutely comprehends the objectivity of facts. The believer is "passive" if he is open to and in submission to the divine decree, but he is consequently called to resist evil – even by violence – so as to participate in upholding the true foundation of humanity: justice. The passive charity which Christian doctrine recommends to one who has been slapped on the cheek shocks Muslim reasoning, which considers it unrealistic and illogical because it is unnatural. The enemy is essentially he who practices evil and enforces injustice. He is, for the same reason, the enemy of God and His law. He cannot reasonably expect true "love" from the believer. The latter is moreover not permitted to "love" an enemy who hates God.[94]

This dynamism of faith, upheld by the conviction of possessing the revealed truth, has left a permanent mark on the Muslim's conception of human

---

[89]See, for instance, Guénon, "Sayful-Islam," who recalls in this regard, more specifically on p. 59, that Christ himself had declared: "I have not come to you bearing peace but the sword," Matthew 10:34.

[90]See, in particular, ibn-Khaldoun, *Mouqaddima*.

[91]Hūd: 118 (Blachère).

[92]al-A'raf: 24.

[93]"... If God did not check one set of people by another, the earth would indeed be full of mischief. But God is full of bounty to all the worlds," al-Baqarah: 251 (Masson).

[94]Galwash, *The Religion*, pp. 108 f.

relations and has equally determined, to a very large extent, the rules of war. Pointless mercy or passive compassion shown to an evil man represents an injustice with regard to the community, a threat to its security, and an infringement on divine will. It is thus that Islam "strikes us with the unbending nature of its convictions and also by the pugnacity of its faith; these two complementing aspects, the one interior and static, the other external and dynamic, essentially stem from a consciousness of the absolute which, on the one hand, makes us impervious to doubt and, on the other, rejects error with violence."[95]

History shows us that no divine or ideological revelation claiming to regulate earthly matters has been able to express itself in an entirely pacific manner since it had to assert itself against the violent reaction of the sociological milieu which it aimed to reform. Urged on by their divine mission, God's various prophets had to resort to violence which legitimized war, simultaneously giving it a character of legitimate defense. The very manner in which they conducted their battles provides an illustrative example of the way man has to struggle in order to let good triumph.[96]

From these examples, and in particular from that of the Prophet Muhammad, we can distinguish three specific characteristics which gives us a better grasp of the Muslim understanding of foreign relations. These three elements – piety, pugnacity, and magnanimity[97] – could at first appear contradictory. In the Islamic perspective they are complementary. Piety is submission to God and unshakable attachment to His law. The combative spirit resides in love of justice, respect for the truth, and a "passionate zeal for the cause of God." Finally, magnanimity, which is not devoid of a certain implacability toward traitors, is a reminder of divine mercy toward man. If nonbelief appears essentially as injustice, the revelation is a mercy and faith a grace.

Thus, it is beyond doubt that in Islam there exists a doctrinal element which is eminently combative and a historical tradition of war. However, violence, taken in its broader meaning, is a legitimate function of justice. "Be it a question of exterior and social order or internal and spiritual order, war should always make an equal attempt at establishing harmony and stability...This is the same as saying that its normal resolution – which is definitely its only justification – is peace."[98] Thus, we find a definition of the *jihad* in the sense implied in the Muslim tradition. Islam not only preached toler-

---

[95]Schuon, *Comprendre*, p. 49.
[96]Abu Zahra, *La conception*, p. 13 f.
[97]Schuon, *Comprendre*, pp. 177-118.
[98]Guenon, "Sayful-Islam," p. 59.

ance but gave it the force of law.[99] Proselytism, no matter how zealous and sincere it may be, could not effectively be implemented by force since it would contradict divine plans, being an expression of human arrogance.

The verse forbidding compulsion in religious matters seems to have been revealed in Medinah, at the very moment when the Muslim community had been strongly structured and no longer needed to fear its direct enemies[100] since it had become the main military force of the Arabian Peninsula. This chronological precision assumes a certain importance since it explains and justifies *a priori* certain reactions of the Islamic community. The prohibition of religious compulsion not only protects nonbelievers from excessive proselytic zeal on the part of the Muslims but, more importantly, it also attempts to counteract any compulsion or persecution which would affect certain loyal subjects – potential believers – whether isolated or within Muslim community. It is also in this sense that the divine injunction should be understood. The Muslim community placed its power at the service of those of its adherents who suffered because of their faith.

Being fundamentally realistic, the Qur'ānic revelation admits violence and legalizes war. However, battle is permitted only to check injustice. The permission to engage in armed combat has explicit motives and is immediately limited. War must necessarily be declared as a form of self-protection or legitimate defense; hostilities must be waged with decency and according to divine ways. Aggression and the initiation of combat without any valid reasons are forbidden: "Fight in the cause of God those who fight you, but do not transgress limits, for God loves not transgressors."[101] Violence is answered by violence, injustice by force.

Other than the defense of the community, injustice and persecution are also valid reasons for authorizing war: "To those against whom war is made, permission is given [to fight] because they are wronged; and verily, God is most powerful for their aid; [they are] those who have been expelled from their homes in defiance of right [for no cause] except that they say, 'Our Lord is God.'"[102] The oppression or exile to which isolated believers in minority groups living outside the Muslim world often fall victim represents a "casus belli" through a sociological or communal assimilation which can be easily understood if one refers to the Muslim conception of the "collective man."

---

[99]"There is no compulsion in religion! The true way distinguishes itself from error," al-Baqarah: 256 (Masson).
[100]Bêchebichy, *Les relations*, p. 18.
[101]al-Baqarah: 190 (Blachère) as well as al-Baqarah: 194.
[102]al-Hajj: 39-40. (Reda).

The formulation of permission itself is full of reservations inasmuch as it poses conditions which are difficult to express. Legal permission can become a moral obligation for the community and for the believers individually, if the facts appear clear and evident. In effect, they may not refrain from intervening in order to put an end to injustice and to reestablish order according to divine plans. This is even more so in the case of persecution of a believer: "And turn them out from where they have turned you out, for tumult and oppression are worse than slaughter."[103] Islam stands to defend not only the Muslims but also persecuted Jews and Christians. This kind of armed intervention characteristically corresponds to what nineteenth-century European international law meant by "humanitarian intervention." This is a literal case of the assertion of basic human rights: security, guarantee of man's person and property, respect for freedom of thought. Islam's military power was the background and guarantee of this assertion.

Ligitimate causes of war are the defense of the community and protection of the oppressed on a general level. The doctrine more precisely defined the various motives which entrusted believers with the authority to take up arms: to safeguard the Muslim faith; to defend, maintain, and consolidate the Islamic community; to counter any plots which seek to turn the believers away from their religion; to guard what is recognized by divine and human laws; to protect one's own person; to right an injustice committed toward one's brothers in religion as well as to monotheists who have paid their capitation taxes. However, man's natural tendencies toward violence, his greed for domination, desire for revenge, material motivation or tendencies of pillage are all considered as malevolent and iniquitous causes. In short, aggression is forbidden.

In practice, the concept of "aggression" is eminently subjective and difficult to define. It would perhaps be useful to give it a psychological meaning: the provocation or triggering of hostilities which aim at dominating or at imposing a certain concept of the world or to steal land and possessions. Inasmuch as it can be defined, the intention plays a determining role. Sometimes it is brash and sometimes discrete, good or bad. It may conceal legitimate aspirations or, on the contrary, acts of violence. Nonetheless, the Qur'ānic prohibition is precise and absolute, having a bearing on all possibilities, since it is not only legal but also religious. Neither the believer nor the community can hide their true intentions or their intimate desires from God Who "knows and hears all."

---

[103]al-Baqarah: 191 (Blachère). This verse permits, in other respects, a better understanding of certain human and psychological aspects of the conflict which since 1948 has torn the Arab and Islamic Middle East.

Islamic literature takes pleasure in recalling and explaining the decisions Prophet Muhammad made when he was leading the growing Muslim community. It is not important whether or not the traditions which are reported seem exaggerated or even fictitious to *certain* critics. The fact that they vividly influence the contemporary Muslim conscience represents the "furtive anticipation of an ideal order"[104] which, when projected, illustrates the conviction of the believers and becomes part of a vision for the future. It would probably not be superfluous to devote some attention to it.

Necessity soon forced the Prophet to organize an army to repel enemy attacks and to dispatch preventive expeditions against hostile neighbors. A man of integrity, a fine politician and brilliant strategist, Muhammad felt the need to "dissuade" the enemies of his community. He had to counter attacks of pillage; he had to ensure peace and tranquility on the caravan routes. Finally, in the context of tribal wars which were tearing the Arabian Peninsula apart at that time, armed forces proved to be of vital necessity in order not to encourage "the enemies of Islam or to endanger the very existence of the state, which was in the first stages of its evolution."[105] Thus the battles, even those initiated by the Prophet, assumed the character of a response to provocation or that of self-protective measures.

The argument is likely. Threatened by the Makkans who feared for the unity and supremacy of their city, by the Jews who refused to see in Muhammad the prophet foretold and who were struggling to preserve the economic importance they enjoyed in Medinah, denigrated by the Christians who raised their cries of impostor, and challenged from the inside by certain inhabitants of Medinah (accused of being "hypocrites" by the Qur'ān), the developing community truly seemed to be in danger. The opposition of established neighboring societies was violent toward both the Islamic community and converts, isolated Muslims who, by their adhering to the faith, had broken the ties of tribal solidarity and protection. These historical considerations and sociological conclusions justify those arguments claiming that the Prophet was obliged to use arms for legitimate defense.

For Muslim literature, the battles fought by the Prophet illustrate the particular nature of Islamic war: it is just in its causes, defensive in its initiative, decent in its proceedings, pacific in its end, and humanitarian in its treatment of the conquered enemy. The manner in which Muhammad waged battles is

---

[104]Abdallah Laroui, *L'idéologie arabe contemporaine* (Paris: Maspero, 1967), p. 103. After this: Laroui, *L'idéologie arabe.*
[105]Esade F. Tugay, *Mahomet, le Prophète d'Allah* (Cairo: Eastern Press, 1951), p. 276. After this: Tugay, *Mahomet.*

of primary juridical importance and still theoretically valid in our time. Recourse to violence is dependent on and made legitimate by the adversary's attitude. The immense magnanimity shown by the Prophet ought to prove that even the battles which he initiated were of a preventive character. The prophetic traditions show this clearly. For example, even before besieging Makkah, when it was yet uncertain as to whether weapons would be issued, upon hearing one of his army leaders singing "today is the day when blood will flow, we will have no pity," Muhammad snatched the banner indicating his military authority from his hands. He then gave it to another soldier well-known for his peace-loving nature, expressly ordering the troops not to revert to arms unless they were attacked.

The expulsion of the Jewish tribes of Medinah, an often-mentioned fact, illustrates the sometimes implacable nature of Muhammad. For Muslim authors this was an indispensable act of legitimate defense. By reconstructing the facts such as Islamic sources tell them to us, we can explain the violent nature of the measure taken with regard to the Jews. Their dogmatic hostility was vehement and bitingly sarcastic. Their great economic importance as well as their cultural superiority over the Medinans gave them considerable influence. Muhammad, who at first offered them the possibility of assimilating themselves into the community of believers as an autonomous entity, was very soon obliged to abandon the hope of converting them or of making reliable allies of them. Ever ready to plot and join forces with the enemies of the Muslims, they were all the more fearsome in that they possessed fortified positions right within the Islamic territory. Faced with the "insolubility" of Judaism,[106] and for the very safety of the community, Muhammad decided to eliminate this force.

Two of the three tribes accused of high treason were expelled and permitted to take their personal estate with them: the one (Bani Nadhir) for having attempted to murder the Prophet; the other (Bani Qainuqa') for having spied for the enemy. As for the third tribe (Bani Qureiza), they had broken an agreement made with the Muslims by trying to rally the neighboring tribes with a view to making a communal attack on Medinah which was besieged at that time. For two weeks the Muslims besieged their fortress, forcing them to surrender. The men were court-martialed while the women and children were put into slavery. On the level of dogma and jurisdiction, the elimination of the Jewish tribes does not in the Muslim doctrine have any particular importance since this was a question of legitimate defense; treason is moreover punish-

---

[106]Edmond Rabbath, "Pour une théorie du droit international musulman," *Egyptian Journal of International Law* (1950):13. After this: Rabbath, "Pour une théorie."

able by death in all known systems of law. Furthermore, the tragic massacre of the men of the Bani Qureiza was not a sanction of the Islamic canon. In actual fact, the Jews under attack requested that an old Arab, known for his wisdom and justice, decide their fate in accordance with Hebrew law. It was the application of the Jewish law which led to the inhuman harshness of this decision.[107]

There is no real need to quote any further examples of the Prophet's behavior, even though they abound in the prophetic tradition. On the other hand, two particular aspects of the doctrine which are of a certain topical importance should be mentioned: the claim to protect isolated believers in the "world of war" and the theoretical attitude toward "internal wars."

It is on the level of protecting isolated believers that the defensive value of Muslim violence is both the most logical and debatable. The argument of intervention for the protection of persecuted Muslim minorities can at first seem to permit all sorts of excesses in practice. We need only to remember the specifically Muslim conception of "collective man" according to which all believers, subject to the divine law, are grouped into one homogenous entity. Oppression imposed upon any one of them represents an attack against the entire community. Furthermore, on a sociological level, the great initial "revolution" of Islam aimed at replacing tribal or blood relations and loyalties in Arabia with a religious bond. By embracing Islam, the individual once again excluded himself from established society, voluntarily placing himself "out of the law." Since he was thus "detribalized," he no longer enjoyed any protection and ran the risk of becoming the victim of the worst arbitrariness, no longer having the preventive guarantee of blood revenge.

The Islamic community had to immediately assert itself as the protector of the Muslims. The assertion of its power and of its protective role assumed a growing importance with the adherence or support of an increasing number of individuals. By extension, attacks on the community were not only intended as persecution of isolated believers but also as a prohibition for individuals to embrace Islam if they so wished. It is in this context that the proselytizing aspect of the religion appears, and it is here that the verse forbidding religious compulsion assumes its fullest meaning. It is indeed "important for one who preaches a sublime cause aiming at defending faith and individual freedom, that mankind be aware of this cause, that each man should have the right to freely choose from among the different doctrines the one which most suits him and is in greatest accord with reason. If a king

---

[107]Tradition reports that Sa'd ibn-Mu'adh, prince of the tribe of Aws, referred to Deuteronomy 20: 10-15, for its "Law of Anathema."

or despot oppresses his people, restricting their freedom and preventing the truth from reaching them, the apostle has the right to smash the barrier which surges up between these oppressed people and his message."[108] Constraint and prohibition of free choice in religion are the very stigma borne by the world of injustice and strife. In this respect, the Qur'ān's attitude is very clear since it does not admit intervention in a non-Muslim country which is tied to the world of Islam by treaty: "But if they seek your aid in religion, it is your duty to help them, except against a people with whom you have a treaty of mutual alliance."[109] Islam committed itself to not threatening non-Muslim communities or imposing its faith upon them, on the condition that they did not persecute their citizens who had accepted the Qur'ānic revelation and acknowledged the veracity of Muhammad's mission.[110]

Classical doctrine is scanty in its indications on the second aspect under consideration in this chapter: the ordering of inter-Islamic relations. This is understandable since the legal doctrine of Islam was constructed upon the myth of a homogeneous community, all believers forming one "nation." Very early on, however, under the pressure of circumstances, the theory of political unity was debated. Muhammad's settling in Medinah put an immediate end to the permanent hostilities which divided the city's two main tribes. However, even before the death of the Prophet, an attempted revolt divided Arabia. Abu Bakr checked it. The more authority and obedience the community leader commanded, the more this idea took root. Ibn Khaldun even goes to the point of considering as just and holy any war waged to confirm central power.[111] Quoting order and justice as their motive and invariably invoking Islamic principles, Muslim factions confronted one another in bloody battles, each party claiming to be waging a just and holy war and at the same time accusing the adversary of condemnable hostilities.

Since resorting to violence is authorized for the defense of the community and for the elimination of injustice, these possibilities can sometimes seem paradoxical in light of the fact that community authority was identified with the caliphate. Injustice is not the exclusive invention of the outside world. Islamic unity was destroyed by religious schisms or, more simply, by political

---

[108]Abu Zahra, *La conception*, p. 22.
[109]al-Anfal: 72 (Blachère).
[110]The first treaties signed by the Prophet explicitly mention it. The accord signed with the Christians of Najran stipulated: "They will not be oppressed as long as they do not oppress anyone." See also the letter of Muhammad to Emperor Heraclius, reproduced by Hamidullah in his *Muslim Conduct*, p. 170.
[111]"The Hand of God is extended upon the community and the one who separates himself falls into the fire," says the Prophet. Notice that the "community" is understood here as the collectivity which implicitly follows all the Qur'ānic principles.

ambitions which were often based on the quest for local or cultural identity. On the legal level, this matter was of great importance since it plainly addressed the problem of the fusion of the spiritual and secular spheres. However, anathema and excommunication were not characteristic in Islam's religious history. The distinction between orthodoxy and heresy was steeped with mutual tolerance. Since the eleventh and twelvth century, under the influence of Imam al-Ghazzali, Muslim doctrine rejected confession, declaring that acknowledgment of men as believers depended solely on their accepting the basic articles of faith. Dynastic differences, even though it was the rejection of Sunni caliphal authority, were not supposed to constitute a reason for exclusion.[112]

Jurists therefore arrived at the point of considering the possibility of "subnationalities," depending on the power they exercised and on the administration and jurisdiction they applied. In this connection, the prophetic traditions give additional elements. In the messages he sent them, Muhammad assured the foreign princes that he would leave their power intact if they embraced Islam.[113] The Qur'ān also admits the division of believers into various political entities, recommending that Muslims give just aid if needs be: "If two parties among the believers fall into a quarrel, make peace between them, but if one of them transgresses beyond bounds against the other, then fight against the one that transgresses until it complies with the command of God. But if it complies, then make peace between them with justice and be fair, for God loves those who are fair [and just]."[114]

In the context of "rules of war," there are terms concerning armed conflicts between opposing Muslim entities. As a matter of fact, the stipulations of classical doctrine appear admirably "modern." They do of course envisage dissidence – "civil wars" – rather than interstate battles. Rebels enjoy *de facto* recognition of their government: their jurisdiction over the territory they command is considered legal and valid for as long as they retain their authority. Neither the leaders nor partisans of the dissident group are responsible or impeachable for the human or material losses caused by the battle.[115] Concern-

---

[112]Ignaz Goldziher, *Le dogme et la loi de l'Islam: Histoire du développement dogmatique et juridique de la religion musulmane*, translated by Félix Arin (Paris: Geuthner, 1958), p. 154. After this: Goldziher, *Le dogme*.

[113]Hamidullah, *Muslim Conduct*, who cites, in other respects, on pp. 266 f., various examples, of which Bahrain and Oman are two.

[114]al-Hujurat: 9 (Reda). One can also see an allusion to the possibility of inter-Muslim wars in an-Nisa': 92: "... If the deceased was part of a group hostile to you and he was a believer ..." (Blachère).

[115]Majid Khadduri, *The Islamic Law of Nations*, Shaybani "Siyar" (Baltimore: Johns Hopkins, 1966), pp. 218-219. After this: Khadduri, *The Islamic Law*.

ing the waging of hostilities, the laws are identical to those governing war with outside enemies, with two favorable exceptions: prisoners cannot be put to death, and property cannot be seized and distributed as booty.

The division of the community was accepted by force of circumstance. However, the doctrine contains few precise legal terms relevant to relationships between Islamic countries or to the treatment of nationals of one Muslim country who chose to live in another Muslim country.[116] The fact that events have not exerted a great influence on legal doctrine can be understood in the general perspective of Muslim law and by historical analysis. In truth, "internal" conflicts which led to the community's becoming fragmented assumed a particular character which defies initial analysis. In contrast to the wars which followed the fall of the Roman Empire and which took place in the eleventh and twelfth centuries in Europe, these conflicts were never motivated by "nationalistic" feelings. It was rather a matter of various *coup d'états* which established new dynasties or divided the Muslim world into an infinite number of small states or autonomous principalities. These political upheavals generally took place without excessive violence and did not have long-lasting harmful consequences for civilian populations. At the same time, no significant breakdown came about in the general political system nor in the cultural unity. The absence of nationalism and the fundamentally Muslim psychological attitude of attachment to the leader rather than to abstract theories or ideologies explain why Islamic "international law" – as opposed to what happened in the Christian West – was concerned with defining and governing relations with territories not under Qur'ānic jurisdiction and not with internal relations in the "world of Islam."

At the conclusion of this discussion dealing with the concept of war in Islam, a final remark is necessary. It would be historically incorrect to claim that none of the wars undertaken by the Muslims were motivated by a spirit of aggression or greed, but this aggressiveness could not be blamed on the religion, regardless of the violence of certain Qur'ānic verses calling for war against the invaders. Legitimate defense was of course not the only reason for the wars which the Muslims began. The desire to dominate, the spirit of aggression, and the attraction of booty were certainly not always absent. The historical explanation of these conflicts is more a matter of political science or sociology than of law. An objective analysis of the doctrine clearly shows that force was not a primordial element of Islamic expansion. The Western

---

[116]Hamidullah, *Muslim Conduct*, pp. 128 f., cites the example of Saladin who bestowed a pension, purse, and self-jurisdiction upon the North African students living in Cairo.

[117]Miguel Palacios, "contacts de la spiritualité musulmane et de la spiritualité chrétienne," in *L'Islam et L'Occident*, Paris (Cohiers du Sud), p. 69.

bias which attributes the rapid expansion of Islam to the sword "should be rejected or reduced to a role of at most a secondary importance which aided and made possible the success of many other factors of a spiritual nature. Without these, the brutal force of the holy wars would have been fruitless."[117] The very fact that the subjugated peoples subsequently rejected Arab rule but retained the Muslim faith constitutes a formal proof.

Magnanimity

The waging of war, both throughout the history of wars as well as in our day and age, is greatly determined by the aim of the belligerent party. The very definition of the conflict unfortunately too often proves to be more important than existing international legislation or generally accepted moral laws. It is impossible to find an all-inclusive definition, whether historical or cultural. Violence can suddenly surge up as a necessity in relation to the image a group has of man and society, of their reciprocal roles or of their mutual relations. Islam has developed an original conception of the world, society, and the individual. The aim of war is strictly defined and determines both the manner of waging battle as well as the appropriate manner of dealing with the enemy.

In the Islamic doctrine, even if war sometimes represents the negation of compassion, it may not in any way stand against virtue and justice since God authorized combat under specific circumstances of legitimate defense. The fact that Muhammad and the prophets who preceded him had to resort to arms proves that violence is legitimate and that it can be committed in such a way as to respect elementary humanitarian laws.[118] The Muslim soldier would thus be guided by the Qur'ānic principles and the example of the Prophet. He would be able to respect the humanity of the enemy since it is not peoples but soldiers who struggle against each other in war. Humanity and bloodbath, justice and violence have to exist side by side on the battlefield.

At the same time, it is impossible to understand the Muslim philosophy which reconciles armed combat and compassion without referring to what at a very early stage proved to be the spiritual climate of Islam. It is also necessary, in this connection, to consider the particular expression of the religion as Muhammad incarnates it for the Muslims. Piety, which first and foremost means submission to the absolute, forces man into humility and, consequently, to generosity. The Qur'ān and Muslim doctrine often associate effort and struggle with patience, generosity, and forgiveness.[119] Humility, re-

---

[118]Abu Zahra, *La conception*, p. 11.
[119]ibn-Taimiyyah, *On Public and Private Law*, pp. 150 f., for example.

sulting from an innate sense of the unseen world, compensates for aggressiveness in the manifestation of power. Piety clears the way for combativity — it is the affirmation of truth by force, and if needs be, by combative force. It is the struggle and effort made against oneself in relation to the world in order to make the divine word apparent. Combative force is always implacable toward those who consciously oppose truth (tyrants and traitors) and foreshadows divine justice. Thus, it cannot be vindictive and, even less, cruel. Thus, piety, which brings about combat, tempers the latter so that the two ways continue to culminate in magnanimity.[120]

Legal doctrine and popular belief are correct in emphasizing the extraordinary magnanimity displayed by Muhammad during the various battles he fought. This beneficence is admirable, not only in the light of the customs of that time, but also by comparison with the actions of the preceding prophets as recorded in the Bible.[121] On the level of doctrine, the requirement that warriors show compassion is expressed in two ways. First of all, the combatant is supposed to go into action motivated by good intentions – that is, he should want to defend the religion and not go in search of booty. Second, with regard to the battle itself, he must apply both forms of the "holy war" which the religion enjoins: the "greater *jihad*," the spiritual battle which compels him to bridle his anger and (baser) instincts and the struggle against the enemy of justice. The validity of the cause in no way implies that the enemy may be annihilated. On the contrary, the war is ever-just on the condition that the battle be waged in a manner imbued with compassion, no matter what the actions of the foe may be.

"O you who believe! Stand up firmly for God, as witnesses to fair dealing, and let not the hatred of others to you make you swerve to wrong and depart from justice."[122] This verse defines and sums up the entire Islamic ruling concerning the manner of waging war. Neither the commander of the army nor the isolated soldier may ignore the humanitarian rules imposed by the Qur'ānic revelation. As a whole, the terms of this revelation seek to define the enemy; to stipulate the formalities which precede the opening of armed conflict; to determine what treatment is given to the vanquished prisoners, be

---

[120]See concerning the explanation of Schuon, *Comprendre*, pp. 117-124.

[121]It is interesting to note on this that the Islamic doctrine rejects the authenticity of acts of useless violence and the cruelty of the Jewish prophets. The Muslims believe, in fact, that the transmission of it is in error and that all the messengers of God who preceded Muhammad and who had been obligated to resort to arms in order to affirm the truth had conducted their hostilities on the basis of humanity, never going beyond the limits imposed by the truth. See Abu Zahra, *La conception*, pp. 14-15.

[122]al-Ma'idah: 8 (Blachère). In verse 2 of the same sura, the Qur'ān warns that hatred does not lead the believers to "an abuse of law."

they soldiers or civilians; and to divide up the war booty. The legal doctrine provides numerous rules which, for the most part, are of a distinctly humanitarian nature: prohibition of inflicting unnecessary suffering, prohibition of excess, protection of personal property and estate. These minutely detailed stipulations are presented in the form of specific examples which are nevertheless sufficiently concordant so as to allow for the establishment of general principles. With the exception of a few noteworthy examples,[123] the rules governing the waging of battles are disseminated in works of science, general jurisprudence, philosophy, history, literature, religious exegesis, or else in works dealing with the military, art, political morality, fiscal treatises, diplomacy, or expeditions.[124]

The established rules covered the whole war process, from the beginning to the end of hostilities. They draw their obligating power from the "fear of God." The prophetic traditions report that "every time the Messenger of God sent an army or a detachment ahead, he personally advised the commander to fear God Almighty and ordered the accompanying Muslims to perform good deeds, that is, to behave with decency."[125] The cornerstone of the entire structure resides in the prohibition of excess. This is at the base of all ethical and legal philosophies of Islam. The instructions of the Prophet, as well as those of his successors, emphasized the necessity for the Muslim soldiers to abstain from needlessly shedding blood or from destroying properties as long as military realities did not call for such actions. Muslim jurists seem to be perfectly aware of having made innovations in the domain of laws pertaining to war.[126]

The prohibition of excess is the very postulation of modern war law. However, since war is considered a sanction in Islamic judicial doctrine, the law of retaliation should be applied. This reciprocity is nevertheless strictly limited by certain elementary humanitarian values. Retaliation had been immediately tempered in Islam, on a general level, by the exhortation to be compassionate and patient.[127] In any event, recourse to retaliation is specifically conditioned by the prohibition of going beyond the bounds of human-

---

[123]Shaybani, for example.

[124]*Ghazawat.* See Rabbath, "Pour une théorie," pp. 9-10. We note, in passing, that the practice of the Muslim leaders, apart from those of the other orthodox successors of the Prophet, did not rest upon legal authority. The importance of precedents which were at times created must not be totally ignored. Hamidullah, *Muslim Conduct,* p. 24.

[125]Khadduri, *The Islamic Law,* pp. 75-76.

[126]Khadduri, *The Islamic Law,* p. 92.

[127]ash-Shura: 43, which recommends mercy and patience. Verse 40 deals with pardon. In fact, the entire passage of this sura merits being cited (36-43), for it eloquently demonstrates the fundamentally peaceful spirit of Islam, in times of war as well as in times of peace.

ity.[128] Moreover, the law of retaliation would not be applicable if it were to bring about the violation of a Qur'ānic instruction.[129] Understood in this light, it prevents the Muslim combatant from resorting to excessive reprisals because of a narrow spirit of reciprocity which takes on the form of revenge.

Islam has minutely elaborated laws pertaining to the manner of waging war. We shall limit ourselves to simply emphasizing them here and shall return to some specific considerations later.

Hostilities must always be preceded by a declaration[130] or an ultimatum so that the enemy is not taken by surprise. Moreover, in an effort to reduce the consequences of combat, Muslim law limits them to strictly military aims, and clearly distinguishes between combatants and noncombatants. By extension, it prohibits needless destruction and the use of arms causing far-reaching destruction,[131] as well as any other indiscriminate measures, such as poisoning food sources or water supplies for such actions would affect civilians not taking part in combat.[132] Ignominious procedures are also prohibited, such as treachery or torture of the enemy (the latter being considered as worse than crime), as well as the use of certain weapons causing unnecessary suffering.[133] Enemies who have laid down arms must be spared; those who have fallen in battle must be respected[134], and human remains must be buried.[135] Finally, among the humanitarian terms of Muslim law there is also the fact that armed combat is limited in its duration: an automatic truce interrupts combat for four months of each year.[136] This interruption should enable the warriors to bandage their wounds sustained in combat and to appease the sufferings of the civilian populations.

In their present-day formulation and systematization, the terms of Islamic wartime law are the result of a judicial speculation which was effected two or three centuries after the death of the Prophet. From the beginning of the Arab-Muslim conquest, however, the warriors of Islam adopted a magnificent

---

[128]al-Isra': 33.

[129]ibn-Taimiyyah, *On Public and Private Law*, p. 175.

[130]This is the "call" *da'wah* of Islam.

[131]As a fire or flood which were, at the time of the prophet Muhammad, the means of massive destruction.

[132]Tradition reports that the Prophet raised a prohibition on exporting corn to Makkah.

[133]The Malikiyyah prohibit, for example, poisoned meat. See Khadduri, *War*, p. 103. Also refer to Hamidullah, *Muslim Conduct*, p. 187.

[134]God forbade Muhammad to avenge the memory of his uncle Hamza upon the corpses of the Makkan soldiers.

[135]After the battle of Badr, the Prophet ordered his troops to bury the enemy's dead so that they would not be left as food for lions.

[136]at-Taubah: 36.

spirit of tolerance toward the nonbelievers and subjugated peoples. At a time when violence knew neither law nor feeling, Abu Bakr, the Prophet's successor, gave his soldiers the following well-known and often-quoted instructions which contain the moral spirit of Islamic law: "Remember that you are always under the gaze of God and at the threshold of your death, and that you will account for your deeds on the Last Day... When you are fighting for the glory of God, acquit yourselves as men, without heaving your backs; but, let not the blood of women, children, or the aged be a blemish on your victory. Do not destroy palm trees, do not burn houses or wheat fields, never cut down fruit trees and do not kill cattle unless you are forced to eat them. When you grant a treaty or a capitulation, take care to fulfill their conditions. As you advance, you will come across religious men who live in monasteries and who serve God in prayer; leave them in peace, do not kill them and do not destroy their monasteries..."[137]

The orders given by Abu Bakr in no way represent pious recommendations. They are strict legal obligations which engage the personal responsibility of the combatant. The soldier of the "holy war" is obliged to present himself "under the gaze of God" sincerely and directly and is subject to the rules of honor and humanity. If strategy – the sign of mastery and intelligence in the art of war[138] – is recommended to him, treachery and trickery are strictly forbidden. The principle of good faith and upright intentions constitutes the moral basis of the Muslim in both combat and all circumstances of his private and public life. Deceit and cheating are condemned as being contrary to the judicial foundations of morality. Certain exceptions are tolerated on the absolute condition that the life of the believer is in extreme danger. However, the limits of moderation always apply. "If you kill, do so in a dignified fashion," said the Prophet. This order is considered by legal doctrine to be the prohibition of treacherous trickery, of torturing the wounded or prisoners, or of killing wounded enemies on the battlefields or leaving them to die by not giving them water or food.

In the same vein of moderation[139] and of respect for man, there is the fact that soldiers of the "holy war" are forbidden to plunder. This prohibition is worth being discussed here, though it could appear secondary in relation to

---

[137]Rabbath, "Pour une théorie," p. 16; and Amir Ali, *Spirit*, pp. 86-87, among others. Abu Zahra cites a tradition attributed to the Prophet: "... Do not kill their old people, the infants or women. Do not be excessive and take care of your spoils; act in the right way and do good ..." (*La conception*, p. 53). See the translation of principal texts reported in Hamidullah, *Muslim Conduct*, pp. 304 f.

[138]Allah Himself is the best in this domain. See al-Anfal: 30.

[139]"He has established the balance. Do not transgress the balance," ar-Rahman: 7-8 (Blachère).

the corpus of Islamic wartime law for it reinforces and illustrates the idea under discussion. The Prophet said: "He who loots or usurps, or who encourages plundering, is not considered as one of us." This prohibition should be placed side by side with the many terms stipulating the rules for sharing booty. It is in this context that the coherence of the revelation and the logic of the prophetic orders become clear. Muhammad actually advised his soldiers who were setting out on a campaign to take care of their booty; according to the Qur'ān, the soldier who is enticed by material gain will not be rewarded: "O you who believe! When you go abroad in the cause of God, investigate carefully, and do not say to anyone who offers you a salutation: 'You are not of the believers,' coveting the perishable goods of this life. With God are profits and spoils abundant."[140] Muslim legalistic literatue, rich in stipulations concerning dividing up booty, imputes numerous declarations to Muhammad in this connection. The great detail with which the doctrine, even from the very outset of Muslim history, treats the distribution of property taken from the enemy constitutes a constraint, a judicial requirement and practice whose strict application, when mutually controlled by all the soldiers, is aimed at preventing the illegal seizing of goods. As such, the innumerable stipulations concerning booty appear to be of secondary importance but represent a practical means of forbidding pillage.

Certain more general terms of Muslim law should be analyzed here. First of all, the enemy must be treated with justice,[141] respect,[142] and compassion.[143] It has been repeated that before battles the Prophet would recite: "O Almighty God. We are your creatures and they are too. Our lives are in Your hands, as are theirs. O God, cause them to be defeated and grant us victory over them." Islamic law which is essentially practical and realistic, does not ask that the combatants "love" their enemy since generosity and charity are impossible without justice. The moderation shown by the Prophet during the conquest of Makkah was not love but magnanimity in his seeking peace and reconciliation. This still does not mean that the enemy is an inferior and damned creature for, like all creatures, he was created by the one God and thus belongs to the brotherhood of men. However, "if humanity unites all men, then truth distinguishes those creatures who submit to obeying God from those who break His laws."[144] Thus, military and wartime commandments

[140]an-Nisa': 94 (Masson).
[141]al-Ma'idah: 2.
[142]al-An'am: 109.
[143]al-Baqarah: 195.
[144]Muhammad Z. Khan, "Islam and International Relations," *The Islamic Review* (July 1956):8. After this: Khan, "Islam."

necessarily imply respect for humanitarian and moral principles. Hostilities are intended to lead to reconciliation; violence has to be checked and limited on personal and geographical levels.

The most obvious originality of the Islamic teaching in the domain of war, is the guarantee offered to noncombatants. This limitation fully corresponds to the spirit of the Qur'ānic revelation which holds man individually responsible; so, the limitation rejoins the concept of "holy war" in Islam, answering those who have taken the initiative of engaging combat. The verse authorizing war is understood and interpreted in these two possible ways. "Fight in the cause of God those who fight you, but do not transgress limits for God does not love transgressors,"[145] means both that war is permitted only to drive back an attack and that Muslim arms must be used only against those who participate in active hostilities. War does not oppose peoples but defenders of faith and those who have attacked them. Therefore, hostilities are limited in their objectives (combatants) and space (the battlefield). Thus, the period of war is reduced.

The Qur'ān not only demands that enemies who do not take part in the combats be shown respect, but that they be shown kindness as well. Women, children, the elderly, religious men, the old and infirm, slaves and servants are protected from any direct attack. The greater part of the legal doctrine seems to extend this protection to adult males who have not had any active part in the hostilities: peasants, workers, merchants, to whose ranks may be added the members of medical and paramedical personnel.[146] In fact, the recognized interpreters of the Qur'ān view the injunction to "help one another with God-fearing kindness"[147] as the duty to cooperate with civilian enemies in humanitarian matters.[148] This is not at all a "modernized" deduction since classical Muslim legal doctrine in effect provided for the permanent neutralization of a health service – women or doctors who were following the wounded[149] of *both* sides.

The prohibition against harming noncombatant civilians implies the ban on certain arms of indiscriminate nature as well as the extent to which the enemy can be harmed. Legal doctrine did not limit itself to expressing a pious oath in this realm but developed precise laws based on plausible examples. By way of illustration, the translation of a legal text relating to Islamic wartime law

[145]al-Baqarah: 190 (Blachère). It is convenient to also note that "transgressors" is understood, at the same time, as a prohibition of aggression and a putting on guard against excess.
[146]Muhammad Hamidullah, "The International Law in Islam," *The Islamic Review* (May 1951).
[147]al-Ma'idah: 2.
[148]Hamidullah, *Muslim Conduct*, p. 279.
[149]Khadduri, *The Islamic Law*.

is of significance.[150] The author[151] very explicitly indicates that, for instance, when besieging a fortress in which there are women or children, the Muslims are not allowed to set fire to nor flood the area. "If the enemy surrounds himself with a rampart of children, he must be left alone, unless he proves to be too formidable an enemy." Is this not precisely the practical expression of the necessary compromise between military needs and humanitarian requirements, the basis of modern law applicable in the case of armed conflict?

The distinction between combatants and noncombatants was applied to Muslims themselves, each category having its own obligations. The first category – the soldiers – is "constantly reminded of the religious nature of their mission, that of being a warrior...in [the holy war], for the victory of Allah; from the latter, apart from submission to the authority of Islam, nothing more is required than the strictest neutrality."[152] The concern for separating combatants from noncombatants is moreover witnessed by the soldiers of the first battles of the Prophet who declared: "The factor which distinguishes us from the nonbelievers is the green turban forming part of our headgear."[153]

Civilian citizens of conquered territories fell under the "protection" of Islam. They could continue to live there freely, subject to their own legislation. They ceased to be directly involved with the development of military operations. Rare are the historical examples showing that Jews or Christians had to endure persecution in the form of retaliation, when the tides of fortune would temporarily turn against Muslim powers. Even at the height of the crusades, resident Christians were generally not molested. The few known exceptions were always the deeds of ignorant people. As for nationals of belligerent enemy states who happened to be in Muslim territory during a war, they were permitted to reside there normally until their permit expired. They were to be neither molested, nor threatened in their person or property, nor were they to be expelled or imprisoned, on the condition that they committed no hostile act against Islam.

In the context of the limitation of hostilities, the institution of the safeguard accorded to foreigners, an integral part of the "holy war," should be mentioned again briefly since it offers the possibility of placing limits on the battlefield. This was achieved in two ways. First, thanks to the respect it en-

---

[150]Baron Carra de Vaux, *Les penseurs de l'Islam*, vol. 3: *L'exégèse, la tradition, et la jurisprudence* (Paris: Guenther, 1923), p. 365.
[151]Sidi Khalil of the Malikiyyah.
[152]Rabbath, "Pour une théorie," p. 17.
[153]Hamidullah, *Muslim Conduct*, p. 236. This distinction of the military nature was eventually misinterpreted in order to humiliate those who had surrendered. See below, chapter 5.

joyed, it must have permitted the establishment of diplomatic channels in order to transmit ultimatums and open negotiations for peace,[154] to communicate the agreement of truces or cease-fires; it also permitted very precise stipulations regulating the conclusion or breaking of treaties. These theoretical hypotheses have very often been put into effect in historical practice and in fact correspond to the modern Islamic spirit and doctrine pertaining to war.[155] Second, during hostilities on the battlefield, there is yet another factor which serves as an obvious limitation on the scope of the conflict: the fact that in the name and upon the responsibility of the entire community, every believer is guaranteed the possibility of granting safeguard to one or several enemies, even if they are situated in fortified positions. This is not a surrender nor even a truce demanded of the enemy. The beneficiaries enjoy this privilege for as long as they abstain from resuming combat. The hostile combatants to whom such a safeguard has been granted do not thereby become prisoners but are permitted to live freely among the Muslims.

Concerning prisoners, the prophetic traditions report the following injunction of Muhammad: "The captives are your brothers and collaborators. It is by God's grace that they are in your hands. Since they are at your mercy, treat them as you treat yourselves with regard to food, clothing, and habitation. Do not demand any work of them which is beyond their capacities, rather, help them to accomplish their tasks." Over and over the Qur'ān mentions that among the actions of great moral value which form an integral part of piety is the kindness which the believer should show toward his captive: "And they feed, for the love of God, the indigent, the orphan, and the captive."[156]

The terms inaugurated by Qur'ānic legislation constitute one of the most lasting and glorious contributions made by Islam to the development of wartime law. Examples of generosity and humanity abound in Muslim history, from Muhammad[157] to Saladin [Salah ud-din] the Great who, according to Arab chroniclers, liberated a great number of crusader prisoners when he realized that he did not have enough food to feed them all.[158] A great deal

---

[154]"If they incline to peace, incline toward them," al-Anfal: 61 (Blachère).

[155]See Abu Zahra, *La conception*; Bêchebichy, *Les relations*; Chalaby, *L'Islam*; and Draz, *Initiation*.

[156]al-Insān: 8 (Blachère).

[157]Tradition reports that the Makkan enemies defeated at the battle of Badr were well treated. At Medinah where they were enemies in captivity, they declared: "Blessed be the people of Medinah. They have given us their horses while they themselves walk. They have given us bread to eat when, haveing little, they content themselves with dates." See Ameer Ali, *The Spirit*, p. 63; Tugay, *Mahomet*, p. 130; and Galwash, *The Religion*, p. 65.

[158]On this very land of Palestine seven centuries later, Napoléon in front of Saint-Jean-d'Acre

of original sources mention this fact.

In order to fully comprehend the original and revolutionary aspect of Muhammad's instructions, one has to bear in mind how far back in time they appeared as well as the evolution of morality: this took place in the seventh century at a period when the tradition in Arabia was to ransom one's captives and massacre those who did not have the means to buy their freedom. At the same time, in the West, the "kind" king Dagobert, planting his sword in the ground after battle, had all of the conquered population who were taller than his sword killed."[159]

The Qur'ān,[160] jurisprudence, and historical tradition provide instructions pertaining to the status of prisoners. It should be noted that the doctrine is not always unanimous and does not always seem to conform to Qur'ānic stipulations,[161] nor to the generally followed practices, if we are to believe historians. According to judicial science, it would be up to the leader of the community to decide upon the fate of prisoners. He had four choices: immediate execution, subjection to slavery, ransom and exchange for Muslim prisoners, and finally, unilateral and unconditional liberation. All the Muslim jurists who retain the possibility of immediate execution of a part or all of the prisoners agree in recognizing that this could only be a question of an exceptional measure taken as a military precaution or in the higher interests of society. Nothing in the Qur'ān either prescribes or authorizes the killing of prisoners. The revelation provides for and authorizes only ransom or liberation. The main early legal authority seems to share this opinion.[162] Moreover, historical tradition shows that neither the Prophet nor his successors permitted the execution of prisoners. On the contrary, it would appear that Muhammad's companions and their troops had some difficulties in accepting Islam's humanitarian prescriptions. For example, after the battle of Badr, the first decisive victory of the Muslim forces, those who requested merciful treatment so as to enhance the prestige of Islam and accelerate its propagation[163] were opposed by those who,[164] in the name of simple justice, demanded the execution of the enemies who had apparently shown a particu-

---

massacred all the Syrian prisoners which he detained, by starving them to death. Abu Zahra, *La conception*, p. 63.

[159]Dermenghem, "Témoignage," especially p. 376.

[160][After the capture comes the time for], "... either generosity or ransom until the war lays down its burdens," Muhammad: 4 (Blachère). See also al-Anfal: 70.

[161]Ghoneimi, *The Muslim Conception*, p. 148.

[162]Khadduri, *The Islamic Law*, p. 91, with the simultaneously opposing opinion which is supported, moreover, only by the jurisprudence and that in default with the Qur'ān.

[163]Abu Bakr, who became the first successor.

[164]'Umar, who became the second caliph.

lar violence toward the growing Muslim community. Muhammad decided to free the prisoners for a certain ransom and to keep those who could not pay the price of their liberty. The latter were freed as soon as they had each taught ten children of Medinah to read and write.

Quartering and subjugation of prisoners have, even up to modern times, been a widespread practice. Reducing prisoners to slavery, apart from the fact that it met economic needs, was generally not motivated by humanitarian considerations but rather by the mythical belief that the victors had the right of life and death over them. This custom could have been inherited by Islam from the Persians and Byzantines, with whom the Muslim troops had violent contacts very early on. Tradition reports that Muhammad accepted that the captured enemies be distributed among the believers as slaves, on the strict condition that they be humanely treated, nourished and clothed just like normal citizens, and that they not be subject to excessively difficult tasks.[165] The prophetic traditions also show how the Prophet, without formally forbidding his combatants to subjugate the members of a defeated tribe, encouraged them to free them by marrying one of their women. In this way, they established relationships with the conquered people.[166]

Given the fact that the Qur'ān did not envisage the subjugation of prisoners of war, it seems likely that this measure must have represented only one form of sanction, based on reciprocity. Taking the era into consideration, one could moreover claim that slavery was a lesser evil which allowed for lives to be saved and provided a form of temporary detention. Furthermore, ransom, exchange or liberation were not only possibilities but binding obligations. The precise Qur'ānic commandment – "...until war lays down its burden..." – indicated the time limit of captivity. At the end of the war, all prisoners must necessarily be freed, on the sole condition that the Muslims held captive by the enemy be repatriated at the same time. Maintaining enemy soldiers in captivity nourished the public treasury through ransom and above all offered the possibility of exchanging them for believers as well as non-Muslim subjects who were being held. In the first treaty concluded between Muhammad and the people of Medinah, one clause already stipulates that the allies should not miss any opportunity to recover their imprisoned relatives.[167] The succeeding caliphs insisted that the Muslim administration apply all its efforts in order to recover captured Muslims.

There were also certain legal terms applicable to Muslim soldiers whom the

---

[165]Khan, "Islam," p. 11, who cites al-Bukhari.
[166]This pertains to one of the "political" marriages of the Prophet. See Abu Zahra, *La conception*, p. 73; Hamidullah, *Muslim Conduct*, pp. 216-217; and Tugay, *Mahomet*.
[167]Article 3. See Hamidullah, *The First Written Constitution*, pp. 41-42.

enemy held in captivity. They had to remain faithful to the Islamic faith, and they were formally forbidden to take part in any war against the Muslim community or to provide the enemy with information of a military nature. At the same time, the doctrine considered it the absolute duty of the Muslim leader to obtain their release by means of an exchange of people, properties, or the payment of a ransom. This requirement became a widespread practice.

Islam regulated the conditions and terms of restitution by means of specific treaties called *fida*. The frequency of battles between Islam and the outside world made this an almost routine procedure. This fact had no small influence in saving thousands of lives and in ensuring the safeguard of those enemy soldiers which warfare had put out of combat.[168] It moreover enabled medieval Europe to become aware of the state of prisoners in the East, whose retrieval then became possible.

Cases of unconditional liberation are not rare in Muslim history. The best-known examples are, first of all, the Prophet's unconditional liberation of all prisoners captured when Makkah was taken, and Saladin who released the Christians who had no means of buying their freedom when the Muslim armies retook Jerusalem.

Taking into account the absolute word of the Qur'ān and the spirit of the Islamic revelation, contemporary Muslim jurists consider that the only possible alternative for the Muslim leader is either to unilaterally liberate the prisoners whom he holds captive, or to exchange them for Muslim prisoners who are in the hands of the enemy or against a certain ransom. This is the interpretation which seems to be the most appropriate in terms of the causes, limitations, and aims of the "holy war" in Islam.

Eternal Principles

Asserting the oneness of God, truth, and the human race, Islam immediately appeared as an ecumenical religion and a political system of universal aims. Since it simultaneously recognized the authenticity of the preceding divine revelations, it conceived of the universe as a single entity having a pluralistic formation. It then came to the point of defining itself in relation to the outside world, thereby giving rise to a bipolar conception of the universe. This division is not based upon geographical or juridical criteria but represents a state to be described rather than a situation which could be subjectively judged, since it emanates from the divine will.

---

[168]Khadduri, *War*, p. 217, notes that these treaties of exchange were numerous mainly during the Abbassid period. Twelve treaties of ransom or of exchange are known in only the first years of the reign of Harun ar-Rashid.

The Muslim world, ruled by Qur'ānic legislation, concretely represents the domain of justice and peace, the *world of Islam*; whereas the exterior countries, if certain conditions are not fulfilled, remain the sphere of oppression and error, the *world of war*. This (latter) world is hostile toward Islam insofar as the believers residing there have neither freedom of conscience nor security of their persons or belongings. Thus, injustice and violence are apprehended from within. The two systems are irrevocably separated by this inherent clash which makes them mutually exclusive. However, the objective division of the world exists in order to encourage men to cooperate and to avoid the exclusive domination of one political entity over the others since God desires harmony and fraternity among peoples.

Peace in justice is the deepest essence of the Islamic revelation. The prophetic tradition reports in this connection that once, in answer to a question, the Prophet defined the "best Islam" as that which "consisted of feeding those who are hungry and of spreading peace among the known and the unknown" [i.e., between believers and nonbelievers] of the whole world.[169] By force of circumstances, and particularly because of its geographical location, the Muslim community was soon compelled to define and maintain neighborly relations based on peaceful coexistence. Rules appeared to determine the terms of these relations. International relations were supposed to remain peaceful as long as the outside world had an agreeable and tolerant attitude.[170] If the universe necessarily had to be divided into two "domains" eternally hostile toward each other because of belief, neutrality would have been inconceivable. However, there is nothing which opposes the idea of a third party remaining uninvolved in hostilities. Accordingly, the Qur'ān forbids Muslims to attack a nation which has not shown any hostility toward them, providing all the guarantees of security.[171]

Islam of course turned out to be proselytic. The nature of its external relations was largely determined by the objective reality of various eras, political ambitions of certain leaders, and strength of arms. On a strictly religious level, these relations should have been characterized by moderation and patience. As the "midway nation," the Muslim community had to accept and acknowledge the existence of other peoples ruled by different laws. Since law is "personalized," the foreigner was able to reside in Islamic territory, permanently or temporarily, adhering to his own laws. Reciprocally, the Muslim

---

[169]Goldziher, *Le dogme*, p. 18.
[170]Hassan al-Ma'amoun, "Quelques principes de l'Islam," *Revue internationale de la Croix-Rouge*, November 1958, p. 598.
[171]an-Nisa': 90.

who entered the "world of war" was obliged to respect the public order of that place. On the level of interstate relations, right from its inception, the Muslim state maintained diplomatic relations with the outside world. However, the profound sense of justice as well as the dynamic and collective apprehension of the concept of compassion encourage the Muslim to reduce the "world of disorder and oppression" to nonexistence. The instrument of this procedure is the *jihad*.

The "holy war" is an effort. First, it is an effort made to curb the passions of the self; an effort which is also communal so as to enforce good and forbid evil; it is finally an armed effort imposed upon the believer individually or upon the community as a whole, as circumstances may require. Its aim is not to impose Islam but to maintain the society's security and to ensure its expansion by making sure that anybody outside of the world of Islam is free to embrace the faith. Nonbelief is punishment in itself. The nonbeliever who does not prevent Muslims from practicing their faith is in need of no other punishment.[172] The "holy war" could not assume a military character other than within the confines determined by Qur'ānic law. It then becomes armed aggression, holy and pious, just in its motivation, waging, and end. Since the traditional doctrine considers aggression a natural trait of man, it describes as iniquitous those conflicts whose motivation lies in the desire for revenge, in rivalry of personal interests and jealousy, as well as in the "tendency for violence or vandalism."[173] The only just wars are those authorized by the revelation and fought "in the path of Allah." Any other form of violence is condemned. In the final analysis, force should theoretically lead back to the existential unity desired by God; to order and harmony, to "soundness," to justice in its broadest meaning. In this nonmilitary context, the "holy war" is a permanent state since man is created in such a way that he must constantly be harsh with himself and others in order to fight his natural tendencies toward selfishness, injustice, and desire for power.

Islam's military history is woven of superior military deeds, of examples of tolerance and magnanimity, as well as of massacres. It is a history of men. The Muslims of today are not wrong in proudly looking back on their past. The Prophet and his successors – in particular the caliph Umar, the great empire builder – succeeded in using Islam to inculcate respect for man and recognition of human values in their combatants, the enthusiastic zealots of a

---

[172]"Be that as it may, the unbeliever who does not forbid to the Muslims to establish the religion of Allah has himself already suffered the disadvantages of his unbelief." ibn-Taimiyyah, *On Public Law*, p. 141.

[173]The raids of razzia. See ibn-Khaldoun, *Mouqaddima*, pp. 56 f.

new religion.[174] The extraordinary examples of humanity shown by – among others – Muhammad at the time of the conquest of Makkah, 'Umar when he rode into Jerusalem, and Saladin in various circumstances during his struggle with the crusaders, incessantly return under the pen of Muslim authors, historians, jurists, or moralists. With the internal dissensions and wars which soon arose, followed in Spain and the Levant by the brutal contact with a Europe which was beginning to stir, the necessities of the moment led to excesses. The invasion of Turkish tribes from the West and then the terrifying waves of Mongols nevertheless did not bring much damage to the Islamic concept of war on the level of doctrine.[175] To claim that all Muslim leaders followed the legal terms governing international relations – both during times of peace and war – would be to display an ignorance of the history of human nature. These violations all the same do not diminish the value of the religious laws which remain immutable. A contravention of the law takes nothing away from its obligating and coercive nature.

Simultaneously based on the concepts of force and compassion, the fundamental principles of the Islamic legal system pertaining to both interstate and internal conflicts may be summed up as follows:[176]

– Prohibition of excess, treachery, and injustice in all areas.
– Prohibition of inflicting unnecessary suffering upon the enemy: no massacres, cruelty, or vindictive punishment.
– Prohibition of uncalled-for destruction, in particular the devastation of civilizations.
– Condemnation of poisoned weapons or of mass and indiscriminate destruction.
– Clear distinctions between the combatants, who in Muslim armies wore a distinctive insignia, and civilians not directly participating in combat.

---

[174]We emphasize, at this stage, that the rules of the law of war do not represent a myth "modernized" by the contemporary Muslim authors who try to prove the concordance of the religion with the present juridical principles. The apostolic tradition is rich in examples. In the fourteenth century, a chronicler compiling the reported anecdotes mentions the recommendations of Muhammad as regards the treatment of prisoners and lets his readers perceive the indignation of the Muslims when coming across their Arab enemies finishing off the wounded on the battlefield. See ibn-Sayed al-Nass, "Des anciennes sources de combat, du comportement des guerriers, et de leur bibliographie" [On the Ancient Sources Concerning Combat, the Behavior of Warriors, and on their Bibliography] in Farag al-Sayed, *Message au soldat arabe* [Message to the Arab Soldier], translated by Mohamed Nasr al-Dine (Cairo: Supreme Council of Islamic Affairs, n.d.), pp. 43, 63. After this: al-Sayed, *Message.*
[175]See the analysis for another period by Sivan Emmanuel, *L'Islam et la Croisace: Idéologie et propagande dans les réactions musulmanes aux Croisades* (Paris: Maisonneuve, 1968), 222 pages. After this: Sivan, *Idéologie et propagande.*

- Respect for those who have withdrawn from battle: the wounded, soldiers granted free passage – safeguard – and prisoners of war.
- Humane treatment of captives who must be exchanged or unilaterally freed when the war comes to an end, on the condition that there remain no Muslim prisoners in the hands of the enemy.
- Protection of civilian populations: respect for their religions – and hence their cultures – and the ministers of the latter; prohibition of murder of hostages or rape of women.
- Affirmation of individual responsibility: abolition of any punishment of persons for a crime which they have not committed themselves.
- Prohibition of reciprocity in inflicting suffering and retaliation which could constitute a contravention of essential human rights.
- Collaboration with the enemy in humanitarian tasks.
- Formal prevention of any act contrary to the stipulations of treaties concluded by the Muslims.

Because they consider the law to be of divine essence, Muslim jurists go by a certain number of idealized norms, refusing to codify practices which could be legal tender. With regard to armed combat, Islam – which may claim the honor of never having known systematic genocide nor concentration camps – proclaims universal rules. It is thus endowed with moderation and wisdom such as could benefit mankind at the present time. All excesses are banned in the name of justice and reason. War is not an act of revenge, but an effort to drive out iniquity and oppression. This is a concept which poses very precise restrictions as to the manner of carrying out military operations, a notion which proceeds from a higher conception of man as such and from the respect due to him as a creature of God. Islamic international law reposes upon solid moral principles which aim to transcend the everyday human reality. The Prophet Muhammad declared this most explicitly: "God Almighty sent me to perfect your character and to make it more dignified."

---

[176]We again take up here the ideas already developed in our short article: "De certaines règles islamiques concernant la conduite des hostilités et la protection des victimes de conflits armés," *Annales d'études internationales*, 1977), pp. 145-158.

Chapter 6

THE REALITY OF ISLAM

> The will to justify one's self, found
> in all our social systems, eventually
> weakens them.
>
> Malraux

The Muslim Awakening and Reform Movement

Since the eleventh century, the political history of Islam has been largely determined by policies formulated in Europe. The Portuguese and Dutch destroyed its trading dominance by discovering and developing new maritime routes; England and France penetrated Islamic territories; and Russia cut the heartland off from the eastern extremities. In the Balkans, Asia, and Africa, European imperialism collided with the spread of Islam, a development which eventually led to Islam's subjugation in those areas. Religious expression itself suffered. A formalistic piety leaning toward bigotry and an unnatural mysticism maintained superstition, stifling Islam's creative originality. A pure reiteration of traditional cultural elements gained precedence over the pursuit of modern "Western style" knowledge, and over scientific research in particular. The faith withdrew into a strict orthodoxy which preserved traditional religious values, but could not assimilate those principles which could have propelled Muslim society along the path of progress that Europe was already following. Consequently, the Islamic vision of the world shrank and intellectual growth was sacrificed to preserve doctrinal unity by the military authorities of newly converted nations. An atmosphere of questioning and doubt led to the conviction that the fate of Islam was profoundly linked to that of the traditional Islamic civilization. The distinction between permanent and transient, essential and superfluous disappeared, and Islam settled into a centuries-long tranquil stagnation, which would be shattered only by the nineteenth-century conquests by the West.

After a long and gradual decline, the Arabs disappeared from the forestage of Muslim history. The Turks, while imitating Western military tactics and adopting its weapons, refused to seriously consider its political or social concepts. Secure in their arrogant pride, they did not realize that Europe was penetrating the empire and suffocating it. This collosal indifference on the part of the government had a parallel among the common people: their understanding of Islam began to disappear, and subsequent reformers did not attack such ignorance.[1]

---

[1] The life of modern Muslims represents "a manifestation against their own religion," 'Abdu, *Rissalat*, p. 136.

It is generally believed that the period of the Muslim world's self-assurance came to an end when Napoleon arrived in the valley of the Nile.[2] The French incursion into the heartlands of Islam forced the Muslims to define themselves in relation to a victorious West. Thus, the link between the East which had fallen into inactivity was reestablished with the West, but unfortunately for the Muslim, Europe came forward not as a partner but as a dominator. Colonization seriously wounded the Muslim pride which then expressed itself with more religious, cultural, and political assertion, invigorated by the fact that it continually was set at odds against European imperialist interests. Leading the forces of anti-colonialism, the Arabs reappeared on the horizon of Muslim history.

Islam asserted itself as the soul and cornerstone of the resistance movements led by a population which, though politically dominated, was not institutionally subjugated. As an element of differentiation and identification, it brought about divergent processes. In effect, the Islamic peoples [of the Arabic speaking countries] expressed their identity by rejecting the twin dominating forces of Christian Europe and Muslim Turkey. The Arabs had to combat both. Allied at first with the West as "Arabs" instead of "Muslims," they turned against Turkey and later against the West when they realized they could not cooperate with the West while it claimed to be their master, as illustrated by the system of mandates and the Balfour Declaration. In Africa, Islam helped create a new society which was non-tribal and more capable of opposing foreign influence. In Asia, a supple and adaptable Islam maintained its hold on its lands and continued to spread in spite of colonial domination. Islam often represented the banner of the struggle against colonialism.[3]

A threefold phenomenon, which came to lead the liberation movement, soon established itself within Islam: reform, identification, and assertion. These three related manifestations constitute the framework of modern history, and their cumulative effect gave the Muslims a dynamic and challenging aspect which had previously been lacking. The search for identity, which is not undertaken without some measure of anguish, simultaneously implies a quest for authenticity and an adequate means of expression. Religious zeal, patriotic fervor, nationalistic feelings and a pan-Islamic aspiration blended to-

---

[2] This affirmation certainly merits being nuanced. One can in this regard mention the work of ibn-Taimiyyah, of Muhammad ibn-Abd-al-Wahab, and of Shah Wali Ullah Dehlvi, for example.
[3] This is true when the Muslim populations are minorities; however, as in the South Asian subcontinent or in Ethiopia, Islam will remain on the defensive. The Muslims in [British] India were able, simultaneously, to liberate themselves from the English tutelage and to form their own communal state. The lot of the Eritrean populations continues to furnish painful elements to the history of contemporary Eastern Africa.

gether in this need to be distinguished from the "other," which at first was the colonialist West and later the industrialized world — capitalist or Marxist. This reaction, especially in the Arab world, is closely associated with religious reform. Thus, Islam opens itself up in order to organize the challenge on a political level. It arms itself with "ideological" instruments intended to strengthen its positions in relationship to the outside world and to solidify the Muslim block. The arguments defy abstract classification since the protest appears as a concrete, pragmatic, and down-to-earth defense of the religion in an intellectual atmosphere bathed in the sacred. The terms of the claim reflect emotions and feelings which are always expressed at the beginning in "Islamic" statements. After the first spark given by an elite influenced by Western modes of thought, the reaction increasingly assumes the character of a popular movement which transforms both its nature and its social color into concepts which the common people understand.

Over the course of its long history, Islam has succeeded many times in repelling outside aggression. At the turn of the twentieth century, however, the situation was very different. The enemy appeared both from the inside – in the form of reactionary autocrats and an inhibited youth – and from the outside in the guise of colonial domination and the strong fascination for material success. Industrial, liberal, and then Marxist Europe was deeply entrenched in the Muslim world thanks to the power of the ideas and institutions which it had produced as well as by the trends and needs which it had created. In its first stage, renovation was accomplished as a sometimes unconscious effort of imitation and rejection of foreign values. The Islamic world while contemptuous of the West's spiritual failure tried to understand its material success. The West, whether directly or indirectly, fragmented the traditional civilization, and the Muslims, because of intellectual laziness or the desire to show off, tried to borrow its systems and ideologies without having the critical nature which would have permitted true assimilation.[4] The reaction toward Europe was ambiguous; it was considered as both "a model and a target."[5] Estranged by colonial domination, then held back by their own economic backwardness, the Muslims were searching for an identity which would protect their fundamental values. Holding fast to their religious tradition so as to resist the cultural hold of the West, they placed the debate on a spiritual and political level. In this light, the West truly projected the image of a spiritual chaos rather than that of a source of examples. In a society cen-

[4]Malek Bennabi, *Vocation de l'Islam* (Paris: Seuil, 1957), p. 73. After this: Bennabi, *Vocation*.
[5]Mohammed A. Lahbabi, *Le personnalisme musulman* (Paris: P.U.F., 1967), p. 102. After this: Lahbabi, *Le personnalisme*.

tered on the spiritual, the borrowings would have had to be interiorized before being truly accepted, for only this would represent an original affirmation. A certain sense of the sacred – the perfection of which derives from an absolute conviction – is in fact present in all public and private events and determines the course of historical evolution. Thus an atmosphere of religiosity is maintained during political crises and social failures, technological upheavals and the encroachment of foreign ideas. To forget this would be to fail to understand the modern aspirations of the contemporary Muslim world.

While the movement of questioning, self-examination and assertion affects the Muslim world as a whole, it is the Arabs who have resolutely taken up the reins of its destiny. At a time when Islam had ceased to be Mediterranean (through its expansion in Africa and Asia), the Arabs returned to the fore ground of Islamic history which they had for almost five hundred years given up to the Persians and then the Turks. There are many reasons for this reappearance.

Although they represent a minority, the Arabs possess the center of spiritual orientation for Islam as a whole – Makkah. Moreover, the cultural and political rebirth of Islam had to draw its arguments from its traditional heritage. The language in which the revelation had appeared was exalted, as were the glorious deeds of historical Muslim heroes who had initially been either Arabs or belonged to Arabized peoples. The intellectuals and the masses of believers found matters for reflection and elements of hope. Claiming the historical legacy to direct the future destiny of their faith, the Arabs reconstituted a solid nucleus around the cradle of Islam – perhaps projecting a mythical image of it – and around the glorified history of its early greatness. The moral and territorial recession of Turkey gave Arabism a chance to assert itself. Modern Arab consciousness jelled on two pivotal points which, though they are distinctly separate for the West, always end up intermingling in Islam: religion and politics.[6]

The Islamic renaissance was largely inspired by the wish to eliminate colonialism. After expelling foreign domination, the next step was to overcome economic backwardness by drawing upon the techniques and certain related knowledge and expertise of the West. The humiliation caused by colonial domination, military and political defeat in Palestine, and economic backwardness helped to make political assertiveness one of the major aspects of the religious quest. Reformers generally avoided breaking with the "ecclesiastic" class of the 'ulema, all the while devoting a large part of their activity

---

*Taha Hussein, "Tendances religieuses de la littérature égyptienne d'aujourd'hui," *Islam et Occident*, (Cahier du Sud), pp. 233-241.

to politics. Aspirations of national dignity, religious reform, and political struggle all became closely interconnected, and each one of these tendencies nourished the others. Expressions of religious superiority were enhanced by memories of past glories and by the desire for doctrinal elucidation. Traumatized by the victory of Western materialism, the Muslims returned to the original sources of Islam in order to assert their identity. It is therefore difficult to grasp the profound upheavals which the Muslim world is currently experiencing if we fix our attention upon the contemporary epoch alone. Historical knowledge and an appreciation of Islam explain collective motivations as well as individual behavior.

The Muslim reform movement has been the object of a great deal of literature. While the intellectual premises are for the most part identical, regardless of the spiritual or geographical affiliations of the authors,[7] the solutions which they put forward vary in their expression and even in their content. Each author claims that Islam cannot be held responsible for the long stagnation and apparent decadence of the Muslim world, but rather that the present problems are the fault of the Muslims' failure to live according to the guidelines of their religion. Their loss of past material prosperity and greatness is due to the fact that they did not respect "half of the divine law." In order to lift the veil of darkness and ignorance which had descended closed upon the Muslim world, it was deemed necessary to reemphasize the perfectly rational nature of the Qur'ānic revelations as well and the profound wisdom contained within the teachings of the Prophet. After all, when the believers lived according to the precepts of the faith – which encourage thought and a critical mind – Islam had asserted itself as the torchbearer of progress.

These arguments, drawn from the past, do not only have apologetic aims but are meant to condition the Muslim conscience. Those intellectuals who sought reform unconsciously aimed such ideas at the masses. The general suggestions they proposed were multiple: to rid religious practices of superstitions and obsolete ideas accumulated over the centuries, to distinguish what was essential from what was secondary in order to retain only the truly elementary doctrines, and to return by an open intellectual inquiry to the original sources of the Qur'ān and the Prophetic tradition.

Two main tendencies developed: one, apologetic and apparently conservative, aimed at defending Islamic values from the encroachment of foreign materialistic civilization; the other, on the contrary, accepted secular princi-

---

[7]See Pickthall, *The Cultural Side*, pp. 38 f., as well as Mohammed F. Jamali, *Letters on Islam Written by a Father in Prison to His Son* (London: Oxford University Press, 1965), pp. 101 f. After this: Jamali, *Letters*.

ples and desired a modern society in which religion would be respected but would cease to be the basis of political thought. There was thus a natural opposition between the "reformers" who clung to their Islamic cultural heritage and advocated a return to orthodoxy (certain formulations of which they nonetheless unhesitatingly rejected) and the "modernists" who advocated the critical assimilation of modern thought by a rationalistic and liberal Islam which would be open to the ideas of Western Europe.

It would doubtlessly be more useful to briefly describe the religious and political theories of the leading reformers than to analyze the similarities and divergencies between the two preceding factions, for their nuances could vary infinitely.

Jamal ed-Din al-Afghani,[8] as the precursor of the movement and in view of his powerful and versatile personality, is a difficult man to describe. Both his expressions and ideas seem to have been varied and spontaneous, and his activities had far-reaching spiritual effects on the Muslim masses. He led the struggle against the prevailing institutions, preached the return of the original Islamic brotherhood and levelled biting criticisms at Western materialism and the apathy of his fellow Muslims. He believed that the only way the Muslim world could successfully resist European imperialism was to unify itself both ideologically and politically. He painted an idealized picture of Islam which went back to the time of the Prophet and his companions, whose military powers and successes violently contrasted with the Muslim world of his own era. Al-Afghani did not formulate a true coherent doctrine; he condemned sterile observance of religious dogma, claimed the individual had a right to discuss traditional theological precepts, and said that the state could legislate in order to answer the growing needs of a complex social organization. He thus tackled the reform of systems rather than of the individual,[9] but his influence was keenly felt and recognized long after his death. In fact, he is considered by history as the precursor of the Islamic awakening, of Muslim fraternity and solidarity against the West; as the flagbearer of anti-imperialism; and as the somewhat haphazard theoretician of a kind of pan-Islamic nationalism.

Al-Afghani's most brilliant disciple was the Egyptian Sheikh Muhammad 'Abdu,[10] whose reasoning was built upon two basic postulations: the absolute

---

[8]Nikki R. Keddie, *An Islamic Response to Imperialism. Political and Religious Writings of Sayyid Jamal ed-Din "al-Afghani,"* (Berkeley: University of California Press, 1968), which presents the English translation of the principal writings of the reformer. After this: Keddie, *An Islamic Response.*

[9]Bennabi, *Vocation,* p. 147.

[10]See 'Abdu, *Rissalat,* and Khadduri, *War,* pp. 60 f.

necessity of religion in the life of the people, and the need to adopt and assimilate the best of what Western science had to offer. Since Islam is in perfect harmony with reason, it could not be opposed to progress. This capacity
to adapt should have permitted it to borrowing Western techniques alone.
Clearly diverging from his master's teachings on this point, 'Abdu doubted
the effectiveness of a reform movement based on anti-colonialist political agi-
tation buttressed with religious arguments. On the contrary, he believed that
the liberation of the Muslim world could take place only through individual
emancipation and called for the abolition of the intellectual sterility imposed
by automatic imitation of badly understood religious dogma. In this respect,
he quoted the warning of the Qur'ān: "God does not change anything in a
people until the people changes itself."[11] He attempted to give all Muslims
a renewed sense of self-confidence by providing the moral basis for a new
kind of society; this would be effected through a return to a purified Islam
which would be capable of assimilating modern developments and advance-
ments and of ensuring social justice on an internal level. It is thus essentially
as a "religious" reformer that his name lives on.

If al-Afghani does not seem to have been sufficiently clear and exact in
setting out his ideas, 'Abdu on the contrary seems to have been excessively
dogmatic. He succeeded in providing the Muslims with a purified belief but
one which nonetheless lacked efficiency since he did not deal with the social
dimension.[12] Wishing to purify the faith of supersitions, and aberrant practices, he urged his fellow Muslims to return to the task of doctrinal interpretation. For him, the success of any reform was contingent upon the Muslims'
reopening of the "doors of speculative effort,"[13] meaning that they should start
to think for themselves once again. Victory over the dominating West and
the rebirth of the Muslim world were not to be achieved through violence but
through the effort of self-evaluation. On the death of 'Abdu in 1905, his dis-
ciples split into two groups, each one representing a particular aspect of the
master's thought.

The Syrian Rashid Reda, dynamic and inexhaustible, gave Arab reformism
a more apologetic, sometimes polemic, tone. He based his thought on the
ideas of Sheikh 'Abdu concerning the necessity of bringing Islam closer to
its original sources, the Qur'ān and the Prophetic tradition, but set his ideas

---

[11]ar-Ra'd: 11 (Masson).
[12]Bennabi, *Vocation*, p. 49.
[13]*Ijtihad*, see 'Abdu *Rissalat*, pp. 108 f. The adjective "speculative" translates the idea in French
poorly for it locates the efforts in an abstraction detached from the practical. A. de Zayas Abbasi
proposes the following as translation of *ijtihad*: "effort of analytic and deductive reasoning in
order to discern the just and correct application of the principle in practice."

out in a manner strongly influenced by al-Afghani. He attempted to give the renovation of the Muslim world a dimension which was political and, for its time, pan-Islamic. It was his opinion that the ideological and political unity of Islam would effectively block Western expansion. That being the case, Reda was devoted to constructing a theory of a restored caliphate which could revive the material and spiritual fortunes of the Muslim community. Though a fundamental rigorist, he did not limit himself to simply recommending a return to traditional prescriptions. He distinguished between the sacred law – immutable and eternal – which regulates an individual's personal life and those laws regulating politics and jurisprudence which could be changed to deal with the ever-evolving concepts of social justice and community property. Legislative elucidation could be effected by the consensus of the *'ulema*, who represented the community and who could meet in a sort of "Islamic parliament." Reda thus reconciled the Qur'ānic concept of consultation and unanimous community consensus in order to show the possibility of establishing an Islamic-style representative government. Reda, like his master 'Abdu, recognized the validity of modern ideas and advocated adopting them. However, he went further than 'Abdu by turning to political activism, preparing for the appearance of a movement which later influenced Islam politics in general, and Arab politics in particular: the "Muslim Brothers."

Claiming to rebuild the Muslim community according to the strictest Qur'ānic principles, which they believed would necessarily provide solutions to the social problems of the time, the "Muslim Brothers" tried to establish a mass movement which could eventually seize power. It is not possible to coherently summarize their doctrine, which ran the range from the simple affirmation of the validity of religious principles to sometimes violent political activism. In short,[14] they saw Islam as a system of morality and social justice containing all the values Muslims need to build a society ensuring their collective well-being and individual freedom. Since Islam contains all the needed answers and shows the way to bliss in the hereafter, there is no need to initiate or assimilate foreign ideas or institutions. It was therefore not a matter of developing a new political program but of applying the correct interpretation of Qur'ānic precepts and concepts — one freed of the anachronisms accumulated by popular belief. Apart from excessive materialism and communist atheism, all foreign ideological systems were present in the very heart of purified Islam.[15] The "Muslim Brothers" apparently were able to give their

---

[14]See Khadduri, *War*, pp. 76 f; and Bennabi, *Vocation*, pp. 141 f.
[15]The religious movements to political and social extensions demand the reestablishment of the absolute rule of the revealed law over the Islamic community is known under other expressions such as the "Dar ul-Islam" in Indonesia and the "Istiqlal" nationalist and socialist party in

doctrine a particular dynamism by somewhat "interiorizing" their program through a near-sanctified act of "fraternization."[16] The movement acquired a truly popular basis and expressed the aspirations of the common Muslim for an idealized society, internally more just and externally more dignified. Notwithstanding the excesses of certain later leaders and in spite of repression (which was extremely severe in some countries), the movement's influence doubtlessly still lives on in the minds of the masses, the educated classes, and those youth who are in search of a rebirth and moral rejuvenation. In all likelihood, the movement has not yet spoken its final words.

The South Asian reform movement seems to have been original. Like their Arab brothers in faith, the Muslims in South Asia demanded a rationalistic reinterpretation of the religious dogmas by which neither the Qur'ān nor the Prophetic traditions would have to suffer. On the whole, they were less traditionalistic than Arab authors. Sir Sayyed Ahmed Khan preached the incorporation of scientific progress and the adaptation of Western institutions into a modernized Islam. To these ends he created a university which was to offer a setting in which "the best of Western thought could be taught in a Muslim atmosphere."

The second influential author was Amir Ali,[17] who based his ideas on an apologetic biography of the Prophet in which he explained how Muhammad, as a man, succeeded in putting an end to the chaos of Arabia and in opening up the possibility of great progress for humanity by proclaiming the primacy of reason. For the author, the life of Muhammad alone offers probing evidence of Islam's capacity to adapt to modern times. Although he was a shi'ite, Amir Ali had a resounding success, even among the predominately Sunni Arabs. However, few of his readers could support him in his claim that the Qur'ān was the personal product of the Prophet Muhammad.

The best known author of the South Asian reform movement was Muhammad Iqbal[18] due to the wide-ranging extent of his knowledge and the fame of his poems.[19] Convinced of Islam's infinite malleability, he advocated that

---

Morocco. See Attilio Gaudio, *Allal el-Fassi* (Paris: Moreau, 1952), in which the Algerian reformer shows himself very much more dogmatic and, consequently, timid in political and economic matters. See also Ali Merad, *Le reformisme musulman en Algérie de 1925 à 1940 Essai d'histoire religieuse et sociale* (Paris: Mouton, 1968), in particular pp. 306 f. After this: Merad, *Le reformisme*.

[16] Bennabi, *Vocation*, p. 141.
[17] Amir Ali, *The Spirit*.
[18] Iqbal, *The Reconstruction*. See also Ahmed, *Iqbal*.
[19] A. J. Arberray, *Aspects of Islamic Civilization as Depicted in the Original Texts* (London: Allen and Unwin, 1964), gives certain English translations of the poem of Iqbal. See chapter XIV: "The Revolt of Islam," pp. 36 f.

the whole Islamic system be reexamined, however, without breaking away from its historical heritage. He demanded[20] that a new form of "spiritual democracy of Muslim aspirations"[21] be established by means of community and individual intellectual efforts. Contrary to Rashid Reda, he rejected the idea of reestablishing the caliphate, arguing that Islam consisted of loyalty to God and His law and not to a political guide for a governmental constitution. Closely associating traditional Muslim institutions and doctrines (sometimes interpreted in allegorical fashion) with Western rationalism, judicial principles and technological knowledge, Iqbal believed that the kind of reform he envisioned could achieve a compromise without any shock.[22]

This extremely brief account of the principal modern Muslim reformers finished, we will now discuss the two main tendencies of Islamic renovation: "reformism" and "modernism."

Reformism does not seek progress in terms of present-day political, social, or technical realities but seeks to understand Islam's "program of action." A return to the original sources does not necessarily mean that the idealized intellectual procedure should ignore immediate realities, but rather that it must develop a way to successfully integrate foreign ideas and institutions into the framework of a Muslim identity proper. Like the reaction against Western domination, a return to past procedures creates a mental process of seeking identification within continuity. The past acts as a mirror which projects the image of an idealized future. The emotional power of the image – sometimes touched up, sometimes mythical – captivates the mind and reveals a nostalgia for a long-gone purity. This quest could take on a truly "revolutionary" character on the religious and political levels and thereby constitute a "renaissance," implying the return of Muslim civilization to its former level of greatness and development. This would free Islam from the theological and legal fetters created by deficient traditional interpretations.

---

[20]Iqbal, *The Reconstruction*, in particular Chapter VI, pp. 36 f.

[21]Gardet, *L'Islam*, p. 321.

[22]Having finished this brief development about the Muslim reformers, it would be convenient to cite the initiative of Sheikh Muhammad Ashraf who launced, in 1948, the publication of a specifically Muslim monthly, *The Islamic Literature*, of which the objectives are the following: "1. to reflect in a valid manner the ambition of Islam to regain its past glory; 2. to present a new interpretation of Islam which would be amenable to changing conditions of the world; 3. to analyze in a critical fashion the present situation by exhuming the hidden treasures of the actual past of Islam, ignorance of which has made the Muslims very uncertain about their future; 4. to be the crucible, for the entire Islamic world, for the exchange of ideas which will again bring Islamic fraternity to the limits of the universe." This initiative was enlarged in the *Editions Ashraf* at Lahore furnishing numerous interesting works. See Alfred Guillaume, *Islam*, 2nd rev. ed. (Harmondsworth: Penguin, 1964), pp. 163 f.

In the Islamic context, any "renaissance" must necessarily begin with a religious reform. However, the reform movement probably made a fundamental error by concentrating its effort on the limited level of dogma and not paying enough attention to the dynamism of a modern industrial society. It failed to effectively channel the enormous emotional and spiritual energy generated by the humiliation of the politically dominated Muslim masses. The happy medium – such an essentially Islamic virtue – between intellectual speculation and political apology remains elusive, and an adequate total expression of modern Islam has yet to be discovered. Such a rediscovery would finally extinguish the temptation to embrace the political and social ideas and institutions of Europe as well as its techniques and knowledge.[23] However, it is most unjust and erroneous to claim, as Western literature too often does, that the spirit of Islamic reform "in truth conceals an ultraconservative attitude ... Progress first of all consists of a return to the ideal past, accompanied by an adaptation to the necessities of the present moment."[24] This is proven by historic comparison. In fact, the humanists who paved the way for the European renaissance quoted the authority of antiquity as the mainstay of their claims. The image which they brandished of this antiquity was also touched-up: for example, Greek slavery and the brutalities of Roman imperialism are never mentioned. Protestantism, which later became an immense liberation movement in Europe, did nothing other than return to the original Christian sources.[25]

The "modernists" come from the same "reformation" line, demanding a purification and revival of the faith, especially on the level of individual conscience. Its "ideology" is not clear for it groups together scanty elements of Western civilization or of Marxism, gathered and accumulated by the intellectual elite. This elite has usually received a foreign education and severed its ties with traditional Muslim civilization. It could appear[26] that such people were more concerned with "Westernizing" existing social structures than with actually transforming the institutions. To a certain extent they helped to aggravate the disorders of contemporary Muslim society by trying to be too "progressive" and not taking into account the "Muslim soul." Essentially pragmatic and empirical, modernism is more affected by transformations from the outside than from the inside. Doctrine seems to be an accumulation of ideas borrowed twice: first, concepts introduced by a Westernized elite, infatuated with liberal thoughts, which believed it would find the remedy for

---

[23]Pickthall, *The Cultural Side*, pp. 170 f.
[24]Jomier, *Le commentaire coranique*, p. 9, which explains the adjective of "moderniste" to which we attach a different meaning.
[25]Lahbabi, *Le ersonnalisme*, p. 93 and Laroui, *L'idéologie arabe*, p. 103.
[26]Bennabi, *Vocation*, p. 64.

colonial domination and internal despotism, and second, Marxist concepts which appeared as a means of defense against new forms of external imperialism and as a solution to the problems of economic development in social justice.

Moreover, on a concrete level, most Muslim governing bodies – that is, those liberated from colonialism – disposed of "national" administrative and political institutions before any reliable substitutes could be found. Thus, Western ideas continued to flow in and the modernizing movement could not find original concepts to stem the tide of alien ideas long enough to permit a successful assimilation of the foreign contributions already present. Failing in that attempt, Muslim reformers continually had to deal with Western systems and concepts imposed upon their societies by history, not by choice. By placing too much attention on the systems to be theoretically reformed, it failed to influence the present realities. It was in search of an immediate solution rather than long-term stability. This group sought to apply rationalism or 'scientific' socialism in achieving a rebirth through participation of the masses, but the latter would not cooperate unless the basic options were "Islamic." Thus, in short, if the reform movement has erred up to now by its excessive dogmatism, the modernizing movement on the contrary has failed to elaborate a coherent doctrine since it was motivated by subjective impulse and not by intellectual discipline.

By means of its most extreme currents, modernism gave rise to a tendency toward the secularization and laicization of the modern Muslim state. In the opinion of certain writers,[27] Islam is an eternal religious truth and an inimitable moral discipline – but one which should not interfere with contemporary political affairs. With the exception of a single victory in Turkey – one which is not necessarily permanent – secularism, which appears as a theoretically easy way out, has not had great appeal among the Muslim masses.

Nationalism and Muslim States

The Muslim world of today has been fragmented into an apparently permanent array of national states.[28] Such a development is not only an important political matter but also a phenomenon which has theoretical repercussions on Islamic doctrine as well as on the reality and practicality of its traditional international conception.

Everyone agrees that the two world wars inflicted deep rifts in history. In

[27]Abdel Razek, "L'Islam," pp. 119-144.
[28]Albert Hourani, *A Vision of History: Near Eastern and Other Essays* (Beirut: Khayats, 1961), pp. 71 f. Or chapter 3 particularly deals with the Arab countries.

the Middle East, the 1914-1918 war brought about important political changes through the dissolution of the Ottoman Empire and, on an ethical level, by the Wilsonian declaration of the right of all peoples to self-determination. The abolition of the caliphate in 1924, following the lying promises of the West which were made to gain Muslim support against Turkey and their subsequent colonization by various European countries, further inflamed their emotions and accelerated the process of nationalism. The antagonism of Western imperialists and later ideological disputes which arose from the creation of communist states helped to reinforce this trend. World War I had freed the Arabs from the Turkish yoke; World War II augmented nationalistic feelings, slowly leading to the decolonization of the vast majority of Muslim territories under European domination. The question then arises as to how Islam, with its ideal of fraternity and universalism and fundamentally "anti-nationalist" character, could have influenced these events.

Since the assertion of nationalism was inseparably linked to the resurgence of Islam, the first movements arose in the shadow of reformist theories – especially that of al-Afghani – which advocated maintaining communal unity through pan-Islamism. Concrete historical circumstances, however, prevented such a development. Islam appeared as the dynamic element while nationalism assumed the form of a mass movement, depending on popular religion to provide the mainstream of revolutionary forces. Despite its universality, Islam stimulated nationalism due to its possession of an immediately transmissible, unique "ideology," upon which the movement's cohesion, identification, and moral unity could be built. Nationalism, even when it was localized, was initially religious.[29] Political effort and national claims were linked to Islam's spirituality which had been able to provide the necessary expressions and justifications for the historical phenomena which it had to accommodate in the past.[30]

It would therefore be appropriate to analyze the pan-Islamic theory as supportive of, or opposed to, nationalism in a threefold perspective: realities,

---

[29]The opposition of the "Dastur" party in 1919 and 1933 to the politics of naturalization which France had undertaken in Tunisia was made with religious arguments. The naturalization process appeared anti-Islamic because it seemed to conceal a preparation for Christianization. Some special cemeteries were established for the naturalized Muslim Tunisians. Even taking into account the political utilization of the incident, the example is significant enough. See Pellegrin, *Islam*, p. 127.

[30]See Bayard Dodge, "The Significance of Religion in Arab Nationalism," in *Islam and International Relation* ed. J. Harris Proctor (London: Pall Mall, 1965), pp. 94-119. After this: Dodge, "The Significance." The author deals very specifically with the Arab world. The example is certainly more convincing but we are of the opinion that it is less exclusive than the earlier one. The identical conclusions could be applied "mutatis mutandis" to other Islamic countries.

The Reality of Islam

doctrines, and feelings. An incomplete view of the phenomenon could lead to serious errors. "Pan-Islamism" did little more than presenting vague ideas of spiritual unity and, at times, reinstating a reinvigorated caliphate through its apologetic writings which attempted to answer the Muslims' needs for identification and defense with regard to the West. The Muslim world's use of Islam as a unifying ideology and an element of solidarity against the outside and as a shield to protect it from the invasion of European concepts and institutions caused pan-Islamism to be seen in the West as "fanatical" or "reactionary." It is true that in the final quarter of the nineteenth century, Sultan 'Abdul Hamid used the rather complicated arguments of the movement to combat the growing desire for independence in his empire's provinces, as well as those of the liberal circles which contested his authority. He forged a theory of pan-Islamic solidarity for purely tactical and political aims – an undertaking which is not in the Qur'ānic spirit of fraternity imposed by the religion – and subsequently advocated by King Faisal of Saudi Arabia. As for Europe, it manipulated the doctrine according to its immediate interests. Favorably disposed to the similarity between the caliphate and Christian medieval feudalism, and by attributing a supposedly spiritual power to the sultan, it thus found a pretext of intervening in the internal affairs of the Ottoman Empire on behalf of its "European-protected" Christian minorities.

The abolition of the caliphate in 1924 put an end to all immediate hopes of Muslim political unity. Pan-Islamism had already fought on all fronts. A Muslim press agency founded in 1914 lived but a brief moment, having been systematically boycotted by the influential milieu of the Western press. Moreover, the newly created League of Nations constantly held it in mistrust because it was a possible rival supranational organization. Whatever its initial validity may have been, the movement was sure to fail for it was opposed to European interests. One must, however, add that further reasons for its failure were: the emergence of sectarianism (especially in the Arab world), claims to hegemony and conflicts over the respective interests of various Muslim territories, as well as the material and financial difficulties which the implementation of the pan-Islamic program would have engendered.

Religious reformers at first violently condemned nationalist movements as opposed to the spirit of the Qur'ānic command to unite all Muslim peoples into one fraternal community based on equality. They nevertheless ended up by adapting to these movements, accepting them as the only immediate way capable of providing modern Islam with its long-sought-for political dimension.

At this stage, the question could be debated from three particular views: the influence of European ideas, the specificity of nationalism in Islamic countries, and the theoretical reconciliation of state nationalism and religious universalism.

European colonialism – in addition to forcing the Islamic world to define itself vis-à-vis the West – imposed political borders upon the future national states as well as their domination upon the inhabitants. Disputes often arose in the framework of given territorial entities. The inability of the Ottoman authorities to lead the pan-Islamic struggle triggered a nationalist movement in the Arab world which was aimed against both the Muslim Turks and the Christian West. The outburst at times expressed itself through violence, then finally broke up into localized forces seeking to throw out certain colonial dominations. These were, in order of importance: French, English, and Turkish for the Arabs; Dutch, British, and Indian in the Far East and, much later, Zionist.

Another very subtle factor of European influence on Islamic nationalism originated in the relatively liberal political system of the colonial nations which could not ignore the calls for independence and national demands. The situation was very different in the Muslim republics of the USSR, for example. Either because of opportunism or immediate political calculation, the demands of the independent Islamic countries still generally avoid mentioning the forty to fifty million Muslims remaining under Russian domination. However, those Muslims could in the future develop a nationalist feeling directed against Slavic domination and the Sovietization aimed at the base of Islam and of its traditional values.[31]

Finally, European influence can again be found in the intellectual formation and the desire to imitate those who unleashed the nationalist awakening. These political leaders, nevertheless, can no longer ignore the Islamic imperatives imposed by public opinion, which lead to their public adoption of the cause of Islam.

The nationalists need popular support to achieve their political objectives and to attempt the modeling of their institutions on those of the West. Once the goal is attained, the expression of nationalism must change because of the constant pressure of the masses who still interpret political programs via traditional Islamic concepts of the individual, the government, and the community. The customary and sentimental religious aspirations of the Muslim

---

[31]The declaration of Sheikh Mustafa as-Sibai in May 1950 during the course of a popular gathering organized in Damascus by the Muslim Brothers is illustrative: "We will have our revenge upon France for all that it has done here [Syria-Lebanon] and in the Maghreb ..., upon England for all that it has done in Egypt, in Palestine and wherever it finds itself present ...; it is the same with our contacts with the United States [due to their support of Israel]. On the contrary, no vengence incites us against Russia." Cited by Marcel Colombe, *Orient arabe et non-engagement* 2 vols. (Paris: Publications orientalistes de France, 1973), 1:104.

peoples have therefore entered into the political arena. The terminology lacks the nuances necessary to better define the phenomena involved.

A brief review of history will help us characterize the specific nationalism of the Islamic countries. Certainly, European nationalism was nourished by an impassioned history of oppression and success which the political entity, real or illusory, experienced throughout its history. It even voiced the legitimate claim of the survival of nations but was, since its origin, very tightly integrated and directed by the merchantilist doctrine which knew how to profit from it. The Islamic territories' nationalism, on the other hand, seems to have been, above all in its first phase, more emotional than reasoned, more spontaneous than led. The territorial divisions before colonization, formed by Islamic history itself, had already allowed some external signs of regional identity. In spite of the progressive decline of its political authority, the caliphate remained its symbol, a development which prevented a similar split on the spiritual level. The empire's immensity and the absoluteness of power had, however, necessitated a strong administration which gradually diluted its authority to the benefit of various local governments and contributed to the appearance of certain nationalist sentiments.

It is still too soon to know whether the process which directed the formation of "nationalities" in the Islamic world is a temporary step or a movement having reached its point of no return. It is very different from the historic experience of the West. The principle of "sovereignty" seems not to have been separated from a truly interiorized feeling. The present Muslim states were brutally formed on the debris of a dissected empire, in terms of colonial borders and according to the domination to be rejected. The undertaking has not been achieved internally but has to a certain extent been imposed and then encouraged by the enthusiasm of the Westernized intellectual elite. This is the reason why the nationalism of political institutions has not fundamentally assumed a form of sentimental solidarity which transcends frontiers and joins itself to the pride of sharing a common faith.

The nationalism of the Islamic countries defies analysis. It has certain very virulent aspects, and others largely universalist. The "citizen" appears obligated to several loyalties: national and Islamic – sometimes regional, as Arabism – or emotional, as solidarity with the Third World. Any idea of a possible subordination of religion to national political institutions or, conversely, of tying civil authority to religious power is automatically excluded, for Islam does not recognize any clergy. The political destiny of Islam, as a religion uniting the spiritual and temporal domains, could however, go hand in hand with the progress made by state institutions.

As it is an original reformist doctrine,[32] it would be worthwhile to mention the concept of double loyalty or double "nationality" in this context since it occupies an important role in the contemporary Islamic scene. The first one expresses itself by religion, culture, traditions, and social customs – in other words, Islam. The "political nationality" corresponds to a situation of quasi-exterior facts imposed by circumstances and, primarily is still evolving, seeing that it strikes no deep identity and does not need the universalist claim of the Muslim. The present nationalism of the Islamic countries would, in such a case, be only a reaction against the foreigner, an expression of impatience in the face of the urgency and the diversity of the problems to resolve and, finally, a raising of sometimes violent and ill-fated claims, since it pits certain Islamic nations against each other.

Nationalism, in its turn, asserts the moral precepts and social spirit of Islam's democratic tradition with great vigor. This period of transition which the modern Islamic world is undergoing could very well funnel into diverse, but Islamized, guises issuing from earlier civilizations, such as the Turkish, Persian, or African. It is very probable that these manifestations will mature through comparison assimilation with Islam under one form or another[33] which could succeed in raising some barriers against excessive nationalism. Its influence will increase with time. National sentiment is to a degree reconciling itself with the unitary spirit of the Qur'ānic message. By refusing to consider the territories but, on the contrary, focusing in on man as the determining criterion, religion will help prevent expressions of extremist particularisms. Each believer and each Muslim people will, in the final analysis, "participate in the equality of rights and of obligations for the good of the community of believers."[34]

As a majority of the Islamic countries have acquired political independence and want to take charge of their own destiny, it seems reasonable for them to give voice to their nationalistic feelings. Indeed, these feelings have never been clothed, as they were in Europe, with ethnocentrism and expansionist ambitions. The political ethic remains deeply communal, and the feeling of collective identity could be explained as being on behalf of the entire Islamic community and not necessarily as being against others at the same time. "The Qur'ān recognizes the happy marriage between universal virtue and collective virtue. It actually teaches that outside of the brotherhood of the faith there is the brotherhood in Adam."[35] The assertion of essential Islamic values, such

---

[32]This was developed by Ben Badis, an Algerian reformer. See Merad, *Le reformisme*, pp. 187 f.
[33]"Arab nationalism" in its present form furnishes a convincing example of this.
[34]Abdel Jalil, *Aspects*, p. 71.
[35]Draz, *Initiation*, p. 81.

as equality and justice, is always active and sometimes even impertinent when it expresses a need to go beyond opening itself to universalism rather than withdrawing into itself. This national feeling thus tries to be neither aggressive nor exclusive: "We respect all nationalisms but we stand beside each community which struggles to assert its nationalism," declared the most committed of the present-day Arab political leaders.[36] This nationalism which tries to be "fraternal" manifests itself in a contradictory and incoherent manner for Western analysis, for it is at the same time characterized according to circumstances by particularism, national aggressiveness, international intervention, and the aspiration of universal fraternity.

Arab nationalism offers an interesting example of Muslim reactions, although these theses have varied in terms of events, in the political personalities who formulate them, and in the personal ambitions which they sometimes hide. The statements have been Syrian, Egyptian, and more recently, Libyan. Its actual meaning is based on the following ideas: independence and national dignity, anti-imperialist struggle, unity and – to a lesser degree – socialism.[37] Historically, however, it has asserted itself in a different fashion, namely as a simultaneous manifestation against European and Turkish domination. After the attempt to unify the Arabian Peninsula by the Wahhabi movement, the first nationalism which appeared in the Islamic world was Egyptian and, paradoxically, incited by Muhammad Ali, a non-Egyptian who tried to join his country with the Sudan and Syria. Despite the bravery of his army, he failed because his project collided with the interests of Great Britain and France. The movement was nevertheless started and could no longer be stopped.

The inability of the Ottoman authorities to lead the pan-Islamic struggle as well as the intellectual withdrawal of the Turks allowed the Arabs great latitude in taking charge of their own destiny. In an earlier time, identification was spun around the glorious cultural heritage. As opposed to the Ottomans, it is not improbable that the Qur'ān's being written in Arabic gave them [the Arabs] a sense of intellectual superiority. Arab nationalism was born in the beginning of the last quarter of the nineteenth century by the revival of literature and a rediscovered interest in history. Religion, still the essential part of Arab heritage, did not play a determining role at this stage. On the one hand, Arabism was actually directed against Islamic Turkey and, on the other, its promoters were mainly Arab Christians from Syria and Lebanon who had

---

[36]Press conference of Col. Qaddafi. See *al-Ahram*, March 31, 1972.

[37]See, in this regard, The Ministry of National Orientation of the U.A.R., *La charte* (Cairo: Service d'état pour l'information, 1962), pp. 25 f, particularly Chapter 9 and 10. After this: The Ministry, *La charte*.

been educated in Western schools. They furnished a base of identification with respect to Europe and the Ottoman Empire, but this was more on a cultural than a doctrinal level.

An Arab political awakening soon followed, and the First World War accelerated it. Sherif Hussein's proclamation of the Hijaz's independence in June of 1916 was greeted as a "day of rebirth" (*yaum an-nahdah*). European manoeuvers which successfully substituted their own colonial domination – through League of Nations mandates – for the Ottoman oppression, created such a shock that the victory of the Kemalist revolution in Turky and its diplomatic successes appeared for a time to be a triumph for Islam.

The struggle against European domination and the Jewish presence in Palestine nourished Arab nationalism and gave it a new coloring by intimately linking it to a renewed Islam. The latter one sought expression from religious justification to political demands. The double deception of the West introduced a new form of nationalism which passed from the control of the princes to the people. In a parallel development, the nostalgia for unity was no longer only sentimental, but it also furnished an awareness of a potentially enlarged force to resist the assaults – real or supposed – of reborn imperialism.[38] Reminders of the humiliation and the economic and cultural aftereffects which it caused,[39] the desire to participate in global life, as those whose destiny was not imposed from the outside, as well as the errantism as regards palestine, drove the Arabs to opt for a "revolutionary" line and to search for aid which might be offered to them *a priori* – that of the Communist democracies. This is why Arab nationalism, in its most aggressive expression, is seen as being opposed to Islamic solidarity, whose promoters do not hide their open hostility to atheistic Communism.

Sherif Hussein, launching the "Arab revolt," tried to justify the legality of his action to the Islamic world by claiming that he was leading it against a "non-Islamic" Ottoman government. Religion came to the aid of politics. Islamic reformism, despite its background of ideal unity, seemed to go hand in hand with the political revolution of national states in the making. Economic immobilization, cultural apathy, social inequalities, and political despotism were declared contrary to Islam. There are many examples from the Islamic past which prove this. Confidence was therefore able to grow, and the ways to the future were opened: it was sufficient to return to the true reli-

---

[38]See the declaration of Col. Qaddafi, *al-Ahram*, May 5, 1971.
[39]"The revolt against colonialism is an inherent natural right of all colonized people, but the profound hatred which our people feel, and do not cease up to the present to feel for the colonizers, finds its justification in this period." The Ministry, *La charte.*, p. 43.

gion. The paths which conducted it there were multiple. Their choice seems
to divide the Muslim peoples and reaffirm the institutions existing in each of
the national states. The programs of action cannot but differ in their formulation and their essence, since they consciously or unconsciously refer to an
idealized image of the original Islamic society.

It must, however, be emphasized that the feeling of the historical unity of
the Islamic community remains lively and cannot be rashly thrust aside, considering the deep divergencies which are sometimes held as a proof of this
unity,[40] as branching expressions of similar currents toward the affirmation
of identity and the social struggle. Even within each national political entity
there is a great deal of tension between liberals, progressives, revolutionaries,
conservatives, socialists, or feudalists. The ideas are too seething to allow a
synthesis to be formed from the affirmation of fundamental Islamic concepts
and the assimilation of borrowed external values. The social rupture provoked
by the demands of modern life and the imperatives of economic development
which force these nations to seek an alignment of foreign doctrines and at
the same time encourage nationalism have already been raised. With time,
however, resounding ideology no longer reflects reality. The society's middle
and lower classes, less influenced by imported ideas, judge all the progress
of modernization by a more Islamic view of the world. Islam is not a statement of abstract ideas because it not only influences the political course of
events but also expresses itself in individual commitment and communal rule.
Not surprisingly, it seems to assert itself more and more as a moderating influence.

For twelve centuries, the caliphate remained the expression of a bond uniting all believers under the direction of the revealed divine law. Political circumstances condoned the dismemberment of the Islamic community into national states. According to economic necessities, historical heritage and political opportunism, various national movements were tried, most of them claiming for national dignity were accompanied by attempts at social transformation. In [British] India, where the Muslims were scattered and lived as minority populations no longer in control of their "historical territory," it took the
form of a communal regrouping around Islam through the creation of a geographically split but Muslim majority state by the name of Pakistan. In Indonesia, Islam was able to join itself to ancestral customs, which accelerated
the process of identification. In Black Africa, it dynamically established itself
as a vector of a superior spiritual civilization and a promoter of new social
structures. In shi'ite Persia, it manifested itself in the form of a pacific and
egalitarian mysticism. The Kemalist revolution established in Turkey a radical
secularism which is, perhaps, not final. As different as it might seem, each
of these manifestations are woven on the same frame and fundamentally preserve the coloring of a dynamized traditional Islam which expresses its am-

bition to furnish adequate solutions to the problems of modern society.

By asserting its own values, political Islam ceases to doubt its reality, its vitality, and its practicability in the face of a world which has lost its spiritual sense and respect for moral values.[42] Besides, a feeling of fundamental unity, even if it is not realized in actions, remains lively. It expresses a deep religious emotion, the conviction of a community of destiny, a hope for the future, and a homogenous vision of societies. The faith has great expectations for itself even with the most Westernized elites, as an expression of a new search for itself vis-à-vis the world. Nationalism thus joins itself with the desire for unity and, moreover, with an always lively awareness of the universalism preached by the Qur'ān. No real contradiction appears at the base, seeing that the existence of diverse nations is strengthened by mutual respect and fraternity among all of them.

Universality and Diversity

It is evident that, even in Islam, religious factors do not have an exclusive monopoly on the influences affecting the social and economic organization of contemporary life. However, Islamic society could never completely separate itself from such a concern. At all levels and in all domains, these factors appear as the criteria of reference and often as dynamic initiatiors. Islam finds again its traditional vocation. In such widely different countries as the Kingdom of Saudi Arabia and the Arab Republic of Libya, it is supposed to form the society's foundations. In the first, the Qur'ān represents the political constitution; in the second, the "revolutionary intellectuals" are called upon to see to it that religion "entirely once again regulates the political, economic and social life, war and peace."[43] With its rediscovered vitality, Islam affirms itself as a social and moral "ideology." There is a specificity in this political claim and spiritual quest which often escapes external observation. For the believers, there is no doubt that the revealed provisions and the values accumulated over the course of centuries can provide a solution to the contemporary community's problems, rebuild the political institutions of Islam, and revitalize its creative originality. In view of the fullness of its aspiration, the reformist and modernist doctrines still lack coherence and uniformity. Thus,

[40]Ibid., p. 125.
[41]Rodinson, *Marxisme*, pp. 575 f., for example.
[42]Bennabi, *Vocation*, pp. 152-153; and Pickthall, *The Cultural Side*, p. 174.
[43]Discourse of Col. Qaddafi, *al-Ahram*, March 31, 1972. It is equally interesting to refer in this context to diverse works of the Academy for Islamic Research which consists of some one hundred *ulema* gathered from about twenty countries with the goal of debating the problems of Islamic society in areas as crucial as finances and investments, insurance, social solidarity in Islam, and so on.

religion no less represents an immense potential force offering an ethical base and an eagerness to go beyond the Islamic peoples. It probably constitutes the best available material for the reconstruction of the post-colonial community. Such is its true spiritual, political, and international vocation. It seems, therefore, useful to analyze which part of contemporary humanity Islam continues to mould.

Statistics relating to the Muslim world are generally elusive, out dated, and incomplete.[44] Six to seven hundred million is probably the most realistic Muslim population figure.[*] It is also equally tricky to provide estimates as to the number of "Islamic" states since an agreed-upon definition of such a state has never surfaced. Before the 1969 Rabat conference was held, the host government had sent out thirty-five invitations. Some countries which had been invited, especially those in black Africa were, however, not really "Muslim" countries. Taking only the criterion of population into account, it can be seen that there are Muslim majorities in approximately thirty nations.[45] About fifty percent of the population of five of the countries invited is Muslim: Nigeria, Malaysia, Mali, Chad, and Lebanon. Five other African countries were invited, although the proportion of their Muslim population was less than thirty percent: Tanzania, Upper Volta (Bourkenia Faso), Cameroon, Sierra Leone, and the Ivory Coast. On the other hand, there are numerically large Muslim minorities in India (more than fifty million), in the USSR (about fifty million), and in China (probably more than forty million). Finally, geographically homogeneous Muslim minority groups are of great interest to the political world today because of their claims for self-government and independence. There are six to seven million Muslims in Eritrea, more than three million in Palestine, and one-half million in various southern Philippine provinces.

In other words, on the international political scene, more than one out of five countries is Muslim and every sixth person is a Muslim. This does not mean that only his external behavior is conditioned by Islamic precepts and norms but that he recognizes the guiding force of Islam in his moral behavior and personal thoughts and that he belongs to a society whose every aspect

---

[44] See the statistics which appeared in *Le Monde* September 21/22, 1969, and above all the remarkable Louis Massignon, *Annuaire du monde musulman: Statistiques historiques, sociales, et économiques*, 1954 4th rev. edition, (Paris: P.U.F., 1955), which is unfortunately dated on the statistic level.

(*) By 1984, the Muslim population had risen to 848.22 million. See Richard V. Weeks, *Muslim Peoples, A World Ethnographic* (Westport: Greenwood Press, 1984). Even if there had been a minimal growth of 11 percent a year, the Muslim population should now exceed one billion.

Tariq Quraishi (ed.)

[45] According to the statistics established by *Le Monde* on the occasion of the conference of Rabat,

has been based upon Islam. This is important if one bears in mind that each Muslim is strongly susceptible to the idea of Islamic brotherhood, and that Islamic countries, if they ever unified, would constitute a bloc with considerable weight in world politics.

Even after decolonization, and despite changes in naval military strategy and the development of maritime transportation, Islam has partial or total control over places of primary importance: the Bosphorus and Dardanelles, the Persian Gulf, Suez and Bab el-Mandeb, Gibraltar, and the Singapore (Straits of Malacca). Its geographical closeness to Black Africa – of which certain parts are Islamic – has resulted in the formation of a mutual bond in the struggle against Western imperialism. Islam also possesses huge natural resources over which it is trying to regain total control – that is, Arabian oil, which is an extremely important element in the world economy. Finally, one has to remember that many of the six to seven hundred million Muslims are young people, giving an image of unity and strength, animated with an almost messianic spirit.

On the religious level, the present dynamism and vitality of Islam can be seen by the number of people who embrace it every year. Islam still spreads faster than most religions, especially in Africa and Asia, where the logical simplicity and flexibility of its doctrine find receptive audiences. This expansion appears to be a direct result of European expansion, for its pacification of territories made missionary work easier and it was seen by the subsequently colonized people as a vehicle of national assertiveness against, and rejection of, the Christian West. Since Islam, as any other religion, carries with it its culture and the bulk of its moral and social values, its ascension and growth are thus steady. More than half of all Muslims alive today live in areas which have never been under the political domination of Islam.

It is worth noticing, moreover, that conversions continued to take place even during the cultural and military decline of the Muslim state. With one exception (the Indian "Ahmadiyyah" sect which was officially declared non-Muslim in 1976), missionary activities were never systematically organized, for a long time remaining the concern only of dedicated volunteers.

The political struggle has been shaping itself mainly under the cover of trade because the Islamization movement seems to have grown faster with the anti-European and anti-Christian feelings aroused during the period of Euro-

---

there were twenty-four countries, to which it is convenient to add the Gulf States, the United Arab Emirates, Bahrain, Qatar, and Oman (and among which, curiously enough, do not figure: Bangladesh, Mauritius, and the Comoroes). Albania is a marginally interesting case since it seems that the net majority of the population might be Muslim.

pean colonial domination. However, it would be too easy and too unfair to see it only as an ideological competition. On the individual level, the movement relies on religious conviction and has grown in two directions during the post-colonial period. On the one hand, there was the geographical and numerical growth of Islam and, on the other, an assertion of Islam as the national religion and its precepts and injunctions as the backbone and fundamental spirit of society.

On the political level, there is a double phenomenon. In Africa and Asia, Islamic civilization is not on the defensive as it is in the Middle East, where contacts with the industrialized Western countries took place in a context of domination. In the former two continents, Islam asserts itself fully in all its potentialities. On the other hand, the political fate of Islam seems to be drawn, once again, to the shores of the Mediterranean Sea. The Arabs appear as the founding fathers of the new spirit, and Islam must define itself vis-à-vis Europe and its material achievements. The thoughts, oppositions, and gropings of the Arabs have a great effect on the Islamic world as a whole, and provide much food for thought.

Islam seems to have a stronger hold over the recently Islamized people who are not hampered by the weight of tradition and who are relatively less influenced by European political and economic doctrines. In the Far East and Africa, Islam, in the face of an economically underdeveloped world, has the task of carrying forward human progress, whereas in the Mediterranean world, it hardly ever asserts the conviction of its strength. In that area, the certain mental reservations it seems to have with regard to the material aspects of civilization cause it to flourish in a retrospective and often apologetic manner.[46] Disregarding for the moment its external manifestations, one finds the same spiritual quests and material ambitions in both areas.

Should we then talk of Islam or Islams? If we did so, Islam's fundamental unity would disappear under a diversity of multiple facets. The insistence of Western historians on studying only the strictly religious aspects of the phenomenon has probably hidden a reality which, according to the Qur'ān, God Himself has determined. When Islam's principles and precepts are correctly understood, it asserts itself as fundamentally "one" religion. However, in its concrete application, it takes on expressions that are extremely varied, a fact which corresponds to different interpretations and to the needs of Muslims to adapt to different regions of the world. Therefore, it is useful to analyze the diverse manifestations of modern Islam according to its geographical and ethnic distribution.

---

[46]Louis Massignon, "Situation internationale de l'Islam," *Islam et Occident*, (Cahier du Sud), pp. 13-18.

"Arabic Islam" is the richest, the most diversified and certainly the most contradictory in its external expressions because it is the most creative in its dealings with completely different economic problems and its direct confrontation with the Western world and Jewish nationalism. In its traditional form, ever, Islam is invoked to support economic growth in a roughly drawn context of social equality and thus tends to preserve a Muslim and Arab character in the society. The "liberal feudals" are faced with several forms of socialism which are more or less democratic. The only characteristic these different regimes have in common is their desire to maintain a specific Arab-Muslim character at all cost. In this affirmation, where conservative or modernist religious tendencies merge and where a local or pan-Arab nationalism along with personal aims for hegemony are entangled, the precise source of arguments is difficult to define.

Following the path of some reformists, the Arabs feel they have a particular mission as far as Islam is concerned.[47] Muhammad 'Abdu, for instance, had advocated the revitalization and galvanization of some Muslim countries in order to make Islam once again one of the great world powers and to give it back its former strength. It is obvious that the ideologies motivating modern Arabic nationalism, which is expressed more emotionally than territorially, and conservative movements such as the "Muslim Brothers," were bound to clash. These same tendencies can be seen between the fundamental unitary conscience and the personal or regional dissensions, which makes true political unity, already existing to a certain degree on the psychological level, practically impossible.

The present period of transition is naturally one of conflict. At stake is the establishment of an egalitarian, efficient, and dynamic society which can control its own destiny. It would be presumptuous to say what the final outcome will be.

Turkey, which controlled the destiny of Islam for several centuries and had a great influence on the Muslim world, is an interesting case study for it is the sole Muslim state which has based itself on secularism. The military success of the "Young Turks" exerted a tangible political influence on the Arab nationalists or elite but these two groups did not support the decision to secularize all state institutions. Yet, the very secularization of laws had a greater influence on the political life of Turkey than on its popular customs and found its expression in a nationalist instead of an anti-religious form. In the beginning, Turkish nationalism was mixed with Arab nationalism. Later on, however, it confined itself to Anatolia, thereby giving the Arabs a chance to ex-

---

[47]Nadawi, *Islam and the West,* and Hazem Z. Nuseibeh, *The Ideas of Arab Nationalism,* 2nd ed. (Port Washington: Kennikat Press, 1972), pp. 122 f.

press their own nationalism to a greater degree. This development also led to the abandonment of almost two-thirds of the Turkish and Turkistan Muslims to communist domination in Asia and Eastern Europe. Looking back, one sees that the secularization of institutions was a decision based on a certain form of resignation or at least triggered by a misled ambition. However, beyond the official secularization of the state, the influence of Islam is still felt among the Turks and tends to spread thanks to modern democratic institutions. Not only does Islam remain a criterion of reference that has to be invoked to justify social transformations, it is also a source of new energy for contemporary Turkish political life. Thus, even for a secularized Turkey, one has to avoid jumping to hasty conclusions about the political fate of Islam.

Iran constitutes a particular example because the shi'ite doctrine is indifferent to and even distrustful of political life. The Safavid dynasty, which forced itself upon Persia as a religion and a movement of national and cultural identification, resulted in the victory of a strong mystical tendency, not that of a truly political group.[48] The distrust that religious people have for governmental authority, whose theoretical "legitimacy" is constantly questioned, persists even now. In addition, the Pahlavi dynasty's accession to power in 1925 did not involve any nationalistic character since the Iranian nation had developed as a separate entity since the fifteenth century. The modernization of institutions and customs did not lead to secularization as had happened in Turkey. The reforms which rely to a large extent on judicial, social, and Western concepts, necessitate a transformation into a specifically Islamic point of view dominated by a quasi-irrational quest for an equality and a brotherhood that are far removed from European democracy. The very audacious modernization process conducted by the Shah was met with such a violent reaction from the traditionalist groups that it almost drove the country to the brink of destruction.

In Africa, Islam is full of dynamism. It is estimated that the number of believers has doubled during the last two decades. Through Qur'ānic schools, Muslim missionaries offer a superior culture to the newly converted people who do not want to adopt the convictions of the former colonial power. Such a development sooner or later leads to cultural Arabization, which is reinforced by usually sending the best students to Qur'ānic universities in North Africa and Cairo. It has often been shown[49] how colonization made conversion to Islam easier by establishing peace among tribes, allowing better com-

---

[48]Seyyed H. Nasr, *Ideals and Realities of Islam* (London: Allen and Unwin, 1966), 184 pages. After this: Nasr, *Ideals*.
[49]Arnold, *The Preaching*, pp. 315-365, particularly pp. 361 f.

munication among people, abolishing slavery, and placing the most culturally advanced black people, usually Muslims, in the administration and the army. However, such arguments, which are true enough, cannot completely explain the present-day vitality of Islam in Africa. One has to study these phenomena more thoroughly. Two characteristics stand out: the first proceeds from religion itself; the second from the particular paths that Islamization took. The logical simplicity of the doctrine and its worldly social and human implications fit perfectly with African traditions. Thus, Islam, which was already established in Africa before the Europeans arrived, spread peacefully among the colonized population due to its widely perceived demand for social justice and racial equality. This was also helped by the fact that most missionary activities which started at the beginning of the nineteenth century seem to have mainly been the work of mystical groups.[50] They organized communities around a single leader, thereby making brotherly cooperation easy in an agricultural society and taking as their own the belief in supernatural forces, which is the immemorial spiritual heritage of Africa. With the development of education, African Islam has tried to purify itself gradually by returning to the original sources and by attempting to lessen mystical influence. It is highly probable that Islam will grow on three levels: on the numerical and geographical level, on the religious and individual level, and on the social and political level.

In Asia, the influence of mysticism and pre-Islamic cultures, namely Hinduism, Buddhism, and animism, was also predominant. "Islam settled in Indonesia without chasing out the first occupants."[51] This feature became very important in the history of Indonesian Islam, where traditional common law stood up to Qur'ānic legislation. Religion played a major role in the anti-colonial struggle and also in the debates that followed independence. Most of the competing political parties claimed to be inspired by a religion reflecting the fierce doctrinal oppositions that went from rigorous integrism, such as the Dar ul-Islam party, to the reformist tendencies of Egypt, and especially of Pakistan.[52] Indonesian Islam is one of the most active for intellectual speculation is not burdened with the weight of tradition. It has shown a lively feeling of brotherhood, of Muslim solidarity, and of "universal humanitarianism." Indeed, the Indonesian group was preponderant in molding the spirit of the Bandung Conference.

It would be useful to concentrate on the case of Pakistan since it is the

---

[50]Ishak, M. Husaini, "Islamic Culture in Arab and African Countries," in *Islam – The Straight Path: Islam Interpreted by Muslims*, (New York: Ronald Press, 1958), pp. 224-252. After this: Husaini, *Islamic Culture*.

[51]André Miquel, *L'Islam et sa civilization: 7e-20e siècles* (Paris: Colin, 1968), p. 396.

[52]P. A. Hossein Djajadiningrat, "Islam in Indonesia," in *Islam – The Straight Path*, pp. 377-402.

only country whose birth resulted from the long desire of creating a state on strictly Islamic principles. When confronted with Buddhism and Brahmanism, Islam in South Asia took specific expressions, especially in rural zones where its orthodoxy merged with a mysticism impregnated with the cult of saints. There was hardly any tension between Muslims and other religious groups in the peninsula until the era of colonization*. The British were fickle in their policy for they encouraged the Hindus at the expense of the Muslims who were, nevertheless, more educated and endowed with a more acute political conscience. Later, when the anti-colonial protest started, they made several attempts to mend fences with the Islamic community. The movement which was to lead to the creation of Pakistan had strong nationalist tendencies at first, and religion acted as its catalyst. The assertion of Muslim identity appeared on two levels: it clashed with the Hindu belief, the members of which constituted the majority, and it equally clashed with the British system and its ethics. In addition, it was linked to the modernist-reformist movement led by Sir Sayyed Khan and Muhammad Iqbal. Muslim political leaders adopted an attitude of temporization toward England for they were reluctant to join the Indian Nationalist Movement, the National Congress, which would have

---

(*) This is not historically tenable.

The Hindu-Muslim enmity is as old as the advent of the Muslim rule in South Asia. The Muslims came as the conquerors of South Asia which reduced Indians to a subject race. And though as rulers the Muslims were generous, the Indians maintained their hostility toward them and their faith. The Indian desire to strike back surfaced during the reign of Moghul Emperor Akbar (1542-1605) when the Hindus converted a large number of mosques into warehouses and bandstands. See *Aurangzeb and His Times* by Zahiruddin Faruki, (Delhi: Idarah-i Adabiyāt-i Delli, 1972) p. 33.

During Jehangir's time (1605-1627) many mosques were "demolished and appropriated by the Hindus, and new temples erected in different parts of the Empire." See p. 37 of the same book. Also pp. 112-113.

During the reign of Moghul Emperor Shah Jahan, the Hindus were forcibly taking Muslim women into their custody for cohabitation: "When the royal camp was at Gujrat... the Sayyids and Sheikhs of the town petitioned the Emperor... Thereupon Sheikh Mahmud Gujrāti was appointed to make enquiries, separate the Muslim wives from their Hindu husbands, and take possession of the mosques."

See also the letter of Mujaddid Alif Thāni (1551-1614) to Nawwāb Sayyid Farid Bukhāri: "You must be aware of what had befallen in the recent past to the followers of Islam in [Moghul India] ... Having come into dominance, the polytheists [Indians] imposed *kufr* (disbelief) on *Dār al-Islām* and the Muslims lacked the courage to practice the injunctions of Islam. If somebody dared [to express his faith], he was put to death..." Abul Hassan 'Ali Nadawi, *Tārikh Da'wah wa 'Adhimat* (Nadwa: Majlis Tehqiqāt wa Nishriyāt-i Islam, 1980) p. 305.

Needless to say, this happened during the Muslim rule in South Asia when the Indians were their subjects and well before the advent of English rule. To say that there was no Hindu-Muslim conflict before the English set their foot in South Asia is at best a myth perpetuated by India.

Tariq Quraishi (ed)

led to the creation of a state in which they would be outnumbered and economically and culturally dominated by the Hindus. The First World War, which led to the dismemberment of the Ottoman Empire and to military occupation of new Muslim territories, brought about a violent reaction among the Muslims in South Asia, who subsequently abandoned their tolerance toward the British and organized the Khalifat Movement – a fiercely anti-British party that was joined later by M.K. Ghandi [a Hindu] and his partisans from the Congress Party. The driving force of the pro-Khalifat movement weakened after Turky abolished the caliphate in 1924. The bad experiences and discrimination endured by the Muslims when the first political actions took place drove them toward a new form of nationalism which relied on religion and on communal solidarity.[53] After independence and the partition of [British] India, two-thirds of the Muslims joined Pakistan while about fifty million remained in India where, after some difficult times, they formed an active minority that clung to orthodoxy.

Recent history calls for the mentioning of Islam's different expressions in the two provinces which previously composed the original Pakistan. In the western part, the influence of reformist thinking, especially Arab, was strong. On the contrary, in the east, British discrimination against the Muslims led to an undeniable cultural decay. Administration, public education, and trade were all monopolized by the Hindus. The creation of Pakistan led, for some time, to a Muslim political awareness, but religion and the social structure remained under Hindu influence. Reformist ideas were difficult to spread. Psychological and administrative mistakes, the arbitrary division of the borders into numerous enclaves, economic exploitation, the obvious social disparities in which the Hindu minority played an important role, the plots of India, and the ambition of the superpowers all generated a new nationalism which eventually gave birth, amid violence, to Bangladesh. The Pakistani experience, which was not approved of by all Muslims, is interesting for it shows the link between a dogmatic reformism and a political nationalism which for historical reasons had to assert itself against both the Western world and Hinduism. Government officials seem to be unsure of the difference between Islamic and secular forms of government. All modern historians seem to recall the search for a practical compromise, since theoretically, society should not be separated from religion. It is certainly premature to predict future political developments. At the present time, problems of equipment, infrastructure, and economic growth remain imperative priorities.

The study of differing geographical "expressions" of Islam should not hide

---

[53]Mazheruddin Siddiqi, "Muslim Culture in Pakistan and India" in *Islam – The Straight Path*, pp. 296-343, particularly pp. 315 f. After this: Siddiqi, "Muslim Culture."

the reality that in general, Islam shows an extraordinary unity and an important uniformity of conviction. The only tangible differences are on the level of popular belief and are mainly due to ignorance.[54] The liveliness and unity of religious expressions are seen in a variety of areas under a variety of forms. On the individual level, the believer profoundly feels the positive aspect of Muslim law and ethics since he is also called upon to build "a kingdom in this world." The divine word which is constantly recalled, the evocation of Muhammad's behavior, and the Islamic statements on traditional wisdom not only guide his behavior and thoughts but also direct him on a uniform and moral path. Of course, the most indisputable "physical" testimony of communal unity on the collective level is the pilgrimage to Makkah which every year brings together hundreds of thousands of Muslims, each showing the same fervent faith and conviction. The Qur'ānic spirit gives birth to a new life which bridges different mental expressions and behaviors and equalizes the social systems in a much more forceful way than political definitions and ideological labels ever could. The influence of the Qur'ān on contemporary "Muslim thinking" remains unquestionably strong. It is the principal source of individual and collective inspiration as well as the last recourse and refuge for the believers.[55]

The Prophet's personality, what he did and said, also contributes to the shaping of the "Muslim soul." No name is more popular and more generally used throughout the whole world than that of Muhammad or its equivalents – Ahmad or Mahmoud. A popular feeling of fervent respect, devotion, and personal faithfulness constitute one of the most stimulating elements in the lives and the thoughts of the Muslim masses, contributing to the maintenance of a certain degree of fundamental communal similarity. It would also be appropriate to talk about mosques, which effect uniformization through their social and cultural importance. They have now regained and even surpassed their primary importance as spiritual and educational centers, featuring libraries and reading rooms. The Friday sermons deal with daily problems such as hygiene, political options, professional awareness, devotion to the community – in short, all matters of importance in underdeveloped countries. This phenomenon in turn contributes to the growth of a certain unity of thought among Muslims.

It is better to consider Islamic unity and diversity in a very general manner, for too precise an analysis would distort the objective situation and make it impossible to predict future developments. Thus, it is necessary to make some

---

[54]Mohammad Rasjidi, "Unity and Diversity in Islam," in *Islam – The Straight Path*, pp. 403-430.
[55]"The Qur'ān is not a mute code for the archives but an oral teaching which roars when one swallows it." See Massignon, *Parole donnée*, p. 237.

statements about the possible bonds between Muslim solidarity and contemporary pan-Islamic inclinations. It is obvious that Islam has never lost its influence on individual believers even during periods of decadence. As for social evolution, the question is whether the source of energy represented by Islam has dried up or not, and how its eventual revival will be realized. Certainly, the materials offered by the Qur'ānic revelation should allow the erection of a modern society. Notwithstanding this, the desire to submit to a divine authority and to keep a spiritual awareness through an ambition which becomes an end in itself seems to have led to a new form of anxiety. A certain confusion over those conceptions and priorities related to the adoption of modern technology has arisen. The hesitations, mistakes, contradictions, and new apologetic temptations appear as natural phenomena throughout this period of transition, but they nevertheless show, better than words, a total lack of trust. Indeed, although the modern trend seems to shape the social and political destiny of Islam, its role remains somewhat limited. Other than its phraseology, which is borrowed from the West or Marxism, there has been no real influence.

It seems that modern Muslim humanism has been searching, mistakenly, for new terminology and concepts other than trying to revive purely Islamic values. These values will probably identify themselves in a more vivid way as society once again finds its traditional balance. The present incoherence should not cause us to jump to conclusions drawn from the outside. Certain reformists make a methodological mistake in interpreting Islam according to foreign ideological criteria and then attempting to remold Islamic values to fit those criteria. The problems of the Muslim world have their answers in its cultural heritage and among its traditional values. Of course, new paths will be built according to foreign concepts, but they will find their place in the global network. Besides, Islam should not limit itself to a certain geographical area, breaking away from a world that is gradually becoming unified. The question is not to reject foreign values, but rather to define the relation of the Islamic world to the non-Islamic human experiences and political ideologies.[56] The game is not over yet. Actually, it has just started. In order to study the present vitality of Islam, it is necessary, first of all to distinguish factual realizations from verbal assertions; second, to confront Islamic theoretical humanism with concrete problems; and finally, to formulate a plan for the future.

The apologetic attitude often disguises a certain anguish over the demands of a developing society. Nevertheless, Muslim universalism has been estab-

[56]Bennabi, *Vocation*, p. 123; Rodinson, *Marxisme*, pp. 129 f.; and Nasr, *Man in the Universe: the Islamic View* "Arabic Background Series" (London: Longman, n.d.), p. 711.

lished and is open to the outside world. Religion galvanizes the believer with its assertions of justice and moderation and thus provides a shield against imported ideologies. Western intrusion, economic delay, and the too rapid growth of cities have probably led to a certain dislocation in the social organization. Traditional values and virtues have always somehow succeeded in surviving and providing a foundation for society. The Muslim world has so far failed to build a unified and coherent ideology. Maybe it will never reach this goal, but it will keep the variety which makes its history so original. Faith still represents to most Muslims an extraordinary moral strength and a social incentive, both of which have always been used according to the particular needs of the given moment. This evidence being accepted, one still has to show how the psychological feeling of communal solidarity, which transcends national frontiers and political differences, manifests itself.

Speculations about the unification of the Muslim world have always been tinged with either a sarcastic skepticism or, on the contrary, with an unrestrained idealism. Debates as to the need of reestablishing the caliphate have polarized theoretical oppositions, and the affectation of intellectual advances in political science has created a greater confusion. One then has to revert to the fundamentally Islamic concept of a "divine government." The sovereignty of Allah is universal and is to be found everywhere in the world, no matter which social systems exist. The secular political state is a definite entity which is limited to one people and one territory. Such powers are not antinomian since man's choice would not go against God's laws. Inside this universal divine government there is, according to the principle of existential unity, a Muslim community, a politico-religious entity based on faith and not on geographical or racial criteria. The latter, racial critera, have never managed to erase local "particularisms." On the psychological level, however, the community has kept its unity. As early as the eighteenth century, the transformation of the Ottoman Empire and the territorial dislocations that followed, two theories began to compete, one monist, the other pluralist. The latter advocated dividing the community of believers into territorial entities, each one being ruled by a caliph who would be responsible for implementing the divine law in his territory. Traditional orthodoxy rejected this theory but nevertheless had to adopt its views, only to witness the existence of political subentities declaring allegiance in a more or less formal way to the central caliphate. In sum, the phenomenon of distortion between a centralist, denationalist Islam and particular original differences is not new; it had been expressed even before the concept of "nation" appeared.

Today, however, it has a new form. Religious conviction, judicial and social duties, and cultural prescriptions are the elements in a spiritual and even temporal community which transcends all borders. This very awareness of brotherhood and collective solidarity comes directly from the revelation, which is the sole foundation of Islamic law. Therefore, there is no contradiction in this kind of dual loyalty to religion and to the state, since the believers feel a togetherness beyond the national government. It is difficult to precisely describe the phenomenon for the aspirations merge, and the limits between the different faiths are not clear-cut: Islamic or national, regional or traditional, political or general. There is always in the back of the Muslim's mind a vague and sometimes illusory idea of the ideal Islamic community. If this question has not always been raised on the level of concrete international politics, it has always remained vivid in the minds of the Muslims. Anarchy and political divisions have in fact never succeeded in dividing the aggregate unity of Muslim thought. The sense of community based on the book survived political disintegration. The apparent victory of secular principles and national sovereignty has never deeply affected the feeling of Islamic solidarity, and the latter feelings seem to be continually expanding. In the last analysis, this awareness of brotherhood has proven to be indestructable, for it does not rely on institutions or on loyalty to one man, but on the conviction of possessing and sharing the ultimate truth. Political solidarity is thus a corollary to religious conviction.

The Islamic community (ummah) thus finds its original meaning as a life style. Moreover, a civilization exists and grows only when it continues to live. The modern Western analysis still has too much of a tendency to make post mortem analyses of the Islamic world. Islam has never remained static, but at times its mobility has been thwarted by external circumstances, reaching its lowest point during the Ottoman reign and European colonization. Today, social institutions have a much larger range of action and power. As a religion of "evidence," Islam has never totally changed the traditional ideas of the peoples who have joined it. It nevertheless has imposed a vision of God, man and society, thereby leaving an everlasting stamp on their attitudes toward life. Thus, a certain conceptual unity, an identical train of thought and feelings, has allowed Muslims from very different social and geographical backgrounds to solve identical problems with diverse solutions – even though they shared similar reactions and attitudes.

The modern "Muslim world" is the result of distinct regional idiosyncracies expressed in the common context of Islamic civilization. It has not yet provided a global political answer to the problems encountered by men and society, but it always seems to define itself in a homogeneous manner in relation to the non-Muslim world. As a people's religion and conviction, and as a cultural and social phenomenon, Islam goes beyond particular manifestations. Each one of its aspirations and problems or tendencies represents in the last analysis its collective testimony as well as the survival of each of its nations.

Indeed, many contemporary Muslim states could not disassociate Islam from their past or even their birth. Most of them must refer to it either for the immediate present or project it as an ideal objective to be attained in the future. Political opportunism, however, has led Muslim people to work separately for their national independence. Individual interests superseded the larger communal ones. After the actual period of crisis and quests for identity, a well-kept nationalism will not last very long for it cannot justify its existence in the Islamic mind or in the history of Islam. This is the reason why it dilutes itself in a larger context: pan-Arabism or pan-Islamism. Even the older religious opposition between sunnism and shi'ism tends to fade away and then to reappear as two different expressions of a sole conception of humanity.[57]

Of course, an analysis that would strictly stick to concrete reality would give a less optimistic view of the situation. Arab disputes have been major events on political scene in the last years. On the global level of Islam, the same unitary aspirations and political oppositions are at play, but they seem diluted by geographical space, linguistic differences, and the specificity of the problems encountered. Several wars had broken out among Arab countries, and Pakistani and Bengali nationalisms have clashed violently. Several Muslim countries fight over territories. Also, the Islamic world has not reacted in a unified manner in disputes involving one or more Islamic states. Political motivations take precedence over religious solidarity, as it is the case in South Asia and in Cyprus, for instance.[58]

Beyond these differences, feelings of unity and attempts at effective collaboration are expressed under various forms. On the political level, for instance, the Islamic General Secretariat is actively preoccupied with the Muslims' situation in the southern part of the Philippines.[59] The Grand Sheikh of al-Azhar made an appeal to the Muslim people and governments, asking them to support the Eritrean people's struggle for independence according to the principles of the United Nations.[60] On the economic level, decisions were also taken but no practical results have ever been seen. Those talks were aimed at the establishment of an Islamic Common Market, an Islamic Bank of Economic Development, a Chamber of Commerce and Industry, more fre-

---

[57]The reformist authors discern an "ecumenical" rapprochement of Shi'ism and Sunnism. We note on the political level that Iran always participates more with pan-Islamic manifestations. See *al-Ahram*, June 24, 1975.

[58]Almost unanimous support of the Arab world for President Makarios, who supplied – we emphasize in passing – a scathing denial of "Muslim fanaticism."

[59]Mission of its General Secretary to Manila. See *al-Ahram*, September 3, 1974.

[60]See *al-Ahram*, January 3, 1975.

quent meetings between Muslim ministers, promotion of tourism, and lastly, the creation of an Islamic university.[61] They advocated the "economic cooperation and solidarity between Muslim countries" by simultaneously asserting their right to control their resources and raw materials.[62] Problems encountered by domestic political organizations, demands for a steady economic growth, plots of the Western world and the USSR as well as the humiliation felt by Islam vis-à-vis a militarily strong India tend to induce a reinforced cohesion in the Muslim world which manifests itself in a new pan-Islamic quest.

Contrary to the reform movement started at the end of the nineteenth century with Indian nationalism and the birth of Pakistan, the new pan-Islamic movement does not push the reestablishment of a centralized caliphate, nor does it advocate enforcing the Muslim judicial system in its "classical expression." Using the vivid feelings of communal unity which exist at the psychological level is both practical and efficient and manages to avoid the emotional reactions of al-Afghani's initiative and those of his followers. Its purpose then is more limited, aiming only at harmonizing the policies of the Muslim states within an enlarged community. It does not strive for the creation of an "Islamic bloc" that would be distinct from the non-Islamic world. It rather tries to lay the foundations for cooperation among Islamic nations. It tends to acknowledge the existence of the whole community and to respect the sovereignty of individual national states.

The conferences of Islamic solidarity have resulted in attempt to solve specific problems, some of which are related to international relations. National differences were settled through the intervention of fellow Muslim states – that is, the reconciliation of Pakistan and Bangladesh took place under the aegis of the late president Sadat during the Islamic Conference in Lahore; Algerian mediation in the Iran-Iraq conflict, Saudi and Algerian intervention between Kuwait and Iraq; and Arab mediation in the dispute between Syria and Iraq over rights to the waters of the Euphrates river. If the Muslim countries do not unanimously support the Arab claims in the Palestinian conflict,[63] they in turn back up the demands for a military withdrawal to the pre-1967 war borders.[64] Apart from rare exceptions, Muslim states make the same decisions about world problems and vote similarly in UN conferences. It is nevertheless difficult to determine what the incentives are, whether there

---

[61]Resolution of the Islamic Summit of Algiers. See *al-Ahram*, August 3, 1971.

[62]See the editorial of the *Egyptian Gazette*, September 27, 1974, on the subject of the Second Islamic Summit in Lahore.

[63]Since certain Islamic countries have recognized Israel – Turkey among the first in the world.

[64]The Islamic Conference of Rabat opened in 1969, in presence of twenty-six delegations having been convoked immediately after the burning of the al-Aqsa mosque in Jerusalem.

exists solidarity among Islamic nations or among underdeveloped and neutral countries, or whether they all have a similar conception of justice and law. In spite of difficult problems, the new pan-Islamic movement seeks to establish a central and permanent institutional body for political, scientific, and cultural cooperation. Political states are progressively integrating into the larger body of the community of the faithful. As far as nationalities are concerned, the use of different languages helps to maintain differences.[65] Some people have proclaimed the establishment of "an organization that would promote Islamic solidarity." This new appellation and the designated institution have not yet received the unanimous approval of Muslim countries, but a General Secretariat of the Islamic Conference was designated in 1969 and established in Jeddah.

A brief summary of the organization's purposes could be illustrated by the declaration its former Secretary General made during the Conference of Ministers of Foreign Affairs in Kuala Lumpur in 1974, for it stated its priorities,[66] such as the settlement of proceedings for the creation of an "Islamic Solidarity Fund" to facilitate economic growth and to improve the standard of living for Muslim countries. In the same spirit, an "Islamic Bank" was created, the currency[67] of which was the "Islamic Dinar," in order to promote Muslim solidarity through economic and commercial collaboration. The ministerial conference also had to debate a proposition which sought to even out the losses of some Muslim countries due to the steep increase in oil prices. The Conference moreover had to consider conclusions reached in several former conferences which dealt with discriminated Muslim minorities throughout the world, the liberation of Jerusalem, and assistance to the believers who are fighting in Palestine and the Philippines. Most problems were eminently material and practical in nature. The religious aspects are usually left aside. They are dealt with by knowledgeable theologians who meet more and more frequently but receive less publicity. In spite of the small amount of concrete results obtained so far, it is useful to emphasize that the sharing of a common conviction has created a spirit of solidarity and a sufficiently strong desire to permit an exchange of views concerning strictly material matters. The pan-Islamic movement, which remains tolerant in order to reach the highest level of collaboration possible, certainly will help Muslim states and will take its place in the creation of a better balanced world order.

---

[65]While the phenomenon is non-existent without the framework of pan-Arabism.
[66]See al-Ahram, June 20, 1975.
[67]This is equivalent to the special drawing rights of the International Monetary Funds.

Toward Islamic Solutions

The current quest for an identity conducted by Muslim countries follows the pattern provided by Europe, and the collective awareness asserts itself mainly in the religious domain. It would be too exaggerated, however, to conclude "that everything has transpired as if the Islamic world were trying to find again the lost and former ideas of the Western train of thoughts."[68] On the contrary, an original assertion exists; it is understood, however, that the scientific and industrial problems are a given and that the main references have to be drawn from Western liberal or Marxist experiences.

The renewal of interest in the Islamic religion, culture, and humanism throughout the Muslim world constitutes a phenomenon which will have an important impact on its development in the long run. Besides the emotional reactions of the people and the groping of reformist or modernist doctrines, there exists a desire to rediscover the totality of Islam. The movement is more general than it at first appears; while progressively asserting itself in intellectual circles, it remains vague in popular consciousness.

In sum, Islam has reached the final step of the threefold function it has had for some years: proselytism in countries which had been under Western political domination and which are now encountering economic-growth problems, providing an ideology which can be used to claim independence and restore national dignity, and offering a realistic and practical plan of social organization for Muslim states. Its role is especially important in those nations which are proceeding from the pre-industrial to the modern era.

Islam, being dynamic, is able to incite new societies. A prime example of this can be seen in Africa. A coherent doctrine embracing cultural heritage by taking into account material and technical underdevelopment still has to be formulated. The struggle is too subtle to successfully reach such an ill-defined goal. A great effort is needed for a more vigorous political reflection. A comprehensive vision for the near future is lacking for most analyses remain primarily sectorial and disintegrating, be they dogmatic, legal, historical, or philosophical. Studies of human behavior and state action have led to the simultaneous consideration of many different aspects of the problem, that is, moral, judicial, psychological, cultural, economic, political, and social. Such studies are essential because Islam is indivisible and should be studied as a whole. Man is an entity and his action is a reflection of his inner self likewise his society is a mirror for profound collective and individual convictions.

---

[68]Laroui, *Idéologie arabe*, p. 37, which aims especially at the Arab East.

One should not exclusively focus one's attention on the social element of contemporary Islamic societies. However, too many writers neglect the fact that one of the main factors behind any Muslim's actions is his understanding of Islam which is still felt as a living link between himself, his destiny, and God. It is dangerous to neglect the importance of Islam's cultural continuity as well as the psychological weight of living by its precepts since both are parts of everyday life. The most vivid Islamic tradition cannot be placed in the narrow frames characteristic of political analysis. It is more a feeling, worthy of respect and taken as a given, than a social phenomenon that needs to be dissected. The former president of Mauritania, when talking about the progressive character of "authentic Islam," put it this way: "We cannot afford to play with what belongs to us. We have neither the material nor the military power. If we did not have any dignity to defend or any moral code to fight for and reintroduce in relations among nations, then we would have nothing."[69]

Through conservation of dogma, Islam has been able to resist the destruction of its political community as well as its alienation by colonization. It is also in the dogma, that incarnation of the past, that contemporary Muslim states find various elements of their identity. This fact explains the great influence of religious tradition and of its guardians, the *'ulema*. This phenomenon is but a partial view of the situation for this inner conviction has ceased to represent a self-conscious feeling; on the contrary, it now asserts itself by claiming to have a role to play in the world, to which Islam has opened itself with ambition and tolerance. It is too easy to see only apology in the affirmation of the validity of the Islamic traditional norms which are held to be quite adaptable to changing conditions and superior to any secular legislation. One has to consider their inner structure to understand how omnipresent they are in the people's minds and how they influence the elite's economic and political decisions. To this extent, the themes debated by recent Islamic seminars clearly show the firm nature of Islam's conviction: " ... the awakening of the Muslim world and its rise tomorrow; the role of Islam in face of modern challenges of invasion and alienation;"[70] ... "the plurality of cultures in the modern world; or the role of Islam in the make-up of modern man."[71]

One has to go beyond Western political concepts to have a better understanding of Muslim options, for these derive from a global vision of God, the universe, and man. The only permanent authority is the Qur'ān. Debates, propositions, or solutions are just temporary arrangements to meet the needs

---

[69]Declaration of President Mokhtar Ould Dada to André Fontaine, *Le Monde*, February 6, 1974.
[70]Seminar of Algiers on Islamic Thought, see *al-Ahram*, July 25, 1974.
[71]Muslim-Christian seminar at Tunis, see *al-Ahram*, November 11, 1974.

presented by particular circumstances. It is therefore difficult to design a definitively Islamic political doctrine, a situation which is made even harder by the fact that the Qur'ān does not set out a clear formulation. Besides, the disputes, ambitions, and rivalries which have marked the course of Muslim history have only confused the issue. If we turn our attention to domestic political organization, economic and social philosophy, and the contemporary Muslim vision of international relations, we can draw some important conclusions.

The word "government" in its modern sense appeared only in the nineteenth-century Turkey. Its etymological origin[72] means "to judge," "make a decision," or "give orders." Yet, Islamic tradition relates that the Prophet declared that "when three persons are out in the desert, they have the right to nominate one of them as their leader." Thus leadership, not authoritative but conferred through a vote, is an essential characteristic of Islam. Still, the structure of executive power and the mutual responsibilities of the ruler and the ruled were never clearly delineated in any doctrine. Muslim political theory has always been limited to describing the moral qualities and sacred duties of a ruler. The essential virtues of the leader[73] are: first, "Fear of God" – the source of all blessings for the community and the "secret" of all wisdom, according to the Prophet's teachings; second, a sense of justice, compassion, and a desire to serve the people and consult them on all important matters. A good leader is one who governs for the people; a dictator governs only for himself.[74] The ideal Muslim state does not exist anymore, but the theoretical concept of equality for all before the law remains vivid in the popular psychology.

Contemporary Muslim states have organized themselves according to basic constitutional structures,[75] very similar to European patterns but nevertheless retaining their specifically Islamic features. It is difficult to determine the extent to which religion influences the writing of constitutional texts. Generally

---

[72]*Encyclopedia of Islam*, vol. 3: *Party, Government and Freedom in the Muslim World*, 2nd ed. (Leiden: Brill, 1968), s.v. "Hukuma," by Bernard Lewis, pp. 23 f.

[73] Amir Ali, *The Spirit*, who cites ibn-Kout Tiktaka, an author of the fourteenth century, see p. 287.

[74]A woman, to whom the founder of the Umayyad dynasty asked why she did not consider it with the same fervor as 'Ali, responded: "Because you value your empire more than man, while 'Ali accepts to govern by using the first as an instrument in the service of the individual." Khan, "Islam," pp. 116-117.

[75]*Encyclopedia of Islam*, vol. 3: *Party, Government and Freedom in the Muslim World*, 2nd ed. (Leiden: Brill, 1968), s.v. "Dustur: A Survey of the Constitutions of the Arab and Muslim States." After this: "Dustur." See also the "Constitutional Proclamation" of the Council of the Yemeni Command, *al-Ahram*, June 20, 1974, which seems to be a good résumé of the constitutional principles of contemporary Muslim states.

speaking, the Islamic spirit is less vivid in the fundamental dispositions of the formerly colonized countries than in those that were never colonized with the exception of Turkey. The compromise between modernization and the traditional circles appears to be permanent. Historical incidences have played a major role in this state of affairs, but one can almost predict that future politicians will not be as easily influenced by imported ideas as their predecessors were because, since they come from the non-elite classes, they will still be attached, to a certain degree, to the traditional Muslim culture. It would be absurd to label Muslim political theory as one that does not advocate liberal democracy or approves of totalitarianism in all its forms. It is more productive to point out the similarities and differences of Islamic political theories when compared with the two dominant forms now found in the world in order to discover features unique to Islam.

Most Muslim countries have accepted parliamentary democracy, a governmental structure also accepted by traditional religious circles. Experience has shown that liberal regimes do not last and are often overthrown by military coups which impose then their authoritative systems on the people. The 1952 Egyptian revolution seemed to represent a popular democratic claim opposed to a dynastic and totalitarian power.[76] Indeed, all the principles allowing establishment of a true "democracy," such as obedience to the law by the ruler and the ruled, the Qur'ānic recommendation for consultation corroborated with examples by the Prophet, the right of the people to choose their political leaders, and a strong feeling of equality among all, are to be found in the philosophical and political doctrines of Islam. These concepts are very close, if not identical, to those of Western democracy. On the other hand, the unchangeable character of the law, the decisive involvement of Islam in social matters, and the positive aspect of a legal community could give birth to a certain kind of economic organization.

This is why some aspects of Marxist philosophy [77] are very appealing, for they correspond to the essential values of Islamic philosophy. On the other hand, Marxist ideology itself is fiercely rejected because, besides its atheism[78], it introduces the "abominable idea" that man is but a social end in himself. A state that would dehumanize individuals can only be tyrannical. Islamic law guarantees people autonomy and inspires them with freedom. Re-

---

[76]Bennabi, *Vocation*, p. 30.

[77]This is so besides the fact that the Communist countries overwhelmingly have taken the side of the Muslim peoples fighting for their national independence.

[78]This is due to the incompatibility of Marxism with Islam or the "sacred principals of the state," in order to retract the expression of the Moroccan Superior Court of Justice, namely that the Communist parties have been prohibited in the majority of Muslim countries.

jecting a dehumanizing dictatorship is thus a concrete obligation, for Islam requires social justice and refuses to conceive of man as just a social instrument. Man is God's witness. The Qur'ān indicates the priority of loyalty and obedience. "Oh you who believe! Obey God! Obey the Prophet and those who have authority!"[79] God represents His law as one that transcends all objective social conditions. The Prophet is the perfect example. "Those who have authority," meaning political officials in the modern sense, appear in the third position.[80] Obedience to them is conditioned by the respect they themselves pay to the original authorities. A dictatorship in the Marxist sense would therefore not be possible, and if a Muslim ruler were to establish one, it would have to perfectly enforce the Law of God and His Prophet in order to be acceptable to the Muslims.

Muslim democracy is thus original. It will, however, be better understood when contrasted with the Western concept of democracy by choosing three particular features: democratic pluralism, the role and power of nominated leaders, and finally, state's intervention.

As a general rule, Islamic political philosophy does not advocate the existence of political factions representing individual interests nor the idea of groups which can argue over the responsibility of powers in a democratic competition. The modern understanding of "party" is quite new to the Muslims, dating back only to the beginning of the twentieth century for the Arabs and the Ottoman Empire, and even later for Iran.[81] Western-style democracy is not compatible with the ideal of social unity preached by Islam for it creates a type of division in society foreign to Muslim political ethics. Multiparty systems reflect twentieth century European liberalism and eventually lead to selfishness and abusive exploitation of one group by another; all of which ideas is contrary to the main principles of Islam. The strictly religious groups, such as the "Muslim Brothers," were always very hostile to such ideas. At the other extreme, the "revolutionary" or "socialist" regimes have also rejected the idea of "class struggle." It is worth noting that neither the legal prescriptions nor the historical experience of Islam show that it has ever advocated the effective participation of the entire community in the political decision-making process and in the governmental responsibility.

A Muslim government is not "theocratic" since its only power is to enforce the rules of the divine law. Thus, its political power is different from that of a democratic regime since it enforces certain institutions and certain moral

---

[79]an-Nisa': 59 (Masson).
[80]Lahbabi, *Le personnalisme*, p. 58.
[81]*Encyclopedia of Islam*, vol. 3: *Party, Government and Freedom in the Muslim World*, 2nd ed. (Leiden: Brill, 1968), s.v. "Hizb," pp. 2-23.

norms,[82] whereas Western democracy allows people to choose the institutions and norms according to the desires of the moment. Islamic legislation, which was imposed by God and freely accepted by Muslims, should prevent a short-lived majority from ruling over an opposed minority. theoretically, the legal interpretation and the election of the leaders are reserved for those individuals who know the divine law and who know the personal qualities and defects as well as moral and physical abilities of that person. However, such a practice is not carried out in contemporary Muslim states. Democracy does not have the same intensity among Muslim people as it does among the Judeo-Christian people for Islamic political ethics are situated between liberal individualism and socialist collectivism.

By contrast, the same analysis shows that the power given to Muslim leaders is usually greater than that of their counterparts in Western countries, but it is never totalitarian as it is in the regimes of Eastern Europe. The ruler has absolute executive power, but he is only a "first among equals," acting under the eyes of God and submitting to the superior authority of the Islamic law and morals. People can criticize the leader, but rebellion for the establishment of a better regime is prohibited[83] as long as the leader is accepted by the community and appears to govern within the limits of the law.

As a result of religious conviction, political history, and traditional culture, a distinction between authority and power has gradually developed. Permanent and absolute authority is the divine law, while power is granted according to circumstances. If the official's intentions are unjust and arbitrary, his power has no validity. This is due to the Islamic concept of double loyalty (to God and the ruler) which allows us to better understand the Muslims' attitudes toward their various national governments.

The political problems and difficulties of the Muslim countries are certainly more numerous and more complex than those of the underdeveloped countries in general. With some exceptions, parliamentary democracy has failed

---

[82]Khadduri, War, p. 81; Chalaby, Islam, pp. 167 f., and Pickthall, The Cultural Side, p. 180.
[83]Oliver Carré, "Le contenu socio-économique-politique des manuels d'enseignement religieux musulman dans l'Egypte actuelle," Revue d'études Islamiques 38/1 (January 1970):122-123. After this: "Le contenu" which analyzes the Nasserite Egyptian regime, but of which the conclusions reveal a general concept in the Arab world that the regime is either republican or monarchical. See al-Harkan, Le dogme musulman, and, for example, the experience of the "directed democracy" of former President Sukarno in Indonesia. "Dustur," pp. 1 f. and, more specifically, p. 39 of the same book (Encyclopedia of Islam, vol. 3: Party, Government and Freedom in the Muslim World). The cases of Iran and Pakistan are a little different, although the role of the Shah was more important in practice than the Constitution of 1906 would allow one to think. For Pakistan, its entire nascent history was marked by the preponderant influence of the army in its political affairs.

everywhere, a situation which is probably due to the "Muslim mentality" still being so impregnated with a sense of the absolute that democratic nuances and compromises are difficult to grasp. Opinions are hardly ever qualified: it is either a violent hostility or an unquestioning acceptance, both elements sometimes occurring in one and the same person. Seen from the outside, the distance between the two positions seems very small. Defending good points or opposing bad ones boils down to conformity or, on the contrary, to animosity which protagonists think they perceive between permanent authority and occasional or "de facto" power. The criterion of appreciation is not only found uniquely in a sacralized interpretation of the situation but more concretely in the moral qualities of the leaders who are most likely to enforce Qur'ānic justice since it is community justice. This last element leads us to a study of the main themes in Islam's economic doctrine.

It is pointless to refute repeated Western allegations as to the inability of Islam to develop a strong economic system as history speaks for itself. Religion is tainted with a progressive enthusiasm, advising men to enjoy the wealth that God gave them and to seek profit within the limits of decency. Islam, be it traditional or reformist, praises the social virtues of trade and industry, but strongly condemns materialism, or "naturalism" as al-Afghani says. Linking the sacred to the secular, Islam seeks to change the economic organization of a society by transforming the present institutions and especially by installing in them strong moral values. It is thus natural that the pioneers of the Muslim awakening should always be preoccupied with economic questions.

Before listing some of the abstract principles, one has to remember the popular feeling of solidarity which continues to manifest itself outside the economic structure: helping the family, protection of small merchants as well as compulsory unpaid work by young people and generally by mystical groups toward the elderly, widows, and orphans. Simultaneously, a feeling of association erases any idea of class struggle inspite of the obvious differences between life styles. The customers of the "bazaar" or "suq" are very much aware of it for merchants sell their products at prices that are fixed according to their clients' imagined or real wealth. The merchant is not hostile to the customer; he is associated with him. It is, in fact, an idealist vision that succeeds in bridging the gap between classes through the fraternal redistribution of wealth.

In this sense, Islam has always been moderately revolutionary from the social point of view. The revealed law allows the community to enforce heavy taxes on excessive wealth or even to appropriate it for the benefit of the less fortunate believers. The task to grant dignity and a decent way of life to all individual members is the community's duty.[84] This shows the central community spirit and the ethical unity of the Qur'ānic revelation.

There is a constant feature in Islamic social philosophy which explains why the "socialism" found in most Muslim countries is not just a more or less imprecise imitation of an imported theory.[85] In an ideal state, there would be no hostility between the haves and the have-nots, nor would there be any opposition between individualism and socialism. The right to private property is guaranteed within limits which vary according to the prevalent objective conditions, but it only represents a social function. That right can be restricted if it deprives some members of the community or, if it was dispensed without taking decency or justice into account. Thus, Islam supresses the "jus usendi and abusendi" by installing an economic system based on morals, a system that divides money between people according to religiously based fiscal policies (i.e. *zakah*) and according to the interpretation of "private property" as being the right to use what God has granted mankind. In one way, Islam has made a link between capital and work. Thus, can we say that Islam is close to socialism?

European experiences have probably had a great influence on Islam by presenting themselves as possible models for the rapid modernization and development of national economies. However, such influences were always in danger of being rejected if they could not be worked into the Islamic concept of what social order should be. Indeed, beyond doctrinal oppositions, political polemics, and legal texts, there exists a homogeneous philosophy throughout the Muslim world. The differences found between Arab "progressivism" and "feudalism" between the Iranian "silent revolution" and "Pakistani democracy" appear to be more tangible in form than in substance. Each system tries to find its own path to the establishment of social equality, and in this quest, material conditions are more determining factors than ideological options.

A collectivist solution is presented under the label of Muslim socialism. This can best be described as a form of socialism which respects private property – a limited capitalism which does not clash with the spirit or the economic doctrine of Islam. The preoccupation to harmoniously merge private property with public interest comes first in the minds of Muslim reformists who seek possible middle way between Western capitalism, which is viewed as inequitable and inadequate for the needs of development, and Marxism

---

[84]al-Harkan, *Le dogme musulman*, p. 38.
[85]Ahmed, *Iqbal*, pp. 63 f.; Chalaby, *Islam*, pp. 293 f.; Sharif, *Islamic Social Framework*; Hussain, *Islam*; Abd-al-Meguid, *Le socialisme arabe*; and Roueni, *L'influence*, among other numerous authors.

which is but a daring simplistic solution that denies any intrinsic and universal value to man. This median would refer to cooperative socialism in those sectors of the economy rooted in Qur'ānic teachings and mutual solidarity. Between the notion of exploitation of man by man and that of the state's totalitarianism is the very form of socialism "which takes its roots in Islam. It is not imported from foreign countries, and allows everyone, rich and poor, to build a society of abundance and justice."[86]

The simultaneous birth of Muslim nations and their inhabitants' desire to safeguard the essential Islamic values through a compromise between liberalism and Marxism makes the elaboration of a coherent ideology more difficult. To the outside observer, there will always be "irrational" or "suprarational" aspects in any Muslim theory to come since the weight of religion will always be strongly felt.

All forms of spontaneous or imported culture are filtered into Islam and therefore bear an Islamic stamp because, although Islamic civilization is built on transcendental and sacred notions, it remains very practical. The progress engendered by the industrial revolution and scientific research in the Western world are very appealing especially to the young people although the spiritual criterion always comes first. The Muslim people are very optimistic despite their material underdevelopment;[87] they trust their past experiences and are stimulated by the Prophet's recommendations.[88] They are moreover aware that it will be through material and scientific progress that Islam will play a part in the organization of the modern world by bringing to it its high conception of moral values.

Muslim states make their contribution to international justice and security by taking part in intergovernmental organizations. It is difficult to understand the original intention of traditional Islamic theories about international relations and to correctly apply them today to meet the internal and external changes which have occurred during the past several decades. Decisions in foreign policy sometimes seem to bear an emotional element which is difficult to analyze. Religious influence is certainly less obvious in diplomatic practice than in domestic matters. A brief analysis would show that the situation has changed too rapidly for the leaders of modern Muslim states to justify their decisions on a traditional basis. It would, however, be incorrect to conclude that the classical doctrine is therefore no longer applicable.

---

[86]Declaration of president Qaddafi Eric to Rouleau, *Le Monde*, June 28, 1975.
[87]Mohammed, Z. Abdel Kader, "Vèrs la lumière," *al-Akhbar*, June 28, 1975.
[88]"In the eyes of God, a sole wise person is preferable to a million worshippers," or again "Religion, this is the reason; no religion for the one who does not possess it."

Indeed, traditional spiritual and moral virtues have not lost any of their value. In addition, a given foreign policy is never exclusively based on abstract national interests; it represents the clear internal organization, ideology and ladder of humanitarian values molded by that particular culture.

Thus, Islam participates in events on the world stage. For example, the Muslim world has always stood beside the peoples who struggle against colonial domination and has always strongly condemned practices of racial discrimination. Besides, the Islamic conception of "peace in justice" has always been considered by the Western world as "Arab intransigence," especially with regard to the Palestinian conflict.

The traditional doctrine is not an unused document. Contemporary students are taught that the Muslim "holy war" is a "purely defensive war." "It is also perceived as a revolutionary war which seeks to liberate oppressed people in neighboring countries and throughout the world."[89] Modern legal writings always furnish a list of solidarity rules between people in case of an armed conflict. As a concrete illustration,[90] one can mention the Ottoman Empire's refusal, due to their respect for the revealed law, to use toxic gas supplied to them by their German allies during the Gallipoli War (World War I). One can also mention the very active and sincere Muslim participation during the last diplomatic conference on the reaffirmation and development of a humanitarian international law applicable to armed conflicts.

Indeed, the influence of Islamic ethics is not limited to Muslim countries, all of which, although sharing the common characteristic of being situated in the developing world and facing different problems, do express similar aspirations, i.e., the assertion of a newly acquired political sovereignty and the desire to control their own national economies in order to chart their own destiny. The same need for dignity makes Muslim countries join the non-aligned movement, the options of which are often unqualified and inherent political collaborations are very diverse. Common solidarity is manifested in a concern for economic growth and, on the psychological level, with a feeling of wounded pride. Muslim countries undeniably have other concepts to offer the world, such as an Islamic humanism which is being brought back to life by modern and logical thinking. The traditional values of faith have spread all over the Third World, and many countries have acknowledged their common destiny. Between the blocs that divide the world, Islam favors neutralism, and in this capacity played a major role at the Pandung Conference. The Muslim world is still not a great political and military power, but it seems to already

---

[89]Carré, "Le contenu," p. 122.
[90]Pickthall, *The Cultural Side*, p. 189.

represent a great moral force on the universal level.

The influence of religion is certainly not felt as vividly in international political matters as it is in decisions pertaining to domestic problems. Can we nevertheless say that, in relations among individuals, the separation between religion and politics is felt more vividly? The controversy over the secularization of Muslim society does not seem to be clearly stated. The problem exists, of course, and has been the cause of heated discussions among Muslims. There may not be a clear-cut alternative though, for it could very well be that religion is but the inner motivation behind political decisions.

For the sake of clarity, one could postulate a "religious Islam" and a "political Islam." This theoretical distinction would not be too far from reality, in light of the profound changes undergone by the Islamic world. Two questions then arise: "Do we have to separate religion from politics?" and "Is secularization of the Muslim community possible?"

The first question has often been raised in essays written by Western authors. To them, the answer is simple, as they refuse to make a comparison with European history. Indeed, in the Western world, such a separation was necessary and logical. The Catholic church was competing with rising national consciousness and it was deemed practical to set aside the ecclesiastical power in order to establish an exclusive temporal authority in society. Freed from its political aspirations, the church could make the changes needed to adopt itself to the newly emerging realities. Nothing of this sort happened in the Islamic world. The revelation makes no distinction between the spiritual and the temporal. Besides, it would be impossible to have any ecclesiastical institution settle religious matters since no such central authority has ever existed. The idea of a divided world, of two destinies, one worldly and one eternal, means nothing to the Muslim people for they are convinced of the unity of God, the universe, and individuals. This will always exist in theory no matter what course politics might take because it is one of the most basic Islamic beliefs.

The second question, that of secularization of institutions in Muslim states, is more difficult to answer. Of course, one could find a million paths and many easy solutions, but one would have to agree on terms and their definitions. Secularizing institutions is not a decision that would endanger Islam, as has been said before; maybe it would be an illogical act that would deprive the revealed Law of its moral and practical content. Traditional Islam finds it unacceptable to free the state from its duty to maintain the ethical strongholds of society, even in its modern national understanding. On the other hand, a reform which would make the Islamic system more compatible with the requirements of modern life is not prohibited. The problem is more defined than it at first seemed. The distinction is not between the spiritual and the temporal but between the two merged realms: the unchangeable prescriptions and those that are susceptible to change. Harmony in human relations is made possible through religious faith, not through human legislation. Secularizing Islamic social life would be a serious mistake today, for man now has destructive powers in hand which, due to the lack of a sincere spiritual conviction, he may not be able to control.[91]

We tend to forget too easily that Muslim countries are in a state of war. No sooner did their anti-colonial struggles end than they were confronted with serious problems such as the quest for national identity, growth, and economic independence. Their active political participation often hides the reality of the struggle. People are in a transitional period but, at the same time, they are looking for stability. They are torn between irrational sentiments for immediate progress and cultural tradition.[92] The Western world judges with extreme severity the "incoherent patterns" of foreign and domestic policies in Muslim countries, not remembering that it took centuries and the most destructive wars in human history for Europe to find a relative equilibrium.

In the course of its ideological elaboration, the contemporary Muslim world has either enthusiastically accepted foreign influences or rejected them with all the violence brought about by wounded dignity. Usually with the passage of time, things get smoother, the traditional culture asserts itself in a more coherent way, allowing assimilation of those foreign concepts which express the real aspirations of the people and provide an answer to local problems. Abstract concepts cease to be symbols when they correspond to the local mentality and traditions. In the long run, Muslim political and economic ideologies should not be replicas of foreign values but should have their own specific stamp. The fundamental ideal of brotherhood or the quest for social justice are not vague feelings invented by man but originate from a moral code devised by God. "When God is King, the secular becomes religious."[93]

Whatever the motivations of those governments who want to modernize the national legal system, the notion of a secular law is still foreign to most Muslims because sacred law remains the ultimate reference for their daily life. Western literature seems to have neglected this permanent aspect, judging institutions in relation to texts. Islam is a subtle and dynamic faith, totally in-

[91]Lahbabi, *Le personnalisme*, p. 107; Jamali, *Letters*, pp. 86 f.; and Hamidullah, "La philosophie juridue chez les musulmans," *Annales de la Faculté Droit d'Istanbul* (Istanbul: 1968), vol. 18, nos 29-32, pp. 137-152.
[92]Laroui, *Idéologie arabe*, preface; and Anouar Hatem, "Pays neufs et traditions arabes en politique étrangère" *Communita Mediterranea: Rivista Trimestriale di Dritte Internazionale e di Politica Economica* 1 (June/December 1968):83-92. After this: Hatem, "Pays neufs."
[93]Pickthall, *The Cultural Side*, p. 190.

volved in all aspects of life. Modern political philosophy tries to recreate on earth a city obeying divine laws, not "mere judicial values but rather an engagement toward, and on behalf of, human beings."[94] The Muslims are aware of the psychological disarray in which industrialized and materialistic nations now find themselves; they also trust the potential economic power of those Islamic states which are situated in the "golden belt of the world."[95] They are thus on their way to gaining that kind of self-reliance which will facilitate the discovery of those new political and economic ideas compatible with the true spirit of the Qur'ānic revelation. When they are finally found, their spiritual kinship with Islam will make them much easier to enforce.

Problems and Perspectives

In our attempt to draw an "objective" picture of the whole situation, we may have shown an excessive optimism by not studying the serious problems encountered by the Muslim world today. A reinterpretation of dogma can only result in a certain amount of anxiety and violence. The debate is still going on between those progressive tendencies which do not take religion into consideration and those moderately progressive traditional religious groups that do. However, contemporary Muslim theoreticians, to be successful, must find a happy medium between definitive conclusions, reached by a political analysis characterized by an insufficient knowledge of Islam, and a too detailed study by oriental historians who will not go beyond mere positive criticism. Such a compromise can only be reached by studying the "Muslim mentality" and its influence on their daily life and behavior.

Of course, it would be presumptuous to summarize contemporary Islamic thought as it is far from being an aggregate whole, ruling as it does over thousands of men in the Middle East, Africa, and Asia. However, studying some of its spiritual and cultural ideas would allow us to better understand its ongoing evolution. Unfortunately, until quite recently, the traditional European ignorance of and contempt for accepted values in dominated or economically weak territories have led them to ignore such an undertaking. They thought that "Muslim states would unquestionably adopt European concepts. In order to stop the Western invasion, the Eastern world saw but one solution: to accept Western influence. It thus becomes greedy and forgets its own value. Today, [1931] it is perfectly clear that self-denial is the most danger-

[94]Lahbabi, *Le personnalisme*, p. 93. See also Nasr, *Man in the Universe*, pp. 706 f.
[95]See the declaration of M. Hussein Tohamei, preceding the opening of the Islamic Conference of Kuala Lumpur, who said: "The role of the Islamic countries will become in the years to come more and more important," *al-Ahram*, June 20, 1974.

ous, the deepest acceptance of defeat clearly seen as a fact."[96] Contempt is
really the worst thing!

Since 1945, Muslim countries have controlled their destiny and have had
the chance to build their social structures on specific foundations originating
from the Islamic vision of man and the world. This process has already
started, but it still has a long way to go. Its evolution will not be hampered
by existing ecclesiastical institutions but rather by a much more powerful
psychological fact: the sacred cultural and spiritual tradition. Islamic law will
always carry a lot of weight in the Muslims' decisions because of its divine
origin. It is naive to expect that the still largely traditional understanding of
Islamic concepts will be able to deal effectively with contemporary issues
right away for the problems to be solved are very complex and no one seems
to have a clear idea of the goals to be achieved. Action seems to be stimulated by the urgency of the problems at hand and by concerns for self-identity. A distortion could be born between the spiritual dimensions and the material realizations. In the confrontation between sacred Islam and the modern
world, facts are known and problems have been raised. Islam today is probably strong enough to meet the challenge. The modernists' and reformists'
legitimate desire to prove it at first led to an easy way out. They were
apologetic, an attitude which has always been denounced as dangerous even
to the writers who sometimes resort to it.[97]

A romantic glorification of the past and of the perfection of the Qur'ānic
revelation could possibly paralyze much-needed original thinking by hiding
the real problems and urging Muslims to be overly optimistic and lenient with
themselves. Going back to the original sources may seem retrospective, even
reactionary, taking intellectual efforts backward instead of forward. Raising
abstract problems sometimes have very little to do with contemporary
realities.

There has always been an apologetic touch in contemporary Muslim political thought. We now have to understand why this has been so. First of all,
it is a cultural defense against external critical judgments, and sometimes it
takes an aggressive character like any reaction. It unconsciously asserts the
wish of formerly colonized peoples to free themselves from the feelings of
alienation with their traditional culture. It also has positive elements of en-
durance and strength which are very stimulating for the whole social structure. When the traditional Muslim thinker declares that the present backwardness of the Muslims is due to their unfaithfulness to God's Will, he does not

---

[96]E. F. Gautier, *Moeurs et coûtumes des Musulmans* (Paris: Payot, 1955), p. 283.
[97]Bennabi, *Vocation*, pp. 54 f.; Fyzee, *A Modern Approach*, p. 54; and Lahbabi, *Le personnalisme*, pp. 101 f.

offer any practical answers; when he claims that Islam is the religion of reason, of human freedom, and of tolerance, he does not solve any problems.[98] He nevertheless provides the material necessary for building a modern Muslim ideology. One should note that it is through theology that the first steps of the Islamic resurgence have been taken. It was the first successful attempt at shaking the colonized Islamic world from its lethargy. Describing the decadence of the "Muslim community," theologians were also thinking of efficiency and material progress for the glory of Islam. The ideologies at work are numerous and sometimes contradictory: some try to keep the traditional heritage untouched, others want to adapt it to new social demands. Gradually, a well-formulated apology unveils the cultural and spiritual resources necessary for the construction of a coherent system.

The contemporary situation is unique. The Muslim world has been invaded by foreign concepts and ideological trends. Islam is not the only reference available to level out heterogeneous influences. The social changes that the Muslim world is undergoing could cause a reinterpretation of religious dogmas. However, social orientation and the believer's involvement are independent of the fact that religious conviction has been questioned or not and do not rely on the renewal of spiritual feeling either since they are very easily patterned after the objective conditions prevalent in Muslim areas and throughout the world. Thus, the problem is not if Muslim states will play a part in the growth of the industrial and technological civilization but whether they will be able to safeguard the specific essence of their personality when doing so.

Experience has adequately demonstrated that imitating imported doctrines has not worked. Only the movements inspired by Islam, a renewed Islam which has not changed the original revelation, will assimilate the different trends and provide syncretic solutions based on moral virtues as the driving force of civilization.[99]

The struggle between contradictory tendencies still continues since each has a different cultural background and must face different material problems according to the countries that compose universal Islam. There are questions which need to be asked, such as: Who really knows what is at stake in the debate between an "Arab Islam" which is engaged in a political struggle[100]

---

[98] See the very severe analysis of Laroui, *Idéologie arabe*, pp. 16 f.
[99] See the different points of view on this aspect in Guillaume, *Islam*, p. 193; Rodinson, *Marxisme*, p. 121; Lahbabi, *Le personnalisme*, pp. 174 f. as well as Laroui, *Idéologie arabe*, and Bennabi, *Vocation*.
[100] In which a certain spirit of objective criticism tends to make way for emotional empiricism especially since the disappointments issuing from the guerillas of Palestine. Bennabi, *Vocation*,

and in a fight for unity, and a "Turkish Islam" which is officially secular, but where the vividness of the popular faith could challenge the secular character of the state?; Who can predict what the relations will be between the "two Islams" and "South Asian Islam," which has partially expressed itself in the Pakistani experience aiming at trying to create a modern and a fraternal Muslim state in which, unfortunately, geographical division and economic problems happen to be stronger than religious bonds?; and what could be said of the African, Indonesian or Malaysian "Islams" which mix ancestral traditions with their Islamic heritage?

These differences are very important. Indeed, Muslim states have a long cultural tradition and have their own conception of man, society, and the world. As soon as they are intellectually ready, they will find the appropriate elements necessary for the construction of an economic, political, and social doctrine that will prevent them from falling into the hands of two threatening imperialistic tendencies: pseudo socialist totalitarianism and Western colonialism. At such a juncture, the present financial power of the oil producing countries could play a highly important role.

Any evolving society changes the expression of its culture. However, a civilization which has not only an "existence" but also a strongly ingrained "essence," such as Islam, will resist change as time goes on. The principles that originally gave birth to the "Muslim mentality" persist. There exists an immutable core in Islam that claims to provide everlasting answers to all fundamental existential problems. A modern Islamic ideology is slowly taking shape according to the prevailing social conditions.

The traditional civilization is still alive in one form or another, either implicitly or explicitly. Reformist and modernist thought has succeeded in introducing Islam to the modern world but has failed to provide a new expression that would allow it to play its role on the international stage. The Qur'ānic revelation has a specific character, but there is nothing original in the reflection or in the interpretation. Only a proud and ambitious Islam has given expression to spiritual values, but it has never succeeded in enforcing them in a new society.

Problems and contradictions were present at the very birth of the Muslim world. They have already been stated in al-Afghani's writings [101] in which he acknowledged the urgent need to adapt to certain European techniques but was against a naive and unconditional admiration of the West. The coming and establishment of Marxism on the political stage in Eastern Europe made

---

pp. 149 f., and Nasr, *Man in the Universe*, p. 702.
[101]Keddie, *An Islamic Response*, in particular conclusions.

the debate even more difficult. The quarrels started even before Muslim territories won their independence. "Religious Islam" continued to progress in this period, while "political Islam" had to undergo radical change so as to function in a world where science was prevailing. The conjunction of the two phenomena is interesting. Islam asserts itself as an essential spiritual force in the convulsed Third World but has yet to show that it can create those situations conducive to economic development in a modern world. It has to fight poverty without overlooking God's laws and man's rights. Islam will have to reach a compromise that will take both the local circumstances and the traditional culture into account. In addition, its technological progress still depends on foreign imports. The relationships which industrialization builds between religious reform and social evolution, and between religious conviction and human psychological problems have yet to be determined. Choosing new criteria or giving new expression to old principles in order to adapt them to new realities is both urgent and necessary. The Muslim world is still in the process of trying to bridge the gap between apology and objective inquiry.

The West's knowledge of Islam is so partial and biased that it fosters misunderstandings and disappointment. Even the best historians have not contributed to making matters any clearer; they only stress its complicated history, unevolving law, and internal polemics. A strictly positive analysis is very limited in scope. This fact has led some historians to start real "archeological work" on a civilization that for a long time would have supposedly remained in a deeply lethargic state. Indeed, it is only recently that they have ceased to study Islam in its religious aspects. Western writers have now started to understand Muslim thought better; they have just discovered that Islamic civilization is a dynamic one going currently through a delicate period of change. By using strictly "objective" and rational criteria, European scientific investigation claims to provide the Muslim world with an alternative, one which, however, would give rise to great tensions: either adhere to Islam and forget about material progress, or adhere to technological progress and forget Muslim values.[102] The possibilities of Islamic thought and its future influence on the world cannot really be predicted by the West because European intellectuals find it difficult to go beyond the Greek or Latin humanist philosophies. They thus retain their narrow view of the Islamic world and are unaware of its actual vitality and energy.

On the other hand, the Muslims often have only vague picture of foreign cultures. This imprecision distorts their perception of the West, and is due

<hr>

[102]See Laroui, *Idéologie arabe*, pp. 120 f., criticizing above all the Anglo-Saxon Protestant orientalists; and Dinnet and Ibrahim, *L'Orient*, p. 17.

mainly to the fact that the Western world has always asserted itself as a dominator instead of as a partner. Muslims have never been able to acknowledge the real ethics associated with technological success since they only saw the material results of those civilizations. The manifestation hid the essence; the immediate utilitarian value covered the idea. This superficial understanding led them to adopt a simplified or even a naive mental attitude: they started to imitate the material accomplishments and tried to instill in them traditional Islamic values. The horrible events of the two world wars caused Muslims to have even deeper feelings of hostility for industrial civilization in general, which they saw as deprived of any spiritual or moral support.[103] It thus revived their faith in Islam. A feeling of appeal and of repulsion followed and still persists, especially among the Westernized intellectuals. In a case such as this, an unquestioned merging of conceptions is less probable than a definite divorce. Muslim humanism will adapt to modern circumstances through a liberated ideology, a careful choice of options, inhibition, and the likes and dislikes it still has toward foreign doctrines. This does not mean it will absorb external influences, but rather that it will undergo an intellectual reform and a profound social transformation in order to assimilate the triumphant technique.

This effervescence is one dimention of the problem under consideration. Since contemporary Muslim nations have combined all the various elements available, their society have been built on chaotic foundations. Such a society still finds it difficult to separate important principles from secondary considerations and to sort out facts instilled by foreign inspiration that are worthy of being accepted, adapted, or rejected. It does not differentiate between the legitimate desire for industrial and technical growth and a clear definition of the objectives. It tries to evaluate the adequacy of Muslim values by comparing them to foreign concepts without, however, successfully inserting them into the concrete realities of the contemporary world. This process of thought accentuates the disbalance in Muslim societies which lean on a glorious past while moving toward an uncertain future. It also enlarges the gap that separates the intellectual elite from the believing masses who are becoming politically more and more powerful. Religion in its most traditional form is always identified in people's minds with political matters. For several legitimate reasons, religious people avoid becoming politically involved and are content with showing the excellence of Muslim values. Things started changing twenty years ago, however. Only an objective and realistic reflection, allowing Muslims not only to become stronger but also to understand each other,[104]

---

[103]Pickthall, *The Cultural Side*, p. 170.
[104]Laroui, *Idéologie arabe*, p. 120.

will facilitate a mass mobilization led by the intact power of Islam.

Some[105] think it is paradoxical, and dangerous even, to merge religious elements with a political philosophy especially in our industrial age. In other words, it is not possible for Muslims to keep a personal and a subjective view of the world. Any ideology alters reality according to an ideal matrix. The matter to be debated is the quality of the model. Muslims hold it as divine and eternal, while an outside objective observer would see it as moral, peaceful, and tolerant. It seems to lead to a "balanced human condition both on a spiritual and a social level."[106] Besides, Muslim states have no other choice, no other emotional source upon which to build their future, than Islam. Muslim thinkers do not have to elaborate an ideology but rather to free Islam from the weight of accumulated tradition so that it will become again what it was originally: the liberation of reason, freedom of thought, and self-expression.

The Muslim intellectual path seems to take three directions: a longing for a glorious – sometimes mythical – past, a subtle argumentation, and a tendency to elaborate doctrines through deduction. It is therefore difficult to envision the future by means of contemporary theoretical debates. Rarely has anyone attempted to give a new interpretation of Islam by going back to the original source of the inspiration.[107] Until now, religion was essentially a bond and a defense. No longer overpowered by traditional orthodoxy, by the Ottoman authority, and by the colonial administration, Islam now asserts itself in the contemporary world. Western intrusion has influenced traditional values and modes of thinking. Muslim people have given a spontaneous answer to materialistic superiority. A genuine desire for constructive and objective criticism seems to prevail over irrational emotion. The religious element endures because the bond between Islam and social organization should not be broken. Thus, political, social, or religious changes follow identical paths, and interaction among them is commonplace. Understanding the divine world derives from the believers' state of mind which itself is patterned after material conditions. Moreover, the Muslim peoples' inner attitude and general behavior originate from their understanding of the Qur'ān.

The duality of the problem accounts for the complexity of the situation. After gaining self-awareness and benefiting from self-affirmation and a geographical expansion of religious conviction, Islam tried to understand itself better in order to find those values which would allow it to control its own des-

---

[105]For example, Majid Khadduri.
[106]Schuon, *Comprendre*, p. 49.
[107]"The reformers are not really going back to the origins of the Islamic thought, no more than the modernists are to the origins of Western thought." Bennabi, *Vocation*, p. 63.

tiny. Absorbed in the need for an innerchange, it has still not found either a political balance or a real position in the world order. It does not even appear as one of the important potential components of modern universal humanism. Though spiritually traditional and materially progressive, it is still in search of ideas that can adequately express its aspirations.

Islam, a social fact and a complete civilization in itself, is not a simple or an isolated phenomenon. One cannot arbitrarily separate the main events of its history from those of world history. The apparent intellectual immobility and passive acceptance of tradition are the result of a society which considered critical minds a danger. Today, due to its flexibility, Islam can maintain a middle position among the communist countries and resist the onslaught of materialistic ideologies. Its flexibility permits it to win over its rivals when it has the occasion to confront them, as in Africa for instance. Its most fundamental value is its religious spirit which is expressed every day in the reflection and personal actions of those believers who are taking part in a technological society. This takeover from religion "is not incompatible with the notion of God first; it is in fact exactly what it means if one wants the ultimate goals of men and their real dignity to be respected. The clash between Islam and the technical revolution (seen as a positive temporal accomplishment) incites the Muslim people while facing this world to deepen their faith in God."[108] Thus, they have to find a new definition of the sacred and the temporal or, more precisely, since the two are related, to better understand their potentials within the Islamic world. Islam will then become the true humanism that it was by selection, adaptation, and assimilation of European, Arabic, African, and Asian cultural elements.

Since the end of the nineteenth century, the internal cultural and political turmoil of Islam has been at the core of its history. It is a new movement which will continue to push forward. It carries with it the most traditional concepts and the most progressive aspirations. The convictions and hesitations, the feelings of hope and certainty, the oppositions and contradictions engendered by debate are signs of ambition and dynamism in contemporary Islam. It will soon regain its millenial vocation of an open religion and will impose fundamental permanent values. "Religious Islam" is gaining ground; "political Islam" is gaining confidence. The first one is stronger since it is the criterion of self-identity and the blood of personal commitment.

At all levels, religious conviction has become an absolute imperative. No Social transformation or material innovation could take place without it. However, being naturally open and tolerant, contemporary Muslim civilization has

---

[108]Gardet, *L'Islam*, pp. 385-386.

no intention of leading a solitary evolution; on the contrary, it wants to act as an active partner in international life. Its unconditional support of anti-imperialistic movements in the Third World and its aspirations for social equity have led it to seek in its fundamental traditions the appropriate sanctions that can be adapted to the needs of the time. Its flexibility is also its firmness, because the ethics prescribed by religion have refused to submit to the *fait accompli*. Demands are more and more affirmed in all Muslim countries with an Islamic moderation. The President of the Islamic Conference in Kuala Lumpur asked the different countries to cooperate "without bad thoughts or arrogance for the glory of Islam so that [our] religion might be a force of peace, progress and growth, not only for the countries and the peoples of Islam but also for the whole world."[109]

Nevertheless, Islam and its future role on the international stage will be determined by the Muslim people themselves. In this context, the Qur'ānic revelation provides them with assurance and strong incentive. "Indeed, Islam has no principal virtue which has not been talked about, no law of order which has not been specified, and no source of charity which has not been perceived. It prepared the road for emancipation, independence of reason in man's research, and, as a consequence of both emancipation and independence, it allowed man to develop to the fullest his natural abilities in order to awaken his will. Those who read the Qur'ān as it should be read will find millions of treasures and riches."[110]

[109]Declaration of Tun Abdel Razzak, reported by the *Bulletin de l'A.F.P.*, June 21, 1974.
[110]Abdu, *Rissalat*, p. 122.

EPILOGUE

Of what meaning to us then are
the concepts and prescriptions
which feign a universal value but
whose value stop at the spiritual
boundary of Western Europe?

O. Spengler

A New International Community

Mr. Abdul Aziz Bouteflika, the Algerian foreign secretary and chairman of the 29th Session of the UN General Assembly, declared that the United Nations had contributed to "the birth of the Third World. The countries that belong to the organization will see to it that they be understood and respected. They want to explain that the world has been made without them, sometimes against them, and that they will help in bringing about real changes without adopting any dogmatic attitude."[1] This statement in itself could very well conclude what we have been saying so far. It gives expression of the need for dignity, of a feeling of injustice, of a will for change, and lastly of a pragmatism that may hide the lack of a real doctrine of substitution.[2]

International law, which was developed in the Western world, settled only matters concerning European relations. Yet, since its birth as a distinct science and until the end of the eighteenth century, people's rights have always been held in a universal perspective. This vision of things gradually became more limited because of the system itself and also because of some historical events. In 1815, the Vienna Treaty reorganized "the world" which then was but a "family of all European nations." From then on, conventional law grew in importance, but the very notion of people's universal rights, which would have benefited people living in non-Christian civilizations, grew weaker.

Back then, nobody found anything wrong with the idea that international law had been elaborated in an abstract way according to the political changes undergone by European countries. its main principles could not have been understood by people belonging to foreign civilizations. The subjects of law would not have achieved in their internal judicial order a level that would guarantee respect for their inalienable human rights as the West defined them. Such a system could thus list and protect regional interests and enforce European laws and rights since it dominated and ruled over the rest of the world. European leaders were therefore able to reject all principles or values belong-

---

[1] *Bulletin de l'A.F.P.,* December 21, 1974.
[2] See Mohammed R. Djalili, "L'impérialisme culturel, entrave à l'épanouissement de l'humanité," *Le Monde diplomatique,* March 1977, p. 33.

ing to foreign civilizations.

By legitimizing the intervention of European law in the affairs of non-Christian countries on the religious, financial, administrative and constitutional levels, the foreign-inspired judicial doctrine deprived them of the very attributes of sovereignty on which their institutional body rested. World War I and the intervention of the United States under President Wilson changed the political and judicial evolution of international relations. The first worldwide conflict was not enough, and eventually it led to a universal crisis that affected every single country. Absolute sovereignty became prevalent again. The unanimous consent of the nations was the ultimate rule for national sovereignty. However, after World War II, and after people became aware of the loss of colonies, people's rights tended to become more universal.

If one randomly reads through the conventional texts pertaining to armed conflicts,[3] one will discover that the history of Europe has essentially been dealt with through agreement, treaties, final acts, declarations, and protocols. This is shown by the chronological unfolding of events, the procedure used during parliamentary conventions, and the quality of the signatories. Indeed, twenty-six multinational instruments were signed from 1856 to World War I.

- A Declaration on Maritime Law Enforcement (1856)
- The Geneva Convention for Amelioration of the Conditions of the Wounded and the Sick in Commissioned Armies (1864)
- The St. Petersburg Declaration on Explosives (1868)
- The Brussels Conference on War Laws and Customs (1874)
- The final Act of the First Peace Conference (1899), plus two conventions and three declarations
- The Hague Convention on Exemption of Naval Hospitals (1904)
- The Geneva Convention on the Wounded and the Sick (1906)
- The Final Act of the Second Peace Conference (1907), plus ten conventions and one declaration
- The Naval Conference of London (1909)
- The Convention for the Establishment of an International Court (1910)

From 1919 (when a number of states joined the League of Nations) until 1950 (when international law became truly applied all over the world and when the colonization movement decreased slowly) fourteen treaties were

<hr>

[3]Dietrich Schindler, and Jiri Toman, *The Laws of Armed Conflicts: A Collection of Conventions, Resolutions and Other Documents* (Leiden: Sijthoff, 1973), 795 pages.

passed,[4] such as:
- Four treaties concerning maritime war: Washington Treaty (1922), London Treaties (1930, 1936), Nyon Agreement (1937)
- The Geneva Protocol Forbidding Toxic Gases (1925)
- The Second and Third Geneva Conventions (1929)
- The "Roerich Pact" on the Protection of Artistic and Scientific Institutions and Historical Monuments (1935)
- The Agreement on the Imprisonment of European Axis War Criminals (1945), and a convention on Prevention and Punishment of Genocide Crimes (1948)
- Four Geneva Conventions (1949)

Since 1950, only one treaty, the Hague Convention for the Protection of Cultural Property During Armed Conflicts, was passed through traditional diplomatic channels.

The preceding list does not need any comments for it speaks for itself. The use of languages is also edifying, showing a common cultural background. French was the only language used until the Washington Treaty was written in English in 1922. The Genocide Convention in 1948 was the first instrument in which the five official languages of the United Nations were equally used.

Besides the chronological repartition and the legal procedure of the treaties, national participation is still more significant. European nations were at the forefront of the international stage until 1950. Today, they represent less than one-fourth of the UN General Assembly. Examples are numerous:
- The Geneval Convention (1864) twelve countries, all of them European
- The St. Petersburg Declaration: seventeen countries, fifteen of them being European, two Muslim: Turkey and Iran (Persia)
- The Brussels Conference: fifteen countries, fourteen of them being European except for Turkey
- The Second Peace Conference: forty-four countries, twenty European and two Muslim countries
- The Geneva Protocol in 1925: twenty-seven countries, eighteen European, two Muslim countries, Egypt, and Turkey. Today, ninety-three states have had access to or ratified it, seventeen being Muslim
- The Geneva Diplomatic Conference (1949): fifty-nine states, twenty-nine of them being European, seven Muslim. On February 1, 1973, 134 states participated in the Fourth Geneva Convention, thirty-five of them were European, twenty-nine Muslim.

---

[4]We do not take into consideration the two conventions of Havana of 1928, signed exclusively by the American states.

Reading the statistics is somewhat difficult, but it brings out a certain amount of interesting abstract pieces of evidence since they take into account neither past historical circumstances nor the present political and military power of the participating states. From the nineteenth century until 1914, many laws related to armed conflict were passed by Europe, which played a major part in such activities. However, roles have changed in the political forum of the United Nations. The coming of newly independent countries on the international stage hardly changed the stream of events, for no existing conventions were rejected. On the contrary, those new states, in reality having no other choice, complied with the legal instruments already in effect. However, a deep change took place in the procedure of conventional creation. The integration of new participants into the existing international political life was implemented within the frame of the already constituted institutional structures. The overthrow of legal and political powers can lead to a modification of the very substance of international law. It would then be endowed with much more power not only on the geographical level but also on the level of fundamental principles.

The world is no longer a huge family of states organized under Western rules. It is now a truly universal society which has not yet, however, found exactly how to express its rights. Most countries that vote in the United Nations today are newly independent states in Asia and Africa. They sometimes contest the conventional instruments which were elaborated without their consent, and they question the common law that has been until now well established. This phenomenon started at the beginning of the twentieth century (in 1907), at the Second Hague Conference, by the Latin American republics whose philosophical concept, strangely enough, had come from European civilization.[5]

Three quarters of a century later, the balance of power had changed so much as to be practically unrecognizable. Indeed, the reactions of certain newly independent states do not spring from a desire to reject the existing international system as a whole, but rather as a hesitation to accept all its principles. The rupture sometimes seems deeper than it really is for challenges to the status quo rapidly take the image of subversion.

The actual influence of the new nations in the international system is difficult to objectify.[6] Schematically, we can note that Europe progressively gave up its opinion that it was the sole center of initiative. Western liberalism was

---

[5]See Green, L. C., *De l'influence des nouveausx Etats sur le droit international.* Extract from the *Revue générale de Droit International Public,* Paris (Pedone), 1970, 29 pages.
[6]Lucien Sfez, "In Bangkok, New Conceptions Marked the 4th Conference of the 'Peace by Law,'" *Le Monde,* September 21/22, 1969.

rejected; Marxism itself appeared as a regional ideological expression, a view which is supported by its absence in the Middle East and Africa and its distortions in Asia. In the quest for an authentically universal humanism, non-European civilizations are expected to make a new contribution.

It might be useful to give a numerical representation of the universalization process of the UN as well as of the influence of its different members. For the sake of clarity, we have uniformly retained the 1977 demographic evaluations – with four billion people being the world's population – and considered 156 "nations."[7]

Outside geographic reference, "Muslim" states constitute a special rubric. The chosen dates were those of the signing of the charter and the period 1945-1950 not because those years saw a spectacular transformation in the composition of the UN, but because they witnessed the elaboration of the principal instruments of an "international ethical system:" The Universal Declaration of Human Rights and the four Geneva Conventions.[8]

The possible interpretations of such a table are several. We will deal only with a few remarks of simple objectivity because they do not take into account political changes that took place in the countries considered.

In 1945, the original members of the UN hardly represented one-third of all nations and less than half the world population: Western Europe, the USA, Canada, and Latin America, sharing a similar judicial and social philosophy,[9] held close to sixty-five percent of the votes, though they composed less than one-fifth of the total world population. Africa and Asia, partly because of European colonization, appeared to be the most disfavored continents.

In 1950, the situation changed a little bit. The members of the UN corresponded to less than forty percent of all nations and represented more than half of the total world population. The number of Asian countries grew significantly. They since then have obtained more than one-quarter of the votes in the General Assembly, while their population formed less than half of the total world population. On the contrary, the non-Marxist industrialized countries and Latin America continued to hold more than sixty percent of the votes, while the people they represented did not reach one-quarter of the total world population.

---

[7]Of which seven were absent from the United Nations: Switzerland for Europe; Rhodesia and Namibia for Africa and, finally, North and South Korea, Taiwan, and "Palestine" for Asia.
[8]One could, in this context, also mention Resolution 377(V) "The Union for the Maintenance of Peace" of November 3, 1950.
[9]We made an abstraction of the nuances atributed to "American International Law."

Today, however, the situation has totally been changed. The present-day UN has universal dimensions. Those that were absent in the 1950's plus Africa and Asia control more than fifty-eight percent of the votes. European socialist countries have seen their intrinsic weight decline, going from 12 percent in 1945 to 7.4 percent in 1977. The industrialized non-Marxist states and the developing countries of South America have about seventeen percent of the votes each. We can moreover deduce from the table that the nonindustrialized countries account for at least twenty percent of the votes, which corresponds to the numerical weight of their population in relation to the total world population. The demographic representation of the Third World varies: the people of Africa represent about one-third of the global population with less than ten percent of the UN votes.

It appears unnecessary to elaborate further, except to remark that the Muslim countries doubled the relative importance of their votes at the UN General Assembly from 1945 to 1977, going from 13.5 to 28.2 percent – a figure similar to that of the Christian countries (the industrialized countries and those of America) and superior to that of liberal and socialist industrialized states together.

The Universalization of Human Rights

The international community "today contains the representatives of more than 100 countries, most of whom are improvised and believe they have grievances and demands toward the older nations rather than having elements of reason and progress."[10] Any movement that destabilizes the existing system is taken as unreasonable and unstable. However, historical experience demonstrates that it is not possible to impose a general juridical order and expect that it will be valid for all times and all places. The propositions that seem unchangeable appear, with the passing of time, to have been only the expressions of a particular era. This phenomenon, of course, marks the body of principles and international regulations; it is a changing projection of subjective and objective elements, the global vision of society by those who compose it and the quest for adapting to current material realities. Differences in the situations of several nations as well as in the nature of various peoples, are manifested in their different ways of expressing identical aspirations. Rules of universal claims and wishes are respected without protest as long as people believe that they can guarantee the imperatives of justice, logic, and utility. If the end of these rules determines their justification, their expression must vary according to material and sentimental situations. It is the concep-

---

[10]Général de Gaulle, while talking to the General Assembly of the United Nations, during his press conference on April 11, 1961.

tion of the world that results in the given attitudes and behavior of individuals and of society. Criteria of good and bad, of prohibited and allowed become obscure when they are put in a new perspective shaped by the different cultures and mentalities that try to define these concepts.

The future international legal order will be determined by the national and regional phenomena, of beliefs, representations, and aspirations, which form the collective conscience. Perhaps the present ongoing evolution of such ideas influences international ethics more than do the external material circumstances which pose essentially technical problems.[11] Values, although having general and invariable premises, are understood only in a temporal and empirical context. The international juridical reality, where formulation appears to be more spontaneous than deliberate, could lead to the progressive embracement of the cultural, moral, and religious expressions of all the people who compose the world community. These motivations which are frequently irrational, exercise a direct and a subtle influence and remain subjacent even if the doctrine[12] does not mention them at all or tries to abandon them as potential obstacles on the path to true universality. No systemization can be advanced in an abstract manner because society is not a simple technical modality arranging mutual relationships but a body organized around an ideology which gives it its direction and dynamism. Any legislation, even an international one, which cannot embrace the different elements of this reality will eventually disappear.

Relations and affirmations take place in terms that are more political than juridical thus participating in a movement characteristic of the twentieth century – namely that law, especially a law of the people, stems from solidifying abstract symbols or traditional convictions into concrete forms of expression. This dispute could make it difficult to apply existing rules and, at the same time, could ameliorate them in conditions of transition and instability. Nevertheless, this is part of a common search for universal rules, based on a harmonized conception of justice and common interest that would transcend cultural differences and national borders, for mankind. The consequences of such a development could, however, be very serious because they would be multiplied by a number equivalent to the number of ideologies engaged in this competition. This is the same mistake which the West committed in the nineteenth century, namely to consider its particular and subjective conception

---

[11]We will consider only the present time, conscious of the fact that, historically speaking, this was above all whe.ı the economic transformations engendered, for example, the abolition of slavery and the progessive limitation of the "right of ownership."

[12]With, however, some brilliant exceptions, of which Wright, "The Strengthening," and Jenks, *The Common Law* are some.

of man and society, limited only to a precise moment of history, as the only authentically universal system available. In fact, "the notion of order which guides juridical thought is an attribute of values, of social and moral imperatives permanent in international relations."[13] The most profound transformation which contemporary international law has known resides in the composition of the community which it is called upon to rule. This state of affairs subjects institutions to a crisis that may be advantageous if it engenders a more authentically universal legal order. A synthesis of diverse aspirations will be possible only because of a certain sense of pragmatism and relativism. A compromise has to be found between cultural tolerance and the imperative stability of existing institutions. Without doubt, it has less effect on the substance than on the interpretation of its principles. The obstacles to be overcome are considerable. The most important of them are: formalism, the principle of exclusive national sovereignty, and the objective inequality of states in the eyes of international law. Various stumbling blocks caused by differences in cultural traditions should also be mentioned.

The principal defect of the contemporary system is probably the formalism that was imposed by a twentieth century Europe enjoying a largely culturally homogeneous and relatively stable era through its maintenance of the equilibrium of various forces. The formalism did not disappear with the two world wars, for it permitted the merging of substance with an understanding of the law and the hiding of fundamental divergences between legal dispositions and the aspirations of a changing world. Trying to protect states through defining their ability, it limited itself to regulating mechanical procedures rather than being concerned with the real evolution of society. Like a body without a soul, the law of the people has never really been defined in a universal dimension nor in a long-term historical perspective. Such a situation has made its adaptation and integrated evolution difficult. Certainly, by its nature, the legal norm will always be out of date because it codifies earlier experiences. The gaps which were enlarged in former centuries cannot, however, be filled by the traditional process of juridical elaboration. We should revert to the more general and vague principles which have already been absorbed in people's moral systems. Stability of the system could thus suffer. This legitimate preoccupation does not, however, lead to a pushing back of deadlines because tensions are already high. Having ceased to be a law of the people in order to become that of the states, international law has come to protect the system rather than the individual and to be preoccupied with the respect for rules rather than for justice. In their search for a logical model, jurists appear to have neglected the fact that international law is also a product of

---

[13]De Visscher, p. 171.

mental attitudes and affective behavior. The formalism of codes and doctrines as well as the politics of "realism," which are based on the concept of national sovereignty have become blurred while confronting contemporary social phenomena of considerable significance related to the interdependence and solidarity of all states.

The principle of national sovereignty constitutes a formidable hindrance to the universalization of law. Born during European history, it will not be abruptly emptied from its substance, but it will necessarily suffer from some limitations. Of course, we should not follow the utopia of those who pretend to organize international relations outside of state sovereignty. This theoretical method reflects an indisputably concrete reality, like the projection of emotional symbols acquiring more resonance in the individual conscience than the very vague sentiment of international solidarity. It is certainly manifested in a way unique to each country and culture. Still, in the newly independent countries, the first affective reaction frequently grows stronger, and sometimes violent, within the national framework. Moreover, the international community is a partnership of nations that are capable of living and developing because the numbers are virtually convinced that they have to respect certain obligations.

The pluralist system, which originates from a nonjuridical and a political vision of relations, remains a fact. However, it was the absolutist conception of sovereignty, discovered and adopted by the European nations in a more or less distant past, that was imposed in the West. The nation became an end in itself, and the legal order was built according to what the holders of power decreed. Positivism reconstructed the universe in the form of partitioned worlds, separated by the will of force and mercantilist ambitions. The moral origins were cut off and the ethical ideal gave way to political necessity. The principle of exclusive sovereignty, accompanied by a continual search for political equilibrium, established international relations on principles somewhat immoral. Force rather than law, and power rather than justice furnished the instruments of diplomacy. The tendency to disassociate the law of the people from universal justice, to bring it exclusively to a positively built order was particularly noticeable during the period from European imperialism to decolonization. Today, it is felt that the burdens of nations have grown more than their rights have, and that such an international community can survive only through interdependence. Certainly, the juridical humanism which gives priority to man before national sovereignty has not been born yet. This brief reminder has the purpose of underlining the fact that if national sovereignty remains a basic pillar of international relations, it will simultaneously represent a considerable obstacle to the universalization of the law of the people.

Any individual, whether he has good or bad intentions, weak or violent ones, aspirations and contradiction, also has the ability to distinguish justice from injustice. This autonomous power stimulates the evolution of the juridical system. Individually or collectively, man elaborates on new ethical criteria without really creating them but rather by specifying the content of old ones. Though being identical in their inspirations, people differ in their expressions according to external – objective or subjective – circumstances. Thus, the traditional culture, religion and ideology, as well as the new material of each society, induce particular meanings that can lead to belief in categorical oppositions. The moral values which are accepted now in the West did not exist a century ago.[14] On the contrary, the original canons of non-European civilizations seem to be unable to evolve rapidly. They cannot continue as the supporting foundation of a homogeneous conception of man, of the group, and of the world.[15] It is useful, therefore, to judge the adequacy of ethical ideas and the validity of juridical institutions by the perspective of relativity since their real significance stems from traditional mental structures and concrete mental conditions. Moreover, all representations of the person and society are open to criticism because, since they were created by man, they are all subjective and relative. All may appear coherent, each with its system, but on the contrary, they are incompatible with each other. The difficulty of forming a common ideal of justice and general principles of ethics is rendered worse by the inability of individuals to recognize a universal mankind, whatever that may be. Personal and national interests affect the spirits more than the suffering of men which is presented as an abstraction.

Institutional divergencies, which seem to vary infinitely according to the circumstances of the moment, are without doubt more visible than intimate agreements, and are certainly more formal than substantial. A certain identity of ethical and legal conceptions in all civilizations and during all eras, all of which proceeded from an exclusive source – man, has been made by recent research in comparative law. However, the transposition of human aspirations in positive law may have obscured the identity of moral convictions and stressed objective oppositions. In the present state of world politics, problems have a new dimension: emancipation of colonial territories induces national ambitions and regional disequilibrium. The big difference in the standards of life of people go hand in hand with violent claims and a conflict of interests. Competition is expressed through conceptions that are really original, or through borrowed ideologies, which makes it difficult to erect a system that has authority and the necessary universal credibility. In a parallel way, the

---

[14]We recall the well-known illustration that the penal law of numerous European states provided for forms of torture and mutilation until the nineteenth century.
[15]Stone, *Human Law*, p. 351, estimates that they could not survive at the international level.

leveling of needs and simple common sense compels the nations to retain institutions which may appear good, thus leading to a progressive engendering of cohesion. A community of sentiments can only be built slowly. Convergencies will increase and grow with the better synchronized evolution of the law of the people, thanks to the interdependence of nations and to the technical facilities of exchange and communications. The particular nature of each people will, according to all probability, hinder complete uniformity in the vision of the world.

The contemporary era, one of profound changes, is particularly interesting because it provides each subject of international law with the leisure to express itself. The transition toward real universalism can be possible only under two conditions. On the one hand, those political entities which have recently been associated with the process of juridical elaboration would not find a pretext for rejecting or contesting the existing institutions. On the other hand, the liberal ethnocentric West and exclusivist Marxism are called upon to stop imagining and judging civilizations according to the images they have made of themselves. They need to discover and accept differences without getting into scandals and without trying to simplify them in order to project other cultures in a distorted or biased manner. Despite its weaknesses, the United Nations offers a material framework favorable for such an undertaking.

First, the UN, through its specialized affiliates, contributes greatly to the reinforcement of international solidarity, thus building a network of juridical relations rooted in a context that is strictly politico-juridical in order to embrace economic, technical, social, and cultural domains. By facilitating the participation of a greater part of humanity in the progress of civilization, UN affiliates offer people the occasion to be aware that they can communicate in universal solidarity. Moreover, although the UN seems to be in a crisis, or ever at the edge of bankruptcy, it continues to embody a certain idea of law and morality. The attacks of which it is the target lead to a question mark which, in relation to new political and ethical conceptions, could lead to the elaboration of more general and universal principles. For the first time in its history, humanity is ready to engage in a dialogue as big as the planet. The exchange will progressively lead to a competition between differing values. The present law of the people is incoherent. The juridical order under formation is growing stronger, but it is still too primitive, too young and too liberal to competently prescribe stable rules. It selects its principles of action randomly, under the pressure of circumstances: the present situation, ideological convictions, and political calculations. Its tools do not permit it to fashion a universal system. On the other hand, we are seeing the disintegration of the law in its older imperative because it is based on the fixed perceptions of a disappearing society.

A strictly formalist conception and an exclusively political organization of international relations have imposed the principle of absolute national sovereignty and, consequently, have pushed certain nations to try to escape from all obligations, as if independence and sovereignty had liberated them from external domination. The law of the strongest comes to dominate since no general authority exists above the nations. When the principal criterion is reduced to power, the axiom of sovereign equality becomes an abstraction, even alien, which allows nations to adopt a policy which is contrary to the ethical inspirations of the system to which they formally refer. Certainly, a policy of equilibrium of forces can guarantee peace and stability. This perspective, however, is too broad to constitute a durable conception of international law, especially if no moral limitations can be used against force. If order were to be imposed by those who derive the most profit from it, the practicability of the system would be questioned. Submission to equality lasts only if the obligatory norms are seen by the people as conforming to justice and to moderation.

In this order of ideas, it is convenient to reiterate how the law of the people was imposed on the world and how it appeared to the colonized people of the nineteenth century. The principles of equality, respect, human rights and peace which were progressively imposed during the nineteenth century in the limited framework of Western Europe were the result of an immense illusion, for it hid the reality of a non-European world victimized by colonial violence. Whereas Western imperialism seized vast territories, a line of generous ideas spread the principle that protection of mankind was a guarantee for the smooth functioning of the law of the people and a condition for international stability. This very doctrinal conception, however, supported the claims of colonization and acknowledged the validity of unequal treaties, which also consecrated the use of force in international relations.

Besides the fact that it was imposed from the outside on a population that was more a victim than a beneficiary, the formal presentation of the legal order made its authentic acceptance more difficult. The positivist jurists of Europe were in possession of a public law which they atrophied by codification. The system was supposed to be sufficient, thanks to the power of legislative creation which the principal actors of world diplomacy had. It was applied to societies which were culturally different and in which considerations of high ethics and community justice were the essential foundations of social life. The West created a pseudo-morality directed at justifying a posteriori its activities. The geographic domain of the law of the people grew, but it was superimposed rather than received in those regions that maintained the fundamental convictions as well as those of their previously established institutions which had proven efficient to their specific needs. The imposition of these formal codes and principles on societies in which the main pillar of the legal system (the nation) did not exist created a profound disequilibrium, thus provoking a gap which has not yet been closed. In fact, the formerly colonized states frequently lack either competent jurists who are still in touch with their national culture or a local intelligentsia which has been nourished by the traditional culture and is also sensitive to the realities of international relations. Moreover, coercion prevented any real assimilation from the outset, thus starting a process of increasing rigidity in the then-current practices whereas, later on, independence and the consecutive desire to participate in international relations forced a rapid acceptance, without compromise, of the operating rules and institutions.

For the near future, we therefore cannot expect from the nations which grew out of colonialism and whose role has grown in the international scene any substantial contribution to the interpretation and reformulation of the law of the people. The doctrinal bind in which these nations find themselves constitutes an obstacle to the universalization of the law. We cannot have premature assimilation and comprehensive reception of external elements. It is difficult to reject norms that, despite their defects, permit participation in international life. In return, it is easy to contest them without having a coherent doctrine with which to replace them. Emotionalism and a desire for quick action tend to supplant national reflection when the number of problems to be solved is multiple and enormous.

Another block to the universalization of international law resides in the objective differences between cultures and is rooted in their individual juridical conceptions. We frequently read in Western literature[16] that the world is divided into three big juridical families, all of which are European: the Romano-German, the socialist (which descends from the first) and the Anglo-Saxon family of "common law." They all, each in its own way, produce certain marginal external systems which represent only transitory remnants of a finished era. Reference here is to a very ethnocentric vision of the situation. For its part, international doctrine, whether naturalist or positivist, remains convinced of the universality of the law in spite of the absence of cultural homogeneity. The First School (naturalist) claims that perception of fundamental virtues and innate feelings of justice are common to all individuals regardless of their civilization. As for the positivists, they are not preoccupied with cultural divergencies, because to them law is limited to a technical procedure and to a factual verification which rejects all subjective aspects.

Indeed, an attitude of extreme gullibility that considers whatever appears to people as good and accepts all national and local representations as real

---

[16]David, *Grands systems*, pp. 27-28 for example, as well as Stone, *Human Law*.

would be dangerous because it would undermine the bases of international organization in an age where universal order is probably a condition for the survival of humanity. This question is put the same way all the time in order to determine whether it is realistic or not to seek to impose a sole and general order on people whose philosophies, needs, and objectives are different.[17] A suitable compromise, which is difficult to find, sometimes hardens positions and contributes to making the universalization of the law less practical because it is not possible to mintain by force a system elaborated by one civilization, even if it is the most materially advanced. A formal extension of the juridical codes which now govern a great diversity of ideologies, economic systems, religious convictions, and traditional values could possibly result in an "etiolation" of the law, which would contribute to its weakening rather than its universalization. In fact, cultural diversity constitutes a considerable obstacle which could be diverted on the condition that we no longer use old tools on a mechanism that transformations have changed. It is therefore on the global intellectual level that our efforts will succeed.

In summary, on the international level, law and ethics are at the same time unique and multiform: unique because they emanate from man, and pluralistic because they reflect particular aspirations projected from concrete material situations through the prism of mentalities. This kind of duality is not contradictory because it is expressed on two different levels. The doctrine is ready to enumerate certain principles that are vague and general enough to be universally accepted: for instance, equity, peace, justice, respect for the person with harmony in the group and a progressive increase in comfort and material security for all men. The ways of realization and the modalities of application would not be determined in the abstract but by going back to the source of the culture. The broad claim attached to practical realities expresses in return concepts that are too rigid to be universal. Their spontaneous birth leads to deformation.

The forum that the General Assembly of the UN offers is tumultuous, passionate, and very incoherent, for it is trying to develop norms that are peculiar to each culture and common to the whole human civilizations. The antagonism of immediate interests frequently takes precedence over diffused manifestations of public conscience. Moreover, the political bipolarity of the world does not favor the discovery of materials that would go along with the edification of an ethical and juridical system which addresses the new types

---

[17]Wright, "The Strengthening," p. 100, recalls that Churchill had proposed the creation of continental "councils" for Europe, America, and Asia respectively, which would constitute groups of states united by a similar culture and problems.

of problems that have appeared in the international community.

Juridical doctrine is employed in order to understand, study, and direct the considerable transformations that take place in the world, but it has to operate through the canons of the traditional law of the people. Europe of the nineteenth century has in fact given support, especially to the contemporary world society, with its theoretical speculations. The inherited framework threatens to break, even though jurists believe they can fix it. Their formation and intellectual course incite them to copy in the international system the form of reasoning applied in domestic law. For most people, the concept of "law" transcends the notion of juridical rule and goes into the context of a moral ideal, personal, or collective. Even in the West, meta-juridical considerations made by public opinion tend more and more to find their way inside the traditional law of the people. The dilemma is dressed in known terms: Should we try to guarantee the prevalence of the law through texts or through ethics? In the first case, the nations would always find articles and interpretations to support their pretentions. In the second case, we risk reaching an enumeration of the formula of universal appearance which tends to harmonize interests and irreconcilable attitudes in an abstract manner.

The bad reputation from which international law suffers results from its inability to create a unanimous conviction about its validity. For historical reasons, it was unable to incorporate cultural diversity, and most of its sources were not that strong. On the contrary, rationalism and positivism have choked a system which does not yet have the ability to absorb new influences. It is thus necessary to return to human reality which is born of the "need of reanimation of the law by injecting irrationality in it."[18]

Several very serious obstacles to the universalization of international law remain. However, tergiversations are not out of fashion. Adaptations should be studied rapidly and accomplished progressively in order to avoid brutal transformations. Social rules take shape and change as a function of the variable that engenders them and always in the last analysis brings them to justice. The international community is in a position of becoming an incontestable reality, but the harmonization of its law is far from effective. Experience has shown that no real choice exists. It is in the interest of nations and mankind to introduce new non-European concepts and experiences into the future juridical body so that it could more accurately express the solidarity and growing interdependence of nations. The period of quiet indifferences is over.

---

[18]Michel Villey, preface in *Dimensions religieuses du droit*, et notamment sur l'apport de saint Thomas d'Aquin, Paris (Sirey, "Archives de Philosophie di Droit," t. XVIII), 1973, VII/507 pages.

Motivations transcending the will of nations have already acquired a pertinence for a future legal order. Perhaps we are much closer to the times when bases of society are constituted by universal ethical forms rather than by force. Traditional hierarchy is multiple and diverse, and so are the ways of politics. Military force represents only one means of pressure. By subtle bargaining and clever propaganda, mediocre or secondary powers gain in prestige and contribute to the shaping of an international system that is better adapted to the contemporary situation.[19] A new political situation should bring about a real spiritual revolution and a regenerated public mentality. The survival of humanity necessitates an endless adaptation of convictions and ideologies to fit changing realities.

Mutual patience and tolerance should be a great help. By adapting the existing rules and ameliorating those whose applications are urgent, we can, without dogmatism or false realism, look at the same time at the moral and legal expressions which different cultures and civilizations have developed and held throughout their history. Indeed, a certain number of concepts which had originally been assumed as fundamentals could also be pushed back some. International security, for instance, cannot be confused with respect for the established order. The law would thus deny its first vocation. The principle of the equality of nations is also being questioned. In a better integrated society, the strictly formal affirmation of equality takes a form of deceit. In the face of real inequality, the most deprived countries claim there is inequality in creation and preferential systems. A modest codification of international law will apparently be realized very soon. The present juridical order, which claims that the status-quo generates rights and obligations thus imposing favorable conditions for the powers that put the system in place, is being contested.

Contesting the juridical order without nuance takes in our opinion a regressive character, which makes the insistence on maintaining the existing system at all cost reactionary. Isolationism, which is an introverted form of national aggressiveness, is unrealistic. Abstract internationalism, which claims to create a society for all men, even without nations, has presented only a prayer that went in vain. Through the effect of actions and reactions on the regional and international levels, universalism is the only concept able to endow the law of the people with a new dimension by accepting the contribution of each legitimate value as a part of a new global human culture.

Only from a formal point of view has the universal legal order supposedly

---

[19]See, for example, the explanation of Stanley Hoffman, *Gulliver Empetre* (Paris: Seuil, 1971), 635 pages.

been achieved. The speed of the process has uncovered different courses of work that have not yet become visible. We have to reveal them *a priori* by scientific research and rational deduction rather than by reaching their unification *a posteriori*. Dynamism is the guarantor of an effective universal system. In the actual state of things, the evolution of the law of the people depends on natures' desire to consider the harmonization of their mutual values for the establishment of a common system. We should therefore remain open to a certain number of attitudes:

- moderation, which means maintaining one's conviction without false dogmatism;
- tolerance of other doctrines which are different from ours or of which we have only little knowledge;
- loyalty toward national heritage and toward outside commitment with real acceptance of equality; and,
- humanism, which requires that each individual enjoy respect for his rights and his dignity, by accepting that the status of the individual may change according to cultural traditions.

This brings us to the last essential principle which somehow crowns them all: the sense of relativism and the empirical approach which implies the search for moral and juridical values that have a general or universal character.

The Muslim "Path"

We have chosen to explain one of the social philosophies that have marked the history of humanity, one which continues to guide the behavior of millions of people. We will not, however, attempt to understand Muslim law in its totality or in its immediate actuality. A general, rather than a positive, analysis will permit us to describe a system with all of its symbols, convictions, aspirations, and suppositions. In principle, "Muslim" law in its original and formal sources should represent the exclusive motivation of the Muslims' attitudes. It was therefore difficult to avoid certain developments foreign to juridical history and, on the other hand, to take a big step back in order not to have the view diminished by established norms that would hide the fundamental concepts of its juridical system and philosophy of existence. This perspective would offer the advantage of underlining the continuity and homogeneity of Muslim law, even though its long evolution saw a break, due to the coding of norms of our era, in the tenth century, after which came a period of stagnation corresponding to the cultural and political collapse of Islam during the fourteenth and fifteenth centuries.

The continued existence of religious convictions permits us to underline the actuality of Islam through examples drawn from the contemporary era as well as from the past. Muslim law has retained only that which was considered unchangeable, not only in terms of rules created or deduced by jurists but also in terms of the expression of a spirituality associated with a particular civilization. The basis of law is provided by divine will. In this sense and in a very general way, Muslim law is ideal and unchangeable. Muslim juridical speculation is thus less interested in the construction of a society than in maintaining communal order. It has grown with the development of society, and its casuistic presentation gave it great flexibility. Juridical expression did not aim at reflecting an image of reality by relying on facts because, on the contrary, it was supposed to guide them as a speculative discipline linked to and dependent on the essential substance of law, the revelation, just like the branches are to the tree. The practical realism exercised within the limits imposed by a superior order should have avoided limiting the law to an abstract ideal or to an inaccessible model of behavior.[20] In brief, the spirit rather than the practice of Muslim law has seemed useful in this regard.

Religions are different in order for us to be able to calculate[21] their impact on the evolution of international laws. The absence of an ecclesiastic hierarchy and the completely derived revelation transcendence probably give Islam exceptional characteristics. On the one hand, there has never been any complicity of the state with the "church" or vice versa. On the other hand, God made His law known. The essence of the Islamic civilization has been the law instead of theology. It has constituted the primordial science and the matrix of social order. It has never been a code of what existed but a reminder of what should be done; nor an image of society but a light that shows to those responsible how they should decide, to the judges how they should arbitrate, and to individuals how they should behave. This indication of the "almost possible" stimulates the will and guides the spirit toward a multiple but homogeneous world. It continues thus to determine to a great extent contemporary political options, even if it has to resort to awkward apologetics.

Islam reappears globally in its traditional aspect in the debate over future conceptions of humanity. Its dynamism rests on the loyalty of the believers and on an attempt for historical rehabilitation of the Muslim community. In order to understand Islamic law in its substance, an account of principles has to be accompanied by research on society developing in its objective conditions. In fact, the environment hides expression of the rules, even when the substance of the law is explicit. Moreover, history, in spite of its vicissitudes and the mistakes of people, illustrates the way in which application of the

---

[20]Contrary to what David claims in, *Grands Systems*, pp. 15 f. whose ideas on the Islamic law are generally the repetition of former stereotypes.

[21]As well as the fact with little success. Cassin, René, "Religions et droits de l'homme" in *Amicorum Discipulorumque Liber*, t. IV, pp. 97-104.

law shapes society and permits prejudice toward future applicability of the system. We have therefore worked as historians without however really trying to reconstruct a strictly factual truth, preferring a blurred image that would not hide the complexity of religious, social, and cultural phenomena involved. We have gone back very far in history and we have gone very deep in the analysis of global data in order not only to fight the most widespread prejudices, but also to fight against the idea – which is apparently well established in the materialist vision of the contemporary world – that civilizations foreign to the Judeo-Christian culture, of which Islam is one, follow the historical course without being able to create long-term motivations. It has appeared indispensable to us to break the interdisciplinary partitioning imposed by Western intellectualism which hinders any synthesis and any objective vision.

It was indeed not a problem to retrace the totality of a history rich with events, fertile and varied in its cultural contribution, and original in its capacity of renewal; in brief, it is the history of a civilization that has many diversified expressions on a uniform and a coherent basis. Maybe, we should make illustrations. The political expansion of islam was comparable to fireworks. Leaping suddenly, it developed and spread out. The sparkling fire fell, quickly or slowly in order to spread out, or to the contrary, to engender a new explosion of light which in turn and in an autonomous way, spread like an initial explosion with similar and different sparklings. At the moment when the picture disappeared slowly, another succeeded it, apparently from nowhere, on a point that is at the same time far from its real originality which is diversity in harmony. Only the global presentation is prodigious.

It is also this concrete image that illustrates the cultural realizations of Islam. From the establishment of the Mosque that the Prophet Muhammad built in Medinah to the splendid Umayyad mosque in Damascus, the road traveled was immense although hardly a century had passed.[22] Islam had certainly borrowed from others but, thanks to a spirit which is thoroughly syncretic, did construct a monument that bears its mark. All its cultural structure is symbiotic: encounter, discovery, acceptation, assimilation, and development. Faith added a proper coloration, coming from a feeling of greatness and harmony as well as from a certain unity of inspirations. The cultural contribution of the Muslim world was immense. The study of direct and specific influences of the Muslim civilization on the resurgence of the idea of law in the eighth-century in Europe has yet to be realized.

Finally, we can also conceive of another image–the least original of all–

---

[22]Jacques C. Risler, *La civilisation arabe* (Paris: Payot, 1962), pp. 147 f. and André Miquel, *L'Islam et sa civilisation. 7e-20e Siècles* (Paris: Colin, 1968), pp. 79 f.

in order to describe the permanence of faith with its expansion toward the south of the globe without resistance. This spread was realized with the quiet persistence and the long obstination that the feeling of acquiring the truth usually gives.

Without any doubt, some forms Islam has seen are dead. Nobody really imagines advocating a return to the era of grandeur, because, first, we should avoid confusion between what is essential and the diverse shapes of the Islamic culture that have existed. The Islamic cultural history was not strongly solidified at the end of the Muslim-Arab "classical" era, to which the succeeding centuries were only appendices. This mistaken and unjust view, which is very much present in Western literature does not allow us to see the liveliness of Islamic principles in the contemporary community.

The Islamic law remains one of the great juridical systems of our time, regulating relations among almost 700 million people and providing inspiration for the establishment of constitutional bases in several countries. The religious conviction rules social matters. The representation which the Koranic revelation imposes is alive particularly in people's minds, with political importance increasing parallelly with the development of certain democratic forms. Any movement takes a religious coloration to the extent that it penetrates the masses. The masses furnish emotions, expressions, and frequently the substance of social order. Religion constitutes vital element affecting relations among individuals, groups and nations, whose efficacy seems to grow progressively. The phenomenon confirms and enforces the practicability of Islamic law and simultaneously contributes to its plasticity.

The contemporary reformist tendencies seek to express an earthly modern ideology integrated by a faith that could run modern political ideas through a matrix formed by the revealed law. Islam is a lively and a dynamic faith which tends to find external expression of its internal force in order to participate in contemporary international life. Its contribution could be fundamental, not only because it has the experience of fourteen centuries in governing relations among people, but mainly because it brings an eminently ethical view of international law, considering in the last analysis man as an ultimate goal of the system. Its spiritual virtues have not ceased to be manifested in the historical development of the community of believers and remain important in the intellectual life of the contemporary Muslim world. The Western intellectual frequently lacks an appreciation of the role played by secular conviction in certain reactions of public opinion and in the political decisions of Muslim states. A certain form of secularism seems to be triumphing in Muslim coutries which are confronting the very real problems of economic development. There is no doubt that they would be mistaken in believing that Muslims seek to establish a society based on secular principles, either liberal or socialist, detached from spiritual conventions and traditional moral principles. Religion cannot be relegated only to the level of individual conscience.[23] We have to be pleased for Islam and for the World.

A Global Essay

It is not sufficient to analyze the law of the people by comparative, logical, or axiomatic methods. It is also not necessary to give a positivist presentation of the norms that are applied in relations among individuals and nations, as only proven effectiveness can give them an obligatory character. In short, a selection of some major concepts which constitute the principal domains of that law relevant to international relations will undoubtedly clarify the entire issue. These subjects may be peace, war, economic or diplomatic relations, and human rights, for example. It is preferable to start any research on this subject in the perspective of global readjustment than form the perspective of speculation on details.

Such a descriptive essay could become creative if, through the clash of ideas, it advanced values that are associated with a moral community of humanity within the framework of what we could call the "natural law of the atomic era." In fact, presenting the elements of a moral and a juridical system that can function effectively when used by several modern ideologies seems more of a matter of formulation than a precisely doctrinal one providing, however, that the presentation is global enough for the employed terms to maintain their proper connotations.

We have attempted to state the ethical principles and abstract axioms that sustain the organization of Muslim society in order to clarify certain values that contribute to the formation of its ideology and participate in guiding individual behavior and in establishing political institutions. Even though it largely connects the spiritual to the secular, Islam is first a religion and is considered as such because of its absolute character. At the same time, it is considered a projection of an ideal that lies between the desirable and the real. Certain antecedents and present variables of action have been stated in order to explain the historical facts and the agonies of the contemporary Muslim community. We have thus relied on original sources, without considering the critiques made by positivist studies. We have juxtaposed rather than looked at literal identification in order to attempt the prediction of eventual convergencies. It seems impossible to appreciate Islamic law, which intertwines so closely with religion, without giving at least a minimum amount

---

[23]See on the contrary the "Third Universal Theory" proposed by President Qaddafi.

of evidence on Islam and the culture that engendered it. By avoiding a strictly juridical perspective and refusing to allow interrogation on a 'theological' level, we have taken Islam as a divine revelation, and the Muslim community as a complex and specific social phenomenon. After all, it is the Islam of convictions and behavior that we are trying to understand. It forms, in the last analysis, the invariant core that has resisted the changes of history. This option sometimes leads to repetitions but does put Islam in its cultural dimension as well as in its immediate objective conditions.

This approach is without question "scientific," but it could appear to anyone that it offers a very traditional image of Islamic culture, if not a "reactionary" appreciation of Islamic law. However, the debate on the "fixed" character of the law concerns its "jurisprudential" part; in other words, it is an autonomous interpretation of the sources rather than of their substance. The quarrel over reopening the door of speculative effort has already been partially won by the reformists. Most Muslims are ready to believe this, as long as their social life will continue to be guided by rules coming from an Islamic theoretical framework. The reformists, even those who feed on naturalist thought, have to preserve the law's character of being perfectly applicable but remaining idealized. Only a defeatist attitude proposes to follow the path of the secularized West, venturing on a path that may prove to be a dead-end road. It is an uncontested reality and a great benefit for the Muslim world that the majority of Muslims refuse to see their law as being deduced from observed phenomena by insisting that future behavior continue to be guided by revelation.

Contrary to what is often found in Western publications, the immutability of Islamic law does not represent an integral immobilism. The acceptance of certain foreign norms corresponding to Qur'ānic principles of justice and fairness, as well as spontaneous legislative creation, made the Islamic order incontestably flexible even before it fell under the empire of Western legal systems. Diverse factors – evident or presumed – are still in use in the natural process of juridical evolution. The political division of the community and the emergence of occasionally nationalist states does not at all involve – beyond the differences of formulation often adhering to a political ideology – a juridical "provincialism." This clearly contrasts with the situation in the Soviet Islamic republics, where the superiority of Islamic law, more or less amalgamated with modern legislation and regional customs, is unquestioned. In this respect, it is not necessary to analyze Islamic law but rather to reveal that which furnishes the masses with a certain form of inspiration and discipline, and to give less consideration to the formal norms than to their spiritual ties so as to present them in all their richness. Islamic society cannot be judged according to the criteria of modern political science but, on the contrary, by the image which it retains from its past and that which it projects into the future. The religious climate creates a true idealism because it is a submission to a transcendental order. It simultaneously engenders a dynamism, since it does not express the society in terms of what is but in terms of what it wants to become.

Even the notion of juridical "comparison" involves the idea that the law has lost its universal value. The procedure could either be a recension of contents of diverse laws or, on the contrary, a search for the true essence of a foreign legal order. We have embraced the second view: trying to discover what are the common concepts, all the while bridling the urge to disclose in each of the Islamic values a feeling corresponding to those in Western civilization. This, in fact, only shows that one will separate for the purpose of adoption those specific principles, taken in their most general scope, which can make the law of men more universal. Of course, when one leaves the Western system, it would seem more prudent to limit oneself to a comparison of codified laws, but comparative research lacks the method. A too systematic approach could lead to confusion and errors. It is not so much the analysis of the positive rules which is important but the questioning of the society's structures which secrete them. By keeping the debate in the social context, one avoids the abuse to which each attempt to generalize lends itself. This is particularly necessary for international law which even though it is the most primitive of all legal orders is now faced with the urgent imperative of attaining a universal dimension.

Globally speaking, Islam reappears in the contemporary world as one of the answers to the questions posed concerning the destiny of man and of society. The internal political evolution of states engenders its own solutions and transformations. All of the convulsions which have agitated the Islamic countries these last decades, regardless of the labels with which they were tagged, have claimed to be authentically Islamic. These movements continue to seek inspiration in the communal past.

The primary originality of the Islamic system is its conception of the social man – a concept which is simultaneously opposed to communism's annihilation of the individual in the group, and to liberalism's view of the individual and society as antagonists. Communal solidarity assures respect for the rights of man both within the group[24] and on the outside since he is considered a subject of international law. To the positivist materialism which dehumanizes

---

[24]Daniel P. Mannix, *The History of Torture* (London: New English Library, 1970), p. 127, mentions, for example, that in spite of the reputation of brutality which the Christian nations have given them, the Arabs and the Turks invented no form of torture.

man, Islam contrasts its spirituality in preventing the state from becoming a *deus ex machina* which the West knows and which the allegedly "socialist" states are striving to impose.[25] The imperative feeling of individual responsibility – a considerable factor of emancipation – prevents man from alienating himself from the over-powerful group. Loyalty is primarily rendered to the faith's ideals and not to the governmental institutions. The affirmation of the supraworldly goals of man tends to submit the state to the law rather than the individual to the political apparatus. In a quite logical manner, Islam recommends, at the international level, the independence of people rather than the self-sufficiency of nations. In brief, its juridical doctrine advocates loyalty, peaceful universalism, realism, and moderation – all of which are virtues conforming to the spiritual nature of man.

Colonization corroded rather than integrated the traditional Islamic juridical system. In spite of independence, Islamic law is still not reconciled with itself, and it continues its search for a compromise between concrete reality and higher principles. Applying its own potentials, Islamic society improvises rather than searches for a rational mode in the solution to its problems. It participates in the encounter of contemporary ideologies but still often reacts with emotions such as bitterness, enthusiasm, or aggression. The awakening of Islam has so far been more of a disordered search than the definition of a method. Of course, the revelation carries a conviction rather than a technique applicable to a modern humanism. During the present period of political instability, economic difficulties, and spiritual anguish, Islamic thought is used not so much to explain the substantial contents of law but to prove the validity of the religion. In its essence, however, Islam continues to assert its traditional destiny, a place of exchanges and of dialogues between cultures. Undoubtedly, it will be able to recover, if one judges it by the prodigious capacity it has displayed in the past to adapt itself and to be reborn.

At the same time, it appears to the Muslims that they will not be able to reach those secular objectives which affirm their spiritual internal force. The immediate expression is therefore more "ideological" than practical and inhibits the appreciation of the jurist who sees in the acts, and not in the opinions, a source of future international law. Nevertheless, the abstract symbol often creates the mystique appropriate to the social action which ultimately generates the law. It is convenient to emphasize that – beyond the slogans which mobilize the popular energies and a sometimes violent dispute of the existing law – Islam does not at all oppose itself to the world, and it does not seek to undermine international stability. Furthermore, the Qur'ān's mod-

---

25Jean-Francois Revel, *La tentation totalitaire* (Paris: Laffont, 1976), 372 pages.

eration makes it an order to the believers not to " ... spread disorder in the land when a just peace has been established."[26]

Owing to the force of circumstances, the future external expression of an authentically Islamic law will be partially impregnated with Western concepts because Muslim jurists, often breaking with the forms of rationalist reasoning, use theoretical supports inherited from positive law. It is certainly not necessary to wait for the rapid appearance of a synthesis of compromise, but the intellectual bearing, by reconciling the methods of reasoning, could contribute to a better reciprocal understanding. The main positive consequence of the soul searching which followed political independence was the orientation of the spirit toward action. Prodded by the apparent antagonism between the authority of tradition and the imperatives of transformation, Islam rediscovered its dynamism. With optimism, it asserted its relevance.

Basing our argument on the double fact that, on the one hand, Islam provides the essential rules of conduct for seven hundred million people and that, on the other hand, the entrance of Islamic states into the international society is too recent to have yet revealed its full significance, we have sought to penetrate to the heart of Islamic culture. For international relations undoubtedly more so than in any other discipline, the ordering of a true cooperation is only attainable on the preliminary condition that the partners know each other and show a true desire to understand. Colonial Europe did not encourage such an openness of spirit toward the Islamic world which it dominated.[27] Of course, the driving forces behind the analysis are not completely dishonest. Still, apart from some rare exceptions – among them Louis Massignon, for example – they lack true humanism because they are unilateral. Too sure of the excellence of its superior material culture, Western orientalism has often, consciously or unconsciously, prevented the establishment of a real dialogue to carry an appreciation of value, a judgment.[28] The attitude seeks to consider as naturally decadent each conviction foreign to its own culture, which leads to frustration and bitterness and, in turn, will contribute to the increased severing of the respective opinions. We have chosen a different line of interpretation, namely: showing the problematic situation as might be done by a Mus-

---

[26]al-A'raf: 56. See also al-Qasas: 77 and al-Baqarah: 205-206.

[27]It is necessary to note that Marxist dogmatism shows itself to be even more closed. The Soviet dictionary manages to group into a few lines, destined to define Islam, all the injustices and aberrations possible: "... Hostility when meeting the infidel, inferiority of women, and legislation on polygamy are the traits characteristic of dogma. Islam justifies its social inequalities and diverts the people from revolutionary combat toward a futile expectation of success in a world to come." M. Rosenthal and P. Yudin, *Dictionary of Philosophy* (Moscow: n.p., 1967), p. 223 (translation).

[28]Laroui, *Idéologie arabe*, pp. 10 f.

lim. This choice is of course perilous and perhaps questionable, but we think
that our research will gain in objectivity because of it.

The Time of Adjustments

On the strictly formal level, the material structure of a world order exists.
In addition, diverse elements which could permit the formation of a juridical
body of universal scope are already laid out. The fundamentally unstable contemporary political reality encourages rapid evolution to avoid revolution and
chaos. The changes in the composition and the distribution of forces and influences require the largest and most diversified foundations for the law of
man. This evidence should force the jurists to adjust their perspective. Flexibility will permit transformations, whereas immobility will lead to confusion.
The immediate present enjoys an artificial stability born of elements which
are more political than moral. It has, nevertheless, proven itself to be favorable. In fact, even if the present equilibrium is that of "deterrent," the atomic
specter finally creates a regenerated climate by showing that the destiny of
nation-states and of civilizations is tied to that of all of humanity. The times
therefore seem to be auspicious for the construction of a new universal law
which would be less of a uniform supranational law than a certain progressive
harmonization of legal systems.

People only envisage the organization of the international community
through the prism of their own conception of man and society. However, on
the broader essential principles, the identity of human nature tends to transcend the particular tendencies of each nation, culture, or ideology. Implicitly,
there is therefore a "natural" ethic constituting a rational hierarchical order.
The diversity of demonstrations or of expressions, which are located at a secondary level of application, does not at all weaken the existence of this "natural" ethic and does not imply either a contradiction or a hindrance. In fact,
this ethic is undisputed in that it takes a higher awareness of their solidarity,
"in that it takes which the people perceive better than their differences and,
finally, that they remain themselves."[29] Thus, the universality of international
law will not be monolithic but one of tolerance, flexibility, and pragmatism
– ruling a society such as it is, with its agreements, contradictions, oppositions, and aspirations. The law of man cannot continue to be what it has represented since the nineteenth century (a self-contained formal system) because
the universal social order issues from the spiritual representations which make
up the world.

The new world order to be constructed will not be only economical, but

---

[29]Jean G. Lossier, *Solidarité: Signification morale de la Croix-Rouge*, 2nd ed. (Neuchâtel: Baconnière, 1950), p. 11.

also juridical and cultural. Forgetting this last level is to court failure. The West, by unleashing in modern times the movement of "modernism," has imposed the preeminence of positive norms on a world which wants to be more and more dynamic, functional, and impersonal. However, the foundations of traditional cultures are always more vulnerable to change than the international legal order which is the most primitive of all the juridical systems. The intellectuals must, in this context, search for possible ways of harmonization. It will be necessary for them to have great generosity and patience (particularly if they are the committed and responsible ones in their countries) to break the routine and to put into motion the immediate concern of national interests in a world ideologically divided between East and West, economically divided between North and South, and globally facing the problems of poverty in nourishment, energy, and certain raw materials. First and foremost, it is their responsibility to jointly devise a pragmatic framework of acceptable universal norms in which the process of elaborating a more universal law could be placed.

It is certainly not easy to totally separate the material contingencies. However, certain fundamental principles of humanity, justice, and security could be defined and the modalities of harmonization developed by creative research which would take into account religious convictions, ideologies, moral motivations and, also, the constitutional provisions as well as the ordering of public institutions in diverse contemporary cultures.[30] Since science progresses more rapidly than mentalities, it will be necessary to wait for those public opinions which are slow to follow the theoretical speculation. Doctrine, however, can base itself on reality, using the experience and understanding that in a society of independent nations, the interest of all resides in the definition and the putting into practice of a juridical order as open as possible to the universal.

Factors such as the variety of civilizations, the opposition of interests, and the legitimate aspirations of individual peoples make it difficult to approve of a diversely expressed feeling of justice and frustrates the establishment of a "universalized" international system flexible enough to win the acceptance of all participants and steady enough to guarantee order. Even so, some approaches can nowadays be fused to reaffirm the authority of the law of man. Certainly, it would be utopian and therefore futile to neglect the importance of ties between law and force. The rivalry of state powers and ideologies prolong themselves and negatively influence the development of law. Tensions in an era of change are unavoidable.

---

[30]The usefulness of such research is, in theory, so evident that it would be sanctioned by Article 9 of the Statute of the International Court of Justice.

One can point out with pleasure that a modest current of modern doctrine tries to grasp the juridical phenomenon integrated with other aspects of social life and of metaphysical speculation including the opposition of public powers, the claim to economic development, and the ties between law and justice. This approach, which previously has been missing, should be encouraged and promoted in the hope that the international discipline of law will stop analyzing a petrified body and take an interest in the study of a system in full bloom. The juridical doctrine will progress to the extent that it can provide a precise view of the reality of things which it claims to order. Thus, it would no longer be only on the level of simple methodology, neglecting the observation of superior evidence such as that of ethical convictions and cultural traditions.

The existence of international organizations offers a concrete framework in which the collective practices of states can be tried. They no doubt contribute to a more rapid development of the law of man or, at least create an apportunity for this to happen. The multilateral agreements progressively take the path of habit, often contested because they have been elaborated without the participation of all. The sum of the specific treaties signed during the last two decades could lead one to imagine a certain unity in the application of law and a harmonization of its intrepretation. Isolated, however, this phenomenon will only have a limited scope and a fragile existence, having to face political ideologies, maneuvers of the strongest states, and reactions of the often-stated national public opinions.

The question is no longer that of transforming the law of man; this has already happened to a very large degree. It is rather a case of transposing a new reality in the doctrine by a creative intellectual effort. The jurists can no longer be satisfied with referring to the practice of states but must draw from the theories and experiences of non-European legal systems which, furthermore, often have a very long and very diversified heritage. They must no longer nurture this tranquil indifference with respect to foreign civilizations. In the main areas of intellectual research, except in intellectual law, one has noticed a change in perspective and a real interest vis-à-vis little-known cultures.[31] It is inconceivable that the law will escape a similar readjustment, especially that part of it which claims to be international. This opening toward universalization cannot be the act of jurists alone but will require a multicultural and poly-disciplinary approach. To the extent which the summoning of historical precedents can constitute an example and create a stimulation, it will be useful to emphasize *mutatis mutandis* that the Western "juridical revolution" of the thirteenth century was initiated by research con-

---

[31]Jenks, *The Common Law*, p. 80.

ducted in universities. The doctrine which was elaborated there sought to order the new relations growing out of the fragmentation of Christianity.

By transcending countries and territories, the efforts of the universities allowed the law to adapt itself to a new and multinational Europe. Would it be utopian to demand the same efforts of the universities of our time which could have the chance to elaborate a doctrine corresponding to our global society? The universalization of the law of man could then no longer be accomplished by idealistic speculation or philosophy, but by scientific research, strengthened by a certain generosity of heart, allowing true communication through the acceptance of the values of others. This preliminary development could constitute an evolution in Western thought which justifies its expansion by evangelism and holds down a permanent reflux of ethnocentrism supported by the material superiority of its civilization. It would equally represent a turning in the Marxist dogmatism which is supported by the most detestable forms of socialist "messianism." If they have to remain blind to the evidence that other cultures are in full bloom and claim a role to play in the organization of the world, the contemporary intellectuals will lack a response to the challenge of our times.

We have, for our modest part, tried to point out the humanism of Islam by analyzing its conception of man, its political institutions, and its internationalist philosophy by returning to the doctrine to explain the acts and by using, at times, Islamic history in order to illustrate the theories. We hope that our undertaking has not been in vain, for we are convinced that the Islamic world – among others – could provide an essential contribution to the formation of the universal community to come. Rather than echoing the defeatist complaint of Dante: "O mankind! By how many thunderstorms and plagues, how many castaways must you be visited by since you have become a many-headed monster" we think that "humanity" has changed its dimension and is necessarily pacing toward integration. Each man, therefore, is responsible for perpetually summoning his "idea" of civilization and his feeling for the universal.

1945: Original Members (51)			Related through states		Related through population	
	Number of States	Population (in millions)	% of members	% of states	% of members states	% of present world population
Non-Marxist industrial states (including Slouth Africa)	13	423,7	25,5	8,3	23,3	10,5
European socialist states	6	317,9	11,8	3,9	17,7	8,1
America (Except U.S. and Canada)	20	264,9	39,2	12,8	14,5	6,4
Africa (without Egypt)	2	28,0	3,9	1,3	1,3	0,8
Asia (including Egypt)	10	767,2	19,6	6,4	43,2	20,2
Total	51	1801,7	100,0	32,7	100,0	46,0
Muslim States	7	136,4	13,5	4,6	8,5	3,6
From 1945 to 1950 = 60 members (9 new)						
Non-Marxist industrial states (including Israel)	16	435,4	26,7	10,2	20,5	11,2
European socialist states	6	317,9	10,0	3,8	14,5	8,1
America	20	264,9	33,3	12,8	12,5	6,4
Africa	2	28,0	3,3	1,5	1,3	0,8
Asia	16	1123,0	26,7	10,2	51,2	29,4
Total	60	2169,2	100,0	38,5	100,0	55,9
Muslim States	11	423,6	18,3	7,4	6,9	3,5
From 1950 to 1977 = 149 members (89 new)						
Non-Marxist industrial states	25	647,7	16,8	16,0	16,7	16,1
European socialist states	11	399,4	7,4	7,1	10,3	10,0
America	26	281,8	17,5	16,7	7,2	7,1
Africa	48	328,2	32,2	30,8	8,4	8,2
Asia (Chinese population replacing Taiwan)	39	2234,5	26,1	25,0	57,4	55,8
Total	149	3891,6	100,0	95,6	100,0	97,2
Muslim States	42	402,8	28,2	26,2	10,7	10,2

BIBLIOGRAPHY

Islam

Sources*

Qur'ān
Translations in the European Languages are numerous. In the French language, we have chosen those of Masson, Denise, Paris: N.R.F. "Pleiade," 1967 and Blachère, Regis (Paris: Maisonneuve et Larose, 1966).

Mohammed 'Abdu, *Rissalat el Tawhid*, Paper on the Moslem Religion. Translated by Michel, B. and Abdel Razek, Mostafa (Paris: Guethner, 1925).

Jamal ed-Din Afghani, *Réfutation des Matérialistes*. Translated by Goichon (Paris, 1942).

al-Bukhari, *L' authentique tradition musulmane*. Translation, introduction, and notes by George H. Bousquet (Paris: Grasset, 1964).

al-Bukhari, *Les traditions islamiques*. Translated by O. Houdas and W. Marcais (Paris: 1903-1914).

Philip K. Hitti, *The Origin of the Islamic State*. Being a Translation from the Arabic Accompanied with Annotations Geographic and Historic Notes of the "Kitāb Futuh al-Buldān": of al-Iman Abdul Abbas Ahmad Ibn-Jabir al-Balādhuri (Beirut: Khayats, 1966). English version.

Philip K. Hitti (ed), *Memoirs of an Arab-Syrian Gentleman* or an Arab Knight in the Crusades. Memoires d'Usamah Ibn-Munqidh. Translation from a unique manuscript. (Beirut: Khayats Reprints no. 7, 1964). English version.

ibn-Hishām, *The Life of Mohammad*. Translated by Guillaume (Oxford University Press: 1955).

ibn-Khaldoun, *Les textes sociologiques et économiques de la mouqaddima (1375-1379)*. Filed, translated and annotated by G.H. Bousquet (Paris: Rivière, 1965).

Ahmad A. ibn-Taimiyyah, *On Public and Private Law in Islam or Public Policy in Islamic Jurisprudence*. Translated from the Arabic by A. Omar. (Beirut: Khayats, 1966). English version.

al-Māwardi, *Governmental statutes*. Translated by Alger E. Fagnan, 1915.

Abdul Hussein A. Muslim, *al-Jami' us-Sahih*. Translated from Arabic to English by Abdel Hamid Siddiqi (Lahore: Ashraf, 1973).

Mohammed H. al-Shaybani, *The Islamic Law of Nations. Shaybani's Siyar* by Majid Khadduri (Baltimore: John Hopkins, 1966). Arabic version.

Mohammed I. al-Shāf'i, *Islamic Jurisprudence, Shāf'i's Risāla*. By Majid Khadduri (Baltimore: John Hopkins, 1961). Arabic version.

Works

General Works on Islam

Publication by Muslim Authors

[299]

Books

Mohammed Aini, *La quintessence de la philosophie de ibn-i-Arabi.* Translation by Rechid Ahmed. Preface by Massignon Louis (Paris: Geuthner, 1926).

Syed Amir Ali, *A Short History of the Saracens.* Being a Concise Account of the Rise and Decline of the Saracenic Power, and of Economic, Social and Intellectual Development of the Arab Nation, from the Earliest Time to the Destruction of Bagdad, and the Expulsion of the Moors from Spain. (London: MacMillan, 1927). Maps and geological tables. In English.

Muhammad Ali, *The Prophet of Arabia* (Beirut: Khayat). In English.

A. M. Alwaye, *The Essence of Islam* (Cairo: Cairo World Press, 1966), 2nd edition.

Mohamed A. Draz, *Initiation of the Koran.* A Historical and Comparative Account arah (New York: Devon-Adair,

Mehdi Badi, *The Greeks and the Barbarians the Other Face of History* (Lausanne: Payot, 1963).

Malek Bennabi, *Vocation de l'Islam* (Paris: Seuil, 1857).

E. Dinet and Sliman Ben Ibrahim, *L'Orient vu de l'Occident* (Paris: Geuthner).

Mohammed A. Draz, *Initiation of the Koran.* A Historical and Comparative Account (Cairo: al Ma'aref, 1950).

Saad El-Dine El-Guizaoui, *On the Margin of Islamic Studies* (Cairo: Conseil Superieur des Affairs Islamiques, 1967).

Tawfik El-Hakim, *L'âme retrouvée* (Paris: Charpentier, 1937).

Tawfik El-Hakim, *Muhammad* (Cairo: Conseil Superieur des Affaires Islamiques, n.d.).

Abdel Hamid El-Sayeh, *The Position of Jerusalem in Islam* (Cairo: Conseil Superieur des Affaires Islamiques, 1968).

Mohammed Essad, *Mahomet 571-632.* Translated by Jacques Marty and G. Lepage (Paris: Payot, Bibliotheque Historique, 1956).

Aly M. Fahmy, *Moslem Naval Organization.* From the Seventh to the Tenth Century A.D. (Cairo: National Publication and Printing House, 1966). English version.

Aly M. Fahmy, *Moslem Sea-Power in the Eastern Mediterranean.* From the Seventh to the Tenth Century A.D., Cairo: National Publication and Printing House, 1966. English version.

Majid Fakhry, *Islamic Occasionalism.* Critique by Averroes and Aquinas (London: George Allen and Unwin, 1958). English version.

M. Hamidullah, *Le Prophète de l'Islam* (Paris: Vrin, 1954) 2nd volume.

Ahmed Hussein, *On conviction and Islam* (Cairo: Conseil superieur des Affairs islamiques. Etudes sur l'Islam, s.d. English version.

Mohammad F. Jamali, *Letters on Islam.* Written by a Father in Prison to his son. (London: Oxford University Press, 1965). English version.

Ismail Kashmiri, *Prophet of Islam Mohammad and Some of His Traditions* (Cairo: Conseil superieur des Affaires islamiques. Etudes sur l'Islam, 1967). English version.

Ebrahim Khan, *Anecdoctes from Islam* (Lahore: Ashraf, 1947). English version.

Abdallah Laroui, *L'idéologie arabe contemporaine* (Paris: Maspero, 1967).

Muhammad Ali (Maulana), *The Religion of Islam.* A Comprehensive Discussion of the Sources, Principles, and Practices of Islam (Cairo: National Publication, n.d.). English version.

Saleh Soubhy, *Pilgrimage to Mecca and Medina* (Cairo: National Press, 1894).

Esad F. Tugay, *Mohammad, the Prophet of Allāh* (Cairo: Eastern Press, 1951).

Publications by Non-Muslim Authors

Books

J.M. Abdel Jalil, *Aspects intérieur de l'Islam* (Paris: Seuil, 1962). 2nd edition. Revised and corrected.

Abdel Malek, Belal Anouar, Abdel Aziz, and Hassan Hanafi (eds), *Renaissance of the Arab World* (Inter-Arab Colloquim of Louvain, Gembloux: Duculot, 1972).

Tor. Andrae, *Mahomet, sa vie et sa doctrine.* Translated by Maurice Gaudefroy-Demombynes (Paris: Maisonneuve, 1945).

Roger Arnaldex, *Mahomet ou la prédication prophétique* (Paris: Seghers, 1970).

Morroe Berger, *The Arab World Today* (New York: Anchor Books, 1964). English version.

Jean-Jacques Berreby, *La péninsule arabique.* (Paris: Payot, 1958).

Jacques Berque, *Le Arabes d'hier à demain* (Paris: Seuil, 1960).

Brilland (de) et Aigrain, *Histoire des Religions* (Paris: Bloud and Gay, 1957).

J.L. Burckhardt, *Voyages en Arabie* (Paris: 1835), 3 volumes.

B. Carra de Vaux, *Penseurs de l'Islam* (Paris: Geuthner, 1923).

Joseph Chelhod, *Les structures du sacré chez les Arabes* (Paris: Maisonneuve, 1964).

Emile Dermenghem, *Les plus beaux textes arabes* (Paris: La Columbe, 1951).

Emile Dermenghem, *Mahomet et la tradition islamique* (Paris: Seuil, 1963).

Henri Desroches, *Sociologies religieuses* (Paris: P.U.F., 1968).

Divers, *Evolution des Pays de civilization arabe* (Paris: University of Paris, 1936-38).

Divers, *Encyclopédie de l'Islam.* 2nd edition, (Paris: Leyde, 1954).

Mircea Eliade, *Traité d'histoire des religions* (Paris: Payot, 1968).

Henry Dumery, *Critique et Religion* (Paris: Sedes, 1957).

Francesco Gabrielli, *Les Arabes.* Translated by Marie de Wasmer (Paris: Buchet/Chastel, 1963).

Demombynes Gaudefroy, *Maurice Mohammed, l'Homme et son Message* (Paris: Albin Michel, 1957).

Demombynes Gaudefroy, *Mahomet* (Paris: Albin Michel, 1969).

E. F. Gautier, *Mœurs et Coutumes des Musulmans* (Paris: Payot, 1969).

Hamilton A. R. Gibb, and J. H. Kramers, *Encyclopedia (shorter) of Islam* (Paris: Masionneuve, 1953).

J. E. Godchot, *Les constitutions du Proche et Moyen-Orient* (Paris: Sirey, 1957).

Phillip K. Hitti, *Précis d'histoire des Arabes* (Paris: Payot, 1950).

Clement Huart, *Littérature arabe* (Paris: Armand Colin, 1902).

Clement Huart, *Histoire des Arabes* (Paris: Geuthner, 1912).

Rene R. Khawam, *Propos des Arabes sur la vie en société* (Paris: Albin Michel, 1964).

Henri Lammens, *The Arab city of Taif During Hegira* (Beirut: Catholic Press, 1922).

Henri Lammens, *The Western Arabia Before Hegira* (Beirut: Catholic Press, 1928).

Colonel LaMouche, *Histoire de la Turquie* (Paris: Payot, 1953).

Stanley Lane-Poole, *Studies in a Mosque*, reprint no. 21. (Beirut: Khayat, 1966). English version.

Alfred Loisy, *A propos d'histoire des religions* (Paris: Emile Nourry, 1911).

Duncan B. MacDonnald, *The Religious Attitude and Life in Islam* (Beirut: Khayat, 1965). Oriental reprint no. 9. English version.

L. Machuel (ed), *Les auteurs arabes* (Paris: Armand Colin, 1912).

Paul Marella, *Toward the Merging of Religions* (Brussels: Foyer Notre-Dame, 1967).

Louis Massignon, *Annuaire du monde musulman* (Paris: P.U.F., 1955).

Gustav Mensching, *Sociologie religieuse* (Paris: Payot).

Andre Miquel, *La littérature arabe* (1969).

Vincent Monteil, *Le monde musulman* (Paris: Horizons de France, 1963).

Vincent Monteil, *Les Arabes* (Paris: "Que sais-je?" 1964).

Vincent Monteil, *L'Islam Noir* (Paris: Reed).

J. D. Pearson, *Index Islamicus. A Catalogue of Articles on Islamic Subjects Published in Periodicals and Other Collective Publications during the Years 1906-1955* (Cambridge: Supplement 1956-1960). English version.

Xavier de Planhol, *Le monde islamique* (Paris: P.U.F., 1957).

F. Rahman, *Prophecy in Islam*. Philosophy and Orthodoxy (London: Allen and Unwin, 1958). English version.

Maxime Rodinson, *Mahomet* (Paris: Seuil, 1968).

Stephan and Nandy Ronart, *Concise Encyclopaedia of Arabic Civilization*. The Arab East (Amsterdam: Djambatan, 1959). English version

Pierre Rondot, *Destin du Proche-Orient* (Paris: Centurion, 1959).

George Sale (ed.), *The Koran, Commonly called the Koran of Mohammed* Translated into English from the Original Arabic with Explanatory Notes Taken from the Most Approved Commentators. (London: Frederik Warne, s.d.). English version.

Nasri Salhab, *On the Steps of Mohammad* (Beirut: Dar al-Kitab al-Lubnani, n.d.).

Savary, (ed), *Le Koran* (Paris: Granier, 1963).

Dominique et Janine Sourdel, *Civilization of Classical Islam* (Paris: Arthaud, 1968).

S. M. Stern, (ed.) *Documents from Islamic Chanceries*. First Series (Oxford: Bruno Cassirer-Oriental Studies III, 1965). English version.

G. de Strange, *Palestine under the Moslems*, reprint (Beirut, 1965). English version

Montgomery W. Watt, *Mahomet à Médine* (Paris: Payot, 1959).

Hanna Zakarias, *Vrai Mohammed et faux Coran* (Paris: Nouvelles editions latines, 1960).

Constantine K. Zurayk, *The Arab View of History* (London: Longman). English version

Articles

Georges H. Bousquet, "Sociological observations on the origin of Islam.": *Studia Islamica* (1954).

Claude Cahen, "Points of view on the Abbaside Revolution." *Historical Revolution*, CCXXX (1963).

Olivier Carre, "The Socio Economic and Political Content of Moslem Educational Manuals in Recent Egypt." *Revue des Etudes Islamique* XXXVIII (Paris: Geuthner, 1970).

J. Castagna, "Bolchevism and Islam." *Encyclopedie de l'Islam*, LI, LII (1922).

Louise Gardet, "Names and Statutes the Problem of Faith in Islam." *Studia Islamica* (Paris: 1956).

Hamilton Gibb, "The Structure of Religious Thinking in Islam." *Institut des Hautes Etudes Marocaines*, VII (Paris: Librarie Orientale et Americaine, 1950).

Hamilton Gibb, "The Reaction Against the Western Culture in the Middle East." *Cahiers de l'Orient contemporain* (Paris, 1951).

Hamilton Gibb, "An Interpretation of Moslem History." *Cahiers d'Histoire mondiale*, I (1953). English version.

G. E. Grunebaum, (Von). "The Spirit of Islam as shown in its Literature." *Studia Islamica*, I (1953).

G. E. Grunebaum, (Von). "Moslem Ideology and Arab Aesthetics." *Studia Islamica*, IV (1955). English version.

G. E. (Von) Grunebaum, "Islam, Essays in the Nature and Growth of a Cultural Tradition." *Comparative Studies of Cultures and Civilization* (London, 1955). English version.

J. H. Kramers, "The Sociology of Islam." *cta Orientalia*, XXI (1953).

Henri Lammens, "The triumvirate Abou Bakr, Omar and Abou Obaida," *Melanges de la Faculte orientale de Beyrouth*, no. IV (1909).

Henri Lammens, "Koran and Tradition." *Recherche de Science Religieuse*, no. 1 (Paris, 1910).

Henri Lammens, "Was Mohammad Sincere?" *Recherche de Science Religieuse*, no. II (Paris, 1911).

H. (Sheikh El) Mamoun, "Some Principles of Islam." *Revue Internationale de la Croix Rouge*, 594 (596) (Geneve, Nov. 1958).

Louis Massignon, "The Salute of Islam." *Jeunesse de l'Eglise*, no. 7 (1947).

E. L. Petersen, "Ali and Mu'awiya, the rise of the Umayyad Caliphate," *Acta Orientalia*, XXIII (1959). English version

Maxime Rodinson, "The Life of Mohammad and the Sociological Problem of the Origin of Islam." *Diogene*, XX (1957).

Pierre Rondot, "Religious Practice in Today's Islam." *St. Missionalia*, Rome, 1961.

Abd-Assamii El-Misry, *Principles of Islam* (Cairo: al-Nahda al-Arabia, 1962). English version.

Tawfik M. El-Roueni, *The Influence of Islamic Legislation on the Arab Unity* (Cairo: Counseil Superieur des Affaires Islamiques, 1966).

El Sayed Farag, *A Message to the Arab Soldier* (Cairo: Conseil Superieur des Affaires Islamiques, n.d.).

Asaf A. A. Fyzee, *A Modern Approach to Islam* (Bombay: Asia Publishing, 1963). English version.

Asaf A. A. Fyzee, *Outlines of Muhammadan Law* (Oxford: University Press, 1964). English version.

Ahmad A. Galwash, *The Religion of Islam*, 4th ed. (Cairo, 1956). English version.

Riad Ghali, *De la tradition considérée comme source du Droit musulman* (Paris: Rousseau, 1909). Arabic version.

Abdallah Gosha, *al-Jihad, the Path to Victory* (Amman: Ministry of Awqaf, 1976). Arabic version.

Mohammad T. al-Ghoneimi, *The Muslim Conception of International Law and Western Approach*. Lay Haye (Nijhoff), 1968. English version.

Muhammad Hamidullah, *Muslim Conduct of State*, 5th ed. (Lahore: Ashraf, 1968). English version

Mirza M. Hussain, *Islam versus Socialism*, 2nd ed. (Lahore: Ashraf, 1970). English version.

Afzal Iqbal, *Diplomacy in Islam*, 2nd ed. (Lahore: Institute of Islamic Culture, 1965). English version.

Muhammad Iqbal, *The Recontruction of Religious Thought in Islam* (Lahore: Ashraf, reprint, 1958). English version.

Ibrahim M. Ismail, *Islam and Contemporary Economic Doctrines* (Cairo: Le conseil Superieur des Affaires Islamiques, 1965).

Kemal H. Karpat, *The Ottoman State and its Place in World History* (Leiden: Brill, 1974). English version.

Allama M. Kifayatullah, *Teaching Islam*. Translation into English by Mahmood Qaderi (Lahore: Ashraf, n.d.), 4 volumes.

Mohammed A. Lahbabi, *Le personnalisme musulman*, 2nd ed. (Paris: P.U.F., 1967).

Soubhy Mahmassani, *The Philosophy of Jurisprudence in Islam* (Leiden: Brill, 1961).

Ali Mazaheri, *La vie quotidienne des musulmans au Moyen Age, (Xᵉ au XIIIᵉ siècle)* (Paris: Hachette, 1951).

Ali Merad, *Moslem Reformism in Algeria from 1925 to 1940*. Maison des sciences de l'Homme (1969).

Mahmoud Mohtar-Katirjoglou, *La sagesse coranique* (Paris: Geuthner, 1935).

Ali Muhajir, *Lessons from the Stories of the Qur'ān*, 2nd ed. (Lahore: Ashraf, 1969). English version.

Mahmoud S. Muhammad, *Islam Condemns Racial Discrimination* (Cairo: Conseil Superieur des Affairs Islamiques, 1967). English version.

Dinshash F. Mulla, *Principles of Mohammedan Law*, 15th ed. (Calcutta, 1961). English version.

Abdul Hassan Nadawi, *Islam and the World*, 2nd ed. (Lahore: Ashraf, 1967). English version.

Sayyed H. Nassr, *Man in the Universe: the Islamic View* (London: Longman, n.d.). English version.

Ali I. Othman, *The Concept of Man in Islam in the Writings of al-Ghazali* (Cairo: Dar al-Ma'aref, 1960). English version.

Muhammad M. Pickthall, *The Cultural Side of Islam* (Islamic Culture), 3rd ed. (Lahore: Ashraf, 1969). English version.

Anwar A. Qadri, *Justice in Historical Islam* (Lahore: Ashraf, 1968). English version.

Omnia Rida, *The Free Arbitre in Islam* (Alexandrie: Commercial Press, 1969).

M. Raihan Sharif, *Islamic Social Framework*, 3rd ed. (Lahore: Ashraf, 1971). English version.

Sa'ed Sheikh, *Studies in Muslim Philosophy*, 2nd ed. (Lahore: Ashraf, 1969). English version.

Haroon Khan Sherwani, *Studies in Muslim Political Thought and Administration* (Lahore: Ashraf, 1968). English version.

Hamed Sultan, *International Law Decisions in Islamic Law* (Cairo: Dar al-Nahda al-Arabiya, 1974).

Ali A. Wafi, *Fasting and Sacrifice in Islam and in Pre-Islamic Religions* (Cairo: Conseil Superieur des Affairs Islamiques, 1966).

Farshta G. de Zayas, *The Law and Philosophy of Zakat*, The Islamic Social Welfare System (Damas: Abbasi, 1960). English version.

Articles

Azzam (Pacha), "Islam and Peace." *Nouvelles de Caux* (Lausanne, Jan. 1952).

Choucri Cardahi, "The Conception and Practice of International Private Law in Islam." *Academie de Droit International.* Recueil des Cours, 1937 (Paris, 1938).

Mohammed A. Draz, "International Public Law & Islam." *Revue Internationale de la Croix-Rouge* (Geneva, March, 1952).

Mohammed Ereksoussi, "Koran and Humanitarian Conventions." *Review Internationale de la Croix-Rouge* (Geneva, November, 1960).

Asaf A. A. Fyzee, "Law and Culture in Islam." *Islamic Culture* (1943). English version.

A. H. Ghalib, "Two Precursors: Saladin and Acoka." *Review Internationale de la Croix-Rouge* (1955).

Muhammed Hamidullah, "Administration of Justice in Early Islam." *Islamic Culture* (1937). English version.

Muhammed Hamidullah, "The Influence of Roman Law on Muslim Law." *Hyderabad Academy Journal* (1943). English version.

Muhammed Hamidullah, "Judicial Philosophy for the Moslems." *Annales de la Faculte de Droit d'Istanbul* (Istanbul, 1968).

Muhammed Hamidullah, "The Quranic Conception of State." *Quranic World.* (Hydrabad, April, 1936). English version.

Muhammed Hamidullah, "The Friendly Relations of Islam and How they Deteriorated." *Journal of the Pakistan Historical Society* (1953). English version.

S. A. Majid, "Muslim International Law." *Law Quarterly Review* (London, 1912). English version.

Ahmad Rechid, "Islam and Law of People." *Academie de Droit International. Recueil des cours 1937* (Paris, 1938).

Subhan, "Jihad and Islam." *The Islamic Literature* (Lahore, December, 1951). English version.

Zafrullah Khan, "Islam and International Relations." *The Islamic Review* (July, 1956). English version.

Collective Publication or of Non-Moslem Authors

Books

R. H. Anshen, *From Religious to National Law.* (New York: Ed. Mid-East World Center, 1956). English version.

A. J. Arberry, *Aspects of Islamic Civilization.* As Depicted in the Original Texts (London: Allen and Unwin, 1964). English version.

Pierre Arminson, *Etrangers et protégés dans l'Empire ottoman* (Paris: Maresq, 1903).

T. Arnold and A. Guillaume, *The Legacy of Islam* (Oxford: reprint, 1960). English version.

T. W. Arnold, *The Preaching of Islam* (London, 1896). Reprint (Lahore: Mohammed Ashraf, 1968). English version.

Jacques Austruy, *L'Islam face au développement économique* (Paris: Ed. Ouvrieres, 1961).

Georges-Henri Bousquet, *Le Droit musulman* (Paris: Armand Colin, 1963).

J. M. Caldwell, A. Gledhill, M. Khaddwi, *Apercu sur les constitutions des Etats arabes islamique* (Paris: Maisonneuve, 1966).

Marie Bernand, *L'accord unanime de la Communauté comme fondement des status de l'Islam* (Paris: Vrin Etudes Musumanes, XI, 1970).

Jacques Berque et al, *Normes et valeurs dans l'Islam contemporain* (Paris: Payot, 1966).

Raymond Charles, *L'âme musulmane* (Paris: Flammarion, 1958).

Jean-Paul Charnay (ed.), *L'ambivalence dans la culture arabe* (Paris: Anthropos, 1967).

Chafik Chehata, *Droit musulman* (Paris: Precis Dalloz, 1970).

Joseph Chelhold, *Introduction à la sociologie de l'Islam* (Paris: Maisonneuve, 1958).

Eugene Clavel, *Droit musulman. Du statut personnel et des successions* (Paris: Larose, 1895).

N. J. Coulson, *A History of Islamic Law* (Edinburgh: University Press, 1964). English version.

Henry Corbin, *Histoire de la philosophie islamique* (Paris: Gallimard, 1964).

Divers, *L'élaboration de l'Islam* (Paris: P.U.F., 1961).

Ceasar E. Farah, *Islam, Beliefs and Observances* (New York: Barron's Educational Series, 1968). English version.

Antoine Fattal, *The Legal Status of Non-Moslems in Islamic Countries* (Beirut: Catholic Press, 1958).

F. W. Fernau, *Le réveil du monde musulman* (Paris: Quesais-je, 1954).

Francesco Gabrielli, *Mahomet et les grandes conquêtes arabes* (Paris: Hachette, 1967).

Louis Gardet, *Connaître l'Islam* (Paris: Fayard, 1958).

Louis Gardet, *La cité musulmane* (Paris: Vrin, 1961).

Louis Gardet, *L'Islam* (Paris: Desclee de Brouwer, 1970).

Louis Gardet and M. Anawati, *Introduction à la théologie musulman* (Paris: Vrin, 1948).

Maurice Gaudefroy-Desmombynes, *Les institutions musulmanes* (Paris: Flammarion, 1950).

Hamilton Gibb, *Les tendances modernes de l'Islam.* Translated by B. Vernier (Paris: Besson-Chantemerle, 1949).

Hamilton Gibb, *Studies on the Civilization of Islam* (London: Routledge and Kegan, 1969).

Ignaz Goldziher, *Le Dogme et la Loi de l'Islam* (Paris: Geuthner, 1958).

G. E. Grunebaum (von), *Islam.* Essays on the Nature and Growth of a Cultural Tradition. (London: Routledge and Kegan, 1961).

Alfred Guillaume, *Islam* (Harmondsworth: Penguin Books, 1964). English version.

Alfred Guillaume, *The Traditions of Islam.* An Introduction to the Study of the Hadith Literature. (Beirut: Khayats, 1966). English version.

Joseph Hell, *The Arab Civilization* (Lahore: Ashraf, 1969). English version.

Basile Homsy, *Capitulations and Protections of Christians in the Middle East* (Harissa: St. Paul Press, 1956).

O. Houdas, *L'Islamisme* (Paris: Laroux, 1908).

J. Jomier, *Le commentaire coranique du Manâr* (Paris: Maisonneuve, 1954).

Majid Khadduri, *War and Peace in the Law of Islam* (Baltimore: Johns Hopkins, 1962). English version.

Georges Labica, *Politics and Religion to Ibn Khaldoun* (Algiers: S.N.E.D., 1968).

Yves LaCoste, *Ibn Khaldoun* (Paris: Maspero, 1969).

Henri Lammens, *Islam*, 2nd ed. (Beirut: Catholic Press, 1941).

Henri Laoust, *Essay on the Social and Political Doctrines of Ibn Taimiyya* (Cairo: French Institute of Archeology, 1939).

Michel Lelong, *J'ai rencontré l'Islam*, 2nd ed. (Paris: Serf, 1975).

Reuben Levy, *The Social Structure of Islam*, 2nd ed. (Cambridge: University Press, 1969). English version.

Y. Linant de Bellefonds, *Traité de Droit musulman comparé* (Paris: Mouton, 1965).

D. B. MacDonald, *Development of Muslim Theology, Jurisprudence and Constitutional Theory* (London, 1903). English version.

Henri Masse, *L'Islam*, 9th ed. (Paris: Armand Collin, 1966).

Louis Massignon, *Parole donnée* (Paris: Union General d'Edition, 1970).

Denise Masson, *Le Coran et la révélation Judéo-chrétienne* (Paris: Maisonneuve, 1958).

Louis Milliot, *Introduction à l'étude du droit musulman* (Paris: Recueil Sirey, 1953).

Kenneth W. Morgan (ed.), *Islam – The Straight Path*. Islam Interpreted by Muslims (New York: Ronald Press, 1958). English version.

Y. Moubarac, *L'Islam* (Paris, 1962).

J. Harris Proctor (ed.), *Islam and International Relations* (London: Pall Mall Press, 1965). English version.

Jacques C. Risler, *L'Islam moderne* (Paris: Petite bibliotheque Payot, 1963).

Robert Roberts, *The Social Laws of the Quran*. Considered and Compared with those of the Hebrew and Other Ancient Codes. 2nd ed. (London: Curzon, 1971). English version.

Maxime Rodinson, *Islam et capitalisme* (Paris: Seuil, 1966).

Maxime Rodinson, *Marxisme et monde musulman* (Paris: Seuil, 1972).

Pierre Rondot, *L'Islams et Les musulmans d'aujourd'hui* (Paris: L'Orante, 1960).

Pierre Rondot, *L'Islam* (Paris: Laforge, 1965).

Franz Rosenthal, *The Muslim Concept of Freedom Prior to the Nineteenth Century* (Leiden: Brill, 1960). English version.

Jean-Paul Roux, *L'Islam en Occident* (Paris: Payot, 1959).

Jean-Paul Roux, *L'Islam au Proche-Orient* (Paris: Payot, 1960).

Joseph Schacht, *Esquisse d'une histoire du droit musulman*. Translated by Arin, Jeanne and Felix. (Paris: Instit des Hautes Marocaines, 1953).

Frithjof Schuon, *Understanding Islam* (Gallimard, 1961).

Wilfred C. Smith, *Islam in Modern History*, 3rd ed. (Princeton: Mentor Books, 1963). English version.

Germain Tillion, *Le harem et les cousins* (Paris: Seuil, 1966).

Emile Tyan, *History of Judicial Organization in Islamic Countries*, 2nd ed. (Beirut, 1961).

Emile Tyan, *Institutions du Droit public musulman*, 2 volumes (Paris: 1954-1956).

F. R. J. Vercheven, *Islam* (London, 1952). English version.

Montgomery W. Watt, *Islam and the Integration of Society*, 2nd ed. (London: Routledge and Kegan, 1961). English version.

Montgomery W. Watt, *Islamic Philosophy and Theology* (Edinburgh: University Press, 1962). English version.

John Williams, *L'Islamisme* (Paris: Garnier, n.d.).

T. Cuyler Young, (ed.) *Near Eastern Culture and Society*, 2nd ed. (Princeton: University Press, 1966). English version.

Gaston Zananiri, *L'Eglise et l'Islam* (Paris: Seps, 1969).

Articles

G. N. D. Anderson, "Recent Developments Shari'a Law." *Muslim World*, (1950). English version).

R. D. Davison, "Turkish Attitueds Concerning Christian-Muslim Equality in the Nineteenth Century," *American Historical Reviews* (1954). English version.

Divers, "A Study in the Islamic Notion of Sovereignty." *Revue de Monde Musulman*, LIX (1925).

Georges Henri Bousquet, "The Mystery of the Formation and Origins of Fiqh." *Revue Algerienne, Tunisienne and Marocaine de legislation et de Jurisprudence*. Vol LXIII (Alger, 1947).

R. Brunschwig, "Medieval Urbanism of Muslim Law." *Revue des Etudes Islamique*. XV (Paris: Geutner, 1947).

W. R. W. Gardener, "Jihad." *The Moslem World*, Vol. II (1912). English version.

Louis Gardet, "Principles and Limits and the Moslem Community." *Economic et Humanism*. n. 2 (1942).

Louis Gardet, "Christian Humanism and Muslim Humanism in Face of Modern Thoughts." *Rech erches et Debats* (October, 1953).

Louis Gardet, "Greek-Arab Humanism, Avicenna." *Cahiers d'Histoires Mondiale II*, II (1954-1955).

Hamilton A. R. Gibb, "Some Considerations on the Sunni Theory of the Caliphate," *Archives d'histoire du droit oriental*, III (1939). English version.

Hamilton A. R. Gibb, "The Evolution of Government in Early Islam," *Studia Islamica*, IV (1955).

Hamilton A. R. Gibb, "Islamic Law in Contemporary Muslim States," *American Journal of Comparative Law* (1959), vol. VIII. English version.

Ignaz Goldziher, "The Principles of Law and Islam," *Historian's History of the World*, vol. III, (New York, 1904). English version.

Clement Huart, "Law of War," *Revue du Monde Musulman*, vol II, (1907).

Edward Jurji, "The Islamic Theory of War," *The Muslim World*, XXX (1940). English version.

Duncan B. MacDonnald, "Mohammadan Law," *Encyclopedia Britannica*, 13th edition, vol XVII (1926). English version.

Louis Massignon, "Respect of the Human Person in Islam and the Priority of the Right of Sanctuary over the Duty of a Just War," *Revue International de la Croix Rouge, no. 402* (Geneva, June 1952).

Louis Milliot, "The Conception of the State and the Legal Order in Islam," *Recueil des Cours. Academie de Droit International*, 2nd vol. (1949).

C. A. O. Nieuwenhuijze, "The Umma, an Analytic Approach," *Studia Islamica X* (1959). English version.

E. Nys, "Law of People in Arab and Byzantiums," *Revue du Droit International et Legislation Comparee*, XXVI (Bruxelles, 1894).

R. Paret, "Contribution to the study of cultural milieux in the Middle East in the Muslim encyclopedia from 850 to 1950 of the Christian Era," *Revue Historique*, CCXXXV (Jan-March, 1958).

D. Santillana, "Law and Society," in *The Legacy of Islam* (Oxford, 1931). English version.

Joseph Schacht, "Foreign Elements in Ancient Islamic Law," *Journal of Comparative Legislation* (1950). English version.

Joseph Schacht, "Islamic Law," *Encyclopedia of Social Sciences*, 7 vol., VIII (1932). English version.

Joseph Schacht, "Remarks on the Transmission of the Greek Thought to the Arabs," *Histoire de la Medecine*, 2nd year, no. 5 (Paris, 1952). English version.

Hurgronje C. Snouck, "Moslem Law," *Revue de l'histoire des religions*, vol. XXXVII (Paris, 1898).

Muslim History and Islamic Contribution to the Evolution of International Morale

Sources

Jawad Boulos, *Les peuples et les civilisations du Proche-Orient* (Paris: Mouton, 1968).

Jacob Burkhardt, *Considérations sur l'histoire universelle* (Paris: Payot, 1971).

Chateaubraind, *Travel Guide from Paris to Jerusalem* (Limoges, s.d.).

Alexandre de Clercq and C. de Vallat, *Guide pratique des Consulats*, 5th edition (Paris: Peadone, 1898).

Abdel Rahman el Djabarti, *Bibliography and Historical or Chronological Wonders* (Cairo: National Press, 1888).

Francesco Gabrieli (edit), *Arab Historians of the Crusades*. Selected and translated from the Arabic Sources. Translation E. J. Costello, XXXVI (London: Routledge and Kegan, 1969). English version.

John B. Glubb (Pasha), *The Course of Empire: The Arabs and their Successors* (London: Hoddernn and Stoughton, 1965). English version.

John B. Glubb, *The Great Arab Conquests*, 2nd edit. (London: Hodder and Stoughton, 1966). English version.

John B. Glubb, *The Empire of the Arabs*, 2nd edit. (London: Hodder and Stoughton, 1969). English version.

John B. Glubb, *The Life and Time of Muhammad* (London: Hodder and Stoughton, 1970). English version.

John B. Glubb, *The Lost Centuries*. From the Muslim Empires to the Renaissance of Europe. (London: Hodder and Stoughton, n.d.). English version.

Rene Grousset, *History of the Crusades and French Kingdom of Jerusalem*, 3 volumes (Paris: Plon, 1934).

Rene Grousset and Emile G. Leonard (directors), *Histoire Universelle* (Paris: Encyclopedia de la Pleiade, 1967).

A. Ch de Guttenberg, *L'Occident en formation* (Paris: Payot, 1963).

Lamartine, *Voyages en Orient*, 2 volumes (Paris: 1911-1913).

Evariste Levi-Provencal, *Histoire de l'Espagne musulmane*, 3 volumes (Paris: Maisonneuve, 1950).

Julius E. Lips, *Les origines de la culture humaine* (Paris: Payot, 1951).

Andre Miquel, *L'Islam et sa civilisation. VIIe-XXe siècles* (Paris: Collin, 1968).

S. Munk, *Mélanges de Philosophies juive et arabe*, 2nd edition (Paris: Vrin, 1927).

Antoine Y. Naaman, *Les lettres d'Egypte de Gustave Flaubert* (Paris: Nizet, 1965).

Jacques Pirenne, *The Great Trends of Universal History*, 6 volumes (Neuchatel: Baconniere, 1956).

Rene Ristelhueber, *God Willing* (Montreal: Ed. Varietes, 1945).

Gustave Schlumberger, *Récits de Byzance et des Croisades*, 2 volumes (Paris: Plon, 1922-23).

Arnold J. Toynbee, *Le changement et la Tradition* (Paris: Payot, 1969).

UNESCO, *Histoire du développement culturel et scientifique de l'humanité* (Paris: La Font, 1967).

Villamon le Venitien and Jean Sommer, *Trips to Egypt in the Years 1589, 1590 and 1591*, vol. 2 (Cairo: Institute Francais d'archeologie due Caire, 1971).

Jacques de Vitry, *Letters of the Bishop of Saint jean d'Acre*, [1160/1170-1240] (Leiden: Brill, 1960).

Alban G. Widgery, *Les Grandes doctrines de l'histoire* (Paris: N.R.F., 1965).

P. Laviosa Zambotti, *Les origines et la diffusion de la civilisation* (Paris: 1949).

Works

Books

Aziz S. Atiya, *Crusade, Commerce and Culture* (New York: John Wiley, 1966). English version.

Charles Bene, *Erasme, et saint Augustin* (Geneva: Droz, 1969).

Vernon J. Bourke, *Histoire de la morale* (Paris: Cerf, 1970).

R. Boutruche, *Seigneurie et féodalité au Moyen Age*, 2 volumes (Paris: Coll Historique, 1970).

Louis Brehier, *La philosophie du Moyen Age* (Paris: Albin Michel, 1971).

Louis Brehier, *Vie et mort de Byzance* (Paris: Albin Michel, 1971).

Claude Cahen, *L'Islam des origines au début de l'Empire ottoman* (Paris: Bordas, 1970).

P. Chaunu, *L'expansion européenne du XIIIᵉ au XVᵉ siècle* (Paris: P.U.F., 1969).

M.D. Chenu, *L'éveil de la conscience dans la civilisation médiévale* (Paris: Vrin, 1969).

Richard Coke, *The Arabs' Place in the Sun* (London: Thornton Butterworth, 1929). English version.

Edward S. Creasy, *History of the Ottoman Turks with a New Introduction by Zeine N. Zeine.* (Beirut: Khayats, 1968), reprints no. 1. English version.

Norman Daniel, *The Arabs and Medieval Europe* (London: Longman, n.d.), "Arab Background Series."

Christofer Dawson, *La religion et la formation de la civilisation occidentale* (Paris: Payot, 1969).

Robert Delort, *Introduction to Sciences Auxiliary to History* (1969).

Divers, *L'Islam et l'Occident* (Paris: 1947).

Divers, *Saint Francois et la Terre sainte* (Paris: Gannereau, 1892).

Divers, *Le siècle de Saint Louis* (Paris: Hachette, 1970).

Georges Duby, *Des sociétés médiévales* (Paris: Gallimard, N.R.F., 1971).

A. Ducellier, *Le miroir de l'Islam* (Paris Coll: Archives, 1773).

D. M. Dunlop, *Arab Civilization to AD 1500* (London: Longman, 1971). English version.

Jean Ebersolt, *Orient et Occident* (Paris: de Boccard, 1954).

Abbas M. El-Akkad, *The Arabs' Impact on European Civilization* (Le Caire: Conseil Superieur des Affairs Islamiques. English version.

Kessmat A. Elgeddawy, *Relations entre systèmes confessionnel et laique en droit international privé* (Paris: Dalloz, 1971).

A. P. Entreves, *Natural Law – A Historical Survey* (New York: Harper and Row, 1965). English version.

Henri-Paul Eydoux, *Saint Louis et son temps* (Paris: Larousse, 1971).

Moustafa Fadel, *Relations of Arabs and Islam with the West and America* (Cairo: Conseil Superieur des Affaires Islamiques, 1969). English version.

Nabih A. Faris (ed.), *The Arab Heritage*, 2nd ed. (Princeton: University Press, 1944). English version.

Gaudefroy-Demombynes and Platonov, *Le monde musulman et byzantin jusqu'aux Croisades* (Paris: Boccard, 1931).

Myron P. Gilmore, *Le Monde de l'Humanisme, 1453-1517.* (Paris: Payot, 1955).

A. M. Goichon, *La philosophie d'Avicenne et son influence en Europe médiévale*, 2nd ed. (Paris: Maisonneuve, 1951).

S. D. Goitein, *Jews and Arabs.* Their Contacts through the Ages, 5th ed. (New York: Shocken Books, 1970). English version.

Alphonse Gouilly, *L'Islam devant le monde moderne* (Paris: La Nouvelle Edition, 1945).

Rene Grousset, *L'épopée des Croisades* (Paris: Plon, 1957).

Rene Grousset, *L'Empire des steppes* (Paris: Payot, 1969).

Romano Guardini, *La fin des temps modernes* (Paris: Seuil, 1952).

E. Guennee, *L'Occident aux XIVᵉ et XVᵉ siècles. Les Etats* (Paris: Collection "Nouvelle Ohio," 1971).

Bernard Guillemain, *L'éveil de l'Europe, An 1000 à 1250* (Paris: Laurouse de Poche, 1969).
Rene Habachi, *Orient quel est ton Occident* (Paris: Centurion, 1969).
A. Hatem, *Suisses et Arabes à travers les siècles* (Geneva, 1969).
Jacques Heers, *L'Occident aux XIVᵉ et XVᵉ siècles* (Paris: P.U.F. 1970).
Johannes Hirschberger, *Abridged History of Western Philosophy* (Lausanne: Age d'homme, 1971).
David G. Hogarth, *The Penetration of Arabia* (Beirut: Khayats Oriental, 1966). English version.

Albert A. Hourani, *A Vision of History*. Near Eastern and Other Essays. (Beirut: Khayats, 1961). English version.
Sigrid Hunke, *Le soleil d'Allah brille sur l'Occident* (Paris: Albin Michel, 1963).
Charles Jourdain, *Historical and Philosophical Excursions Throughout the Middle Ages* (Frankfurt: Minerva, 1966).
M. H. Keen, *The Laws of War in the Late Middle Ages*, 4th edit. (London: Longman, 1970). English version.
B. Lacroix, *The Historian of the Middle Ages* (Montreal: Institute d'Etudes Medieval de Montreal, 1966).
Stanley Lane-Poole, *Saladin and the Fall of the Kingdom of Jerusalem* (Beirut: Khayats, 1964). English version.
Stanley Lane-Poole, *The Mohammadam Dynasties* (Beirut: Khayats, 1966). English version.
Stanley Lane-Poole, *The Moors in Spain* (Beirut: Khayats, 1967). English version.
Paul E. Laurent, *The Islamic Culture in the South of Netherlands* (Cairo: Conseil Superieur des Affaires Islamiques, 1967).
Maurice Lombard, *L'Islam dans sa première grandeur* (Paris: Flammarion, 1971).
Bernard Lewis, *Arab in History* (Neuchatel: Baconniere, 1958).
Guy Le Strange, *Palestine under the Moslems*, reprints no. 14 (Beirut: Khayats, 1965). English version.
Anouar Louca, *Henry Dunant et les origines chevaleresques de la Croix-Rouge* (Geneva: Association Suisse-Arabe, 1971).
Robert Mantran, *L'expansion musulmane (VIIᵉ-XIᵉ siècles)* (Paris: P.U.F., 1969).
Louis et al Massignon, *L'Islam et l'Occident* (Paris: Cahiers du Sud, 1947).
Frederic Mauro, *L'expansion européenne (1600-1870)* (Paris: P.U.F., 1967).
Joseph-Francois Michaud, *Histoire des Croisades* (Paris: Laffont, 1970).
Montgomery (vicomte d'Alamein), *Histoire de la guerre* (Paris: France Empire, 1970).
Cecile Morrison, *Les Croisades* (Paris: "Que-sai-je?" 1969).
Sir William Muir, *The Caliphate: Its Rise, Decline and Fall* (Beirut: Khayats, 1963). English version.
Ignacia Olague, *Les Arabes n'ont jamais envahi l'Espagne* (Paris: Flammarion, 1969).
Zoe Oldebourg, *Les Croisades* (Paris: Gallimard, 1965).
De Lacy O'Leary, *Arabic Thought and its Place in History* (London: Routledge and Kegan, Trubner's Oriental Series, 1939, 1968). English version.
Henri Pirenne, *Mohammed and Charlemagne*, 5th ed. (London: Unwin, 1968). English version.
G. Quadri, *La philosophie arab dans l'Europe médiévale* (Paris: Payot, 1960).
Ernest Renan, *Averroës et l'Averroïsme*, 2nd ed., XVI (Paris: Camann-Levy, n.d.).
Jacques C. Risler, *La civilisation arabe* (Paris: Payot, 1962).
Steven Runciman, *A History of the Crusades*, 3 vol. (Cambridge, 1951-1954). English version.
Abram L. Sachar, *Histoire des Juifs* (Paris: Flammarion, 1973).
John J. Saunders (ed.), *The Muslim World on the Eve of European Expansion* (Englewood Cliffs: Prentice Hall, 1966).
John J. Saunders (ed.), *A History of Medieval Islam*, 2nd edit. (London: Routledge and Kegan, 1966). English version

B. Schnapper and H. Richardot, *Histoire des faits économiques jusqu'à la fin du XVIIIe siècle*, 3rd edition (Paris: Dalloz, 1971). English version.
Haroon K. Sherwani, *Muslim Colonies in France, Northern Italy and Switzerland*, 2nd edit. (1964). English version.
Amir H. Siddiqi, *Studies in Islamic History* (Karachi: Jamiyatul-Falah, 1967). English version.
Emmanuel Sivan, *L'Islam et la Croisade* (Paris: Maisonneuve, 1968).
G. Jean-Louis Soulie and Lucien Champenois, *Le Royaume d'Arabie Saoudite, face à l'Islam révolutionnaire 1953 to 1964* (Paris: Armand Collin, 1966).
Georges Spillmann (general), *Napoléon et l'Islam* (Paris: Librairie Academique Perrin, 1969).
Gaston Weit, *Grandeur de l'Islam* (Paris: Table Roude, 1961).
J. Wellhausen, *The Arab Kingdom and its Fall*. Translated by Margaret G. Weir (Beirut: Khayats, 1963). English version.
J. J. Waardenbourg, *L'Islam dans le miroir de l'Occident* (Paris: La Haye: Mouton, 1963).
Jean Wolf and Peirre Heim, *Les très riches heures de la civilisation arabe* (Paris: Cujas, 1969).
Philippe Wolff, *L'éveil intellectuel de l'Europe* (Paris: Seuil, 1971).
Quincy Wright, *A Study of War*, 2nd edit. (Chicago: University Press, 1969).

Articles
C. H. Alexandrowickz, "Treaty and Diplomatic Relations Between European and South Asian Powers in the Seventeenth and Eighteenth Centuries." *Recueils des Cours*, A.D.I. The Hague (1960). English version.
J. Basdevant, "Two Little Known Conventions on the Law of War." *Revue Generale de Droit International Public* (1914).
Pierre Boissier, "When the Red Cross Does Not Exist: Outline of a Story of Health Services in Western European Armies Till 1859." *Revue International de la Croix Rouge* (551, 1960; 1, 1961).
Reda Chalaby, *Henry Dunant, the Founder of the Red Cross in North Africa*. [excerpts from some of his texts]. (Geneva, May, 1970).
C.I.C.R. "A New Step in the Development of Humanitarian Law." *Revue International de la Croix Rouge* no. 163. (Geneva, January, 1970).
Henri Coursier, "Studies on the Formation of Humanitarian Law." *Revue Internationale de la Croix Rouge*. no. 389-391-396-403 (Geneva, May, 1951). "Christianity" (December, 1951), "Law of People" (July, 1952), "The Red Cross."
Henri Coursier, "The Problem of Slavery," *Revue Internationale de la Croix Rouge*.
Henri Coursier, "Prohibition of Torture," *Revue Internationale de la Croix Rouge* (Geneva, September, 1971).
Yolande Diallo, "African Traditions of Humanitarian Law." *Revue Internationale de la Croix Rouge* (Aug. 1976).
Divers, "New Forms of Conflict." *Annale d'Etudes Internationale*. Vol. 3 (Geneva: I.U.H.E.I., 1972).
G.I.A.D. Draper, "Potential Discipline and the War in the Medieval Ages. Contribution of the Medievel Ages to the Development of the Humanitarian Law" *Revue Internationale de la Croix Rouge* (1961).
E. Everard, "Neutralization of a Country Hospital in XVIII Centuries." *Revue de la Croix Rouge* (Geneva, Aug. 1971).
S.V. Fitzgerald, "The Alleged Debt of Islam to Roman Law." *Law Quarterly Review* (1951). English version.
W. J. Ford, "Members of Resistance Movements of International Law." *Revue Internationale de la Croix Rouge* (Geneva, October, 1967, November, 1967, January, 1968).
Hamilton A.R. Gibb, "The Influence of Islamic Culture in Medieval Europe," Buletin of John

Rylande Library (1955). English version.

Hamilton A.R. Gibb, "Arab-Byzantine Relations Under the Umayyad Caliphate." *Dumbarton Oaks Papers*, XII (1958).

Andrzej Gorbiel, "Protection of War Victims in Polic Legislation Until the end XVIII Century." *Revue Internationale de la Croix Rouge* (June 1975).

L. C. Green, "On the Influence of the New States on International Law" Excerpt from *Revue Generale de Droit International Public* (Jan-March, 1975).

Muhammed Hamidullah, "Place of Islam in the History of Modern International Law." *Journal of Hyderabad Academy*, vol II (1940). English version.

R. Lopez, "Oriental Influence and the Economic Awakening of the West." *Cahiers d'Histoire Mondiale* (1953).

Henri Myrowitz, "The Goal of War, Means of war, the law of war – Reflections on the occasion of the centenial of the Declaration of St. Petersburg." *Revue Internationale de la Croix Rouge*, no. 600 (Geneva, December, 1968).

Monchanin, "Islam and Christianity." *le Bulletin des Missions*, no. 1 (1938).

M. W. Mouton, "History of Law and Customs of War Until the Middle Ages." *Revue Internationale de la Croix Rouge* (1958).

E. Olivier, "Notes on Hospitals of the Middle Ages in the West" *Revue Internationale de la Croix Rouge* (1958).

R. Vaultier, "Ancestors of the Geneva Convention." *Presse Medicale* (May, 1951).

J. C. de Watteville (ed.), "One Century Before Solferino." *Revue Internationale de la Croix Rouge* (Geneva, December, 1951).

Quincy Wright, "International Law and Ideologies." *American Journal of International Law*, (1954). English version.

Pierre Viau, "The End of Classical Humanism." *Options Humanistes*.

Michel Taube (baron de), "Studies on the Historical Development of International Law in Eastern Europe," Chap. II: The World of Islam and Its Influence in Eastern Europe. *Recueil des Cours de l'academie de Droit Internationale*. The Hague, Vol. XI.

INDEX

ACKNOWLEDGMENT

Faced with the impossibility of mentioning everybody, the author thanks primarily:

- His numerous Arab friends from Yemen, Saudi Arabia, the Gulf, Algeria, and especially Egypt, all of which have offered him a brotherly hospitality over the span of many years;

- Mrs. A. and Mrs. F. de Zayas Abbasi, authors residing in Damascus, whose very precise and detailed remarks were of utmost use;

- Mrs. Omnia Rida and Ms. Samia Ahmed Ali, of Cairo, for their sometimes vivid but always pertinent critiques;

- Professor Hamed Sultan, member of the Institute of Egypt, former Dean of the Faculty of Law at the University of Cairo; Professor Mohammed Talaat al-Ghoneimi, Director of the Department of International Law at the University of Alexandria; and Professor Mohammed Talbi of the University of Tunis;

- His Eminence Dr. Ma'rouf al-Daoualibi, President of the Muslim World Congress; and Dr. Mouloud Belaouance, President of the Algerian Red Crescent; who, despite their multiple occupations and heavy responsibilities, have found the time to read the manuscript and to advise the author; and

- Dr. Ahmed Mohammed Ayyoub, whose frank friendship has constituted a permanent encouragement.

The author, of course, solely assumes all responsibility for the opinions postulated and the occasional errors and lacunas which may appear in this work. He apologizes for them to the below-mentioned, famous Muslim people:

- Professor Jacques Freymond, former Director of the University Institute of Higher International Studies (I.U.H.E.I.) at Geneva, who has proved a veritable "master" and without whose advice and encouragement this study would not have been realized;

- Professor George Abi-Saad of the I.U.H.E.I., and Professor Anouar Hatem, former Ambassador of Syria and Director of the Modern French Institute at the University of Fribourg (Switzerland), who have benefited the author with their vast culture;

- Professor Jean Pictet, Vice President of the C.I.C.R., whose personal brilliance has opened the author to the humanitarian ideal;

- Mrs. Nagwa Kami who has diligently typewritten the first draft of this text, and, especially, Ms. Maria Macheret, the author's aunt, who took upon herself the typewriting and final arrangement of the manuscript, the harmonization of the bibliography, and the proofreading of several trial copies;

- His family, particularly Claude, his wife, for her generous comprehension and her infinite patience; his parents who have ever since instilled the author with the idea that personal happiness resides in the respect for the fellow being; as well as Mr. and Mrs. Camille Kher, who offered him discrete assistance on a daily basis;

- Finally, the numerous speakers encountered, both in a personal and official setting, who ingratiated the author with their convictions, their examples, their advice, and their experiences.

DATE DUE

APR 1 '91			

HIGHSMITH #LO-45220